AND THE SEA IS NEVER FULL

ALSO BY ELIE WIESEL

Night
Dawn
The Accident
The Town Beyond the Wall
The Gates of the Forest
The Jews of Silence
Legends of Our Time
A Beggar in Jersualem
One Generation After
Souls on Fire
The Oath
Ani Maamin (cantata)
Zalmen, or The Madness of God (play)
Messengers of God
A Jew Today
Four Hasidic Masters
The Trial of God (play)
The Testament
Five Biblical Portraits
Somewhere a Master
The Golem (illustrated by Mark Podwal)
The Fifth Son
Against Silence (edited by Irving Abrahamson)
Twilight
The Six Days of Destruction (with Albert Friedlander)
A Journey into Faith (conversations with John Cardinal O'Connor)
From the Kingdom of Memory
Sages and Dreamers
The Forgotten
A Passover Haggadah (illustrated by Mark Podwal)
All Rivers Run to the Sea
Memory in Two Voices (with François Mitterand)
King Solomon and His Magic Ring (illustrated by Mark Podwal)

ELIE WIESEL

AND THE SEA
IS NEVER FULL

Memoirs, 1969 –

Translated from the French by Marion Wiesel

HarperCollins*Publishers*

HarperCollins*Publishers*
77–85 Fulham Palace Road,
Hammersmith, London W6 8JB

www.**fire**and**water**.com

Published by HarperCollins*Publishers* 2000
1 3 5 7 9 10 8 6 4 2

First published in the USA by Alfred A. Knopf, Inc.
Copyright © Eliron Associates, Inc. 1999

Originally published in France as ...*et la mer n'est pas remplie*
by Editions de Seuil, Paris 1996
Copyright © Editions du Seuil 1996

Elie Weisel asserts the moral right to
be identified as the author of this work

Marion Weisel asserts the moral right to
be identified as the translator of this work

Photo credits for insert:
page 1, and page 6, top: White House Press Office; page 2, middle,
and page 5, bottom: Elie Wiesel Foundation for Humanity;
page 6, bottom: Boston University. All other photos are from
the personal collection of Elie and Marion Wiesel

A catalogue record for this book is
available from the British Library

ISBN 0 00 255674 X

Set in Weiss

Printed and bound in Great Britain by
Clays Ltd, St Ives plc

For Inge and Ira

*W*hat profit hath a man of all his labor which he taketh under the sun? One generation passeth away, and another generation cometh; but the earth abideth forever. The sun also riseth, and the sun goeth down, and hasteth to his place where he arose. The wind goeth toward the south, and turneth about unto the north; it whirleth about continually, and the wind returneth again according to his circuits. All rivers run to the sea; and the sea is never full; unto the place from whence the rivers come, thither they return again. All things are full of labor; man cannot utter it: the eye is not satisfied with seeing, nor the ear filled with hearing.

ECCLESIASTES

Contents ⌐

CROSSROADS 1

SCARS 45

ON HUMAN RIGHTS 85

ON LEARNING AND TEACHING 99

REVIEWS AND POLEMICS 115

ON BECOMING A SPEAKER 139

OF MADMEN AND VISIONARIES 157

CARDINAL LUSTIGER, MY FRIEND 165

A MUSEUM IN WASHINGTON 177

WORDS OF REMEMBRANCE 207

THE BITBURG AFFAIR 225

FROM SIGHET TO OSLO 251

ENCOUNTERS 275

CHRONICLE OF A DEPOSITION 297

THE GULF WAR   303

FRANÇOIS MITTERRAND AND
  JEWISH MEMORY   311

THREE SUICIDES   343

UNDERSTANDING   353

THE ANATOMY OF HATE   367

THE DESTINY OF SARAJEVO   385

AND YET   401

GLOSSARY   413

INDEX   417

Photographs follow page 214

Crossroads

A CHRONICLE has it that the celebrated Rabbi Shneur Zalman of Lyady was locked up in a St. Petersburg prison after being denounced by a foe of the Hasidic movement as an agitator against the Czar.

One day the warden came to see him in his solitary cell, and this is what he said:

"I am told you are a rabbi, a Master. So explain to me a passage I fail to understand in the Bible. It says in the Book of Genesis that, after having bitten into the forbidden fruit, Adam fled, so that the Lord had to ask him: 'Ayekha, where are you?' Is it possible, even conceivable, that the Creator of the world did not know where Adam was hiding?"

Whereupon the rabbi smiled and answered: "The Lord, blessed-be-His-name, knew; it was Adam who didn't know."

And Rabbi Shneur Zalman went on: "Do you believe the Bible to be a sacred book?"

"Yes."

"And that it speaks to all mankind, of all times, therefore also to ours?"

"Yes, I believe that."

"In that case, I shall explain to you the real meaning of the question God asked of Adam. *Ayekha* signifies: Where do you stand in this world? What is your place in history? What have you done with your life, Adam? These are fundamental questions that every human being must confront sooner or later.

"For every one of us, the book of life goes back to Adam. It is he who embodies the mystery of the beginning. But it is to each of us that God speaks when He says *Ayekha*."

• • •

. . . To write, to write about oneself, one's past, one's burden of memory, is somewhat like that: to keep alive this first question in the Bible.

As I reread my notebooks, I question their subject as he is propelled from page to page, event to event. At which crossroads is he now? What perils lie in store for him, what voices is he following? Where is he going: toward solitude or his need to escape from it?

Before me, always, is the photograph of the house in which I was born. The door that leads to the yard. The kitchen. I want to go inside, but I am afraid. I want to look at the house, if only from afar. With all that has happened to me, it is essential for me to remember that place.

In the first volume of my memoirs,* I tried to describe the secret, almost reclusive life of a young Talmudist-turned-writer when he returned from the death camps. My peaceful childhood, my turbulent adolescence, the uncertainties of my formative years. Full stops and shaky beginnings. Wanderings, wrong turns, changes of direction. Years marked by messianic dreams and challenges, ecstasy and mourning, separations and reunions. A little girl with golden hair, a wise and loving mother. An ailing and defenseless father. Moshe the Madman, Kalman the Kabbalist. Shushani and his mysteries. Saul Lieberman. The Lubavitcher Rebbe. Sighet, Auschwitz, Paris, New York: each place a world unto itself. My journal ended on April 2, 1969, in Jerusalem when my life took another turn, this time toward hope. Toward Marion. I got married.

☙

*T*HESE DAYS *I dream a lot, more than ever before. It all comes back to me with unexpected clarity rendered sharp and painful by the fear of awakening. An immense garden is in bloom. It is spring. I look at the blue and red sky. A window opens and my grandfather appears. I hear his voice ordering the sun to set, for mankind is waiting. He knows how to make others obey, my grandfather. Night falls and suddenly the garden is transformed into a house of prayer. A huge, motionless crowd waits silently for services to begin.*

I am afraid I have forgotten the first verse of the first prayer. I

*All Rivers Run to the Sea (New York: Alfred A. Knopf), 1995.

look for a familiar face. All the faces are veiled, lifeless. I am panic-stricken. I step backward, toward the exit, but a voice inside me tells me I mustn't. Mustn't what? I don't know. Perhaps what I mustn't do is wake up.

꩜

The days move slowly, the years take flight. I work on two or three projects at once. Writing becomes an obstacle course. Have I become more self-critical? I used to rewrite some texts three times; now I sometimes agonize over the same page for hours before tearing it up in a moment of clear-sighted rage.

These are feverish, convulsive years, woven from aborted attempts and exalted renewals. My life now unfolds under the dual sign of change on a practical level and loyalty on the level of memory. Inside me happiness and distress seem to spark a fire that is both somber and luminous. Could it be that I fear happiness?

Notwithstanding my doubts about language, and perhaps because of them, I plunge deeper and deeper into the whirlwind of the words I try to capture and tame. I cling to the notion that in the beginning there was the word; and that the word is the story of man; and that man is the story of God. If praying is an act of faith in God, then writing is a token of trust in man.

I write more than ever. I pause at every page: That which I have just written, have I not said it elsewhere? And I go on writing because I cannot do otherwise.

I have a wife I love, and yet I write not about love but about solitude. I have a home filled with warmth, and yet I write about the misery of the condemned. Around us, our circle of friends becomes larger. I no longer boycott social events with the old determination. With novelists we discuss politics, with politicians we speak of art. Miraculously, I don't suffer from writer's block, the familiar complaint of those around us. Nor is a lack of topics one of my problems.

Madness and laughter are constant themes in my work. Ever since I heard Moshe the Madman and his song, I am unable to free myself of either—nor do I want to.

The mystical madmen of Sighet, the beggars, bearers of secrets—drawn to doom, they all appear in my fictional tales. But I am afraid to follow them too far, outside myself or deep within me.

Sometimes to elude them, other times to confront them, I work; never have I worked as hard: essays on the Bible and the Talmud, analyses of Hasidic tales, novellas, outlines of novels.

Travel no longer tempts me. I prefer to stay at home and study. There was a time when I considered family life an obstacle to literary creation. I was convinced that it was impossible to be both a good husband and a committed writer. Well, I now assert the opposite. For only now do I fully understand the expression *Ezer kenegdo*, which God uses in the Book of Genesis when He speaks of wishing to create Eve to serve as Adam's "helpful opposition." I owe much to Marion. She knows how to suggest, to correct, to critically evaluate texts and decisions.

Still, extraliterary pressures soon make themselves felt. In fact, they are not always negative.

With Saul Lieberman I continue to study the wealth of talmudic texts; with Abraham Joshua Heschel I share the beauty of Hasidic tales. We visit my sisters Hilda and Bea in France and Montreal. Serious, even tragic events take place in the world, while in my private life I discover the vulnerable but dazzling joy of a man who beholds the first smile of his child.

This may well be the time to open parentheses: This volume is different from the preceding one, both in approach and intent.

Until now I have attempted to narrate mostly that which I see within myself; from here on I am also obligated to turn my attention to those who have been judging me.

If, for me, the first volume is a kind of formative work, the second evolves under the sign of conflict. So do not expect a discreet and passive stance from me. The introvert will yield to the extrovert.

And yet I shall omit things that are too private, too personal. I shall not speak of certain friends and other persons I have met who have marked me, for better or worse, since the seventies. All that I hope to include in a separate volume, "My Masters and My Friends."

On the other hand, I shall break a vow I made in *All Rivers Run to the Sea*. I shall take a stand against some of my adversaries, those who have, in my estimation, transgressed the limits of dialogue, having chosen obfuscation as their weapon and "demonization" as their goal. In most instances, it is not my person that is targeted. But in others, less numerous, I am the target, either as a symbol of something or as a witness whose testimony is troubling. Of course I have always rejected the notion of myself as a symbol. Symbols can be repudiated or even erased with impunity. Man is something else, a human being, not a symbol.

What I have said earlier I now reiterate: I detest polemics, but there comes a time when *Shtika ke-hodaya dami,* as the Talmud says, "Silence easily becomes acquiescence."

One must be willing to say no to lies, no to rancor. Will I succeed in being less mean than the mean ones, less perfidious too? I hope so. I have learned not to respond to rudeness. Why stoop to that level? A Master advised me, long ago, never to use a hatchet in my responses.

Let us close the parentheses.

We left off on Tuesday, April 2, 1969, after a wedding ceremony in the Old City of Jerusalem; let us stay there one more moment.

We had, in fact, thought of getting married a day earlier, but at the last minute Marion chose to postpone the ceremony by a day: "April first doesn't sound right," she said laughing. "Our friends will think we're not serious."

The day before the wedding is hectic. In Jerusalem one rarely is allowed to rest. Why would anyone call Jerusalem the City of Peace? What an idea! In Jerusalem you are never left in peace, not even on your wedding day. Friends and strangers come knocking at your door without warning, to ask whether you need anything, or whether you would like to meet this mystical merchant in Mea She'arim or that exotic madman near the Wall.

At 6 on Tuesday the telephone rings. It is Teddy Kollek. The dynamic mayor of the city is inviting me to breakfast. Half asleep, I tell him that just like on Yom Kippur, on his wedding day the bridegroom-to-be is forbidden to eat or drink before the ceremony. "Come anyway," says Teddy, "I need to talk to you. It's urgent." With him everything is urgent, since everything concerns his city. In truth is there in all the world a city that lives more with urgency than Jerusalem?

This time the mayor is wrong—our talk could have waited. But he is preoccupied with current events. Who isn't? He seems more so than anyone else, more so than appears warranted. He fears a hostile initiative by the U.N. to internationalize the Holy City. He would like to preempt it by creating a worldwide commission or association for the defense of the universality of Jerusalem. That is his reason for getting me out of bed on my wedding day. I tell him that his idea seems good, but that there is no hurry and, anyway, the name of the association would have to be changed; the one he has in mind is too long. I suggest "The International Committee for Jerusalem." He accepts. Can I go back to my room now?

By now it is after 7, and the ceremony is set for 11 a.m. I need to prepare myself. But no, Teddy is not done with me yet. Now he needs names of important people for this committee. Whom does he have in mind? It's up to me to find them. I run to get my address book; he knows his by heart. At 9 o'clock, he finally allows me to prepare for my wedding. My nephew Steve, Bea's son, joins me in my room. I shave and change my clothes. Twenty-five years later, I shall keep him company his entire wedding day.

An unforgettable Passover: In an ultrakosher Jerusalem hotel, my closest relatives celebrate a Seder conducted by my Master and friend Saul Lieberman. Bea is there with her husband, Len, and their two children, Sarah and Steve; Hilda with her son Sidney. I read the story of Exodus, and Lieberman dazzles us with his commentaries. But I have trouble concentrating. It has been a long and mentally exhausting day. I feel the presence of some, the absence of others. Which weighs more heavily? I think of my last Seder at home, far away.

The telephone does not stop ringing. No, it isn't Teddy again. The callers are colleagues. Every one of them has an idea, a project to propose. A paper on American-Jewish literature? If I am to believe my caller, the cultural fate of Israel—perhaps even the God of Israel—is at stake. I don't have time? Then how about an interview on that very subject? There follow interviews for radio, for a morning paper and an evening paper. Haïm Yavin, a national television star, a young, earnest man who does not as yet know how to smile, would like me to appear on his weekly show. I'm to take questions from four intellectuals, one of them the poet Haïm Gouri, translator of *Night*. When? The day after tomorrow. It won't take long, he promises. I ask around; my friends think it is a good idea. Very well, let's do it. The questions are easy, the comments typical. The goal of the writer? To testify. To say "Amen," which signifies: "That is how it is, that is how it was." I quote Malraux: "To leave a scratch on the surface of the Earth." All goes well. No trap, no arrow. Not yet.

A few minutes before the end, Yavin decides to provoke me: "What do you feel, you whose mind overflows with memories, when you meet Arab children in the Old City?" What I feel now is the blood draining from my face. Fortunately television is not yet in color; the television audience does not see me blanch. I try not to show my embarrassment as I respond: "It does actually happen that I come across Arab boys and girls. They ask me for money or chocolate. But sometimes they ask for nothing; all they want is for me to look at them. They want the Jew in me, thus the victor, to confront their defeat. And then, in the face of their suffering, their humiliation, I lower my eyes."

The telecast elicits praise and criticism. Moshe Sneh, the Communist member of Parliament, stops me in my hotel to tell me that he approves my words. What he says moves me, for to me he represents a living enigma. How could this Polish Zionist leader, this former chief of the Haganah, this brilliant mind, this fervent Jew, become a supporter of Stalin? Public opinion casts him as a renegade, or worse. I would like to spend an hour with him to question him, to get to know him better, and perhaps to understand him. But I don't dare intrude thus upon him. Will he ever return to his own? Will he ever find his way back to his roots? I know that later he instructed his son Ephraim, a young general and future minister under Yitzhak Rabin, to recite the Kaddish over his grave.

Marion and I had intended to stay another week or so in Israel, but we change our plans. Too many people to see, too many places to visit, too many invitations to accept or decline. Here it is just as traumatic to say yes as to say no. Marion reminds me that I am no longer a bachelor and that if I don't wish to become one again on the spot, I had better take her away, anywhere.

Before we leave, we meet with Paula and Noah Mozes, Dov and Lea Judkowski, Ruth and Eliyahu Amiqam (all from "my" newspaper, *Yedioth Abronoth*). They fall in love with Marion. We pass many pleasant hours. I visit Binyamin Halevy, the Supreme Court justice. We have known each other for some time. His daughter, Ofra, one of the young beauties of Jerusalem, was a friend of Nicolas, my comrade since 1945.

A handsome man, the judge. He has sharp features, contrasting with his warm gaze. He is refined, elegant. I had had several opportunities to discuss with him the two trials in which the Tragedy was central, those of Rudolf Kastner and Adolf Eichmann. Halevy presided over the first and participated in the second. I remember his resounding conclusions about Kastner, the Zionist leader who he said "sold his soul to the devil" in Budapest. And I remember the questions he asked, in German, of Eichmann.

But now I feel like discussing religion with him. For beyond the esteem in which I hold him professionally, he intrigues me as a man. A practicing Jew, he had opened the Kastner trial with his head covered by a *kipa*. But then suddenly, toward the middle of the trial, he appeared bareheaded. My question: What had precipitated the religious crisis revealed by this act? What had provoked it? A word of the accused, a gesture of the prosecutor, the tears of a survivor? Or perhaps a point made by Shmuel Tamir, former officer of the Irgun and future minister of justice under Menachem Begin?

He does not answer. Instead he asks *me* a question in strictest confidence. Begin has offered him a seat in the Knesset. What to do? Forsake justice for politics?

Who am I to advise him? The skeptic in me distrusts politics and, even more, politicians. In the end the judge succumbed to temptation. And came to regret it.

The Côte d'Azur. I love that place of bliss. I love the climate, the atmosphere, the free spirit of its inhabitants. We frequently go there to spend a few days or weeks in the small villages around Nice, Monaco, or Cannes. Hours spent reading, walking, listening to music. The saying is true: One can live like God in France—that is to say, not badly at all.

We settle down to spend the summer in a house Marion found in Roquebrune. I am working on *The Oath* while at the same time preparing my Hasidic lectures. The writer Manès Sperber and his wife, Jenka, spend some peaceful moments with us. I have already spoken of my ties to Manès. I love to listen to him, and he loves to teach. Adler, Trotsky, Silone: He knows so much on so many subjects. Thanks to him, I make considerable progress in oenology. I also owe Manès everything I know about the behavior of mosquitoes, though I still don't know why, even in the middle of a crowd, I remain their chosen target. To console me he says, "It is always the females that bite. And then they die." Of happiness?

Marion has discovered a villa close to ours, "La Souco," where Malraux lived during the Occupation. She would love to buy it. I discourage her, and that's a mistake. I have come to realize often that her instincts are good, her intuition infallible. Had we followed them more often, her husband would be a wealthy man today.

For a change of scenery we drive to San Remo, where Yossel Rosensaft and his entourage of Bergen-Belsen survivors welcome their

Israeli, English, and American friends. They sing and laugh, laugh and sing, even as they evoke their dark memories of long ago.

I rise before the others, around 6 a.m., to go down to the Hotel Royal's swimming pool, where the instructor gives me lessons I desperately need. I tell myself that if one day I have a son, it will be incumbent on me, in accordance with the injunction of Rabbi Akiba, to teach him to swim. Best to be prepared. I am a poor student and tend to flee as soon as I hear steps approaching. Consequently I still don't know how to swim.

The past resurfaces. I remember the day when I first discovered the Côte d'Azur. The immensity of the sea at Bandol. My first trip as a journalist. The immigrants who came from the displaced persons camps. A young girl named Inge. My excessive shyness. My first journey to Israel. All that was long ago, in 1949.

Marion is eager to go home. So am I. We must return to New York, where little Jennifer is anxiously waiting for us. Marion's daughter is often sad, but it is easy to make her smile, so easy.

Here I am, a married man, responsible for a family. For the first time, at age forty, I experience daily life with a woman. In the old days, in Sighet, people married at eighteen. A twenty-five-year-old single woman was considered a spinster, and a thirty-year-old unmarried man a confirmed bachelor. What was the hurry? Were they really mature enough to lead independent lives at such a young age? For me, the discovery of life as a couple includes a series of challenges and traps. I must unlearn certain habits, acquire new ones, learn to bring together two sets of friendships, solder two natures, forge a complicity. There are innumerable problems of adaptation. Will love solve them? What is happening to us happens to everybody. The husband seems always to be cold, while the wife insists on turning on the air-conditioning. She can spend hours in a store; he becomes restless after five minutes. He regularly attends synagogue; she hardly ever does. She loves movies; he is immersed in his books and only occasionally "sacrifices" himself and accompanies her to a film. Never mind. They love each other. Even the disagreements are a source of wonder. Doesn't a life in common signify discovery and sharing? Whatever they undertake, they do together, in perfect harmony. Even their trivial and, mercifully, infrequent quarrels are worthwhile: They allow for stimulating reconciliations.

My friends are happy to see me happy. They've had to wait long enough for this. Rebbe Menahem-Mendel Schneerson of Lubavitch had often scolded me, quoting Scripture: "It is not good for man to remain alone." Among the letters I received from him before my marriage, there was one in particular that made me smile. Three strong pages on theological topics like "Is it possible to believe without believing in God?" followed by a simple question that he said "has nothing to do with theology: Why don't you get married?" I told him that the question actually had a lot to do with theology. . . .

Saul Lieberman, too, pushed me toward marriage in his own way: by describing to me the often tragic fate of bachelors in talmudic literature. Abraham Joshua Heschel had limited himself to a few allusions. When we returned from Israel, he and his wife, Sylvia, hosted a dinner in our honor. On meeting Marion, he gave her his trust with characteristic warmth. That day, in his wonderfully courtly way, he crossed half the city to find orchids for the new bride.

As for me, I try to remember why I was so fearful of "losing my freedom." Was I afraid to detach myself from the past and its ghosts? Afraid of a stability I confused with complacency? No doubt these fears were real, but they were of secondary importance. Why did I wait so long to create a home? True, I worried about not being able to support a family, but was there a deeper reason, a general lack of confidence in the future?

Back home people would have said that I was waiting for my *zivvug*, the being who was destined to be mine in the civil registers on high.

A story, why not?

When the famous German Jewish philosopher Moses Mendelssohn reached the age to be married, it was natural that the richest, most beautiful, most cultivated young girl was chosen for him. Both sets of parents declared themselves delighted and saw no need to consult the two intended. An agreement was reached as to the wedding date, and the cream of society and the most notable rabbis were invited.

On the day of the wedding, following custom, the bridegroom gave a *drasha*, a lecture, that his friends interrupted at intervals with appropriate songs. In another room, the bride and her friends were being entertained by the best musicians and minstrels of the region.

At the moment when the groom had to raise the veil of his bride-to-be, he was dazzled by her beauty. Unfortunately, at the same time, she saw him and fainted. For the philosopher was as famous for his ungainly appearance as for his erudition. He had a small, pointed nose, bushy eyebrows, two dissimilar eyes, and a hump. One can understand the bride's reaction. As soon as she came to, she asked for her father and said, "I'd rather die than marry him." The father begged her to relent, to be patient and obedient. To no avail. The mother also pleaded. In vain. Both lamented: What a scandal, what a shame, all these guests, the uncles, the aunts, what will they say? In the end Moses' father had to tell his son. The groom was not a philosopher for nothing: He had guessed everything. "I understand," he whispered. "Please explain to her that I am not angry. In return, I'd like to speak to her alone; I'd like her to give me fifteen minutes. Thereafter, she'll be free to return to her parents."

In those days such a request seemed preposterous. What? Two young people alone before the wedding? Still, the rabbis agreed. A quarter of an hour, no more. Mendelssohn welcomed the young girl, smiling. He invited her to sit down and to listen to him. "I shall tell you a talmudic legend," he said.

> Before coming down to Earth to be born, every soul is escorted by an angel. Together they leave the heavens, while a divine voice announces: The son of so-and-so will be the husband of so-and-so's daughter. . . . Well, when I heard this voice, I turned to the angel and told him that I would like to meet my future wife. "Impossible," answered the angel, "that is strictly forbidden." Since I was born a philosopher, I knew how to defend my cause. "Listen," I said, "if you don't show her to me, I shall simply refuse to go down to Earth." That's when the angel panicked: "You cannot disobey. This command comes directly from God. Don't you know that it is He Who keeps souls in a coffer that none other can open?" "No matter," I said. "Either you show her to me, or I stay here." Eventually this angel gave in, making me swear that I would never betray him. Then he showed me the woman God had, perhaps inadvertently, chosen for me. And when I saw her, I fainted. To say that she lacked beauty and grace would be charitable. . . . She had a hump, her nose was crooked, better not dwell on

it. . . . In a rage I began to shout, "I don't want her, do you hear me, I don't want her; I'd rather die than live one day at her side!" "It's my fault," sobbed the angel, "I shouldn't have given in. I shall be punished, and the punishment inflicted on angels is the worst of all. . . ." I felt sorry for him and offered him a deal: I would consent to go down and marry the young girl, but on one condition: that I could take her ugliness upon myself.

And the beautiful girl believed him. And her wedding to the philosopher was celebrated with great joy.

Bit by bit I move away from professional journalism, which no longer satisfies me. I feel like changing—if not my profession, then my workplace and my schedule. I still visit the U.N. on a regular basis. In the absence of great speakers, its discourses and goals lack vision. I have to force myself to "cover" its political and diplomatic events. Its cast of characters is usually uninteresting. In truth, my heart is no longer in it. Even scoops no longer excite me. I propose to Gershon Jacobson, my colleague with ties to the Lubavitcher movement, that he take over. Dov Judkowski, my boss in Tel Aviv, agrees. But how will I manage financially? I still send weekly columns to *Yedioth* and occasional special features to the *Forverts*, for whose news desk I stopped working some time ago. I am tired of repeating the same formulas, just changing the names. "Mr. X met last night with ambassador Y. . . ." "It appears that . . . Z formally denies that . . ." I feel my vocabulary getting poorer and poorer by the day. Fortunately, there are my studies with Lieberman, my walks with Heschel.

And yet there would be plenty of topics for a journalist with a passion for his profession. While years ago space was allotted to me parsimoniously at *Yedioth*, today I could command as much as I'd like. Noah Mozes is happy: The daily has increased in size, circulation, and influence. But Dov advises me to give up my column; he thinks I should be writing more "serious" material. At the *Forverts*, my editors are more indulgent; they would publish my thoughts on the theological dimensions of Chinese gastronomy if I so chose.

The times are dramatic—intervals of freedom punctuated by brutal interventions. The sadness of the 1968 Prague Spring: "Wake up, Lenin! Your children have gone mad!" A demented Australian youth sets fire to the El Aksa Mosque in Jerusalem. Richard Nixon sinks ever more deeply into the filthy war in Vietnam, the wretched legacy bequeathed to him by his predecessors. Two hundred thousand demonstrators converge on Washington to vent their anger. The bloody name of My Lai drips over the headlines: How could a lieutenant wearing an American uniform coldly order the massacre of a hundred or more men, women, and children? An officer explains that there are times when it is necessary to save a village from Communism by destroying it. A tragic conclusion.

Meanwhile the Concorde triumphantly soars over the Atlantic. Modern man moves faster and faster without knowing how to utilize the time he saves. In France, in an ultimate gesture of contempt, General de Gaulle steps down, slamming the door behind him. Justice Abe Fortas resigns from the Supreme Court for having accepted a $20,000 bribe from a shady businessman. Then comes Chappaquiddick: Does young Mary Jo Kopechne's death signify the end of Teddy Kennedy's presidential dreams? As for man's first walk on the moon: I spend a sleepless night on the Côte d'Azur waiting for the historic moment. I explain to Marion: "One day we may have a child and he will ask us what we were doing when the first man 'conquered' or 'liberated' the moon. What will we answer? That we slept?"

Then there was Woodstock: 400,000 young people gathered to experience the ecstasy of collective rebellion. Joy, love, and freedom all in one. The thrill of learning that Beckett has been awarded the Nobel Prize in literature: But where does Godot fit in? How I would love to decipher their silent dialogue.

Not content to change just my marital status and place of residence, I also change publishers in America. Through Lily Edelman, B'nai B'rith's director of educational programs, I meet Jean Ennis and Jim Silberman. Jim is editor in chief of Random House, and Jean heads its publicity department. They introduce me to their chairman, Robert Bernstein, a tall, attractive man with red hair, whom Marion perceives as the reincarnation of Huckleberry Finn. Soon I am their author. Lily offers to translate *A Beggar in Jerusalem* with the help of her husband, Nathan, professor of Romance languages at Columbia University. The result does not satisfy Jim. I take back the manuscript and try rewriting it, but my English is not up to the task. I turn to Marion. She reworks the translation.

It is 1970. The publication by Random House of *A Beggar in Jerusalem* goes smoothly, perhaps as a result of its winning the French Prix Médicis. There are enthusiastic reviews in the *New York Times*, the *Washington Post*, and other newspapers throughout the country. This is the first time that one of my books gets such a reception.

A Beggar in Jerusalem does not make for easy reading. I conceived of it as a sort of collage, every chapter a separate tale. Together they were to be more than the sum of their parts. My intention was to contain in one tale basic elements of both Jewish history and my own. To recount the Six-Day War, I called upon characters from my earlier novels, biblical figures and Hasidic Masters, mystical madmen and roving visionaries: I summoned them all to the Wall in Jerusalem. I even invited a certain Joshua of Nazareth to take his place there. Shlomo the Blind, who had previously met him, had predicted what his disciples would make of his teachings. And the son of Joseph the carpenter began to weep, saying over and over: "This is not what I wanted, this is not what I meant to happen. . . ." But it was too late.

Of all my novels, readers say this is the least accessible. It requires explanations I feel incapable of providing. American tourists, returning from Israel, wrote to complain that they had gone to the Wall but had not encountered "my" beggars.

In *One Generation After*, published in France in 1970, I return to the Six-Day War, which has a place in the collective memory of more than one people. There I recall a conversation with Colonel Motta Gur, the liberator of the Old City of Jerusalem, about a radio broadcast of his that had touched the Israeli public so deeply that it was rebroadcast several times. I asked him if he was religious.

He seemed incredulous: "Of course not! For God's sake, why would you think that?"

"Because your account was suffused with religious overtones."

His expression was one of bewilderment: Where on earth did I get that idea? Suddenly, the roles were reversed; now he was interrogating me:

"Did I speak of God?"

"No."

"Of the Bible?"

"No again."

"Did I discuss issues other than those relating to the confrontation? Did I quote the Torah?"

"No."

"There! You see? Your question is groundless. All I did was tell a story. My own."

But what a story. It has elements of prophetic delirium. Listen: Under his command, the paratroopers began to run through the Old City, from one street to the next, from one turret to the next, obeying an irresistible force. The situation was mad, exalted, insane. Every soldier knew, however obscurely, that he had lived only for this moment, for this race. Then, in the midst of the roaring battle, Gur's voice was heard shouting his report to headquarters: "The Temple Mount is in our hands!" And everywhere—on every front, in every house, in every place of business, in every yeshiva—officers, soldiers, children, and old men wept and embraced. And there was in these tears, in this explosion of emotion, something unreal that set the event apart, this event that changed forever those who lived it, and the others as well.

Motta Gur shrugged and said: "You make it sound too poetic; that's not my style."

"So for you it was nothing but another war episode, a battle among so many others?"

"I won't go that far. After all, Jerusalem was not only a military objective. It was something else. Jerusalem is . . . Jerusalem."

"What is it that makes Jerusalem . . . Jerusalem?"

"Why, its history, of course. It is Jewish, isn't it? It touches me, it . . . it's part of me!"

"Jericho, too, has a past linked to ours. So does Hebron. And Gaza. And Bethlehem."

"Enough of your comparisons! Jerusalem cannot be compared to any other place."

I was smiling. He had fallen into the trap. Here he was speaking in mystical terms.

"Strange," he said at the end. "What started as a strictly military operation ended as something else entirely. Suddenly we were fighting as if in a trance. We understood at that moment that our true objective was no longer to occupy this or that strategic position, but to liberate history itself. . . .

"But, no, I'm not even religious, surely not observant. How many times do I have to tell you? Yes, I occasionally go to synagogue. So what? My children go; I accompany them. What does it prove? Only that I fulfill my duty as a parent."

I met him a few years later. He pretended to be angry; he scowled: "If you knew what problems you caused me. . . ."

People close to him told me how, after the battle was over, he came home to his wife and children and spent several days and nights sobbing. Never explaining.

Many years later, in 1995, a victim of cancer, fearing the inevitable decline, he committed suicide. All Israel wept for him.

In the Bible, one generation represents forty years. But I collected and published the texts that compose *One Generation After* twenty-five years after the Event. That is what I sometimes call the Holocaust, for the latter name does not seem adequate.

Some scholars contend that I was the first to give the term "Holocaust" a modern usage by introducing it into our contemporary vocabulary. Why did I choose that word over another? At the time I was preparing an essay on the *Akeda*, the sacrifice of Isaac; the word *ola*, translated as "burnt offering" or "holocaust," struck me, perhaps because it suggests total annihilation by fire and the sacred and mystical aspect of sacrifice, and I used it in an essay on the war. But I regret that it has become so popular and is used so indiscriminately. Its vulgarization is an outrage.

In truth, as I have said over and over, there is no word for the ineffable. *Shoah?* This biblical term, now officially used in Israel, seems equally inadequate. It applies to an accident, a natural catastrophe striking a community. As such it has appeared in official speeches and in the press since the very beginning of anti-Jewish persecutions in Nazified Europe, long before the implementation of the Final Solution. Clearly the same word should not be used to describe both a pogrom and Auschwitz.

After the liberation, Yiddish-speaking survivors referred simply to "the war" or the *Churban*, a word that signifies destruction and recalls the ransacking of the First and Second Temples in Jerusalem. Yet with the passage of time I become more and more convinced that no word is strong enough or true enough to speak of Auschwitz, Treblinka, Majdanek, . . . And yet.

In *The Town Beyond the Wall*, I divided society of that time into three categories: the killers, the victims, and the spectators. Later, in my first speech at the White House, I observed that if we allow the victims to be relegated to oblivion, we would in fact be killing them again.

As the years go by, this witness grows increasingly weary of correcting "experts," of trying to limit the trivialization of memory, of fighting public indifference. Hate crimes, religious wars, ethnic conflicts, collective violence, the rise in xenophobia and anti-Semitism—to think that we had imagined that the demons would no longer come howling in the night.

These may be the reasons for the pervasive feeling that a grave error has been committed, that something has gone awry. We must have been wrong to trust mankind, wrong to hope that we could defeat death by remaining faithful to its victims. Perhaps we should have remained silent, so as not to violate the secret entrusted to us by the dead. Perhaps we were wrong to expose the mystery of Auschwitz to the inevitable profanations we are forced to witness more and more frequently.

༅

*M*Y GRANDFATHER *continues to haunt my dreams. Hands clasped behind his back, he wanders through the Beit Midrash as if he were looking for someone. He is alone. But not completely: I am keeping him company. But he is alone nevertheless. From time to time he stops, picks up a book, and, with an air of deep concentration, leafs through it. He puts it down, and I, in turn, open it. A shiver runs through me: All the pages are blank and faded. I utter a frightened sound, but my grandfather signals me to be silent. And to come closer. He stands before the Holy Ark. Inside are human beings instead of the sacred scrolls. I cry: "But they are dead, Grandfather, they are all dead." My grandfather nods as if to say: True, we are all dead. "But the sacred scrolls, Grandfather, where are they? With the dead?" My grandfather doesn't answer. Panicked, I turn and prepare to run away. I run toward the exit, but it is blocked. I rush to the window, but it opens on a wall. A stranger has scaled it; he is sitting on top. Eyes wide, I try to identify him. It is my grandfather. In his arms he holds the sacred scrolls. He cradles them as if they were his grandchildren. I lean over to capture his song and I fall, or rather I feel that*

I am falling, only to find myself at the very spot where my grand-
father had been sitting. I don't know how, but now I am the one who is
holding the scrolls. I want to rock them, but I don't know the song
that filled my dream.

∾

In Israel, the so-called war of attrition is devastating. In Munich,
where an El Al plane is attacked by Arab terrorists, killing one and
wounding eleven, the Jewish Center is set on fire. A Swissair plane
explodes: Forty-seven people, passengers and crew, lose their lives.
Violence becomes more frequent, more intense. Planes are hijacked.
We witness the massacre of Palestinians by the Jordanian army and
the birth of the Black September movement.

One evening, having been invited to Golda's home, Marion and
I arrive to find her distraught. The army has just shot down five Soviet
MiGs that had violated Israeli airspace. Golda fears reprisals. Chain-
smoking as usual, she complains: "These Russians, what do they want
from us? Why are they always against us, always on the enemy's side?
Why do they provoke us? Is it war they're looking for? With a small
state like ours?"

Next day, in the restaurant at the Knesset, we chat with Ezer
Weizman, the former air force commander, a minister without portfo-
lio in Golda's government, and the future president of the State of
Israel. "Everybody is worried," I say to him. "Aren't you?" No, he is
not. The enfant terrible of Israeli politics is, as General de Gaulle
would say, "sure of himself" and of *Tsahal*, the army. "The next war will
not last six days but six hours," he tells us. "The plans are ready, success guaranteed." "Then why is Golda so worried?" I ask. Weizman
shrugs as if to say: What can you expect of a woman who has never
done military service?

An hour later we have coffee with General Bar-Lev, commander
in chief of the army, and famous for his strategic genius. I first met this
brilliant military man in New York, where he was doing postgraduate
work at Columbia University. He is a fine man—intelligent, reserved,
sophisticated, and loyal. His speech is slow and deliberate; his gaze,
penetrating. He inspires confidence and is admired by the military,
respected by the politicians, trusted by the public.

We discuss the current tensions. He is nearly as optimistic as

Weizman. He whips out his pen and scribbles numbers on a paper napkin. Of course, he says in his low, halting voice, there are those who are afraid—not of the Arabs, naturally, but of the Russians. Those Russians are powerful. Their numbers are overwhelming. But they are far away. What would be dangerous for us would be a war with infantry and armored vehicles. . . . If the Red Army sends more than a hundred thousand soldiers, that might pose a problem. . . . But they would need transport planes. . . . And, yes, their pilots are good. But ours are better.

I must admit that I was frightened by his calm. I thought to myself: The entire world is afraid of the Soviet Union, but he is not. France fears the Russians, Washington is wary of them, China distrusts them, and the tiny Israeli nation is fearless. If Bar-Lev's equanimity had been based on a belief in divine intervention rather than in strategic arguments, I would have better understood his attitude.

Let us stay another moment with *One Generation After,* whose French title, *Entre deux soleils,* was suggested by Manès Sperber. What does it mean, "Between two suns"? It means dusk, the mystical hour worshipped by Hasidic dreamers. At that hour on the first Friday of Creation, according to *Pirkei Avot, The Ethics of Our Fathers,* ten things were introduced into human history: the abyss that swallowed Korah and his accomplices; Miriam's well, which accompanied the Children of Israel into the desert to heal them; the mouth of the ass that answered Balaam; the rainbow in Noah's time; the manna; the staff used to effect the biblical miracles in pharaonic Egypt; the *shamir,* the tiny worm that split the stones used in the construction of Solomon's Temple; the rectangular shape of the letters engraved in the Tablets of the Law; their capacity to be read at four different angles; and the tablets themselves. Certain sages add the demons, who were also created at this hour between daylight and darkness. And the tomb of Moses. And the ram Abraham sacrificed instead of his son Isaac on Mount Moriah.

This title reflects, less clearly than the American, the content of this work, which deals, however sketchily, with generational conflicts and also the fate of children of survivors, their dramatic confrontation with their parents' past. There is the tragic story of one young man, the son of a distant cousin from Queens. He was twenty, a student of literature, filled with literary dreams. One morning he rose, took his typewriter, and walked into the sea.

• • •

Years after the publication of *One Generation After*, I am invited to address the first meeting of "the Second Generation," that is, the children of survivors. Facing these young men and women, some of them now fathers and mothers themselves, all caught between their parents' wounded memory and their own hopes covered with ashes, I have difficulty hiding my emotions. For these people belong to my internal landscape: I look at them and see them through the prism of the past. Some of them were my students at City College. They affect me deeply because every time I see them, I cannot help but see other children through them, behind them, marching in the distance toward the blazing abyss.

I look at these young people and tell myself, tell them, that *they* were the enemy's target as surely as were their parents. *They* were the ones he had hoped to annihilate. By killing Jews, he hoped to prevent their children from being born.

I tell them the talmudic legend of Rabbi Shimon bar Yohai and his son Eleazar. Fleeing the Romans, they found refuge in a cave and stayed there twelve years. When they emerged they were unable to conceal their astonishment: The world outside had not changed. So angry were they that their eyes burned down all that they looked upon. As a result, a celestial voice ordered them back into the cave for another year, at the end of which the son was still angry, though the father was not. And the Talmud comments: "Whatever the son's gaze wounded, the father's gaze healed."

Rembrandt's beautiful painting of Abraham and Isaac comes to mind. It shows them, after the test, embracing with a tenderness that must have moved the Creator and his angels.

Is there a tenderness more profound, more intense, more human than the one that links the survivor to his child? What goes on in the mind of a son who watches his father praying or simply staring into space? What are the thoughts of a daughter who senses the pain of her mother, who has lost two infants to the executioner? Surely there comes a moment when such children become their parents' parents.

My thoughts turned toward them once again when I wrote *The Fifth Son* and *The Forgotten*. I speak to them even when I think I am speaking to others.

In *One Generation After*, I try my hand at a new literary genre. My wish: to convey the essential in the form of dialogue alone. Dialogues between individuals separated by death—or life. Brief questions and clipped answers. I wanted these dialogues to be anonymous. Voices. No, I wanted them to be echoes that reach us from far away. I strain to hear the last conversation between a young boy and his little sister, a grown man and his mother, a Hasid and his grandfather. He is a witness who grasps at scraps of dialogue with the dead man inside him. He wants every word to contain a sentence, every sentence a page, every page a book, a life, a death, and the history they share.

—*Hey you! You look like you're praying!*
—Wrong.
—*Your lips don't stop moving!*
—Habit, no doubt.
—*Did you always pray that much?*
—More than that. Much more.
—*What did you ask for in your prayers?*
—Nothing.
—*Forgiveness?*
—Perhaps.
—*Knowledge?*
—Possibly.
—*Friendship?*
—Yes, friendship.
—*The chance to defeat evil? The certainty of living with truth, or living, period?*
—Perhaps.
—*And you call that nothing?*
—I do. I call that nothing.

*

—*Will you remember me?*
—I promise you.
—*How can you? You don't even know who I am, I myself don't know.*
—Never mind; I'll remember my promise.
—*For a long time?*
—As long as possible. All my life perhaps. But . . . why do you laugh?
—*I want you to remember my laughter too.*
—You're lying. You laugh because you're going mad.
—*Perfect. Remember my madness.*

• • •

—Tell me . . . Am *I* making you laugh?
—*Not just you. No, my little one, not just you.*

I make my first trip to Norway, a nation that will become important to
me in my life as writer and activist. Must I mention the awful, embarrassing fact that in Sighet I knew nothing of this nation and its people? Norway for me was one of those places of which I didn't even
know that I knew nothing.

Invited by the publishing house Aschehoug to promote *The Jews
of Silence,* I go there rather skeptically. No sooner have I landed than a
journalist advises me to meet Johan Borgen. Who is he? And why
should I make his acquaintance? The journalist explains that when *The
Town Beyond the Wall* had come out a few years earlier, it was warmly
received, largely because of a very favorable article by this great writer,
the revered dean of Norwegian letters. "He is our own Mauriac," the
journalist tells me. "Evidently he has taken you under his wing." This
explains the presence of the large number of journalists at a press conference organized by Max Tau, my editor at Aschehoug. I speak of
Russian Jewry's plight; of their struggle, nonviolent but determined; of
their hopes, nourished by their thirst for identity as much as by their
need for freedom. The Norwegian people are always on the side of the
victims, and I sense this among the listeners. Norway is one of the rare
countries to have opened its doors to "displaced persons," the sick ones
who were rejected by the big Western powers at war's end. It is easy to
become attached to this country, to these rather reserved men and
women who are respectful of your moods, your need for privacy and
friendship. Like the British, they favor understatement. In Norway,
reticence is a national virtue. (Do you know the story of the young
Norwegian who was so in love with a woman that he finally told her?)

For me a city, a country, is first of all a face. Oslo has many.

Professor Leo (his friends call him Sjua) Eitinger is the author of
an important study on the psychosomatic effects of the Holocaust on
its survivors. I speak of him in *Night:* He was present at my knee operation at Buna concentration camp. He is a distinguished-looking man.
His gaze is open, his voice authoritative. "I have read your testimony,"
he says. "I believe we come from the same place." Astonished, I ask:
"From Sighet?" "No. From a place that could be called anti-Sighet."
"Auschwitz? Buchenwald?" I whisper. "Both." Suddenly an image

comes back to me: the infirmary. That voice, I recognize that voice. "It's you who . . . ?" He smiles: "Possibly." I tell him that I owe him a debt of gratitude. "For taking care of you?" No. For showing me that even *over there* it was possible to have faith in mankind.

During that same trip, I meet someone who is in fact from Sighet. Better: We attended the same *heder*. Surprised, I call out to him: "What are you doing here?" He bursts into laughter. "And you?" he asks. Haim-Hersh Kahan left with the first transport, together with the town's rabbis and my two mad fellow disciples of Kalman the Kabbalist. After the liberation he returned to Sighet via Vienna and Budapest. How did he come to settle in Oslo? Like all survivors' stories, his had much to do with chance. On his way to the United States, he went through Sweden, where he met a beautiful local Jewish girl, Esther. Haim-Hersh stayed in Scandinavia, went into business, and made a fortune; he now plays an important role in Oslo's Jewish community. He still sings as he did long ago and tells stories of times that only he and I remember.

And so death did not triumph everywhere. Nor did evil. Old bonds are renewed, and new ones are formed.

Max Tau, my editor, is an original. Small, agile, and ever watchful, he appears to be in constant fear of missing something—a rumor, a thought, an encounter. To him I owe the Norwegian publication of my first books. He introduces me to my translator, Gerd Host Heyerdahl, poet and professor at Oslo University. Max, a writer and Jewish immigrant of German origin, had fallen in love with a Norwegian, Tove (taller and less talkative than he), and with Norwegian society.

Since I don't know his language and he doesn't know mine, he speaks to me in German and I respond in my Germanized Yiddish. In company he pretends to understand everything, but in reality he hears nothing for the simple reason that he's deaf, which does not prevent him from participating in the conversation. He laughs at the right moment or becomes serious when required. What upsets him about me? My refusal to "forgive." A Germanophile, he has introduced the important German writers to Norway and proclaimed himself an advocate of reconciliation with Germany. When he obtains a German literary prize for me and I tell him that I do not feel right about accepting it, he does not conceal his hurt.

We have a shared admiration for the great Greek writer Nikos Kazantzakis, author of *Zorba*, whom he has known and celebrated for years, and about whom he tells me a thousand anecdotes and tales of adventure.

And then there is Borgen, my ally, my friend. I owe him in Norway what I owe François Mauriac in France. Borgen lives two hours outside the capital and goes only rarely to the city. His house is isolated, protected. There are flowers everywhere. Several large, light-filled rooms. A few small cubicles—reminiscent of ancient monastic cells—are reserved for guests.

The friendship is instantaneous. From the first encounter, without preliminaries, we go straight to the essential. We speak of writing and of death, the eternal in the moment, the word and despair.

Long and thin, almost emaciated, Borgen radiates an air of rigor and flawless character: Nothing, neither honors nor adversity, can bend him. His intelligence is sophisticated, demanding.

His wife, Martha, is strange. People tell me that she was once one of Oslo's most beautiful women. Now she insists on dressing like a witch, possibly to chase away the demons she believes in and whom, in order to blunt their evil powers, she hides in secret places in her enchanted garden. She lives only to protect her husband—from the living, of course, as well as the demons. After my second visit she confesses to me that her love for Johan is absolute and that she will do anything to keep it intact. I have the feeling that she sees a rival in every being her husband might love. In short, she is jealous of everybody, including me.

They have a beautiful daughter, Anne, a novelist who lives in Oslo. Her brother, Espe, does not leave his father's side. Borgen tells me that years ago Espe was the victim of a serious accident. His body broken, his brain damaged, he lay day and night without regaining consciousness. The doctors said he would never recover, but Johan rejected their verdict: The word "never" did not suit him. Riveted to his son's bedside, he held his hand. Day and night, he clasped his dying son's hand in his own. How is one to explain the transfusion of energy and strength that occurred? Slowly, Espe came back to life.

And here he stands before me, smiling as he gazes at his father. There is between them a bond of tenderness, trust, and wisdom that I feel privileged to witness.

Johan is already ill when we first meet. How does he manage to be stronger than the cancer that is gnawing at him? He suffers in silence. And when we walk along the beach, we speak of other things. He is not religious, but the words we use are. He seems to know how to cope with the body's failings. But the failings that attack the soul, the evil inherent in life—how is one to banish them without denying life itself? Could the saints possibly know secrets that are inaccessible to mortals? Is that what saintliness means: the art of freeing oneself from all temptation, therefore, from all human traits?

I am told that before he died, Borgen asked for a glass of champagne. He raised it to his family, turned his eyes toward the absent or perhaps toward absence, and emptied the glass after uttering the usual *skol.*

It was his last word.

In 1970 the free world is stunned and outraged by the Leningrad trials.

A quixotic episode. Heroic as well? No doubt. A group of young Russian-Jewish daredevils decided to hijack a commercial Aeroflot plane to Scandinavia. From there they intended to continue to Israel. Their effort was part of a larger plan devised in Jerusalem in hopes of attracting world attention to the plight of Soviet Jews. It was a dramatic but dangerous idea: You don't play games with the KGB. The group was awaiting the green light from the Israeli authorities, when an informer who had infiltrated the dissident movement gave them away. The group's members were arrested, imprisoned, judged, and condemned by a Leningrad tribunal. Several death sentences were pronounced, provoking waves of protest in all the capitals of the West. The largest demonstration took place in Brussels in February 1971, bringing together eight hundred delegates from thirty-eight countries. At the head of the Israeli delegation was David Ben-Gurion—an imposing presence, regal but melancholy. The lion of Judea was too old. Though physically still vigorous, he was barely coherent. Many of us regretted that he had been pulled out of retirement.

In my brief address I told a Hasidic tale: Rebbe Uri of Strelisk knocks at the door of his friend Rebbe Moshe-Leib of Sassov and asks for his help: He is collecting funds to enable a poor young girl to get married. However, since he himself knows only impoverished people, he has been unable to gather the required sum. Could Rebbe Moshe-Leib offer him some advice or help? And the Rebbe answers: "I, too, beloved brother, meet only those in need; I don't know any rich men. Therefore I cannot give you any money. All I can do for you is dance.

And that should be sufficient." "In conclusion," I said, "let me tell you that on Simhat Torah in Moscow, I have seen these young Jews dance. It was indeed sufficient." I speak of their courage wherever I go. In Paris I find myself seated next to filmmaker Claude Lanzmann and his young colleague Efrem Sevella, just arrived from Moscow. In flavorful Yiddish the young man recounts the struggle of the scientist Mikhaïl Sand in confronting the Soviet regime. Sevella explains that his comrades had all pitched in to enable him to "ascend" to Israel. He speaks with emotion and conviction. But a few years later, Sevella publishes in France a vicious book, *Farewell Israel*. Every possible negative statement about the Jewish state can be found there.

These demonstrations of solidarity were not in vain. They succeeded in obtaining the commutation of death sentences. In time, all the accused arrived in Israel.

These events have left me with a manuscript, an unpublished novel called "The Trial of Krasnograd." Together with my diary, it remains in my private *genizah*. Soon I begin work on the story of Paltiel Kossover, the proud but star-crossed hero of my book *The Testament*, which deals with the Communist experience, not the Holocaust. You see, mostly I keep my word. I stay away from the "forbidden theme."* At this moment I am also working on *Souls on Fire*, a book I live and retell with joy. I put into it everything I received from my grandfather Reb Dodye: his love of his people, his passion for songs and stories. As I write, I see him on a Friday night as he enters the light-filled house with dancing steps. He sings and I sing along with him into my very prayers and silences. It is with him and his youngest daughter, my mother, in mind that I compose my Song of Songs in homage to Hasidic tradition; it was their tradition and it remains mine. This explains why that particular book occupies a special place in my work and in my life. More than my fictional tales, it is linked to my early life, to my childhood. I have said it often: Hasidism is a world that is mine; it contains my murdered dreams but also my efforts to bring them back to life.

How to define Hasidism? A group in revolt against the establishment? A mystical sect? A religious movement with social overtones?

In my novels Hasidism becomes framework and vantage point; the Besht (the Baal Shem Tov) or Rebbe Levi-Itzhak of Berditchev

*See *All Rivers Run to the Sea*, pp. 150–1.

comes to the rescue of my characters, just as they responded to my requests long ago.

A strange destiny, that of the Hasidic movement. It survived the Holocaust, whereas the majority of its followers became its victims. The killers succeeded in assassinating millions of Hasidim but not the ideal of Hasidism, which is now popular once again, especially with the young.

As the apotheosis of an evolving humanism, Hasidism places the emphasis on the sacred aspect of man and that which makes him human. In a society dominated by the awesome magic of technology, young people discover with wonder the Beshtian precept that the mystery of the universe resides in man, just as the secret of life resides in life itself.

And then, let us not overlook the sociophilosophical elements: Our generation resembles that of the Baal Shem Tov. Just as in his time, it is necessary today to build on ruins, to hold on to something—another human being, a faith. Hasidism? An antidote to resignation. What is its lesson to its disciples? Is it difficult to sing? Never mind. It is because it is difficult if not impossible to sing, to pray, to hope that we must try. Even if living in a world dehumanized by its own guilt is difficult, never mind. Let one person, just one, extend his hand to a beggar, a fugitive, a refugee, and life will become meaningful for others. Evil exists? Death is triumphant? Never mind. Nothing is as whole as a broken heart, said Rebbe Mendel of Kotzk.

There is in Hasidism a quest for nature's beauty, a glimpse into its secrets. In his youth, the Besht was a tutor. He accompanied children to *heder* and taught them not only to sing but also to see. He prevented them from moving too quickly. Look at this tree, he would say; and the sky; and these mountains. At a time when Jewish children were used to walking fast, fearful of being assaulted by hooligans, the Besht made them slow down, to take in the beauty of the landscape. A human being in God's universe, that is a thing of beauty.

Yes, I do like to celebrate the movement that personifies celebration.

But celebration of what? Of Torah? Yes. Of God? Yes again. Of life? Even if it is made of poverty, misery, and suffering?

These are troubling questions that I discuss in another volume, *Somewhere a Master.* In it I describe the great Masters' challenges to the sadness and despair in which they and their disciples lived. How did they succeed in overcoming the pain they must have experienced as they listened to a barren woman, a father reeling under the burden of debt, the parents of a dying child? How did they manage to keep their faith intact as they confronted the injustices that befell their followers and the entire Jewish people?

My generation needed to hear their answers and to follow their example.

Thanks to my Hasidic tales, I am able to speak publicly with less apprehension. I emphasize their wisdom and humor. To shed the image people have of me—the messenger returned from over there— I try to elicit a smile or even laughter. As much as I resist speaking about the Tragedy, I delight in opening the gates to the Hasidic garden. To my surprise, there is an audience for this kind of pilgrimage. Unquestionably, people prefer stories and anecdotes to scholarly analyses. And so I try to combine the two by encouraging the public to reflect.

I care about people learning to savor the meaning of the Hasidic message in particular, of the messianic wait in general. I feel good when I evoke the fervor and wealth of a tale by Rebbe Nahman or a parable of Rebbe Mendel of Kotzk. There I feel no need to censor myself. I am less fearful of revealing what ought not to be revealed. There is no danger of blasphemy. I know what words need to be said; I only have to repeat those I heard from my grandfather's lips.

—Sing, Grandfather. I beg of you. I need to hear you sing.
—*I cannot.*
—Make an effort. Try, Grandfather. You always said one had the right to fail, but not without trying.
—*I cannot. Not anymore. I cannot even try.*
—I shall help you.
—*You cannot help me any more.*
—Are you forbidding me to try?
—*I am not forbidding you anything, my little one. I am only telling you that I can no longer sing.*
—Not even for me?
—*For nobody.*
—For God? For God, whom you have loved?
—*Not even for Him.*

—Why, Grandfather?
—*That's how it is. We cannot help it. Neither you nor I.*
—Is that your punishment?
—*No. It has nothing to do with punishment.*
—Then what does it have to do with, Grandfather?
—*I am dead, my little one. The dead no longer sing.*
—What about me, Grandfather . . . ?
—*What about you?*
—May I then sing for the dead?

The Jewish tradition tells us that it is through study that we may—no, that we must—honor the memory of the dead. We study a Mishna, and in so doing affirm our attachment to those who have preceded us in this quest.

Is that why my passion for study continues unabated? Indeed, it grows. King Lear is mistaken: One is never too old to learn. To rediscover ancient texts is to celebrate them; to celebrate them in their diversity, their timeless beauty. Prophetic, talmudic, philosophical, poetic, ethical celebrations. One must approach Jewish tradition through its fervor and present it with the help of its illustrious and inspired thinkers.

That is what I strive to do in my *Messengers of God.* The book is based on lectures delivered at the 92nd Street "Y" in New York, at Boston University, and at the Centre Rachi in Paris. Adam or the mystery of the Beginning, Cain and Abel or the First Murder, the near-sacrifice of Isaac, the return of Joseph, the metamorphosis of Moses, the ordeal and triumph of Job—every chapter requires months of research. There again, Saul Lieberman is indispensable. I submit to him every essay and solicit his critical comments, which I carefully take into account. I say nothing, publish nothing, without his *Haskama,* his consent.

In my notebook I write:

As a child, I read the biblical tales with a mixture of wonder and anguish. I imagined Isaac on the altar, and I wept. I saw Joseph prince of Egypt, and I laughed. . . . Jewish history unfolds in the present. Unlike mythology it affects our life and our role in society. Jupiter is a symbol, but Isaiah is a voice, a conscience. Zeus is dead without having lived, but

Moses remains alive. His exhortations, delivered long ago to a people about to be freed, resonate to this day; his Law commits us. Without a Jew's memory, his determined collective memory, he would not be a Jew or would not be.

If Judaism, more than any other tradition, demonstrates such loyalty to its past, it is because it fulfills a need. Thanks to Abraham, whose temerity guides us, thanks to Jacob, whose dream intrigues us, our survival, prodigious in many ways, has maintained its mystery and significance. If we have the strength and the will to speak out, it is because our ancestors express themselves through every one of us. If the eyes of the world so often seem fixed on us, it is because we evoke a bygone era and a destiny that transcends it. *Panim* in Hebrew is used in the plural: Man has more than one face. His own and that of Adam. The Jew is haunted by the beginning more than by the end. His messianic dream is linked to David's kingdom. He feels closer to the prophet Elijah than to his next-door neighbor. What is a Jew? Sum, synthesis, vessel. Every ordeal endured by his ancestors affects him. He is crushed by their sorrows and invigorated by their triumphs. For they were living creatures, not icons. The most pure, the most righteous among them was subject to moments of ecstasy and despair, and we are told about them. Their holiness defined itself in human terms. That is why the Jew remembers them, because he sees them at the crossroads of their existence. Anxious, exalted, singled out, they are humans, not gods. Their quest informs his own and influences his choices. Jacob's ladder disrupts his nights. Israel's anguish increases his solitude. He knows that to speak of Moses means to follow him into Egypt and out of Egypt. Whosoever refuses to tell his story stays behind.

This is true for all our ancestors and their journeys. If the near-sacrifice of Isaac concerned only Abraham and his son, their ordeal would be limited to their own suffering. But it concerns us. . . . Somewhere a father and his son head for a burning altar; somewhere a boy knows his father will die before God's veiled gaze; somewhere a storyteller remembers and is overwhelmed by an ancient and nameless sadness; he wants to weep. He has seen Abraham and he has seen Isaac go toward death, and the angel, intent on

singing the praises of the Lord, did not come to rescue
them from the quiet, black night.

Quatre maîtres hassidiques (Four Hasidic Masters) and Cinq portraits
bibliques (Five Biblical Portraits), which are part of the Célébrations, are
entrusted in America to Jim Langford, editor in chief of Notre Dame
Press, for I am close to the Catholic university of Notre Dame, and to
its president, the liberal Theodore Hesburgh. Our dialogues both private and public are ecumenical and fraternal. Both of us are devoted to
the same principles of tolerance. I respect his faith as he respects
mine, and the fight against religious and political fanaticism has never
failed to unite us. We have always confronted the merchants of hate
together. Our signatures can be found at the bottom of many a petition in support of human rights. Eventually I welcome him to the
President's Commission on the Holocaust, created by President
Carter. Ted is a believer of the kind I favor. No one could hope to
have a better interlocutor or a more faithful ally.

For the moment, since I belong to no organization or movement, I
feel free. When I take a stand, I commit to no one but myself. Sometimes I am right; often I am not. So what? I learn from my mistakes. To
enhance discipline and intellectual rigor—that is the goal. To be more
demanding of myself. And of others? The problem is that I don't like
to polemicize for fear of offending. When it does happen, I am ill at
ease; but never mind, I start again. When the subject is one that is
essential to me, I have difficulty controlling my anger even though I
may instantly regret it. But I don't always understand my hosts. Why
do they invite me? Why do they want to hear me say things that will
surely displease them? Who knows . . . ?
    Once, speaking to an important women's organization, I barely
contain my disappointment. The organizers had asked me to divide
my address into two parts: the Holocaust and Soviet Jewry. On the
day of the lecture, they express concern: "Please don't take too long;
we are planning to devote a few hours to receptions for our regional
delegates." Strange: The angrier I get, the more I show my displeasure, the more people applaud. I say things that shock and hurt, things
that should prevent the audience from swallowing their meal. Instead
they applaud and congratulate me . . . after the meal.
    It's all inexplicable to me.
    I don't understand, and yet I find myself unable to refuse the var-

ious invitations that reach me through my agent, Lily Edelman. My friends mock me: "Just because another Jew asks for you, you don't have to accept." They are not altogether wrong. It's true that I always carry around the feeling of owing something to my people.

That is how it happens that I accept the invitation to address the Council of Jewish Federations. Its annual assembly, an important event that brings together donors and organizers of many kinds, is held in a different city every year. This year, 1971, it takes place in a big hotel in Kansas City, Missouri. My address is scheduled for Saturday night.

Since I must spend Shabbat there, I decide to use the time to gauge the mood, study the topics under review, meet the different committees. In short, to find out what preoccupies the leaders of North American Jewry. I shall then adapt my words to their concerns.

Why not confess? I was immediately overcome with a feeling of estrangement, as though I found myself attending a huge gathering of union leaders. The discussions center exclusively on budgets and fund-raising, old and new methods, statistics and forecasts. Everyone is a specialist in some field. How does one approach the millionaire who remains aloof? Who should be delegated to see him, and when— in the office in the morning or at home at night? So much for the spiritual atmosphere I was expecting.

Friday evening, the immense dining room is divided in two. In a corner a few tables have been reserved for those who observe the Jewish dietary laws.

The next day, in a small drawing room, I witness the strangest, most exotic Shabbat service of my life: In addition to prayers and the Torah reading, we are treated to a ballet in which beautiful young girls perform dances that, no doubt, have a religious basis. As I am accustomed to a different style of prayer, I feel somewhat excluded.

All afternoon I am solicited by delegates who are lobbying for one thing or another. Each asks me to include in my presentation the particular project he or she has come to defend, "in the name of what is dear to us": Russian Jewry, support for Israel, child care, Jewish education in high schools, retirement homes, cultural associations. . . . They are funny, all these emissaries, militants, or bureaucrats, working for just causes and for odd ones. To them I appear as intercessor, mediator, defense attorney—in other words, a man of influence. I am not so sure, but how am I to explain this to them? Oh well, they will come to realize it eventually.

The evening begins with the pious chanting of the Havdalah, the prayer celebrating the separation in time of the profane and the sacred, and the end of Shabbat. Then comes the hour when dinner is served. There is the din of three thousand people crowded into the hall. People say hello, call to each other, leave their seats to greet acquaintances; the waiters do their work with difficulty. All the former federation presidents are seated at the dais. I sit to the right of the current president, Max Fisher, a superwealthy industrialist from Detroit who is close to both Presidents Nixon and Ford.

Suddenly I hear feverish whispering behind my back. Polite, I try not to listen. Delegates approach Fisher, evidently trying to persuade him of something. I have no idea what it's about, but I begin to get worried. I sense a crisis looming. Intrigued, I question my neighbor to the right. Oh, it's nothing, he answers. Whereupon a group of young people come over to our table. "We are students," they tell me. "We come to ask you not to be annoyed with us: We are leaving the hall to protest, not against you, but against the leaders of this organization. We are observant and after the meal we wanted to recite together the *Birkat Hamazon* [the customary grace after dinner]. They wouldn't let us."

I turn to Fisher: "Is this true?"

"Yes," he says, unperturbed.

"But why?"

"Because the prayer is not listed in the program."

For a moment I am speechless. Then I try to explain to him that he should be pleased rather than annoyed: After all, what were these young people asking for? The power to control the council's budget? No. They were requesting permission to sing a prayer that would last no more than three to five minutes. The gentleman remains unmoved: "I've made a decision; I've announced it to my colleagues; I cannot retract it without losing face."

I persist. I point out to him that if this becomes public, as it inevitably will, he might look ridiculous to the entire Jewish community. However, I do understand his predicament. So here is what I propose: Let him announce that the guest of honor wishes to recite the traditional prayer; it would be discourteous to refuse. Max acquiesces. The incident is closed. The crisis is averted.

After dinner he invites me to have a drink with him, alone. "I owe you something," he says. "What would you like?" This is my chance to act as intercessor. I repeat the delegates' requests: more spirituality for this kind of gathering; more deference for the observant; priority for Jewish education, for Jewish memory; an initial budget of $100,000 to found a council for Soviet Jewry. . . . Max takes notes. All my requests are granted. Years later we will confront each other during the Bitburg affair. Still, in Kansas City, it is thanks to a simple prayer rescued in extremis that the most important Jewish organization in America became more Jewish.

We spend the winter of 1972 in Miami. Marion is pregnant and travels less. I don't have a choice. Long-standing commitments force me to shuttle between Florida, New York, and other places.

It is during this time that I become embroiled in a political incident as pointless as it is absurd, and one I still regret today. It created a furor in Israel. I find myself, quite unintentionally, in an adversarial situation with Abba Eban, minister of foreign affairs in Golda Meir's government.

There was a time when we had a cordial professional relationship. I admired his learning, his talents. As a young ambassador to Washington and the U.N. he elicited respect and admiration from his colleagues. A brilliant speaker and intellectual, Eban could be convincing even when he himself was not convinced.

The story is told that in the mid-fifties Ben-Gurion asked him to defend Israel's position in a delicate affair. And even though Eban disagreed with that position, he defended it so well that Ben-Gurion told him: "In truth, I myself had doubts, but then I read your arguments, and you convinced me."

Unquestionably, he was a great diplomat who represented his government with superb skill and ability. He brought honor to the state and to the people of Israel. I was attracted by his sharp wit; I appreciated his Jewish and classical erudition; I admired his televised appearances, his lucid analyses of international affairs, and the elegant way he had of eluding delicate questions. He was somebody I would have liked to know better, more intimately.

But then, the incident occurred. In fact, the word "incident" is inadequate. "Political scandal" would be more precise.

Its genesis was as follows: Having just returned from a lecture tour in the Midwest, I am spending a day in our Manhattan apartment catching up on a week's mail when the telephone rings. The Israeli consul general—in New York—is on the line. "This concerns Minister Eban," he informs me. "Are you aware of what is happening to him?"

No, I'm not; I have been out of town. Could he enlighten me? He can and does. During a broadcast with the famous television interviewer David Frost, Eban was said to have answered the question, What do you think about the Nazi criminals who are still at large? by saying that after the Eichmann trial, the problem no longer interested him, or something like that. Allegedly he had repeated this several times. "You can imagine the uproar in Israel," says the consul. "Menachem Begin and the entire opposition condemn his insensitivity and are calling for his resignation. Golda is furious. A censure motion has been introduced in the Knesset. Eban claims that only a statement from you can calm the storm."

My answer to the consul is that, not having seen the telecast, I am hardly in a position to intervene. He understands and transmits my reply to Eban. One hour later he calls back: Eban has suggested that I read the transcript of the interview; perhaps then I could testify on his behalf. I accept, though I make the point that there is a critical difference between the spoken word on-screen and that presented on the written page. The consul insists that I read the transcript. I do. I study it, and I am appalled. Eban is, after all, hardly a novice in such matters, yet he had shown unbelievably poor judgment. I call the consul and express my regret at not being able to help his boss. "But," I add, "it is inconceivable that a man like Eban, or, for that matter, any Jew, could show such insensitivity to Jewish memory and to those who remain faithful to it." In other words, I cannot believe this is what he meant; surely, for once, he had misspoken. I suggest that the program be telecast in Israel. Let the public judge.

A few days later I happen to be visiting Jack Mombaz, the Israeli consul general in Toronto, where I have come to lecture, when Marion telephones to tell me that once again the consul in New York is trying urgently to reach me. In the presence of his colleague in Canada, I return his call. He assumes an official tone: "I have been charged by my minister to communicate the following message to you." And he proceeds to read a statement that Eban plans to make public within the hour. It is a most flattering statement about me, thanking me for having come to his aid. As I listen, I feel the blood rushing to my face. I resent being manipulated. How am I to react? Protest? Expose the lie? My anger and agitation render me speechless. The consul asks, "Can you hear me? Are you there?" I don't answer. He repeats his questions; I remain silent. Only after a long pause am I able to speak again. "You of all people know the truth; I never said anything that could be interpreted as a defense." He denies nothing. My indignation does not surprise him, but he adds: "Try to understand him; he is fighting for his political survival." He is right. Eban's statement, resting on my "defense," saves him from being censured by the Knesset. Golda Meir's government, if by a remarkably small majority, remains in power.

I could publish a correction, if only for the record. But I don't. First of all, Eban could have been acting in good faith: How could I be sure that his consul, out of loyalty, had not distorted my comments? And why hurt a man who has been pleading our people's cause for so many years and with such distinction? He deserves special consideration. One does not condemn a man who, under desperate circumstances, resorts to the kind of behavior that he himself would normally find reprehensible. One does not condemn a man for a single misstep. After all, Eban occupies a place of honor in the diplomatic history of the Jewish state. To the friends calling me from Israel who are surprised if not shocked by my "defense" of Eban, I reply: Reasons of the heart are sometimes as important as the *raison d'état.* One does not push down a drowning man. Let's turn the page.

The Israeli ambassador in Washington, General Yitzhak Rabin, is not close to Eban; that is well known. Still, he approves of my conduct. As does Gideon Rafael, Israel's former ambassador to the U.N., appointed by Eban to serve as director general of his ministry. While in the United States on an official visit, Golda, too, congratulates me: "You know that I don't like the guy, but Begin and his clique treated him savagely; you did well to defend him." There being limits to my tolerance, I give her a summary of what actually happened. I did not defend Eban and deserve no congratulations. She does not seem surprised: "You did well anyway."

This conversation takes place during a reception given in her honor by her diplomatic representatives in New York. Suddenly I glimpse Eban. He must have seen me in conversation with Golda. He does not come over. A little later he walks up to me. He shakes my hand with uncharacteristic warmth. He, too, thanks me. He adds a few comments on the scandalous accusations hurled against him by the opposition. He appreciates my support. What could I say? I say nothing.

A week or two after this reception, I read in *Yedioth* a long interview with Eban on his foreign policy. He speaks of this and that and suddenly tells of having met me in New York, where, he says, I expressed my indignation at the way he had been treated. Stunned, I reread the article. I fail to understand why, if the incident is closed, he is reopening it. And why does he put words in my mouth? His political career is no longer in jeopardy, the government is no longer in danger. Why this new provocation?

My friend Eliyahu Amiqam, a journalist, is visiting New York. I show him the interview, which disturbs him as much as it does me. He asks me for an interview to clarify the matter. Detesting polemics, I hesitate. The counterattacks that provoke more counterattacks are not my style; and then, despite everything, I still have great admiration for Israel's spokesman. Eliyahu understands my arguments but restates his own: Truth must be reestablished. In the end, I accept his reasoning. The interview is published, triggering a whirlwind of declarations, commentaries, explanations. The affair is once again at center stage. Once again there is a tempest in the Knesset. A new censure motion is introduced by the opposition. The uproar is reminiscent of the notorious political quarrels between fanaticized blocs and groups. The government is in danger of toppling. Golda herself intervenes. In her address she speaks of her affection for me and of the friendship that binds us, but she defends her minister. Naturally she prevails. Her coalition represents a solid majority, and Eban is rehabilitated. Next, his entourage aims its heaviest artillery at me. The attacks come from unexpected quarters. I am punished for past errors and forgotten slights—letters I failed to answer, books I neglected to praise, phone calls I did not return. The gloves are off. I had no idea that so many people in Israel were waiting to take potshots at me.

With hindsight, I think that I may well have been unfair to Eban: How could anyone be sure that one of his subordinates did not embellish my comment to gain favor with him? And in the absence of an immediate correction on my part, Eban could have interpreted my silence as acquiescence.

We become reconciled in 1985. His letter of support, at the time of Bitburg, heals many wounds.

Marion and I have seen him often since, with his wife, Suzy, at the home of mutual friends. At this point, Eban is no longer minister. Why did his former political allies shunt him aside? Why did they betray him? After all, they had made certain promises to him.

Eban loses no time. He quickly turns to television. His programs on Jewish history are popular. His books sell well. He is never short of projects. I like listening to him as he tells of the war years in London and Cairo. His memories, touched with irony, his encounters with the

great protagonists of late-twentieth-century American history, are fascinating.

Since his arrival in the United States he has had occasion to encounter outstanding people in all strata of American society. He has met Truman, Eisenhower, JFK, senators, writers, scholars. It was he who conveyed David Ben-Gurion's invitation to Albert Einstein to come live in Jerusalem, where he would surely have been elected president of the State of Israel. The legendary Princeton scholar wisely refused. His reason? He did not know Hebrew.

Eban does know Hebrew, as well as Arabic and French. As analyst and spokesman of Israel's policy, he has had no equal.

Meyer Weisgal was another man who had no equal in his realm—a colorful character charged with energy and bubbling over with imagination. It was impossible not to like him. His white mane reminded one of Ben-Gurion; in fact he was close to Chaim Weizmann, the legendary British scientist who became head of the World Zionist movement and eventually president of Israel. Weisgal was Weizmann's right hand, and the prestigious Weizmann Institute of Science in Rehovot was built through his efforts. His clever and witty repartee helped him obtain unheard-of sums from the rich, sums no one else could extract from them.

Meyer considered Weizmann his god, his "secular Rebbe," his guru, and his savior. Possessive in the extreme, he disliked anyone who did not fully appreciate "the boss." As for those who claimed to revere Weizmann, Meyer was infallible in his ability to detect insincerity.

It was said that he was less admiring of Chaim's wife, Vera. He found her too mannered, too aristocratic. He said she was a snob who deigned to speak only to God, and even to Him only when she felt like talking to someone. Referring to a woman who had recently lost her famous husband, he said: "As a wife, she was not so terrific, but as a widow, she is unsurpassed. . . ."

His autobiography is a small masterpiece. I praised it in the *New York Times*. Later, when he was desperately ill, Meyer recovered his will to live when I persuaded him to write a second volume of memoirs. "Will you help me?" he asked. Of course I was ready to help him. Twice a week I went to see him with a little tape recorder. He spoke; I asked questions; he answered, rummaging in his memory for anecdotes, stories of his youth and the years spent at Weizmann's side.

Unfortunately, much of what he had to say he had already published. Even so I became enthusiastic as we recorded certain unpublished details. I don't regret those weeks, those months I devoted to him. On the contrary, I remember them with a sense of fulfillment.

I am working on *The Oath*, a novel about a Jew and his community accused of ritual murder at the beginning of the twentieth century. The days and months rush by. And the dreams and the memories. Does memory become richer, or does it shrink as man leaves his early experiences farther and farther behind? What makes it surge back? How does one follow its upheavals? And how does one assimilate the traces it leaves behind?

I am fascinated by everything that touches on memory, its mystical force. Memory desires to encompass everything, but it merely illuminates fragments. Why this recollection rather than another? And what happens to all that I have already forgotten? And then: What is the relationship between individual memory and collective memory? Which enriches the other, and at what cost?

Memory is a key element in my work and my quest, but in truth I am painfully aware of how little I know of its nature. It is to me what poetry was to Aristotle: More than history, it contains Truth. To me it is indispensable. To write. To teach and share. Without it what would I be? Without it life has no meaning.

June 6, 1972: Elisha's birth. A dawn unlike any other. It will mark my existence forever. This little fellow in the arms of his mother will illuminate our life. I look at him and look at him. And as I look at him I feel the presence of others also seeking to protect him.

Eight days later: the Brith Milah. "Let's sing, I order you to sing!" shouts the old Hassid of Ger. It's not every day that one attends a circumcision. The ceremony takes place under the sign of Abraham and, as such, is meaningful enough for the prophet Elijah himself to attend as guest of honor. It is on "his" chair that the eight-day-old infant is circumcised.

The men and women present come from different worlds. The former secretary of the Warsaw community, Dr. Hillel Seidman; the violinist Isaac Stern; the editor Jim Silberman; and Rabbi Abraham Joshua Heschel. Assimilated intellectuals and militant Zionists. And, of course, special emissaries from the Lubavitcher Rebbe, who, from his residence in Brooklyn, writes me that his heart and soul are over-flowing with joy. Saul Lieberman calls from Jerusalem to tell us just how much he participates in our celebration: I have never heard him so excited.

The mother is in an adjacent room: Tradition, with the intention of protecting her, ordains that she not be present when her son gives his blood to enter into the Covenant. A messenger shuttles back and forth to keep her informed.

The father seems elsewhere, lost in thought. Whom is he trying to reach, to assuage? "Don't," says one of the Hasidim, shaking him. "Do you hear me? You cannot give in to melancholy, not today! Don't forget, we have recovered a name, that of your father. Now your son will bear it! That is what we must celebrate!" The celebration continues for hours, and the melody of that ceremony still resonates inside me.

The Hasidim are shouting: Open yourselves to joy! Easily said. For my generation, no joy can be whole. I look at my son, who will never know his paternal grandparents. Silently I beg them to protect the one who has been called upon to assure their continuity. Protect him, beloved ancestors. Thanks to him, the line will not become extinct. It is a line that goes back far, all the way to the Sh'la. And to the Tossafot Yom Tov. And to Rashi, thus to King David.

Protect your descendant Shlomo Elisha ben Eliezer ben Shlomo Halevi. Guide him to the right path. And may he make you proud of what his soul becomes. Mother, protect your grandson. I don't know where you are resting, but please lean over his crib and help me sing him lullabies. Tell him your wondrous and strange tales that made me sleep peacefully. And you, Father, protect his dreams. Help him live his child's life. Help me.

"May this little one grow up and enter the world of study, marriage, and good deeds." It is Heschel who recites this customary prayer.

Beloved ancestors, please say: Amen.

So here I am, responsible for a family. A father. Even more than before, I think of my own father. Will I be able to follow in his footsteps? All his life he strove to help the needy, the anguished, the humiliated. And when the end came, nobody came to console him, not even his son in whom he had placed such hope.

He had done everything, within the limits of his meager possibilities, to save his brethren and sisters and to make the world around them warmer, more welcoming. I feel sorry for you, Father. I admire you; I love you; but I feel sorry for you: How naive you were, how innocent. Did you really believe that mankind would cease denying itself by denying you? That man could, that man would, transcend his condition?

The failure of my father and of all he symbolized long made me fear having a child. I was convinced that a cruel and indifferent world did not deserve our children. When I expressed this fear during a radio broadcast, I was violently reprimanded by Georges Levitte, the wonderful intellectual humanist to whom so many French writers, both Jewish and Christian, are deeply indebted.

It was Marion who persuaded me otherwise. It was wrong to give the killers one more victory. The long line from which I sprang must not end with me.

She was right.

And now? Because of my father and my son, I choose commitment.

Scars—

*S*TOP DREAMING, *a voice in my dream tells me this morning. It is time to act. The voice repeats the last words: to act. I want to ask: Can one not act and dream at the same time? But I don't dare open my mouth. I am afraid to wake up. I prefer to dream. Where is this voice coming from that breaks down the walls protecting my slumber?*

Whose voice is it? It has fallen still, but I can hear it. A man's voice.

That of my father? Too harsh. My grandfather? Too sharp.

Suddenly I remember: It is the voice of a beggar I once wanted to follow. I was young, a child still. He laughed, and I asked him why. "To make you laugh," he answered. Then he changed his mind and began to shout: "Would you rather I make you cry?" Making myself small, very small, I said: "What I'd really like is for you to make me dream."

What is more important, asks the Talmud, what is essential: thought or action? The opinions are divided, but in the end all the Masters agree: Study comes first, because study incites action.

As a Jew, I question myself about the role of the Jewish writer. Is it to make readers spill one more tear into the ocean? What must the writer express, and to what end? Which story should be told, and to what audience? Some are convinced that he must devote himself exclusively to his writings, that his influence and his power derive more from his art than from his deeds. This may have been a valid notion long ago. Poetry does not prevent the torturer from beating his victims, and the greatest novel in the world remains powerless before a fanatic. Thus the need to act. But in what area, and by what means? And where does one begin?

Of course, the fight against anti-Semitism remains a priority. It is, after all, the most ancient collective prejudice in history. Its virulence and its capacity to survive remain inexplicable. It is said to be as old as the Jewish people itself. The Talmud detects its first signs at the time of the Revelation at Sinai. Even in antiquity Jews were hated, especially in the higher echelons of society. What did Cicero and Seneca have against the Jews? If one is to believe Flavius Josephus, Apion the Greek reproached the Jews for "belonging to a tribe of lepers capable if not desirous of contaminating the entire world." Tacitus is annoyed with them because they show for each other an "obstinate attachment, an active commiseration in contrast with the implacable hatred they feel for the rest of mankind. Never do they eat with strangers, never do they live with foreign women." Apion and Democritus accuse them of ritual murder. Since then anti-Semitism has become more modern, though it retains the same irrational arguments. One has only to compare those of Pharaoh's counselors in the Bible to those of Haman in the Book of Esther, of Torquemada, Hitler, and Stalin: Their delusions are the same. All were convinced that the Jews were always greedy, determined to achieve political and religious domination and thus to control the affairs of the world. They see Jews everywhere and ascribe to them terrifying mystical powers. At the same time, they have contempt for those who appear helpless. In other words, the anti-Semites hate the Jews because they believe them to be strong but despise them when they perceive them to be weak.

The anti-Semite resents the Jew both for what he is and for what he is not. He blames him for being too rich or too poor, too nationalistic or too universal, too devout or too secular. In truth, he simply resents the fact that the Jew exists.

Thus, for a Jew, anti-Semitism remains the enemy. But it is not the only one. There are other hatreds, other exclusions, other human communities targeted. There is misery on all continents—hunger, ignorance, intolerance, silenced political prisoners, nuclear proliferation: Which of these challenges requires our immediate intervention?

And war, which mankind seems incapable of eliminating or at least restraining, more than fifty years after World War II. What is war? A perverse lack of imagination, of memory? A fascination with the end, with death? How to understand this madness that leaves so many graves in its wake?

. . .

Having virtually given up journalism—not without regret—I turn to teaching.

Once again fate intervenes at a crossroads. I owe my appointment as Distinguished Professor of Jewish Studies at the City College of New York purely to chance.

One evening in a Manhattan hotel, after a lecture on behalf of Soviet Jewry, Rabbi Yitz Greenberg takes me aside. He speaks to me as head of the Jewish Studies department at City College. He wishes to recruit me. To teach what? Anything I want: Hasidic texts, Jewish or Holocaust literature, talmudic subjects. "Things that, in any case, you deal with in your work."

I am very fond of Yitz. I have known him since the early sixties, when he was teaching at Yeshiva University. He is as tall as a basketball player, with a lively and open mind; his discourse is sharp but not aggressive. As he tries to convince me, I realize that if I accept I shall become a father and a professor in the same month.

I accept.

Two days later I find myself in the office of the young dean Ted Gross. He seems pleased, and so am I. It has all happened very fast. The contract has been drawn up; all that remains is the signature. Smiles, handshakes, congratulations. I am proud, I don't deny it. City College is not just any college. It is a place of real distinction.

Is this a new career? Let us say it's a new path. As for the goal, it will not change.

I prepare myself like a student, rereading texts I thought I had known and fully understood. At the same time I put the final touches on *Le serment de Kolvillag* (later translated as *The Oath* in the United States), which is due to be published by Le Seuil in France in 1973.

Also on the agenda, inevitably, are a few trips. With Elisha, of course. In Israel, we meet friends from the newspaper for which I worked from 1950 to 1972. Dov and Lea, Noah and Paula, Eliyahu and Ruth: peaceful, comforting moments. Nostalgic as well.

Elisha in Jerusalem. How can I describe my happiness, my pride, as I carry him in my arms walking with Marion through the narrow streets of the Old City? And as I place his tiny hand on the Wall?

For the editors of *Yedioth Ahronoth* these are heady times: Circulation is up from one week to the next, as are salaries. I make my old friends laugh when I point out to them my poor luck as a journalist: Since I left, *Yedioth* has become better and richer.

As a result of the "war of attrition," the atmosphere in the country is heavy. The security of the state is not yet in question, but the euphoria of 1967 following the Six-Day War has dissipated. Five years have passed and there is ever more talk of Palestinian terrorism. Nobody has forgotten the attack at Lod Airport committed by the Japanese Kozo Okamoto, linked to the PLO: twenty-five killed, among them the internationally renowned scientist Aharon Katzir. That was at the end of May 1972.

In early September of that year, during the Olympic Games held in Munich, Palestinian terrorists belonging to the Black September movement assassinate eleven Israeli athletes. The public follows the tragedy live on television.

The Games continue the very next day. And the whole world applauds.

In a difficult address given a few weeks later, before the leaders of the United Jewish Appeal (UJA), I speak of the implications of this wanton murder.

We must never forget that Munich is not only the capital of Bavaria, but also a symbol. Munich symbolizes the failure and cowardice of the West, its abdication before the powers of evil. It represents the triumph of paganism, of the gods of violence, of fanaticism and death. Munich equals shame. In 1938 the Munich agreements prefigured Dachau, the ghettos of hunger and fear, and the death ramp at Birkenau.

September 1972. The Jewish year begins badly—for Israel in general, for me and my family as well.

One morning, I am in the middle of teaching a class on Rebbe Nahman of Bratzlav when a secretary rushes in to tell me of an urgent call waiting for me at the office. I run to the phone afraid to breathe, afraid to say the word that will force me to listen to what follows. On the other end, my brother-in-law Len is silent. Then he gives me the news: My sister Bea is ill, gravely ill; they have just operated; she has cancer. Len is sobbing. Frozen, I cannot speak for a long moment. Never have I heard my heart beat so loudly. I fall into a chair and ask: "What can be done?" The physician in Len is pulling himself together: "Nothing unfortunately, nothing." I ask him whether Bea knows. No, she doesn't. Besides, she is still in recovery.

I return to my class. My students look at me, perplexed. They can sense my distress. I tell them: "Let's go on, shall we?" But they look at me and remain silent. I don't know how, but I make them speak. "Where were we?" I don't know and they, evidently, don't either. Fortunately, the moment to conclude comes soon.

Back home, Marion places Elisha in my arms to console me.

I begin a series of shuttles between New York and Montreal. Bea knows she had a tumor but believes it to have been benign and thinks it was successfully removed. That is what she says to me.

But then why this shadow in her gaze?

And then comes another blow. My sister Hilda loses her husband, Nathan, a gentle, infinitely kind man.

Hilda tells me: They were on the road. Nathan was driving; suddenly he stopped and asked for a piece of candy—he who had not eaten sweets since childhood. The next moment he was dead.

Born in Tarnów, Poland, he had emigrated to France between the wars. A fervent Zionist, he dreamed of living in Israel. He will be buried there.

Bea calls me from Montreal; she does not feel up to attending the funeral. She asks me to understand; she is afraid. Of course I understand: Cancer is frightening, and so are cemeteries, even to someone as brave as my sister. "Explain to Hilda that . . ." No need to explain. Hilda understands. I accompany her to Israel; I am at her side at the cemetery. The entire Israeli family is there.

By chance, at the cemetery entrance I meet Moishele Kraus, the former cantor of Sighet. At my request he sings the prayer for the dead at the open grave. A distant relative gives a brief eulogy. It is my first time attending a burial in Israel. I didn't know that here men are buried only in their *talit*, without a coffin. It is also the first time that I hear the Kaddish recited here, so different from the one said by the orphan every day of the first year of mourning. It seems heavier, harsher. It is frightening. I am glad Bea did not come.

In the United States, the presidential campaign is in full swing, noisy as ever. And this time around, mean.

Robert Bernstein, head of Random House, is intent on my meeting one of the candidates for the Democratic nomination, the senator from South Dakota, George McGovern. Marion and I are invited to dinner in a quiet restaurant.

The senator makes a good impression. He appears to be a man of integrity, obsessed not with power but with the use he might put it to. He speaks softly without moving a muscle in his face.

I ask him: "Why do you want so much to be president? The campaign is harrowing; it depletes you. After all, you are an influential and
respected senator. Wouldn't it be wiser to strengthen that position,
which is unanimously respected?"

McGovern responds: "Nixon must be defeated. He is evil incarnate. And I am the only one who can beat him."

How naive of McGovern. He did not realize that he was the
only one who could not defeat Nixon.

Moreover, the sitting president is doing rather well. The Watergate scandal is still to come. Foreign policy dominates the news. Sure
planes are bombing Hanoi and Haiphong, but isn't it Nixon who,
together with his national security adviser, Henry Kissinger, makes
historic visits to China and Moscow? Not only will Nixon take the
elections, he will win by a large margin.

The night the results are announced, I see young students weep.

It was in 1973 that *Le serment de Kolvillag (The Oath)* was published in
Paris. It is a bleak novel, devoid of hope. With the exception of the
later novel *The Forgotten*, it is without doubt the most depressing fictional tale my pen has ever committed to paper. While working on it,
I am deep in a depression that on the surface seems unwarranted.
Things are going well, both professionally and personally. Marion has
become my translator, so I no longer worry about the English-
language editions of my work. Our one-year-old son's smile delights
me. Teaching is exciting; my books are being bought by an increasing
number of publishers abroad. Robert McAfee Brown at Stanford University, John Roth at Claremont, Harry Cargas in St. Louis, Lawrence
Langer in Boston, and Irving Halperin in San Francisco all incorporate
my books into their programs. And yet I sense disaster. As the writer
Cynthia Ozick observes: "It is as though, in your novel, you foresaw
the Yom Kippur War and the exasperating solitude of Israel." In truth,
never has the Jewish state been so close to catastrophe.

Why did I set the action of this novel at the beginning of the
twentieth century? To dissociate it from my personal experience, to
distance it from the era of *Night*?

The theme: A young stranger wishes to die, and it falls to a wan-
dering old man named Azriel to dissuade him. What can he tell the
young stranger that will renew his will to live? He tells him a story—
his own, the one he had vowed never to reveal.

Through this story Azriel describes the life and destiny of an annihilated Jewish hamlet. It is all there: friendship and hatred; fanaticism and terror; the chroniclers and their fate; the tensions between societies, religions, and generations; testimony and silence; silence above all; silence as means and as end.

October 5, 1973. The Yom Kippur War, terrible and shattering. We learn the news during services. Rabbi Joseph Lookstein, dressed in white as was the high priest of long ago, asks the congregation to pray with increased fervor. In the middle of the *Musaf* service I am called outside: I must urgently call the Israeli Mission. I remove my *talit* and go to the synagogue office. A diplomat requests a statement for the press. Is it true that the Germans often chose the Day of Atonement to heighten their campaigns of brutality against the inhabitants of the ghettos? As a rule I am wary of such analogies. But today I say: Yes, the Germans knew the Jewish calendar and used it against us. I return to my seat. The congregation is deep in prayer, reciting the *Amidah*. And I realize that this is the first time since liberation that I have violated the sanctity of the holiest day of the year.

The year 1973 contains more bad omens than promises. Yasir Arafat is reelected to head the PLO. In Chile, Salvador Allende is assassinated by the enemies of democracy. In Southeast Asia the war continues: Tons of explosives fall on Laos and Cambodia. In Paris the negotiations between Henry Kissinger, representing Nixon, and Le Duc Tho, Ho Chi Minh's emissary, seem to be going nowhere. In America, the general public follows the news from the various fronts with resignation. But there is a new interest: Watergate. And the forced resignation of Vice President Spiro Agnew, indicted for accepting bribes from private companies.

And now, the war against Israel.

This one is unlike the others. In past wars, the Israeli army had always imposed its own rhythm, its own strategy. In this war, the adversary managed to deliver the first blow, unleashing a striking offensive.

Depressing days, oppressive nights. I have trouble concentrating as I face my students. Rebbe Nahman and his princes, the Besht and his legends, no longer hold my thoughts, which leap toward Suez and the Golan on fire. The news reports from Israel are crushing. What am I to do? How could I help? Write articles, make speeches? The time for that is past.

As always, when Israel lives through a crisis I feel like the medieval poet Yehuda Halevy, who said that his heart was in the East though he himself lived far away, in the West. Though I reside in Manhattan, my thoughts are elsewhere, across the ocean, in the land of our ancestors.

I spend hours listening to the radio, reading the newspapers, watching television. I play with Elisha, sing him his favorite melodies, drink in his smile, but not even he can lighten my mood.

Less than a week before the start of hostilities, Palestinian terrorists had attacked an Austrian train transporting Russian-Jewish emigrants. Was it meant as a diversion? There were rumors to that effect. The incident forced Golda Meir to make a quick, unpleasant trip to Vienna to meet Chancellor Bruno Kreisky, who, she told us, didn't offer her so much as a glass of water. Another rumor: An Israeli spy in Egypt was said to have sent secret information about a planned Syrian-Egyptian invasion. Were his Israeli handlers too preoccupied with the crisis in Vienna to react? Third rumor: The same spy or another highly placed agent of the Mossad was said to have sent on Yom Kippur eve even more precise information, specifying that the offensive would be launched on the afternoon of Yom Kippur. It appeared that a low-level officer, having misinterpreted the information, took the initiative to designate 6 p.m. as zero hour, which was four hours too late. It was whispered that the staff generals were still with Golda and Moshe Dayan when the Egyptian artillery opened fire on the defenses along the Suez Canal.

At the time these rumors were not known in Israel, at least not by the public at large. Overwhelmed by the gravity of the news coming from the battlefields, Israelis felt, once again, isolated and abandoned.

Western Europe was a disappointment. Not a single country— not even France, Great Britain, or Germany—authorized the giant American planes, crammed with arms, to refuel at their airports. An unforgivable stance. On every front the war favored the aggressors. There were terrible battles on the Golan, a bloody retreat in the Sinai. On land and in the air, Tsahal (the Israeli army) was enduring unprecedented losses in human lives and equipment. And the world let it happen.

One more rumor, a persistent one: It was said that Golda had given the order to ready the ultimate option. That was why the White House suddenly gave in to the Israeli government and established an aerial bridge for military use between America and Israel . . . to prevent the first nuclear conflict since Hiroshima and Nagasaki. Of course, Israel has always denied possession of atomic weapons.

A Socialist leader told me that he had witnessed a London meeting of the Socialist international leadership urgently called by Golda Meir, shortly after the Yom Kippur War. A frosty silence hung over the hall when she began to settle accounts with her ideological and political comrades: How could they have betrayed the only democratic state in the Middle East? How could they have turned their backs on the sole Socialist government of the region? She ended with a few words that sent shivers through the audience: "What did you think?" she asked. "That confronted with death, Israel would go down alone?" It seems nobody applauded Golda. Nobody came to pay their respects. Had she shamed or frightened them by alluding to the nuclear capacities of Israel?

In the end, after the tragic failures of the early days, Tsahal astounds the world with its military genius. The invading armies are defeated. After crossing the Suez Canal, Ariel Sharon's tanks advance toward Cairo. And in the north, Israeli troops push to within thirty-seven kilometers of Damascus.

And yet the mood in Israel is oppressive. The evening news shows the handsome faces of the many fallen soldiers and officers. Never before has the State of Israel suffered such losses. Sadat's surprise attack has shaken the Jewish state to its core.

At the very onset of hostilities I decide with Sigmund Strochlitz, my survivor friend from Connecticut for whom Bendin remains as alive as Sighet is for me, to show our solidarity by organizing a trip to Israel for a group of influential American Jews. The plan is to bring along medical supplies for the army, which, according to press reports, are dwindling fast. We draw up a list of some hundred names among the wealthiest and most respected of the American Jewish community. Forty decline immediately. Twenty promise to think about it. Thirty say: Maybe. In the end, Sigmund and I are the only ones. Marion would like to go, but then decides to stay with Elisha.

The El Al flight is filled with Israelis going home. The first rows are occupied by Abba Eban and his entourage. They work throughout the flight. From time to time a crew member brings them radio dispatches.

Silence falls over the plane as we land. Our first visit is to Sigmund's relatives, children of survivors. He rings the doorbell. The door opens and, not expecting his visit, they almost faint. They mention names: This one is in the Sinai, another is en route to the Golan. As for me, I go to see no one: I call no cousin, no friend. I would be ashamed to tell them that I have come for just one day, one night.

We take rooms at the Tel Aviv Hilton. It looks empty and dark. In the morning we join a group of foreign journalists heading for the northern front. Our escort is a young officer I know only by name, the future minister Amnon Rubinstein. On the bus someone calls out my name. I look up and see André Schwarz-Bart. By a strange quirk of fate, we are always together, André and I, whenever there is reason to testify for those who live within us.

I whisper my impressions into my pocket recorder. They are meant for Elisha. If he listens well, he'll also hear the sound of mortars.

I want to go up to Jerusalem to meditate at the Wall. Impossible. A quick trip to the Sinai? Impossible. Ask friends to intercede? Surely they are mobilized. The only planned visit of our lightning trip is to the military hospital Tel-Hashomer, to hand over the medical supplies to my friend Dr. Bollek Goldman, codirector of the hospital. Bollek takes us on his rounds. Before the severely wounded, he describes their heroic military feats. He introduces me to an officer from a prestigious tank division. From between his bandages his eyes are scrutinizing me. He whispers unintelligible words. Bollek leans over him. "He has read your books," he says. "He wishes to shake your hand." I hesitate. "Go on," Bollek urges me. I step forward and hold something resembling a hand. The wounded man's lips are moving. He whispers to me and no words have ever moved me so much.

Back in New York, I intently follow the aftermath of this war that the Israeli press has dubbed *Hamekhdal*, the war of incompetence. People are angry. Golda wins the elections but loses the confidence of her party. As a result she must resign to make room for her young ambassador to Washington, General Yitzhak Rabin.

The wounds of this conflict have never healed. Headed by Justice Agranat, president of the Israeli Supreme Court, a High Commission of Inquiry was named to assess the responsibilities of those who failed to foresee and prevent the aggression. This commission responds to a real need; the country is confronting a crisis of confidence. Every day it is shaken by a new "affair." Politicians accuse one another, generals justify themselves. Israel no longer trusts its leaders. Did it also lose pride in its army?

• • •

Two years later, Marion, Elisha, and I are staying at the Sharon Hotel at the beach in Herzliyya. One day I get a call from General Eleazar, "Dado," as Israelis fondly call him. I had met him at the home of General Haim Bar-Lev, his predecessor and faithful companion during the Six-Day War, but I hardly know him. The Yom Kippur War had marked the end of Eleazar's glorious military career, the Agranat Commission having forced him to resign as commander in chief of the army. "Are you also avoiding me?" he asks. "Of course not," I protest. "I respect your privacy, that's all." He wants to meet. "When?" I ask. "Right now," he says.

Dado arrives a half hour later. It is the first time I see him in civilian clothes. He has an open face with deeply etched features. His gaze is direct. We sit down in a corner of the lobby. He comes straight to the point: "I don't know whether you know what is going on here. But you should." From his briefcase he pulls several files and lays them out on the table. "Here are a few documents. Top secret. If any one of these had been submitted to me at the time, I would have had a clearer view of the situation. And the danger. These documents were received during the weeks preceding the start of hostilities by subordinates at Military Intelligence who gave them little credence. According to their chief, General Eli Zeira, the Arabs were neither ready nor capable of launching another war against Israel. I am not saying that he and his team should be blamed. I was their superior; I assume full responsibility for what they did. But why were *my* superiors white-washed?"

For three hours, he pleads his innocence. Finally he bursts into sobs. After he leaves I tell Marion: "I have just seen a man with a broken heart."

For a whole week I am ill, shaken by violent bouts of fever. My body aches; I hallucinate. What is wrong with me? Bollek Goldman, who has become a devoted friend, comes running from Tel-Hashomer. He can find no medical explanation for my ailment. Could it be psychosomatic? He comes to see me every day. His presence does me more good than his medications.

A short time later, swimming in his pool, Dado has a heart attack. He dies instantly. His military funeral is almost a state funeral. Did the government suddenly feel guilty? In Israel as everywhere else people mistakenly believe it is possible to make up for injustices with pomp and circumstance.

Later I question several members of the Agranat Commission:
Why had they been so severe with Dado and so indulgent with his
superiors? If one is to believe them, the commission's charter forbade
them to go beyond the military and to implicate the politicians. This
was mined and dangerous terrain. I insist: "Was it just? Was it fair?"
Their embarrassed replies do not satisfy me.

As for Golda, I saw her only one more time. Bitter, frail, she did
not forgive those who had pushed her out. As a rule, Golda never for-
gave. As Jacques Derogy and Hesi Carmel observe in their excellent
book Le siècle d'Israël: "Everything she believes in is white, everything
she rejects is black."

Now that she had fallen, did she expect me to defend her against
her many political adversaries? Unfortunately, I could not. For I
believe that because I am not an Israeli citizen, I must not interfere in
Israel's internal affairs. Moreover . . . Golda had not convinced me.
Surely she was not the only one responsible for the disaster of the
early days, but she should have borne some of the onus. The Agranat
Commission should not have whitewashed the government. One day
I said to Golda: "At war's end, why didn't you offer your resignation?
The people of Israel would not have accepted." Golda did not see it
that way. She resented my question. In any case, since the Eban affair
we had been less close.

I ask Moshe Dayan if he had agreed with the Agranat Commission's conclusions. Yes, he had. And does he not feel responsible for
what happened? No, he does not. And after a moment he adds
very quietly: "If I had felt guilty, I would have put a bullet through my
head."

Dayan remained a stranger to me as long as he was commander
in chief or minister of defense. Only later did ties develop between us.
With rare exceptions I tend to appreciate political men and women
more when they are out of office. I felt closer to David Ben-Gurion
after he left office to live at Kibbutz Sde Boker. He seemed more
human, more vulnerable. The man who had hated the "Stern Gang" to
the point of throwing its leaders into prison now became a close
friend of Yehoshua Cohen, the old Stern Gang member with a legendary "terrorist" past.

I remember my first encounter with Moshe Dayan. He was in the
United States on a lecture tour and called me from Miami to invite me
to lunch. "Just you and me," he said. "We'll be able to talk quietly." We

made an appointment at the Regency Hotel in New York. The purpose? He explained: "As you know, all my life, I have fought against the enemies of Israel. Now I want to work on behalf of the Jews outside of Israel." He told me his plan: to study from multiple angles this Jewish community that had survived, to understand the reasons for its endurance. If it were possible to discover which elements had saved it from extinction, we could apply this knowledge whenever the Diaspora found itself in difficulty.

The idea was bizarre. The destiny of a people cannot be reduced to a sociological or scientific formula; it contains mysterious, if not mystical, factors. But he believed in it. He gave up this project only when Menachem Begin, acceding to power in 1977, named him minister of foreign affairs. Later, if Begin was able to conclude a peace treaty with Sadat, it was largely due to Dayan.

The annual UJA conference is to take place in late 1973. For the second time its director, Irving Bernstein, invites me to give an address. His argument is almost the same as in 1972, after the massacre of Israeli athletes in Munich: "The Jewish community is going through a moral crisis. It is therefore important that . . ." He is right; the Yom Kippur War still weighs heavily on our individual and our collective consciousness. What to say to our distraught friends from Israel? The theme becomes clear: "Against despair." To be a Jew means not to despair, even when it seems justified.

An example: In a sealed cattle car an old Jew cries out: "Today is Simhat Torah, the festival of the Law. We must rejoice." He pulls a small Sefer-Torah from his bag and begins to sing. Another example: In a barracks, *over there,* men are wondering how to celebrate the festival of the Torah without a Sefer-Torah. One of them glimpses a young boy and signals him to come over: "Do you remember what you learned in *heder*?" "Yes, I remember *Shma Israel*," the boy replies. "Then recite it." "*Shma Israel, adoshem elokhenu, adoshem ekhad. . . .*" Hear, O Israel, the Lord is our God, the Lord is One. . . . "Good," says the man, lifting up the boy, as if he were the Sefer-Torah itself, and he begins to dance and sing the traditional prayers.

In our tradition celebrating life is more important than mourning the dead. The law is strict: When a wedding procession crosses a funeral procession, the former has the right-of-way.

Rebbe Nahman of Bratzlav—you may remember my love for his

teachings—often said: *"Gvalt yidden, seit eich nisht meyaesh. . . ."* For the love of heaven, Jews, do not despair. . . . In his memoirs, the historian Emmanuel Ringelblum refers to a Bratzlav *shtibel* inside the Warsaw Ghetto. Over its entrance was the same inscription: JEWS, DO NOT DESPAIR. For a Jew, who bears a four-thousand-year-old memory, despair is equivalent to blasphemy.

Invited soon after to address the annual FSJU (French UJA) conference in Paris, I develop the same theme: the struggle against despair. The speaker who follows me to the podium is the Israeli ambassador, Asher ben Nathan. I did not know that he had just lost a son in battle. Had I known, I would have remained silent.

In 1974, after the Yom Kippur War, Israel is constantly shaken by revelations of scandals linked to the military debacle of the early days of the war. In the United States it becomes impossible to open a newspaper without feeling shame and distress. Israeli morale is at its lowest, and it affects ours in the Diaspora. Irving Bernstein comes to see me several times, accompanied by other leaders of the Jewish community, urging me to speak up. One morning Irving arrives with an invitation to address the board of governors of the Jewish Agency, which is about to meet in Jerusalem. "It is a kind of a superparliament of the Jewish people," explains Bernstein. "It includes Israelis and non-Israelis. For you, for us, it is the ideal platform." I ask Golda's advice and that of my Master, Saul Lieberman. Both urge me to accept, though Lieberman warns: "They will be sure to criticize you. But that is the price one pays for living in the Diaspora."

As I prepare my speech I strive to be frank without hurting my listeners. How am I to put my questions so as not to offend them?

After arriving in Jerusalem the same day as President Nixon— you can imagine the traffic!—I call Golda and read her my text. She is not pleased and admonishes me: "Is that all you have to say to them? Why don't you remind them of what they did to me?" Taken aback, I reply: "Golda, I haven't come here to fight for you, but for those of us in the Diaspora."

To say that my words were well received would be not an exaggeration but a lie. Of course the listeners applauded, but out of courtesy, with little enthusiasm. The next day the Israeli press settled its score with me: "How dare someone who lives in America tell us what to do! Since when is a Jew from the Diaspora entitled to preach to us?" The following is part of what I managed to say:

There are questions we must ask ourselves at times, and we must do so without complacency. They may well irritate you; would you prefer self-censorship? Pushkin claims that a beautiful lie is superior to a debasing truth. I don't agree: Truth alone elevates man, even when it hurts. The task of the writer is, after all, not to appease or flatter, but to disturb, to warn, to question by questioning oneself.

All this, as you may have guessed, is the prelude to a few criticisms. I dislike having to articulate them; it is a role that does not suit me. Yes, such is the price I must pay for living in the Diaspora: I never criticize Israel outside Israel.

We are Jews, you and I. You are Israeli; I am not. You represent a state, a group, a nation, with its structures and institutions; I represent no one but the characters I have created or who have created me. You have found; I am still seeking. You have been able to make the break; I have not. As a Jew assuming his Judaism, why have I not settled in the land of our ancestors? That is a question you have asked me often. It annoys you, and I understand why. The Diaspora troubles you. Just as Israel challenges its validity, it represents a challenge to Israel. We are united by the past, divided by the present. Whose fault is it? We blame nobody. We each have our contradictions. Each solves them or claims them in his own way. Yet you show your disapproval in periods of crisis, while we tell you of our concern in periods of calm.

What is this all about? Our arguments are well known. Let us start with yours. Opposed as you are to the Diaspora—historically, philosophically—you say that its Jews are riddled with complexes and paradoxes. In spite of being personae non gratae for centuries in numerous countries, they still choose to stay there—to cling to what? What was it that prevented us in the seventeenth and eighteenth centuries from following a Rebbe Gershon Kitiver or a Rebbe Mendel of Vitebsk to the Holy Land? Between one pogrom and the next, one massacre and the next, we knocked at exile's every door rather than return to our home.

Later, during the emancipation, our newly acquired civil rights led us to dilute or even shed our Judaism rather than use it to fulfill ourselves. The historian Simon Dubnow stresses the point that upon contact with individual liberties, Judaism weakened. Once admitted into the Christian milieu, the Jew often came to look upon his Judaism as a blemish, an obstacle. Emancipation drove us to assimilation, not to nationalism; it brought about a setback rather than a rebirth of our spirituality. Instead of revolutionizing our own history, we set out to change that of others. We absorbed every culture, excelled in every tongue, interpreted all the signs, and took part in every battle; no other people has, either by necessity or vocation, been as universal or as universalist. We hoped to save humanity even as it was bent on our destruction. We were determined to accept nothing less than absolute salvation for all nations; we exerted ourselves more for others than for ourselves.

Israel belongs to all Jews. But is the reverse true? How, then, is one to explain our reticence to join you there permanently? You condemn us. At worst, you consider us hypocrites; at best, you consider us weaklings. Nor do we think that you are entirely wrong. Israel exists, and we live elsewhere; therein lies an anomaly. Of course, there are all sorts of alibis, excuses, justifications to be invoked: We help you, we act, we use our influence on your behalf. What would Israel do, what would Israel be, without the Diaspora? Yet the fact remains: The Jewish people, dispersed as it is, does not live in a state of siege, while you, in Israel, have made your homes on the front lines; your children, not ours, confront perils every day; you, their parents, not we, endure anguish every night.

If you reproach us for our failings, you are right. We don't deny them. As we stand before you, we feel inadequate.

As for us, for what do we reproach you? This may sound absurd and surely unjust to you: We blame Israel for having happened too late. Too late to save the millions and millions of Jews who needed its protection the most. I know it is not Israel's fault. And yet it hurts. Not only do I wish to love Israel, I want to admire it, hold it up as an example, find there what cannot be found elsewhere: a certain sense of justice, a certain sense of dignity. I want to find there a society ruled by a vision of probity, justice, and compassion.

It is a paradoxical yet understandable demand. The more we in the Diaspora fall prey to materialism, the more we yearn to see idealism flourish in Israel; the more passive we are, the more we would like Israel to be creative; the more earthbound we are, the more anxious we are that Israel be ethereal and sovereign. In short, we would like Israel to be what we are not. And if we sometimes voice our disappointment, it is because its reality dangerously resembles ours. Perhaps Kafka was right: Man's weakness lies not in his inability to obtain victories, but in his inability to make use of them.

We follow your current events and frequently fail to understand them. The tone of your debates, the recriminations, the animosities remind us of other societies, other lands. Is it wrong of us to expect so much of Israel? To place you on what amounts to a pedestal?

Try to understand us as we try to understand you. In a world gone mad from feeding upon falsehood and greed, we look upon Israel as a haven where the cycle of cynicism and nihilism will be broken. As people who live in a discredited, disintegrated society, we see in Israel proof that man can and must win the battles within himself. Call me romantic or naive, but I see Israel, surrounded and besieged by hatred, as an ancient laboratory eternally renewed. I see Israel as a country in which victory does not necessarily signify the defeat of the enemy and in which true triumph means triumph over oneself. And in which friendship is possible and irrevocable. And in which everything that is tainted by banality, by vulgarity, is outside the law.

Are we wrong to raise you so high, thus asking Israel to be a model nation? Are we wrong to seek there signs heralding a social messianism or a messianic humanism? And to ask you—though we dislike interfering in your internal affairs—to disagree less frequently and less noisily? And to prepare a friendlier welcome for new immigrants? And to treat Russian Jews as brothers, even when they change their minds on the way and decide to settle in

America? Are we wrong to ask you to adopt a more Jewish attitude toward Palestinian Arabs and, particularly, toward Israeli Arabs? To be less intransigent, more receptive? From Israel we expect no more, no less than the impossible.

Let us open our eyes, my Israeli brothers. As a Diaspora Jew, I live the life and the destiny of Jerusalem. And I should like you to understand us. We are responsible for each other; you do not deny it. If the principal task of the Diaspora is to protect Israel, yours should be to become a new source of life to the Diaspora. Let us assume the dialectics of our so singularly Jewish and so Jewishly singular condition: that we both live on two levels simultaneously; that we both lead a double life; that we be each other's heart and conscience, constantly questioning and enriching each other. Without the Diaspora, Israel would have no one to question and no one to be questioned by. Without Israel, the Diaspora would know nothing of victory but the anguish that precedes it.

In these extraordinary times our generation is at once the most blessed and the most accursed of all. Some thirty years ago Jewish heroes wept every time a courier brought them a weapon; today strategists marvel at the Jewish army's military genius. Fifty years ago nobody imagined that Russian Judaism could survive Communist dictatorship; today we are witnessing its rebirth. A generation ago we discovered the ruins of the world and the dark side of God; today it is on them that we are building future Jewish history.

This speech of 1974—which in my mind remains valid even now—was one I had prepared with great care. I weighed every word, every question mark. I knew that I was treading on mined terrain. But, I did not deliver the speech . . . at least not in its entirety. For a strange thing happened: During the first half, while I was saying *mea culpa* for myself and my fellow Jews in the Diaspora, the Israeli officials were listening, their faces beaming approval. As soon as I began the second part, suggesting that Diaspora Jews also had a few reproaches, the mood in the hall turned. It was as if a wind from Siberia had frozen my listeners' features. The contact had been broken to the point that I asked myself what good it was to continue, to hurl myself against this human wall. In any case I would not be heard . . . and so I, too, broke

the connection. I set aside my prepared text and improvised a different conclusion. I needed to finish. I had to get out of there.

The following year I receive a call from Pinhas Sapir, former
finance minister and acting president of the Jewish Agency: He would
like to pay me a visit at my home in New York. I tell him that I will
gladly come to his hotel; after all, he is someone I respect, and he is
my elder. Nothing doing. He insists on coming to my home, accompanied by his entourage. Without preamble he tells me: "I heard you
last year, but I was not present at the debate your speech provoked. I
know that my colleagues attacked you severely, and I know that they
were unjust. That is why I wanted to come and see you today. To offer
you our official apologies and, especially, my own."

Sadly, this remarkable man died shortly afterward during a ceremony in an immigrant village, clasping the holy scrolls in his arms.

In spite of his soothing words, the incident in Jerusalem stays
with me. I still don't understand my inability to criticize Israel. Perhaps I am guided by the readings of the biblical and talmudic commentaries. Is it not said that even our teacher Moses was punished for
having been too harsh with our people?

It is a troubling subject. I shall return to it.

It was only in 1995 that I discovered that the Six-Day War was not as
noble as I had thought.

I had been so proud of the moving simplicity of "our" officers,
the bravery of these soldiers who, to quote my friend André Schwarz-
Bart, "fired and wept." But in August 1995 the Israeli press is filled with
articles describing assassinations allegedly perpetrated by Israeli soldiers and officers at the beginning of June 1967.

Yedioth Ahronoth, which by now has become the leading paper in
the country, prints an article by Gabi Baron. He reports on what he
himself saw near the airport of El 'Arīsh, which had just been won. In
a hangar, 150 prisoners waited on the ground, their hands behind
their necks. I read:

> Next to the fence guarded by the military police, there was
> a table at which two men dressed in Israeli military uniforms
> were seated. They wore blue helmets and their faces were
> hidden behind antisand goggles and khaki kerchiefs. Mili-
> tary policemen went to fetch a prisoner and led him to the
> table. There ensued a brief conversation we could not over-

hear. Then, the prisoner was led one hundred meters from the hangar and one of the policemen handed him a shovel.

I saw the man dig a hole for fifteen minutes. Then one of the policemen ordered him to throw the shovel out of the hole. And then, one of them took his machine gun and fired three or four shots. The prisoner fell and died. A few minutes later another prisoner was taken to the same hole and shot. A third died in the same way. I myself was present at ten or so executions.

Military specialists have explained that the army had no choice: It feared the fedayeen, those terrorists who wearing the Egyptian military uniform operated behind the Israeli lines. Or then: In the desert, in the midst of a campaign, what is one to do with "useless mouths" . . . ?

How I regret today not having known these facts, this horror, when I met with Moshe Dayan. Had he not been minister of defense during the Six-Day War?

Bad news from Canada. Bea is not doing well. My poor sister is still fighting, but she tires quickly. The treatments exhaust her. She is suffering terrible pain. She spends the High Holy Days at the hospital. I visit her often. She is coughing a lot. She bites her lips as she tells me slowly how she had been able to hear the sound of the shofar on both days of Rosh Hashana. What is she thinking? That the heavenly court's judgment on "Who shall live and who shall die" must have been pronounced? She is pale and weak, my wounded, generous sister. She speaks in a broken, staccato voice. Her gaze is veiled. Whenever she removes her oxygen mask to speak to me, she gasps for breath. But she must confide in me how much she worries about her young children, Sarah and Stevie. I beg her: "Don't speak; I understand you without words." Oh yes, I do understand her. And I ache.

1973. On November 13 and 14, at Carnegie Hall, "*Ani Maamin, a Song Lost and Found Again*" is performed by an orchestra and choir under the baton of Lukas Foss. I had conceived this cantata, for which Darius Milhaud composed the score, for the centennial celebration of American Reform Jewry. It was commissioned by Al Ronald, a German Jew and former member of the Office of Strategic Services. I loved to listen to his tales of espionage, of parachuting into Germany.

The victim of a fatal heart attack, he had pursued happiness with such zeal, my special friend Al.

I have never worked at such a pace. In less than a week the prose poem was completed and sent to the composer in Paris.

Ensconced in his armchair near the window in his Paris apartment, Milhaud asks why I chose this theme, this legend, over others. I tell him that since childhood I have felt a special tenderness for this twelfth article of faith proclaimed by the great Rabbi Moses Maimonides.

As children we had sung the original melody at *heder* and at the yeshiva on every holiday. For me it was a call to faith and an affirmation that even though he was late, the Redeemer would make his appearance one day.

Later I learned that Jews on their way to Treblinka and Birkenau had sung that song, as if to defy death. And I failed to understand: How could they believe in the coming of the Messiah *over there?* From where did they draw their faith in divine kindness and grace?

Then I sometimes question the child within me: What in the world was the Good Lord doing while His people were being massacred and incinerated? When He veils his face, as in the times of the biblical Malediction, what does he see? And then I ask myself: What were our ancestors, the patriarchs Abraham, Isaac, and Jacob, doing while their descendants were humiliated and sent to their death? Were they not, according to our tradition, our protectors and intercessors? Why didn't they shake the celestial throne with their prayers and drown it in their tears?

God. Of all the characters in Scripture, said Saul Lieberman, God is the most tragic. It is not sacrilegious to feel sorry for Him. He, too, needs Redemption. Thus it is for Him, too, that we recite *Ani Maamin*—yes, I believe with all my heart in the coming, however belated, of the Messiah. *Ani Maamin?* I believe? In what? In whom? In the coming of the Messiah? Whom will he deliver? Who is there sufficiently worthy to make him come and save a humanity that has doomed itself?

These are thoughts that come to my mind every year as we commemorate the anniversary of the Warsaw Ghetto uprising. The speakers recall the heroism of the fighters and the faith of the martyrs. And to conclude the ceremony the *Ani Maamin* is sung as if to emphasize that the dead, at the moment of dying, had maintained their faith.

Is it possible that in the midst of hell the victims kept their faith in a better world? Some witnesses answer affirmatively; I have no right to contradict them. We know that a principal goal of the fighters was to show the world that Jews were capable of taking up arms "to defend and save Jewish honor." This expression often appears in their letters and testaments. We also know that those who were lucky enough to escape from the ghettos cared more about alerting their unfortunate brothers outside than about their own survival. All were filled with *ahavat Israel*, love for their people. That was why these young Jews risked their lives. And in the death camps there were Jews who took it upon themselves to become chroniclers and historians, writing and collecting testimonies so that future generations would remember and judge.

And yet there are other documents that reflect total despair. In their solitude Jews realized they could count on no one, that they counted for no one. The free and "civilized" world had handed them over to the executioner. There were the killers—the murderers—and there were those who remained silent. Does that explain the so-called Jewish passivity during the Holocaust? Perhaps Jews refused to fight for a world that had disappointed and betrayed them? Such pessimism is irreconcilable with *Ani Maamin*.

But then which approach is more justified? Both are, equally. There were Jews who prayed for the Messiah, and others who were ready to send him away. There were those who clung to the belief that all was not lost, and others who proclaimed that humanity was doomed. To say, as I do in my cantata, that the silence of God is God, is both an admission of resignation and an affirmation of hope.

The whole question of faith in God, surely in spite of man and perhaps in spite of God, permeates this cantata:

> In those days, even as the heart of the world was being consumed by the black flames of Night, three angry old men appeared before the celestial court, asking to be heard.
>
> Abraham, Isaac, and Jacob—the three forefathers of a people consecrated to God by God—were desperate. Their mission had been to roam the lands near and far, gathering the echoes of Jewish suffering in the world, and make them known in heaven. They wanted to bring it to an end.

Abraham tells what he sees on an earth drenched in blood, and the choir responds: "Pray for Abraham." Isaac describes what he sees, and the choir responds: "Pray for Isaac." Jacob tells us what he observes, and the choir responds: "Pray for Jacob." And God? The choir concludes:

> *Ani maamin*, Abraham,
> Despite Treblinka.
> *Ani maamin*, Isaac,
> Because of Belsen.
> *Ani maamin*, Jacob,
> Because and in spite of Majdanek. . . .

Ani Maamin, a song found again? This subtitle implies that I had found it, lost it, or at one time rejected it. This is what happened: One Passover evening in the seventies, my childhood friend Moshe-Chaim Berkowitz turns to me and asks: "Do you remember the melody for *Ani Maamin*, the one we used to sing at the Wizhnitzer Rebbe's?" Suddenly it comes back to me. Winter 1943. We are spending Shabbat Shira—whose biblical readings remind us of the Red Sea crossing—at the Rebbe's court. Toward the end of the afternoon I become aware of a man, small in stature, wearing *shtreimel* and caftan. He stands alone in a corner, near the stove. I know he is a relative of the Rebbe's. He comes from Galicia. How did he manage to cross the border? I don't dare ask. Suddenly he begins to hum *Ani Maamin;* it is a melody I have never heard before, and I find it both beautiful and heartbreaking. I close my eyes. In the huge study hall there is silence. Like everyone else I hold my breath. The men draw closer, forming a circle around the singer. We all wait for him to repeat the melody. That is the custom; that is how Hasidim learn new songs.

But the Rebbe's relative prefers to speak. He tells a story, his own, of what he has seen and endured on the other side, in occupied Poland. After every episode he stops and sings anew the same haunting tune of *Ani Maamin*, as if to tell us: Remember not only my stories but also my song. In the end we learn it. But since Auschwitz it had eluded me. Yes, I had forgotten it, as had Moshe-Chaim. And it was at the same moment, one Passover eve, in the middle of the Seder, that we both found it again. It is one of the most hauntingly beautiful Hasidic tunes I know. To this day, when I sing it I close my eyes.

Does this mean that I have made peace with God? I continue to protest His apparent indifference to the injustices that savage His creation. And the Messiah? He should have arrived earlier, much earlier. Perhaps Kafka was right: The Redeemer will come not on the last day but on the day after.

And what about my faith in all that? I would be within my rights to give it up. I could invoke six million reasons to justify my decision. But I don't. I am incapable of straying from the path charted by my ancestors. Without this faith in God, the faith of my father and forefathers, my faith in Israel and in humanity would be diminished. And so I choose to preserve the faith of my childhood.

Did I say "choose"? In truth, it is not a real choice. I would not be the man that I am, the Jew that I am, if I betrayed the child who once felt duty-bound to live for God.

I never gave up my faith in God. Even *over there* I went on praying. Yes, my faith was wounded, and still is today. In *Night*, my earliest testimony, I tell of a boy's death by hanging, and conclude that it is God Himself that the killer is determined to murder. I say this from within my faith, for had I lost it I would not rail against heaven. It is because I still believe in God that I argue with Him. As Job said: "Even if He kills me, I shall continue to place my hope in Him." Strange: In secular circles my public statements of faith in God are resented.

From Montreal, another urgent call. Bea: Is there a nobler soul, a more charitable spirit? Though gnawed by cancer, my beloved sister never complains. She repeats over and over: "Not to be afraid, not to be afraid." But I am afraid for her. As long as she did not know the nature of her illness, she seemed to hold fast. She remained active, went to her office between treatments. Why did the oncologist have to tell her the truth? She continues to repeat that all will be well, that we should not worry. But now when I visit the hospital I notice that she can barely smile. The last time I saw her, she spoke of her two children, Stevie and Sarah, more passionately than ever.

We are in Italy when, at the end of August 1974—according to the Hebrew calendar, the twenty-ninth day of the month of Ab of the year 5734—I receive the news. My brother-in-law Len is crying into the phone. I remain mute until I pull myself together to call Hilda but am still unable to move my lips. "What is it? What is it?" she asks. I finally whisper: Bea. Hilda cries out. A foolish thought crosses my mind: Just today I recited the prayer for the coming month; I must have prayed badly.

Marion is with me. So is Elisha. Does love console? I am inconsolable. Does love soothe? It soothes and is indispensable. We speak of Bea—her last visit with us, our last conversation. Language is cruel: We are already speaking of her in the past tense.

I fly to Montreal via New York. At La Guardia Airport, all the flights are booked. I run from one counter to the other, imploring the airline clerks. Finally I secure a seat.

Steve and Sarah have arrived from Israel, where they had been vacationing. Hilda is here too. I see people I know, others I do not. Bea had many admirers and friends. She was loved for her kindness, her compassion, her sense of humor. One of her friends tells me that a few days before her death, Bea had told her that she was terrified. She had seen our parents in a dream. They were expecting her.

And that was it. Life. Death. Three children from Sighet had been reunited after the war, and now only two of us are left. A thought tears through my brain: We had never spoken of her experiences *over there*. Now it is too late.

I tear my clothes as is the custom. I recite the traditional prayer: "Blessed art Thou, our God and King of the Universe, Judge of Truth." The family slowly follows the coffin. I see nothing, nobody. All is dark around me, darker still inside me. I speak to Bea, entrusting to her messages and tears for our parents. "You will see them again. In three days your soul will rise to heaven, tell them . . ." The eulogies. The interment. The sense of irreparable loss. And later, traditional meals: How to touch them? The services, morning and evening. How to hold back the sobs as Steve recites the Kaddish? The ancestral rites. The condolences. It is the first time I am able to observe a week of mourning.

Seated on a low stool sitting shivah, I listen to the visitors who come to comfort us with the traditional words: "May God comfort you together with the mourners of Zion and Jerusalem." Each has a story to tell about Bea. Her altruism, her integrity. No one had ever seen her angry. As for me, I remember her at home, in Sighet. When she fell ill with typhus, she had stayed in a room that was off-limits to us. Later I admired her resourcefulness, her courage. She was always ready to undertake missions most men considered too dangerous. Her work in the displaced persons camp. A walk through Paris with her: I look at the photograph. She wears a beret.

Certain midrashic texts suggest that the soul of the dead floats through the house during shivah. And I can indeed feel my sister's presence.

Often, when I lecture in Montreal, I go to her grave to recite a psalm. Engraved on her tombstone are the names of those dear to us who never had a grave of their own.

For Israel and the Jewish communities of the Diaspora, 1974 ends on a note of defeat. Yasir Arafat's appearance before the U.N. General Assembly was an indecent spectacle. The sight of this terrorist in uniform preaching morality to all of mankind—"In one hand I hold an olive branch, in the other, a gun!"—was distressing. Has the world forgotten the attacks, the assassinations committed by him and his minions?

I publish an article in the *New York Times* and *Le Figaro*, "Why I Am Afraid: Ominous Signs and Unspeakable Thoughts." Here are excerpts:

> I admit it sadly: I feel threatened. For the first time in many years I feel that I am in danger. For the first time in my adult life I am afraid the nightmare may start all over again or that it has never ended, that since 1945 we have lived in parentheses. Now they are closed. Could the Holocaust happen again? Over the years I have often put the question to my young students. And they, consistently, have answered yes, while I said no. I saw it as a unique event that would remain unique. I believed that if mankind had learned anything from it, it was that hate and murder reach beyond the direct participants; he who begins by killing others, in the end will kill his own. Without Auschwitz, Hiroshima would not have been possible. The murder of one people inevitably leads to that of mankind. . . .
>   . . . There are signs, and they are unmistakable: the sickening sight of a diplomatic gathering wildly applauding a spokesman for killers. The scandalous exclusion of Israel from UNESCO. The arrogant self-righteousness of certain leaders, the cynicism of others. The dramatic solitude of Israel. The anti-Semitic statements made by America's top general. Anti-Semitism has become fashionable once more both in the East and in the West. . . . Is it conceivable that Hitler could be victorious posthumously?

... And so, the idea of another catastrophe is no longer unthinkable. I say it reluctantly. In fact, it is the first time I say it. I have chosen until now to place the Holocaust on a mystical or ontological level, one that defies language and transcends imagination. . . . If I speak of it now, it is only because of my realization that Jewish survival is being called into question. . . .

... And so I look at my young students and tremble for their future; I see myself at their age surrounded by ruins. What am I to tell them? I would like to be able to tell them that in spite of endless disillusionments one must maintain faith in man and in mankind; that one must never lose heart. I would like to tell them that, notwithstanding the official discourses and policies, our people does have friends and allies and reasons to advocate hope. But I have never lied to them; I am not going to begin now. And yet. . . .

Despair is no solution. I know that. What *is* the solution? Hitler had one. And he tried it while a civilized world kept silent. I remember. And I am afraid. . . .

Some twenty years later, as I transcribe this text, I wonder whether I was right to be so wary of Arafat. Yes, he was responsible for deadly terrorist activities, which it was my duty to denounce. But at the same time, he was a freedom fighter in the eyes of his people. I was asked to meet Arafat many times. Was I wrong to refuse? Are those who claim to have chosen peace over terror not to be believed? Is Arafat, therefore, to be looked upon as a moderate, a peacemaker, the head of a nascent state rather than of a clandestine military organization?

Summer 1974. We are on Long Island, in the Hamptons, the village of Amagansett, where Marion has transformed a ruin into a beautiful country house. I work badly and fitfully because I spend hours in front of the television watching the Senate and House investigations into the Watergate affair. What we are seeing is the vitality of the nation's democratic institutions at work. The once-powerful witnesses stand humbled before the investigators. Isolated from his faithful and arrogant lieutenants, the President of the United States seems to be alone in his fight for survival. The dismissal of his attorney general for having refused to fire the prosecutors is dubbed the "Saturday Night Massacre" by the media. Nixon makes an astounding statement on television, that he is "not a crook." The Supreme Court orders him to hand over the tapes of his conversations with his aides. The threat of impeachment. This is the stuff of Greek tragedy: the fall of a "hero" who has displeased the gods. All we can do is watch. His last speech. His farewell to the weeping White House staff. His flight to California, his arms raised in a sign of victory. The bland confirmation of his successor, Gerald Ford.

It is a turbulent year in every sector of American society. The public is repeatedly shaken by bizarre happenings, both at home and abroad. The young heiress Patty Hearst, abducted by terrorists, appears to have embraced their cause: You see a photo of her in the act of robbing a bank! There is talk of brainwashing, of rebellion against the class loyalties of her parents.

The greatest of Soviet writers, Alexander Solzhenitsyn, is forced into exile and finds refuge with the German writer Heinrich Böll. In France, Georges Pompidou dies in office and is succeeded by Valéry Giscard d'Estaing. He has beaten the Socialist candidate, François Mitterrand, by 1 percent of the vote. In West Germany, Helmut Schmidt defeats Chancellor Willy Brandt, one of whose advisers had turned out to be an East German spy.

Northern Israel is under attack. The children of the villages and kibbutzim near the Lebanese border sleep in shelters; Arab shells kill eighteen inhabitants of Kiryat Shmona. Saboteurs are infiltrating the country from Lebanon and Jordan. There are far too many casualties on both sides. The worst of the attacks, the most heinous: eighteen children assassinated in the village of Maalot. Why do the terrorists target defenseless civilians? Their cowardice evokes horror. Is there ever a victory when the victims are children? I tell myself that though one day there may be peace between Israel and its neighbors, those responsible for the monstrous crime at Maalot will never be forgiven.

Notwithstanding the Syrian artillery's attacks, the northern villages refuse to evacuate their children. Members of the elite units of the Israel Defense Forces (IDF) track down the saboteurs. Marion and I spend an afternoon on a military base, and at nightfall watch the soldiers depart for the nearby border. We wonder how many will return.

Nonetheless, there does appear to be some progress in the Middle East. The "step-by-step" policy of Secretary of State Henry

Kissinger is praised in Israel when things go well, decried when things go poorly. It is around this time that I meet Kissinger, the first Jew to hold the premier U.S. cabinet post. His cold intelligence, monotonous voice, heavy German accent, and amazing analytic powers seduce and disturb. Foreign policy experts and Hollywood stars do everything and anything to be counted among his intimates. The Orthodox Jewish community is wary of him. They resent his having married a non-Jewish woman on Shabbat and his having taken his oath of office on a King James Bible.

Golda Meir likes him—though the story goes that she jokingly told Nixon, "My minister of foreign affairs speaks better English than yours." She was, of course, referring to Abba Eban.

Kissinger is annoyed with Yitzhak Rabin, Golda's successor as prime minister, for refusing to make certain territorial concessions in the Sinai that had been requested by Sadat. Two observation posts at the Mitla Pass are at issue. Israel does not realize the gravity of the situation, he says with great conviction. After a round of fruitless negotiations in Jerusalem, Kissinger, before boarding his plane at Lod, makes a statement to the press expressing his concern about the future of the Jewish state. For the first time in his career, he is seen shedding tears.

Back in Washington he reports to President Ford, who, apparently at the secretary's urging, decides to reassess American policy toward Israel. It is easy to imagine the uproar in Israel. The fanatics accuse Kissinger of treason. He claims to wish to save Israel in spite of itself; he claims the very survival of the Jewish state is at stake. One day, much later, he confides in me that toward the end of the Yom Kippur War, as Ariel Sharon's tanks surrounded the Egyptian Third Division, the Red Army had five thousand paratroopers ready to intervene.

In the summer of 1975, Marion and I board a military helicopter with Arthur Goldberg. The former Supreme Court justice and U.N. ambassador during the Six-Day War has been invited by the Israeli government to conduct an inspection of the contested zones in the Sinai. The general and colonels on board detail Rabin's position, namely, that it is necessary to keep the two strategic passages until peace agreements have actually been signed. I understand nothing about military strategy, but I trust Rabin. As for Goldberg, he advises caution. A few years later, Menachem Begin gives back all of Sinai to Anwar Sadat, who at the time might well have settled for less.

• • •

In Southeast Asia, the hostilities cease: the first military defeat in American history. I happen to be in Secretary Kissinger's office when an aide brings him a message. His face turns somber as he reads: The last American soldier has just left Saigon. He remains silent a long moment, then mutters something about the price of hostile public opinion and the restlessness on American campuses.

It is the start of the brutal Khmer Rouge regime under its leader, Pol Pot. Strangely, many leftist intellectuals offer the regime their support.

Early July 1976. America readies itself for its bicentennial. There are official ceremonies, parades, military processions, hundreds of tall sailing ships. The past is evoked to better appreciate the present. But on this Fourth of July, Americans are less preoccupied with their nation's history than with the events taking place in the distant land of Uganda, where an incredible surprise operation is being carried out successfully by an elite commando unit of the IDF.

It all began on Sunday, June 27, when a band of Arab and German terrorists diverted an Air France plane en route from Paris to Lod via Athens and forced the crew to land at Entebbe Airport in Uganda. There were 230 passengers on board, 83 Israelis among them.

The world's eyes turn to "Dr. Marshal Idi Amin Dada," the outrageous dictator of this impoverished country. Will he help the hostages or the terrorists? Nobody knows. For this fat, jovial, but ferocious character—rumor has it that he throws his enemies into crocodile-infested waters—it is the perfect opportunity to star on the international stage.

It seems he has some indebtedness to Israel, where he trained as a paratrooper. This does not prevent him from siding with the hijackers, who demand the liberation of forty-seven of their comrades who are imprisoned in Israel and Western Europe.

Whose idea was this hijacking? Was it the PLO's initiative? Then how does one explain the participation of several young Germans of the Baader-Meinhof group?

Israelis are tense. Should they negotiate with the terrorists? That would be contrary to Israeli policy, which is never to validate terrorists' status by dealing with them directly—yet sacrificing the hostages was unimaginable.

Meanwhile, the terrorists proceed with the help of Idi Amin to separate the Israelis from the other hostages. They free the French but hold the Israelis.

Rabin asks his cabinet whether to negotiate. There is tension between him and his defense minister, Shimon Peres. The vote is unanimous: Yes, but only if a military option is excluded. The leaders of the opposition, including Menachem Begin, share this point of view. Human lives count more than principles. Rabin consults General Motta Gur, the army's commander-in-chief and liberator of the Old City of Jerusalem, as to whether a military operation is feasible.

In New York, with our Israeli friends Raphael and Dina Recanati, we discuss our concern that a military move is not viable. We wonder how the army could possibly transport units that far—some 2,200 miles—into hostile territory. And even if a commando unit reached Entebbe Airport, how could one prevent the terrorists from killing the defenseless hostages? In the end, we all agree: A military rescue is out of the question. None of us is prepared for Israeli logic: that *because* the operation seems impossible, it will be undertaken—and brilliantly executed.

What was the Mossad's role? To provide information and photographs. And whose idea had it been to load into the giant plane a black Mercedes identical to the one in which Idi Amin liked to parade? Carried out with clockwork precision, the mission is successful. Tragically, there are four casualties: three hostages and the Israeli colonel Yoni Netanyahu. Four families are in mourning, but there is dancing in the streets of Tel Aviv. Begin, the opposition leader, congratulates Rabin.

It meant much to me when, months later, Yoni's father, Professor Ben-Zion Netanyahu, author of a superb volume on the Inquisition, brought me letters from his son in which my work is mentioned. I then read in his posthumously published diary references to my novels.

In America there is less talk of the bicentennial than of Entebbe. Not since the Six-Day War has there been such a show of admiration for the Jewish state.

Among the hostages was a survivor of the camps. At one point he walked up to one of the German terrorists and showed him the tattoo on his arm: "It may have been your father who did this to me; the Germans wanted to murder me and my family. Now *you* will do the job?" The terrorist did not answer. But when the Israeli attack started, the hostage saw the terrorist aiming his gun at him. "I am convinced that in that final second, what I had said kept him from pulling the trigger," said the survivor.

In 1977, the arrival of the Egyptian president Anwar Sadat in the Israeli capital turns history on its head. By then Yitzhak Rabin is no longer prime minister and Shimon Peres is no longer in charge of defense. Astonishingly, Menachem Begin has been elected to head the new government and selects Moshe Dayan as his minister of foreign affairs. Who could have imagined that the hawk from the right and the military man from the left would bring about a peace that the left had pursued unsuccessfully since 1948?

It all begins on November 9, when Sadat addresses the People's Assembly in Cairo and states: "I am ready to go to the end of the world if it will prevent one of my sons, be he soldier or officer, from being wounded. I repeat: wounded, not killed. Israel will be surprised to hear me declare before you that I am ready to go to them, to the Knesset, in order to speak to them. . . ."

That very day, Yossi Ciechanover, at that time a high official in the Defense Department and a friend of Dayan's, is in my home. We discuss Sadat's speech. I tell Yossi that Dayan must take Sadat at his word. Let Israel invite him to Jerusalem. Yossi rejects the idea, saying it won't work. In retrospect, I think he may already have been aware of secret negotiations between the Israelis and the Egyptians.

I remember: It is Shabbat. Marion and I are with our friends the Recanatis. Transfixed, we watch television, tears running down our cheeks. In Israel, night has fallen. Lod Airport is brightly lit. Egyptian flags line the tarmac. It all seems surreal. The presidential plane, escorted by Israeli military planes, appears. It lands. We are silent, afraid to breathe, afraid to wake up. The plane's door swings open. Is it really Sadat, who only four years earlier had ordered the attack on the Jewish state on the holiest day of the year, Yom Kippur? He slowly walks down the steps and reviews the honor guard. The military band plays the two national anthems. And here is Sadat saluting Menachem Begin, Arik Sharon, Ezer Weizman—and Golda, who not so long ago on her hospital bed had told me that she did not want to live to see the day when Begin would be in the cabinet. But it is Begin who welcomes the enemy leader in order to make peace. Begin, the man of the right, and not she, the former head of a leftist government.

We stay there for hours watching the live telecasts. Commentators describe what they see without seeming to believe it. At a loss for words, they hide behind their own incredulity. I scan the faces of the crowd shown on the screen—anonymous faces, looking awed. The warmth of their welcome moves me as much as the illustrious visitor's arrival. After all, among them there must be orphans, widows, bereaved parents of the Yom Kippur War. And yet there appears to be no anger. On the contrary, they welcome Sadat as a friend come from afar, a brother who has overcome dangerous obstacles.

The next day: Sadat in the Old City, Sadat entering the El Aksa Mosque, Sadat addressing the Knesset.

I admire his instincts, his courage, and I refuse to think of the difficulties that await him and his Israeli counterparts on the road to reconciliation. Will we finally learn to celebrate peace just as our ancestors glorified war?

A leap into the future. Nearly a decade later I invite a young woman to speak on the Koran to my students at Boston University, where I now teach. She is Camelia Sadat, the daughter of the Egyptian leader. I eventually become her Ph.D. adviser and she becomes my friend.

Let us take a few steps back. The year 1977 started badly. In January the French government freed the Palestinian terrorist Abu Daoud before Israel could start extradition proceedings. Throughout the world this scandal provoked an unprecedented wave of protest. In the United States there were calls for a boycott of French products. With the financial help of a few friends I arranged for a full-page ad in the *New York Times*, in the form of an open letter to Valéry Giscard d'Estaing, president of the French Republic:

> Dear Mr. President:
>
> It is because of my love for France, and my respect for its people, that I feel compelled to express to you my sadness and my indignation—shared by many other Americans—over your handling of the Abu Daoud affair.
>
> Although born in Eastern Europe, I owe France more than I owe my own native land. I owe France my secular education, my language, and my career as a writer.
>
> Liberated from Buchenwald, it was in France that I found compassion and humanity. It was in France that I found generosity and friendship. It was in France that I discovered the other side, the brighter side, of mankind.
>
> I was proud of France.

France, to me, represented humanity's highest values in a sterile and cynical society. It evoked Rousseau and Bergson, Proust and Zola, Camus and Mauriac. It symbolized an inspiring quest for justice and brotherhood. In France, I thought, the word humanism does not make people laugh.

Yes, I was proud of France.

France, the birthplace of revolutions against tyranny. France, the ally of our American independence. France, the herald of human rights. France, haven for the persecuted. France and its freedom fighters. France and its Resistance. France and its response to Dreyfus.

No nation had so much prestige. No culture was as readily accepted. No example as universally extolled.

And now, Mr. President?

Now, what has become of France?

Its moral leadership is gone, and its luster tarnished in the eyes of men of conscience. In fact, few countries have lost so much prestige so quickly. What has become of France?

It has betrayed its own traditions.

France has become as cynical as the rest of the world.

Why did your government free Abu Daoud?

And why so hastily?

He lied under oath about his false identity.

Why wasn't he held until Germany or Israel would offer evidence of his crime?

Why was he allowed to leave Paris in the comfort of a first-class airline seat, when 11 Israeli athletes left Munich in coffins?

Your prime minister claims that the courts were not politically motivated. Does anyone believe him in your country? Not in mine.

In my country we believe that France quite simply, and quite shockingly, yielded to killers' blackmail, oil merchants' bribery, and the chance to sell some fighter planes. And in doing that, France deliberately humiliated the victims' widows and orphans, and insulted the memory of their dead.

Are you surprised the world responded with dismay and outrage? Your own people rose to speak out against you.

Because while you have visited Auschwitz, you have forgotten its lesson.

But then, in truth, one should have expected nothing else from France today. In recent years the signs have multiplied. Offensive statements. Sneering remarks. Sudden policy reversals. Strange alliances. Broken promises. One-sided embargoes. The Cherbourg affair. The Mirage sale. French governments have rarely missed an opportunity to demonstrate their hostility to Israel and the Jewish people.

France even abstained on the infamous resolution equating Zionism and racism.

For ideological reasons?

Much worse: purely for money.

Yes, Mr. President, I used to be proud of France and what it stood for. I no longer am.

Written in the heat of the moment, this letter, regrettably, contained one error: I was wrong to reproach France for having abstained from voting during the infamous resolution equating Zionism to racism. I quickly corrected the error subsequently: France had actually voted against this resolution.

In 1993 on a Paris–New York flight, I find myself sitting next to the former president of France. He asks me what I am working on. I tell him: my memoirs. And I add: "I am afraid it contains pages that may displease you." He asks why. I say, "Abu Daoud." "You must let me explain," he replies. "We were ready to extradite him to Germany, since it was there that he committed his crime. But Bonn didn't want him."

In late 1995 the American press reports that Abu Daoud has sold his memoirs for a substantial price. In the book he admits to having participated in the massacre of Israeli athletes in Munich. Where is he now? In the West Bank.

I write every morning. I take notes, I make entries in my personal diary. I sleep less. I read a lot—on planes, in cars. I read very few novels, preferring essays on contemporary history, especially World War II; also, the new philosophers, deconstruction in literature, semiotics.

Writing, teaching, lecturing. Every evening, every morning, I tell myself: The danger lies in trying to do too much. Tomorrow I shall be more prudent, more parsimonious with my time. I never am.

Writing becomes more difficult, more exhausting, more pressing. I need solitude. Silence. I become acutely aware of the ambiguity of words. Always the same questions, the same doubts: How to express that which eludes language? I erase, I rewrite. I fill the wastebasket with superseded drafts. Will I be discerning enough to know when the well runs dry? I redo a single page again and again, until, in the end, I decide on the first draft.

When man is witness to the alienation of his language, when, to quote Rabbi Israel of Rizhin, the parable and its meaning no longer have anything in common, a door has been closed. Literature ceases to be a beacon of salvation or even a means of introspection.

Aesthetics or ethics: Does literature belong to either realm? If one is to believe the Midrash, Adam, when he composed a song for Shabbat, was already making literature. But didn't Eve anticipate him by telling stories about forbidden fruit and snakes? What is certain is that this couple, the first in history, opened the way to future creators. In the end, they could not escape ethical imperatives. Knowledge compels man to choose between good and evil, life and nothingness. Moses—who was as great a writer as he was a legislator—told his brother Aaron to remain *"bein hakhaim vehametim,"* between the living and the dead, and death backed off. The writer creates a link between the living and the dead; he protects one from the other.

A writer cannot detach himself from his story: He is responsible for it to the end. Jeremiah feels guilty for the destruction of the Temple: He is not sure of having found the words needed to change man and revoke the decree.

In New York, at the 92nd Street "Y," I continue my annual lecture series, begun in 1966, on the Bible, the Talmud, Hasidism, and Jewish tradition.

I remember my first lecture at the "Y." There were two of us on the program, the novelist Jean Shepherd and myself. The auditorium was nearly full, but after she spoke many people left. Never mind, I told myself, while counting the few friends and strangers scattered through Kaufmann Hall; so they won't invite me again.

In truth I was disappointed, because this center is among the most prestigious in New York. Resigned, I walk onstage. I sit down at a carved wooden table. I read a page from *Les Juifs du Silence,* the origi-

nal French edition of *The Jews of Silence*. Does anyone in this hall speak
French? No matter; they probably won't stay anyway. I read and com-
ment in English on a passage from *The Town Beyond the Wall*. Please
God, make this torture come to an end. In desperation, I evoke
Beethoven, of whom it was said that he not only composed his sym-
phonies but also the silence that followed them.

Finally it's over.

Only it wasn't. Since then, over more than thirty years, I have
given more than 120 lectures at the "Y".

I am invited to speak at the Sorbonne. My lectures on Rebbe Nahman
and the talmudic Master Elisha ben Abuya are given in the very
amphitheater where, long ago, I listened so intently to my professors.
I still have trouble overcoming my stage fright. My migraines don't
help. Before every speech I remember the words of our sages which
Saul Lieberman used to quote: "It takes less than three years for man
to learn to speak, and seventy to learn to remain silent."

On Human Rights

IN MY DREAM I am looking for my father, who is no longer look-ing for anyone. I see him leaning against the cemetery wall. He sees me and begins to cry, weakly, like the child he is becoming. He comes closer and rests his head on my lap.

Dawn is breaking. In the distance a few ghosts emerge from shelters. "Come," I urge my father, "let us follow them." They lead us to a large, brightly lit synagogue. A stranger goes before us and blows out the candles. Now it is dark. I no longer know where I am. "Father," I whisper, "where are you?" He takes a deep breath and bends down as if to examine the plowed soil. I no longer see his face. Yet, while I still know who he is, I no longer know who I am.

The Jewish writer as activist is the theme of *The Testament*, whose original French title, literally translated, is "Testament of an Assassinated Jewish Poet." Biographical novel? Bildungsroman? No: I am not the novel's Paltiel Kossover, the Jewish Communist poet. I have never been attracted to Communism. Nor have I been a soldier in the Red Army or a prisoner of the NKVD. But I became fascinated with Paltiel's story in 1965, on my first trip to the Soviet Union. I needed to understand the transformation of a young Talmudist into a fervent disciple of Marx and Lenin. The Holocaust is almost totally absent from this novel, except for half a page where I describe Paltiel going through Majdanek. Is that when he became a Jew again? Had he ever ceased to be one? He lived as a Communist but died a Jew. In this novel I explore the soul and conscience of the repressed Jew, one who has exiled himself to the margins of Judaism.

Kossover's portrait is loosely based on the Yiddish poet Peretz Markish and the Yiddish novelist Der Nister, both executed in August 1952 on Stalin's orders.

One day at the University of Geneva, after a lecture on Rabbi Akiba, a young professor shyly approaches me: "So you knew my father," he says. He is Shimon Markish, the son of Peretz, who had recognized his father in Kossover. "I am so sorry," I tell him. "I know and admire your father's work, I wish I had had the good fortune to meet him." We spend hours talking. He confirms what I had only imagined about the internal conflicts of a Jewish writer yearning for justice in an unjust society.

One of the main tenets of my life has been: *"Lo ta'amod al dam reakha...."* Do not be indifferent to the bloodshed inflicted on your fellow man (Numbers 19:16). Not to take a stand is in itself to take a stand, said Camus. Moses rediscovered himself as a Jew and as a man when he defended a Hebrew beaten by an Egyptian and then one beaten by another Hebrew. Had he remained a neutral spectator, he would not have become God's prophet and the leader of his people.

I take part in countless rallies for Soviet Jewry toward the end of the sixties. I go every time I am asked. I tell the mostly young audiences that the young Jews of Moscow are mad, completely mad. Do they really believe that they can defeat the Soviet dictatorship with their songs and their dances? And the rest of us, do we seriously believe that we have the power to influence Brezhnev's policies? But, I tell the audiences, the great Moses Maimonides was right when he said that the world survives thanks to its madmen. The liberation of Soviet Jewry has become my most urgent cause.

A huge meeting takes place in Paris to protest UNESCO's policy of discrimination against Israel. Isaac Stern, Abba Eban, Artur Rubinstein, Manès Sperber, and Mario Vargas Llosa take part. Delegates from some twenty countries express outrage that an international cultural organization would betray the very ideals it was created to serve.

The atmosphere is tense. When my turn comes to speak, I throw out an idea that I consider pragmatic if somewhat outlandish: "Let us adopt a resolution, here and now, declaring that this body will supersede UNESCO." I explain with some bravado: "Since so many distinguished scientists and great writers and musicians are with us, doesn't that signify that we *are* UNESCO?"

Of course, I am joking. But some of the participants take me seriously. Eban speaks up: He opposes my plan for foreign policy reasons. Others want to think it over. The distinguished French philosopher Raymond Aron takes me aside in the corridor: "Do you really want to do this?" I reassure him. He thanks me, laughing.

An hour later, a frantic phone call from an associate of the director general of UNESCO: "Don't do something that could ruin us. . . . Let's negotiate. . . . Everything will fall into place." Some time later we organize another meeting, this time to save Jews in Arab countries. Same participants, same arguments. I ask Raymond Aron: "So, we are starting over again?" He answers: "No. We merely continue. It is they who are starting over again."

In the early eighties, the writer Tahar Ben Jelloun asks me to use my influence to help free Abraham Sarfati, a Jewish political prisoner whom the king of Morocco refuses to release. I discuss the matter with President Carter's staff, with senators, journalists, friends. All my efforts are in vain. When Sarfati is finally freed in 1991, I am pleased. Though I do not share his political convictions—he is a Communist—I admire his courage. Soon after, I am saddened by his declaration: "Israel and the Jewish people are a mythical state and people. The Western Left deludes itself; to achieve peace, Zionism must be fought."

I ask myself: Had I been aware of his anti-Israel position, would I have tried to help him? I hope I am not deluding myself when I answer in the affirmative. Whether I agree with Sarfati's ideology has nothing to do with my duty to fight for his civil rights.

Still, I am bitterly disappointed.

In 1980, on the 18th day of the Jewish month of Sh'vat, I find myself in the dusty village of Aranyaprathet, on the border between Thailand and Cambodia, looking desperately for nine Jews. This day marks the anniversary of my father's death. I need a minyan, a quorum of ten men, to recite Kaddish in his memory.

I had arrived a few days earlier to participate in a march for the survival of Cambodia, organized by the International Rescue Committee and other humanitarian organizations. A hundred or so men and women represent the United States and Europe. Among them are intellectuals and civil rights activists. Bayard Rustin is here, as are Liv Ullmann and Joan Baez; and journalists, countless journalists. I wish I could ask my fellow inmate from the camps, Reb Menashe Klein, what one does in a case like this. Does one have the right to postpone the prayer? Surely he would say: "What are you doing so far away on a day when you should be in synagogue?" For Reb Menashe, a Jewish prayer or a page of Mishna takes precedence over all else.

As for me, I believe that when human beings suffer I have no right to be elsewhere. How could I have refused to go to the place where the refugees from the Cambodian massacres were dying of hunger and disease? I had seen them on television: skeletons with terror-stricken eyes. They had left behind parents, brothers, or children. All were imprisoned, tortured to death.

The atrocities committed by Pol Pot and his Khmer Rouge had reached new lows even in the bloody annals of Communism. In the name of a perverse "progressive" ideology, an entire country had turned itself into a slaughterhouse and sealed the gates.

The dazed survivors stare into the cameras. I see nothing but hunger, despair, and resignation. Just weeks before, they had faced their torturers, beaten and humiliated.

"What are *you* doing here?" asks Henry Kamm, a former refugee from Hitler's Austria and a Pulitzer Prize–winning *New York Times* correspondent. There is no need to respond to his rhetorical question; he knows the answer: We are both here to see what we can do for these victims of American bombs, Vietnamese rifles, and most cruelly, torture at the hands of their own people, for whom the teachings of Pol Pot had replaced those of Moses, Jesus, Muhammad, *and* Buddha. It was the Jew in us who, since the discovery of the mass graves in Cambodia, felt the need to tell these survivors that we understood.

I have encountered obstacles both real and imagined when I have had to recite Kaddish, and I often wondered how it was possible to sanctify God's name inside the kingdom of the dead. I recall my father, his features distorted by pain and anguish. I recall other fathers, other children. I watch them fly toward the gaping heavens and wonder: Who is saying Kaddish for them?

Finally I succeed in gathering the nine men I need: Henry Kamm, Rabbi Marc Tanenbaum, the writer Guy Suarès, Bernard-Henri Lévy, several Israeli doctors. . . . Surrounded by chaos, a few steps from the Cambodian border, we say the *Minha* prayer. My voice trembles as I say the prayer for the dead.

Suddenly I hear behind me a young doctor who repeats the prayer after me. His eyes are filled with tears. Afterward I ask him:

"For whom are you saying Kaddish?" He looks at me and doesn't answer. "Is it for your father?" "No." "For your mother?" "No."

He points to the border: "It is for them."

I am reminded of something from the Talmud: "Be proud, Abraham, be proud of your descendants. Look: they do not forget anyone."

—Kaddish is a beautiful prayer, is it not?

—*Very beautiful. It is the Jewish song of memory.*

—Are you reciting it because you love to sing or because you love to remember?

—*Both.*

—To recite Kaddish is to remember that one comes from somewhere, that one did not emerge from nothingness.

—*I know where I come from, and to whom I owe my life.*

—You recite Kaddish in order to remember your father?

—*Not only my father.*

—Is it out of a need to submit that you recite Kaddish?

—*I do not consider Kaddish an act of submission. And I have not submitted.*

—Is Kaddish not linked to death? And does death itself not imply submission?

—*I repeat: Kaddish has nothing to do with death.*

—Only with God?

—*With God and with His orphans.*

—Who are they?

—*We all were; you still are.*

—And God? An orphan, He too?

—*He more than anyone.*

A rescue mission at the Nicaraguan border. I am to meet Miskito Indians expelled from their homes by Daniel Ortega's repressive regime, the latest "forgotten" in our society, which often practices apathy and selective solidarity.

To reach them is complicated and exhausting. There are no direct flights. The New York–Tegucigalpa connection is via Miami. At the suggestion of John Silber, president of Boston University, I am accompanied by Professor Joachim Maître, who knows the region well. We meet foreign diplomats, we have secret encounters with the opposition. Then we cross the jungle, the last stretch by kayak. I can hardly believe I am doing this, I who have been known to lose my way in my own neighborhood and don't know how to swim.

Why has this leftist regime uprooted these peaceful Indians? Because they live too close to the border? Is that a reason to extract them from their native environment? And why do so many civil rights activists look the other way? Because Daniel Ortega is of the left and violently anti-American, anti-imperialist, and therefore untouchable? Still, the Miskito Indians have succeeded in arousing the sympathy of a few journalists and intellectuals in Europe and America. I discuss the situation with François Mitterrand, who listens well. I do believe that he interceded. In the end, the Miskito were allowed to return to their homes.

My extraliterary activities take more and more of my time and energy. But I feel I have no right to turn away from them. Clearly I have less time to work on my novels, but there are more important things. I explain this when, in 1982, I refuse to take part in a colloquium whose subject is close to my heart. Organized by two Israeli professors of psychiatry, this symposium on genocide, which I am to chair, is scheduled for early June in Tel Aviv. Everything is set. Scholars and historians from several continents have accepted our invitation, among them Armenians. After all, they have ideas on this subject which has touched them closely. How could one forget the massacre of their parents and grandparents at the hands of the Turkish army?

At the last moment, we encounter a major hurdle. Under pressure from Turkey, the Israelis urge me to revoke our invitation to the Armenians. I refuse. It would be too humiliating. And to humiliate is to blaspheme. The pressure increases. I am given to understand that even if a single Armenian participates in the conference, Israeli-Turkish relations will suffer. And that there would be consequences for Jews in certain Arab countries. Jewish emissaries from Istanbul confirm this to me with documents. No matter. I will not offend our Armenian guests. I resign as chairman. To Richard Eder, the *New York Times* correspondent in Paris, I explain why: "A human life weighs more than all the books written about human life."

The war in Lebanon breaks out a week before the conference opens. I suggest moving the conference to Paris or Amsterdam. "But what about the Armenians?" ask the organizers. I say: invite them, of course. Now that the venue has changed, Israel cannot interfere.

Unfortunately, my suggestion is not accepted. The conference takes place without the Armenians.

I know that Israel had to heed Turkish threats and that the ethical demands on Jews in the Diaspora are not necessarily those imposed on Israelis. Still, I am left with a sense of failure.

The war in Lebanon brings increased hostility toward Israel throughout the world. Passing through Paris in mid-June, I am invited to appear on the one o'clock news. I am meant to help restore some balance to the news commentaries on the Middle East. At the end of the program I ask: Why doesn't anyone ever speak of the sadness in Israel? As I leave the set, I am accosted by an angry reporter who says: "Today, you shouldn't have . . ." "Shouldn't have what?" "You shouldn't have defended Israel. Today it was your duty to denounce Israel and to support the cause of its Arab victims!" Back in 1967, this same journalist—Julien Besançon—was considered an admirer of Israel. He had written a powerful book on the Six-Day War.

In America too, the campaign against Israel has become mean. Arthur Hertzberg, a Conservative rabbi, chooses the day before Yom Kippur to publish a violent attack in the *New York Times* headlined: "BEGIN MUST GO." He condemns the prime minister and Israel as if it had been the Israeli army, and not the Christian militia, that perpetrated the terrible massacre of the Palestinians.

It is a time of celebration for our enemies. They exploit the Lebanon war to their own ends. A synagogue in Copenhagen is bombed. The monstrous *Protocols of the Elders of Zion* is distributed in Stockholm. Anti-Semitic statements appear in the German press. In the past, anti-Semitism flourished in the ranks of the extreme right; today, it is found as well in the extreme left.

After World War II, some of us really believed that anti-Semitism too had died in Auschwitz. We were wrong. Hitler is dead, but anti-Semitism is alive and well. It just goes by other names—most frequently, that of anti-Zionism.

South Africa, 1975. My first journey to this land, my first encounter with apartheid—the racial and racist hatred, the arbitrary arrests, the daily killings; the evil determination to jail entire peoples because of their color; the misery of Soweto. The original crime of apartheid is to have legitimized hatred in the name of racial superiority. To hate under the apartheid regime does not constitute a violation of the law;

it is the law. But once unleashed, hatred knows no boundaries. Hate begets hate.

Back then, South Africa was a region without hope. Day after day: riots, repression, funerals. With ancestral dignity families carried their dead to their final resting places. Those armed policemen who surrounded them, had they no respect, no decency, as they faced a community in mourning?

Another subject that does not let go of me: the excluded, the rejected, the marginalized.

In 1985 in Arizona, I participate in the first conference to explore statutes of political asylum or "sanctuary" for the illegal "economic refugees" from El Salvador and Guatemala. Another conference on refugees, in Washington, deals with the larger problem. I remained stateless too long not to be concerned with the fate of those without a land. Long after refugees have been accepted, they remain uprooted.

For the refugee, distances are meaningless. Though one may live a single kilometer from the border, it might just as well be the other end of the world. On one side there is life and happiness; on the other, misery or even death.

The notion of sanctuary has changed over time. In the Bible, the term is *ir miklat,* or the city of refuge. In those days, only someone guilty of involuntary homicide could take refuge there.

The tradition I claim for myself places the sanctuary not in space but inside man. Every human being is a sanctuary, for God resides there. And nobody has the right to violate it.

In certain countries, refugees are called "illegals." That word is offensive. A human being is never illegal. His deeds can be, but not his essence.

Another preoccupation: terrorism. We must put an end to it to save democracy. During the French Revolution, the regime of terror lasted less than a year, and those who were responsible for it ultimately became its victims. Are we to infer that only terror can do away with terror?

Terrorism has but one goal: to reduce the adversary to a state of slavery. Terrorism targets the anonymous citizen as much as the political rival. Terrorism does not attempt to convince but to dominate, subjugate, crush.

In a terrorist regime, man is no longer the unique creation with infinite possibilities, but a cipher or puppet. But then how is one to explain the attraction that terrorism exerts on certain minds? Is there a romantic element in the terrorist adventure? What comes to mind are the revolutionary Russians of the early twentieth century, the anarchists, the nihilists.

In Dostoyevsky's *The Possessed*, the terrorists refrain from attacking the governor when they see that his children are with him. Today, Hamas does not hesitate to attack defenseless children. The hijackings, the massacre of schoolchildren in Maalot, the assaults on buses in Jerusalem. . . . And elsewhere—in India, Sri Lanka, Lebanon, Northern Ireland—the goal is always the same.

In the Middle East, the terrorists' aim is to sabotage peace. One day an international tribunal will condemn them not only for having assassinated innocent people, but for having committed "crimes against peace," to use the words of the Nuremberg tribunal.

One cannot speak of suffering or terror, of evil and disaster, without evoking the destructive demons unleashed in Hiroshima. Auschwitz and Hiroshima: One evokes the end of mankind, the other the apocalypse of our planet. Both symbolize the curse that, more than fifty years later, continues to weigh upon us. From now on, we will live with the frightful knowledge that the impossible has become possible. Evil has been unleashed, and nothing seems able to contain it. Shimon Peres spoke without hesitation of "the two holocausts" of the twentieth century: Auschwitz and Hiroshima. He shouldn't have. Hiroshima was a cruel, inhuman decision, but it was part of a response to Japanese aggression and a global military strategy. It was intrinsically linked to the war in the Pacific. Auschwitz was conceived as an operation that carried its own justification: genocide. True, the death camps had been built during the war, but they functioned independently of the war. One can even say with certainty that, from a strictly military point of view, Auschwitz impeded the Nazi war effort. Thousands of soldiers employed in the concentration camps could have been more useful on the battlefields. The trains that transported Jews from all corners of occupied Europe were needed by the Wehrmacht for their troops. But the Final Solution was, for Hitler, an absolute priority rooted in his deadly and perverse philosophy rather than in his military strategy.

Auschwitz implies the past, whereas Hiroshima announces the future. And it was Auschwitz that made Hiroshima possible. Hitler's

Germany had decided to exterminate an entire people, and the world did not object. Both end and beginning, Auschwitz marks a turning point in history. As does Hiroshima. The bomb that annihilated Hiroshima has become a kind of divinity; it is written with a capital letter: the Bomb. Its shadow falls over the entire planet, leaving no place to hide.

In 1987 Marion and I go to Hiroshima. At a meeting with high Japanese officials I feel compelled to say: "I shall never forget Hiroshima, but you in turn must never forget Pearl Harbor." Our hosts are clearly unsettled by this remark.

We meet *hibakusha*, survivors of history's first nuclear bombardment: men and women with ravaged memories, wounded souls. I ask an old man: "Where were you when . . ." "Not far away," he says. Just far enough. "And you, Madam, where were you when . . ." She was home with her children, who were torn from her by a storm of ashes. I empathize with the survivors' sadness. And their determination. All are committed to the struggle against atomic weapons. Like them, I feel the weight of the threat. There are too many rockets, missiles, and bombs stockpiled in too many arsenals. How is one to protect oneself against a military Chernobyl? How is one to prevent small nations from collecting weapons that the major powers should be destroying?

We leave this haunted city with the image of a shadow on a stone step. At the moment of the explosion, a woman was entering a bank. Only her shadow remains, imprinted on the stone. If by some accident we miscalculate, the same fate may be in store for us. And we may not even leave a shadow.

In December 1995, in cooperation with the prominent Japanese daily *Asahi Shimbun*, the foundation that bears my name organized an international colloquium in Hiroshima. Some fifty men and women, politicians and thinkers, gathered for three days of intense debate on the theme "The Future of Hope."

The question remains open.

On March 5, 1985, I am invited to testify before the Senate Foreign Relations Committee, which is debating the ratification of the Genocide Treaty. Filled with apprehension, I think of the past and its shadows. Had there been such committees to inquire into the tragedy of European Jewry?

When I find out that Jesse Helms is chairing the session, my instinct is to turn around and head back to New York, for this southern senator and I clearly have few ideas in common. As I wait for my turn, I notice that he hardly listens during the early testimonies. And when he introduces me to the committee I realize that he has no idea who I am. He reads a text evidently prepared by his aides: Everything in it sounds false, even my name. To my surprise, when I begin to speak, he actually seems to listen.

I plead for ratification, which means placing genocide outside the law. We owe it to our children. It is up to us to protect them from the dread that inhabits our nightmares. Yes, I know this treaty will not bring back our dead, I say; for them it is too late. But at least by signing we would be remembering. Not to remember would mean to betray them. And if we forget them, we too shall be forgotten.

Senator Helms remains silent for a long moment. He then thanks me in such flattering terms that the entire committee takes notice. Is it the first time he has heard a Jew expressing himself as a Jew? Or is it just a display of southern courtesy? After my testimony, Helms and other members of the committee including Christopher Dodd and Rudy Boschwitz put me through a friendly but intense interrogation. Helms: "Aren't you afraid that, one day, the State of Israel will be accused of genocide of the Palestinians?" "I accept the challenge," I tell him, "I have faith in Israel." Amazingly, at the conclusion of my testimony, Helms interrupts the session to escort me to the door.

Buenos Aires, December 1996. A small gathering in a central square of the capital, opposite the courts. Dozens of men and women meet here every week, holding candles and photographs. They come together to demand justice, or simply to weep. These are the relatives of the Jewish victims of recent terrorist attacks. Expressing their sadness and anger, they come here week after week. They ask: "How is it possible that the assassins remain at large?" The prosecutor in charge of the cases claims to know their identity but to lack proof. President Carlos Menem speaks of logistical problems. He tries to explain, but is not convincing.

Does the writer need to go to the end of the world to testify when he does so in his writings? This is a question that preoccupies me as I struggle to find more time for my literary work. What am I to do, become a recluse? Sleep less? Limit the traveling? Learn to say no? Marion's reaction to my good intentions? She laughs.

On Learning and Teaching⟶

*T*O QUOTE A TALMUDIC sage (Rabbi Hanina, according to the Tractate of Taanit, or Rabbi Yehuda Ha-Nasi, according to the Tractate of Malkot): "I have learned a great deal from my masters, but I have learned much more from my colleagues, and above all I have learned from my pupils."

This statement reflects my own feelings about teaching.

In the mid-sixties, I receive a warm and exciting letter from a dean at Yale, offering me a position. He does not know me personally, nor has he checked my qualifications to teach at an institution of higher learning. The offer is attractive: two courses per semester—one on literature, one on Hasidic thought—a salary three or four times what I am earning, a stimulating environment, a prestigious title at one of the most renowned universities in the world. For a young writer who still has trouble making ends meet, it seems unbelievable.

I immediately send off an enthusiastic response. Back in my apartment on Manhattan's Riverside Drive, I find myself pacing as I consider my new duties. Feverishly I go over possible topics for the first semester. Which texts of Rebbe Nahman will I suggest to my students? How can I make them discover the intensity of the Besht's fervor? Suddenly I am content with the world around me, and even with myself. After all, how many boys from Sighet have ever been invited to teach at Yale? My worries are over. My insecurities vanish. Long live academia! My fellow journalists at the U.N. have never seen me so ebullient. I am asked if I have just won the lottery. I say: "No, but . . . " I tell them what has happened. In his usual friendly, supportive way, the reporter Dick Jaffe ventures: "It's Yale that won the lottery, not you."

Just then I am asked to go to Paris, where my publisher, Le Seuil, seems to require my presence. El Al offers me a free ticket. Fortune is smiling on me. My new novel has not disappointed. That splendid radio station France-Culture proposes a series of interviews. Why not? I am in no mood to refuse anything. Then, suddenly, during one of the recording sessions, I begin to have doubts: What shall I do at Yale? Once I begin I will have to continue; therefore there would be no more solitude, no more trips, no more adventures. No, I couldn't give up all that. I wasn't ready. But how does one say no to Yale? And what about the "famous" argument: How many boys from Sighet have ever been invited to teach at Yale? In my tiny hotel room as I respond to the reporter's questions, I am struck by the obvious answer: It's certainly true that very few natives of Sighet have ever been invited to Yale, but how many among them have refused the invitation?

I am close to all my students; my door is always open to them. I try to make them my friends even though at first they intimidate me, as I probably intimidate them. Will I succeed in guiding them as I teach them? I take my responsibilities very seriously. Every hour of lecturing takes four hours of preparation. Never have I studied so much. Though I may not be the best lecturer at the university, surely I am one of its most diligent students.

As an adolescent I dreamed of becoming a writer and a teacher. Today, I am both. The itinerary has not corresponded to my dream, but its starting point and goal are the same. Could it be that an individual's fate is sealed from the moment he takes his first step?

At the very beginning, I become aware of a strange fact: Nearly all of my students are children of survivors. It takes me awhile to understand that for them I am a substitute for their fathers. Since their fathers were unable or unwilling to share their past with them, they turn to me and take an interest in mine. Later it is the parents who come to see me, to talk to me about their children. I thus become a human bridge between two worlds.

How was I to speak to my students about those years of darkness without shifting the burden to them? How was I to convince them that in spite of everything, mankind deserves our faith?

I remember a student, a nineteen-year-old girl, who, holding back her tears, asks me a question that is troubling her: "Will my father remain a survivor the rest of his life?" I give her a text by Jean

Améry in which he says: "Just as someone who has been tortured remains tortured, so does a survivor remain a survivor forever."

A student despairs of being able to make her mother happy: "I have never seen her smile," she says. Another student: "My parents love me too much; their love is too heavy to bear." Still another: "My parents' sadness prevents them from loving each other." Outside the classroom we speak more about their personal problems than about the work.

Another student appears in my office and bursts into sobs: "Every time my parents look at me, I know it's not me they see." His father had lost his first wife and children. His mother, too, had seen her husband and children disappear. They had met in a camp for displaced persons shortly after liberation; they had a son, my student. His experience became central to my novel *The Fifth Son*.

In class the mood becomes oppressive whenever we touch on subjects related to the camps. At times I still feel compelled to teach the history and literature of the Holocaust. Since very few other professors are teaching the subject, I have no choice; all the more since the director of Jewish Studies has insisted that at least one of my courses be devoted to the topic. Sometimes the students remain seated, heads buried in their hands, unable to go to their next class to listen to lectures on biology or physics. I too feel the weight and destructive force of the theme; I sleep poorly. Even though I know how to share, there are limits. I feel that I cannot and should not be completely open. In speaking of the victims, how can I prevent a student from identifying me with them? How does one speak openly and restrain oneself at the same time? I tell my students: "Together we are going to encounter madness on a global scale. We must take care not to be contaminated." I also say to them: "What are we about to learn here? To read, to weep, to dream the end of the dream. And later, to fall down, but also to rise again, to take one step and then another."

I read and reread the great classical and medieval texts of Jewish martyrology: the persecutions during the reign of Emperor Hadrian, the public executions, the forced conversions. I hope to discover how the experience of those past ordeals eventually became integrated into history. I search for examples. I find none. *Valley of Tears* by Mordechai HaCohen of Avignon? The Crusades along the entire length of the Rhine, the expulsions, the pogroms, the massacres, and collective suicides? No analogy can hold. In those days disasters were localized and salvation possible, through either escape or conversion. During the Night all gates were sealed. And yet my students want to learn, to acquire my knowledge.

We read the diaries of Anne Frank and Moshe Flinker, the poems of Theresienstadt's children. The innocence, the wisdom, the maturity, of these children make my students curse the world that allowed *this* to happen. We analyze the diaries of Emmanuel Ringelblum, Chaim Kaplan, and Shimon Huberband, and the letters of Mordechai Anielewicz. Sometimes we stifle a sob as we hold up a bloodstained image, so that a new generation may know, so that humanity may remember.

Ringelblum had a committee of one hundred chroniclers inside the Warsaw Ghetto. Disguised as members of the cultural religious circle Oneg Shabbat, they would gather every Saturday. Together they became the memory of a besieged Jewish community. They knew and described the degradation of hunger, the cold, the exhaustion of the elderly, the ravages of disease, the cowardice of the informers, the profiteers patronizing the cabarets—yes, there were such people. All this in the ghetto. And on the other side of the walls were the *Shmalezowniks*, the Polish informers who patrolled the streets looking for "Aryan" Jews, whom they recognized by their sad eyes. Inside were the orphaned children and their cries of agony. Ringelblum describes the despair but also the spiritual resistance of poorly armed men and women. And the fact that the first bullet fired by the resistance was aimed at the converted Jewish policeman Sherinsky. And what about Adam Czerniakow, the president of the Jewish Council? Was he right to commit suicide?

Kaplan wrote his diary in Hebrew, his last words a cry of anguish: "If I am caught, what will happen to my testimony?"

Rabbi Huberband had a thousand and one stories about the courage and faith of the victims. His stories even tell of nonbelievers sacrificing themselves to honor God: by attempting to save sacred scrolls from burning synagogues.

And then there are the shattering, harrowing accounts by Zalmen Gradowski, Zalmen Leventhal, and Reb Arye Leib Langfus about their hapless comrades in misfortune: the members of the *Sonderkommandos* detailed to burn the corpses of the Jews gassed at Birkenau. These are writings of unbearable intensity written by dying men, every account a poem, every poem a prayer. How did these writers manage not to lose their minds? Where does one draw the strength to take in the deeds they report? If there is such a thing as incandescent words, theirs are. I tell the students: "If these people had the strength to write them, we must have the courage to read them." To teach their writings is to respond, however inadequately, to their desperate call for justice.

For some twenty years, long before the publication of their testimony, *Voices in the Night,* for which I wrote the preface, I was haunted by these fiery pages. How can one forget the *Dayyan,* the rabbinical judge, and his description of the transport from Bendin? Inside the gas chamber, a rabbi who begins to dance and sing. . . . I read and reread those lines and I want to . . . I no longer know what I want to do. Not to sing ever again? Two Hungarian Jews ask a member of the *Sonderkommando*: "Should we say the *Vidui?*" He answers: "Yes." And so one of them removes a bottle of spirits from his bag, shares it with the others, and they all drink with joy—yes, the chronicler indeed wrote "with joy." And they called out: "*LeChaim*—to life!" Yes, that is what the chronicler wrote: "to life!" As for me, there grows inside me a silence so immense that it will taint all future joy.

The rabbinical judge's account goes on. Naked children are marching to their death, the Rabbi of Boyanne shouting in the face of an SS killer: "Do not imagine that you will succeed in annihilating the Jewish people!" At the height of his exaltation he puts on his hat and roars, "*Shma Israel*"—Hear, O Israel, the Lord is our God, the Lord is One. A Slovakian woman, already undressed, on the threshold of the gas chamber, proclaims loudly: "A miracle is still possible. . . ." I feel for Reb Arye Leib Langfus a tenderness, a love close to pain.

In his account of Treblinka, Yankel Viernik wonders if he will ever laugh again. As for Gradowski, he doubts that, if he survives, he will ever again be able to weep.

Silence reigns as the students study. Silence reigns as the instructor teaches. Silence reigns as the dead burst into the room, bathed in a dim, hazy light. They evolve in a universe parallel to our own, within a creation on the other side of Creation, and perhaps of the Creator Himself. They are on the other side of language. A striking fact: The killers succeeded in finding words to describe the crimes; the victims did not. They failed to find the words that would allow the memory of their suffering to survive them.

These courses were necessary, essential, but I would not teach them very long. Young professors take up where I leave off.

• • •

Three years later, I resign from City College and join the faculty of
Boston University, where, to this day, I hold the Andrew W. Mellon
Chair in the Humanities, and continue to teach in the departments of
philosophy and religion. As University Professor it is my privilege to
choose not only my course topics but also my students.

It was John Silber, the formidable Kantian scholar, who convinced me to join his faculty. At the time he was president of Boston
University; he is now its chancellor. His powers of persuasion are
quite extraordinary.

Silber is not only superbly intelligent but also patient and determined. This is how he persuaded me: "Above all, you are a writer,
aren't you?" Indeed I am. "Then you need time to write, don't you?"
Indeed I do. "Come to Boston, and you will teach only one course per
semester and deliver three public lectures."

The advantage seemed considerable; at City College I had to
teach two courses. And so I accepted—but I miscalculated. My
weekly trips from Manhattan to Boston would take twice as long as
the six hours spent at City College.

I liked John from the beginning: a man of integrity, unafraid of
being unpopular. We became close very quickly. A brilliant debater,
he does not tolerate hypocrites. In twenty-five years, this incorrigible
optimist has succeeded in transforming a second-rate school of
higher learning, deep in red ink, into one of the best universities in
the country. Still, I might not have succumbed had it not been for
the fact that a new admissions policy had lowered standards at City
College.

How was I to announce my resignation to Ted Gross? He proved
to be understanding. "The academic world is very mobile in the
United States," he reassured me. I telephoned Yitz Greenberg, who
was spending a sabbatical year in Jerusalem. He too understood. In
fact he did not stay on at City College either.

In Boston too, my students bring me joy. To witness the awakening of
knowledge, that unique light of understanding, of recognition—is
there a more beautiful moment for a teacher? As you look on, a veil
seems to lift from your students' gaze. Suddenly they seem open to an
idea, able to admire a poem, to resolve a literary or philosophical
enigma. Is there a more creative, more gratifying kind of happiness?

I give biblical, midrashic, Hasidic lectures. I teach the Book of Job: the Jewishness and non-Jewishness of the character. The role played by Satan. The tragedy of Job's wife, his children's death, his betrayal by his friends. Where is God in all this? And the absurd, inconceivable end: Job, once again, the head of a large family? Are we to believe that he will regain his happiness? And what about his children: How do they cope with their predicament? Do they know that they are but successors, surrogates?

The Besht and his disciples. The place Hasidism assigns to exuberance, to friendship, to stories. The Besht or the value of simplicity in human relations. The Besht and the victory over anonymity. The Besht and the quest for meaning.

The great Masters: the wisdom of Rebbe Pinhas of Koretz, the wrath of Rebbe Mendel of Kotzk, the anguish of Rebbe Bunam of Pshiskhe. Every student has his favorite Master. As for me, I love them all.

We embark on the comparative study of ancient texts describing the deaths of the great Masters—of Moses, Socrates, Buddha, Jesus, Muhammad, as well as Giordano Bruno. Might Sylvia Plath be right? Is there an art to preparing oneself for death? Is there a death that is anything but solitary?

There are countless other themes: friendship in ancient and modern times, fervor and madness, faith and rebellion in literature, the complex relationships between Masters and disciples from antiquity on, attitudes toward evil and suffering: indifference or empathy, resignation or rebellion, active despair or passive despondency, the dehumanization of the executioner as opposed to the humanity of the victim. Can evil ever be transformed into virtue? Does suffering ever lead to redemption? We delve into ancient and modern texts. We explore Babylonian literature and the Book of Proverbs.

And then there is my passion for Kafka: Kafka and Aesop, Kafka and theology, Kafka and psychology, Kafka and politics, Kafka the literary figure, Kafka the philosopher, Kafka and women, Kafka and the Jews. An unexpected consequence of my passion for Kafka: The Saudi daily *Al sharq al-Awsat* accuses me—in 1993—of taking part in a conspiracy with Max Brod, who, sadly but unbeknownst to them, has been dead for quite a few decades, a conspiracy that, it claims, aims to conceal the alleged anti-Zionist leanings of the Prague author and to portray him as a fervent Jewish nationalist.

We explore suicide in literature. We evoke King Saul, a man as obsessed by death as David is by life, and Seneca, who understood, as he watched the procession of Jewish warriors, prisoners of Rome, that the spirits of the defeated were higher than those of the victors. We study *Anna Karenina*, works by Stefan Zweig, Anne Sexton, Arthur Koestler, and Primo Levi. We probe the subject of death as temptation, seduction, or escape.

We find enchantment in the universe of Rebbe Nahman of Bratzlav. Enthralled we read his stories, follow him in his journeys. Princes and madmen, lost princesses and raving beggars: How is one to resist them? Each tale contains others, creating concentric circles whose fixed center is the deepest core of man, the individual self at the heart of the collective self, the memory of memory. In all these tales we deal with human beings, not specifically with Jews—haunted creatures looking for one another, for themselves in others; survivors of disasters; messengers and beggars; vagrant children with princely pasts. All of them are searching for love.

In his tale "The Seven Beggars," we find this beautiful passage:

> At the center of the world there is a mountain and on the mountain there is a boulder, and out of the boulder there flows a spring. Now, every thing has a heart, a heart that is a complete being with a face and arms, and legs, and eyes and ears. And this heart is alive, burning with desire to rejoin the spring at the other end of the world, on the other side of the abyss. This heart suffers: the sun follows it, leaving it parched. To survive, it imagines the spring, but the more the heart imagines it, the more its desire to approach it grows. But, as soon as the heart comes close to the mountain, its peak disappears before its eyes and with it the spring. Then its soul takes flight, for it lives only by the love it has for the spring. And if this heart were to stop beating the whole world would be reduced to nothingness. Thus it remains far away, on the other side of the abyss, protected by a bird with widespread wings, doomed to look upon the spring while knowing that they will never be one.

Rebbe Nahman becomes our friend, our support, our Master. Sometimes we take an entire semester to analyze a single tale. That is because I am still influenced by Shushani.* Rebbe Nathan of Nemirov's account of Rebbe Nahman's death moves us to tears. At the end of the school year I invoke Rebbe Nahman's protection for my students. On a trip to Uman in the Ukraine to visit his tomb, I implore his intercession for my family and for the people of Israel, with, again, a special plea on behalf of my students.

I find great satisfaction in being there for the graduate students whose doctoral theses I supervise. Among them are Rabbi Nehemia Polen's work on the "holy fire" of a Hasidic Master killed by the Nazis; Alan Rosen's essay on "The Theme of Catastrophe" in Shakespeare; Janet McCord's thesis on the suicides of writers who were Holocaust survivors; the Jesuit priest Jean-François Thomas's analysis of the work of Edith Stein; Joe Kanofsky's analysis of Rebbe Nahman's influence on Kafka; Yosef Wosk's work on the Midrash; Marilyn Feingold's study of problems in contemporary education. And my longtime friend Yossi Ciechanover's "Suicide in Rabbinical Law," which he started under Saul Lieberman and finished under my aegis.

Shortly after my arrival in Boston, I learned that Dr. Silber was controversial among certain members of the faculty who resented his "authoritarian" methods. I deliberately stayed out of this conflict. My attitude was a result of my New York experience: To please Yitz Greenberg, I had agreed to chair the executive committee of our department, though I had warned him that I would never vote against anyone. If any candidate hoped to obtain a post or a promotion, at least one vote—mine—would be his from the outset. Yitz thought I was joking, but by year's end he released me from this duty, to the great joy of the other committee members.

In the more than twenty years I have spent at Boston University, I have attended only one plenary meeting of the academic body. I did so at Silber's request: "My opponents," he told me, "are going to propose a motion of censure against me. And it will pass. Their arguments will be in bad faith, lies. That doesn't bother me: My position is not in jeopardy, I have the Board's support. What does upset me, what revolts me, is that they are also accusing me of anti-Semitism."

The meeting was stormy, spiteful. It may have been academic, but it was hardly intellectual. One after the other, professors took the microphone to accuse their president of being, in turn, Genghis

*See *All Rivers Run to the Sea*, page 118.

Khan, Torquemada, and Stalin. When my turn came, I told them: "I left City College for this university because John Silber is its president. Today I learn from rumors that he stands accused of anti-Semitism. If that is true, let someone prove it, and I shall hand in my resignation on the spot. I shall never serve here or anywhere under the authority of an anti-Semite." The faculty did vote on a motion of censure, but there were no more references to John as an anti-Semite.

When John Silber retired as president, he was succeeded by Jon Westling, a Rhodes Scholar who shares his passion for excellence. As chancellor, Dr. Silber continues to be actively involved in the affairs of the university.

In early 1980 I am invited to Yale as a visiting professor by its legendary president, Bart Giamatti. I suspect he knows nothing of my misadventure with his institution some fifteen years before. But I remember. And so I accept his offer. First of all, Yale tempts me for the old reason: How many yeshiva students from Sighet . . . Secondly, I still feel guilty toward Yale; I remember that as I accepted a doctorate *honoris causa* from the university, the then president had said to me: "Come join us, help us learn."

Together with the dean of humanities, Peter Brooks, and his colleague Geoffrey Hartman, both professors of English literature, we establish my program: a weekly course per semester—twenty students at most—and a monthly course for faculty members.

For the first course I choose the topic: "Faith and Rebellion in Ancient and Modern Literature." For the second I decide on the Book of Job. I know this book inside out. After all, I expounded on it for two years on French television.

Peter and his colleagues try to convince me to admit at least fifty students to the first course. Stubbornly I refuse, telling them that in order to work seriously it is vital for the students and their professor to keep the class small.

On the eve of my first class at Yale, I spend the night in New Haven, to take in the ambiance. At the suggestion of Peter Brooks, Geoffrey Hartman makes a final plea. Why turn away students who want to learn? I hold to my refusal.

The next day I visit the hall where my lecture is to take place. It is huge, frightening, profoundly empty. My assistant, a young doctoral student, reassures me: "It's always like this: The students come in large groups to do their 'shopping,' to size things up. Then they may go elsewhere."

I go out for coffee and come back five minutes before the hour. I almost faint; the hall is still empty. Anxious, I run to the bathroom to wet my face. I think of how ridiculous I will look. After all my talk about wanting "only" twenty students, I will be left with one: my assistant. I linger at the sink and hesitantly return to the big room. Did I take a wrong turn? The room is packed. It is impossible to get in. I ask a student: "What course is this?" He bursts out laughing, "Why it's yours."

There are now three hundred students waiting for me. I panic. What am I going to do? I beg them to leave. I spell out the details of my arrangement with the administration. In vain I warn them, I threaten them—the course will be difficult, demanding. They will have to read two books a week and write as many papers. They will have to write a major essay each semester. But they are not to be deterred.

Astonishingly, the Yale experience turns out to be one of the most stimulating and fruitful of my academic career.

The faculty seminar also provides a few surprises. I was counting on a simple run with no ambushes. After all, I know the Book of Job better than my own books. What I didn't know was that Marvin Pope, one of the world's greatest experts on Job, was teaching at Yale. As for Bill Hallo, another professor, he is well known for his work on Babylonian and Sumerian sources. In fact, he shows me the connections between Job and the texts on the "Suffering Righteous." And so I find myself every month having to work harder than ever to lecture before this unreasonably talented, erudite audience.

I go on teaching—I'll go on to the end. I have taught courses at Florida International University; at Eckerd College, also in Florida; and lectured at various American universities large and small. It is my vocation just as much as writing. The writer in me is a teacher, the teacher in me a writer. What is important is the ability to transmit, to have something to transmit, to have someone to transmit to.

My major problem with teaching in Boston has to do with distance: an hour by plane. And the weather: In winter, flights are often affected by snow. Delays then become intolerable. The train? Five hours each way. Too much, too tiring. Perhaps I should try to find a position

closer to home? Closer? Why not in New York? An incredible opportunity presents itself. John Sawhill, president of New York University,
informs me that a mutual friend has offered to underwrite a chair if I
agree to occupy it. The terms are excellent, better than those at
Boston—higher compensation, fewer teaching hours. There will be
no more grueling trips, no more worries about the weather. I could be
in class in ten minutes. And best of all, the university would provide us
with an extraordinary place to live, the kind Marion loves—a town-
house in a Greenwich Village mews. A document is drawn up. All we
have to do is sign it. But how am I going to tell John Silber?

We develop a strategy: I'll see John and explain to him that, contrary to what we had anticipated, and in spite of my promise, family
reasons prevent me from moving to Boston. Considering that I hold
the Mellon Chair at Boston University, it would seem inappropriate
for me to continue living in New York indefinitely. Surely he would
agree that this was a problem. Rather than prolong the situation,
shouldn't we confront it now? Thus we would part as friends. What
could he possibly say? At that point I would call Marion from the corner telephone booth to give her the green light. She would inform
Sawhill, and then everything would fall into place.

The following Monday I knock at Silber's door. Despite being
busier than many heads of state, he has agreed to see me. I tell him
that I have a serious problem and in a few words bring him up to date.
As wily as the king of foxes, he eyes me silently and then, surely
thinking he'll please me, cuts me off: "No problem, I'll rewrite our
contract. If I must choose between one day a week and nothing at all,
I'll take one day a week." Though he has just pulled the rug from
under my feet, he is surely awaiting a sign of gratitude.

Calling from a telephone booth, I tell Marion: "I couldn't disappoint him. You understand. . . ." No house in the mews, no short com-
mute—I am staying where I am.

To this day John Silber does not know what our friendship
cost me.

But I hope he knows how much it has brought me.

On December 29, 1994, John's son David dies of AIDS. I knew him.
Earnest, delicate, a good listener, he spoke little and radiated tenderness. His parents adored him; his many sisters loved him. He worked
in the theater, mostly off-Broadway. There was the promise of a luminous future.

His funeral draws a huge crowd. There are moving words from those who knew him well. His father gives the eulogy, and it is shattering. Every speaker adds an image, a shade to David's portrait: the child, the adolescent, the dreamer. Nobody knew he had been so strong, nor so vulnerable. Even those who knew him best did not know him well enough. He had a gift for laughter—and love.

In his eulogy the university chaplain reveals that it was David himself who had "stage-managed" the funeral; it was he who had cast the parts, he who had chosen the biblical text and the music. "Let us applaud him," says the chaplain, "this is David's last stage appearance. Let us applaud the final performance of this great actor."

With tears in our eyes we applaud for a long time. We are reluctant to stop, eager to compensate for all the applause he should have received.

Reviews and Polemics⸻

I N A BOOK OF MEMOIRS one speaks about oneself but, inevitably, also about others. How is one to write without voicing judgments?

The only negative reviews I have written have been related to plays, movies, or television shows dealing with the Holocaust. As a rule, I prefer to praise, but it isn't always easy.

I demolished, as they say, the *Holocaust* series broadcast by one of the networks following an astounding media blitz. Though reluctant to provoke a scandal, I allowed myself to be persuaded by editors of the *New York Times* to offer my opinion in its pages. Had the producers presented their series as a work of fiction, I would not have reacted so strongly. But since it was presented as a documentary, I felt it my duty to object.

My piece had enormous repercussions. The *Times* had to devote an entire tightly set page to the letters that poured in. The scriptwriter responded; I replied to his response. In short, the debate had been opened, and rather violently.

This is what I wrote in the *Times*:

> The story is gripping, the acting competent, the message compelling—and yet.
>
> The calculated brutality of the killers, the silent agony of the victims, the indifference of the outside world—this TV series will show what some survivors have been trying to say for years and years. And yet something is wrong with it. Something? No: everything.
>
> Untrue, offensive, cheap: as a TV production, the film is an insult to those who perished and to those who survived. In spite of its name, this "docu-drama" is not about what some of us remember as the Holocaust.

Am I too harsh? Too sensitive, perhaps. But then, the film is not sensitive enough. It tries to show what cannot even be imagined. It transforms an ontological event into soap-opera. Whatever the intentions, the result is shocking.

Contrived situations, sentimental episodes, implausible coincidences: If they make you cry, you will cry for the wrong reasons.

Why is the series called "Holocaust"? Whoever chose the name must have been unaware of the implications. Holocaust, a TV spectacle. Holocaust, a TV drama. Holocaust, a work of semi-fact and semi-fiction. Isn't this what so many morally deranged "scholars" have been claiming recently all over the world? That the Holocaust was nothing but an "invention"? NBC should have used the name in its subtitle, if at all.

The network should also have been more rigorous in its research. Contrary to what we see in the film, Jewish refugees who crossed the Russian border before the German invasion were not allowed to go free but were arrested, interrogated, and jailed; Auschwitz inmates were not allowed to keep suitcases, family pictures, and music-sheets; Jews do not wear prayer shawls at night; there is a blessing for Torah-reading and another one for weddings— the Rabbi who performs the wedding in the film recites the wrong blessing.

Other, more serious irritants: Mordechai Anielewicz, the young commander of the Warsaw Ghetto uprising, is shown as a caricature of himself; stereotype Jews and stereotype Germans; the exaggerated emphasis on the brutality of Jewish ghetto-policemen and Jewish Kapos; the obsessive theme of Jewish resignation.

Are we again to be subjected to debates on Jewish passivity versus Jewish heroism? They were painful yet fashionable during the Eichmann trial; why renew them now? During the Holocaust, even the victims were heroes and even the heroes died as martyrs.

But I am more disturbed by the overall concept of the production. It tries to tell it all: what happened before, during, and after. The beginning and the end. The evil majority and the charitable minority. The bloodthirsty SS and Father Lichtenberg. Himmler and Eichmann, Blobel and Franck, Hoess and Nebe: hardly a name is omitted, hardly an episode obliterated. We hear their ideological discussions, we see them at work. We learn how they all used their abilities, their inventiveness, and their patriotism to achieve a perfect system of mass murder, for it took many talents on the part of many highly educated persons to bring about a catastrophe of such magnitude.

On the opposite side: the first signs, the first decrees, the first warnings. Expropriation, confiscation, deportation. The ghettos. The manhunts. Hunger. Fear. The shrinking universe will ultimately be reduced to the gas-chambers. But together with the dying victims, we are shown the fighting heroes: partisans, resistance groups, armed insurgents. Courage and despair displayed by both believers and non-believers: It is all there.

Too much, far too much happens to one particular Jewish family and too much evil is perpetrated by one particular German officer. Members of the fictional Weiss family experience the Kristallnacht, euthanasia, Warsaw, Buchenwald, Theresienstadt, Babi-Yar, Sobibor and Auschwitz. Somehow the most famous—or infamous—events and places have been rearranged to fit into the biographies of two families. Thus, Joseph Weiss helps save Jews at the Umschlagplatz in Warsaw, his brother is purchasing weapons for the Underground, his wife teaches ghetto children Shakespeare and music, his son is among the artists who clandestinely prepare their own testimony in the form of drawings, his daughter perishes as a victim of euthanasia, his youngest son Rudi survives Babi-Yar and joins the Jewish partisans in the Ukraine, where he participates in the armed uprising of Sobibor—and more, and more. Whatever happened anywhere, happened to this family. And more so.

The same applies to Erik Dorf: he too is everywhere. We find him involved in every salient event. Who advises Heydrich on how to deal with Jewish insurance claims after the Kristallnacht? Dorf. Who supervises the mobile gas units? Dorf. Who happens to be at Babi-Yar during the mass executions? Dorf. Who prepares the plans for Auschwitz? Dorf, again. Who purchases Zyklon B gas from respectable German industrialists? Dorf. It is simply too much action for one man, any man. One cannot believe that such a person existed—and, indeed, Erik Dorf did not exist. Neither did the Weiss family. In this "docu-drama," the principal characters are fictitious, whereas the secondary ones are not. Yet, for understandable artistic reasons, *all* are treated as authentic. On this level, the implications are troubling and far-reaching: how is the uninformed viewer to distinguish the one from the other? Chances are he will believe that they are either equally true or equally invented. The private lives of the two families are so skillfully intertwined with historical facts that, except for the initiated, the general public may find it difficult to know where fact ends and fiction begins. This would, of course, defeat the very lofty goal the film's creators have set for themselves.

In film as in literature, it is all a matter of credibility. Were the film a pure work of fiction or straight documentary, it would achieve more. The mixture of the two genres results in confusion. And occasionally in scenes that I, for one, found in poor taste. One striking example: We see long, endless processions of Jews marching toward Babi-Yar—with "appropriate" musical background. We see them get undressed, move to the ditch, wait for the bullets, topple into the grave. We see the naked bodies covered with "blood"—and it is all make-believe.

Another example: We see naked women and children entering the gas-chambers; we see their faces, we hear their moans as the doors are being shut, then—well, enough: why continue? To use special effects and gimmicks to describe the indescribable is to me morally objectionable. Worse: it is indecent. The last moments of the forgotten victims belong to themselves.

I know: people will tell me that film-making has its own laws and its own demands. After all, similar techniques are being used for war movies and historical re-creations. But the Holocaust is unique, not just another event. This series treats the Holocaust as if it *were* just another event. Thus, I object to it not because it is not artistic enough but because it is not authentic enough. It removes us from the event instead of bringing us closer to it. The tone is wrong. Most scenes do not ring true: too much "drama," not enough "documentary." In all fairness, I must add that many Jewish and non-Jewish organizations supported the project and promoted it among their members. But they did so even before they could view the programs. This does not mean that people will not be moved. Some who saw previews have been profoundly affected. And I know, don't tell me: the film was not meant for viewers like me but for those who were not there or not even born yet, those who are only beginning to discover the reality of death-factories in the heart of civilized Europe.

You are right, of course. But—and it is an important but—I am appalled by the thought that one day the Holocaust will be measured and judged in part by the NBC TV production bearing its name. Listen to what one of the study-guides, prepared by the National Council of Churches, has been telling its readers: " 'Holocaust' may come to be known as the definitive film on the Holocaust in terms of meticulous accuracy, totality of material presented, and its use of carefully selected archival footage. . . ." Though surely well-intentioned, such misleading, complacent statements are dangerous: It simply is not so. The witness feels here duty-bound to declare: what you have seen on the screen is not what happened *there.* You may think you know now how the victims lived and died, but you do not. Auschwitz cannot be explained nor can it be visualized. Whether culmination or aberration of history, the Holocaust transcends history. Everything about it inspires fear and leads to despair. The dead are in possession of a secret that we, the living, are neither worthy of nor capable of recovering.

Art and Theresienstadt were perhaps compatible in Theresienstadt, but not here—not in a television studio. The same is true of prayer and Buchenwald, faith and Treblinka. A film about Sobibor is either not a picture or not about Sobibor.

The Holocaust? The ultimate event, the ultimate mystery, never to be comprehended or transmitted. Only those who were there know what it was, the others will never know. It was easier for Auschwitz inmates to imagine themselves free than for free persons to imagine themselves in Auschwitz.

What then is the answer? How is one to tell a tale that cannot be—but must be—told? How is one to protect the memory of the victims? How are we to oppose the killers' hopes and their accomplices' endeavors to kill the dead for the second time? What will happen when the last survivor is gone? I don't know. All I know is that the witness does not recognize himself in this film.

The Holocaust *must* be remembered. But not as a show.

In the course of the fury unleashed by the show, I discovered that the producers had consulted with well-remunerated "expert advisors": two SS officers. Not one survivor.

What to do? I am partial to documentaries. *The Eighty-first Blow, Night and Fog, The Partisans of Vilna,* and, of course, *Shoah,* which I helped with a long and favorable review in the *Times.* I wished to acknowledge the enormous effort and devotion of Claude Lanzmann. His film remains a monumental achievement. Nonetheless, certain passages were controversial. For example, the way he dwells on the *Todeskampf,* the death struggle, in the gas chambers. Am I too steeped in Jewish tradition, which considers death a private event whose secret is to be respected? That is why Moses died alone, far from people's sight. And then I cannot, I don't want to, accept Lanzmann's images of Jewish mothers climbing over their children to breathe another second. Of course this is not meant as an overall criticism of Lanzmann—far from it; I understand that he wanted to show the degradation conceived and programmed by the Germans. The *Sonderkommando* is a German invention, not a Jewish one. All its members were forced to do their brutal tasks. They, too, were victims of the killers. And no one has the right to judge them. In my preface to *Voices in the Night,* I tried to express all the tenderness I have for them. True, some members of the *Sonderkommandos* refused to comply; Greek deportees chose to be shot rather than feed the ovens. I was told that the Chief Rabbi of my town,

Rabbi Yekutiel-Yehuda Teitelbaum, threw himself into the flames for the same reason. But his gesture does not diminish the others' worth. And it is partly in memory of their martyrdom that I wrote of Lanzmann's film with unmitigated praise.

Other performances on screen or stage, have dealt with this subject. And every time I felt that the memory of the Holocaust was tainted by either the images or the language, I raised my voice. I don't regret it. Since nobody else protested, it was my duty to do so. And whenever I hesitated, there was always someone to remind me of my own words: Silence signifies consent. Just as there was always someone to resent me. And some grudges are tenacious. Because I disliked *Sophie's Choice* (the film, not the book), and said so in print, William Styron and I no longer speak. I also voiced my disappointment with *Ghetto*, a play about the Vilna Ghetto, which provoked an acrimonious response from its author, the Israeli playwright Joshua Sobol. Yet when I decried certain segments of the television series *The Winds of War,* the author of the novel on which it was based, Herman Wouk, understood my reaction. It is always the same problem: Auschwitz cannot be depicted; the veil covering this dark universe cannot be lifted.

I know that some of the writers who have introduced the Holocaust into their work take exception to my "purist" attitude on the subject. They consider me, unjustly, a kind of censor-inquisitor who watches scrupulously over a territory that, they believe, is theirs as much as the survivors'. They suppose, wrongly, that I claim exclusive rights for myself and my fellow survivors. That is not the case. In literature as in philosophy, there is no "game preserve." Anybody can write on any subject, and even on any individual. But I maintain that no one, myself included, is authorized to speak on behalf of the dead; no one may appropriate their memory. Those who accuse me of arrogance because I demand the respect due the dead understand nothing of my motives: I plead for humility, for more prudence, more reserve in both behavior and language.

Unfortunately, there are suddenly too many Holocaust scholars who know the answers to all our questions, too many experts who, from one day to the next, become judges and critics, deciding who deserves to write and who doesn't, who is sentimental and who isn't, who should be read and who shouldn't. We have come to the point where Jewish survivors no longer dare to speak up. The others always know better.

• • •

In France, one of the most vociferous adversaries of the survivors is Jean-Marie Domenach. Wasn't it he who in September 1989, in connection with the controversy surrounding the Carmelite convent in Auschwitz, led the slander campaign against "certain Jews" he accuses of "Judeocentrism," in other words, of being too Jewish? Surely he was a participant. It is difficult for a Jew to speak of Auschwitz without leaving himself open to criticism, as it is difficult to speak of Israel or Judaism without provoking outbursts of hate.

As regards myself, the attacks and insults come from many sources. I upset a lot of people. I am disliked by racists and anti-Semites of the reactionary right as much as by certain young intellectuals who need to prove their independence of the establishment.

Another intellectual who has chosen to attack me is Alfred Grosser, a Germanist. He denounces me in one book and in many statements to the press for not having devoted my Nobel acceptance speech to the Kurds gassed by the Iraqis. Evidently he does not fear ridicule; one or another of his friends or ideological cohorts should have reminded him that I was awarded the Nobel in 1986, while the monstrous crime against the Kurds was committed two years later, in 1988.

As for Jean-Marie Domenach, his statements are ugly in both substance and form. What annoys him most in today's France? That "the dividends of Auschwitz" are "collected" by certain Jews for political, literary, and other reasons. I don't know which of Domenach's writings will survive, but this "original" phrase will remain. One will say "Domenach" and will inevitably add: "Oh yes, 'the dividends of Auschwitz.' "

A warning to historians and theologians, philosophers and psychologists, novelists and poets: A Domenach is waiting around the corner. If they write about Auschwitz, he will accuse them of doing so to enhance their careers. The witnesses, the chroniclers, the survivors? They forfeit their right to evoke their suffering, to look backwards: Domenach will chastise them for "profiteering." Of course, he will say he did not mean them but "certain" others. In a handwritten, not very coherent letter addressed to me, he said that his remarks were meant for Bernard-Henri Lévy and Zeev Sternhell, not for me.

If one follows the trajectory of Domenach to its grotesque conclusion, a former member of the Resistance should never again speak of the Resistance, nor should a rabbi speak of the Talmud, or a priest of the Evangelists; each could be accused of collecting "dividends."

Domenach's ignorance actually surprises me less than his impudence. By what authority does he give advice and lessons to the Jews? Who is he to lecture us? What right has he to tell us what is appropriate? What does Domenach know about Auschwitz? Has he no shame? What exactly does he want, that Jews like myself remain silent?

Let us go back to those who accuse me of Judeocentrism; namely, that I am exclusively interested in Jews; that I fight only for their rights; concern myself only with their affairs, their happiness, their survival. What if that were so? Having seen and experienced the isolation of Jews in danger, would it not be natural for me to attempt to oppose it whenever it reappears? Isn't it normal for a Jew, a survivor, to devote himself to his people first?

In my Oslo speech I outlined my position: Jewish destiny is my priority, but that priority is not exclusive. Indeed, I can say in good faith that I have not remained indifferent to any cause involving the defense of human rights. But, you may ask, what have I done to alleviate the plight of the Palestinians? And here I must confess: I have not done enough.

Is an explanation in order? In spite of considerable pressure, I have refused to take a public stand in the Israeli-Arab conflict. I have said it before: since I do not live in Israel, it would be irresponsible for me to do so. But I have never concealed how much the human dimension of the Palestinian tragedy affects me. I speak of it in *A Beggar in Jerusalem*. I refer to the Arab children's eyes, so sad, so frightened. They troubled me and saddened me. This I stated not only in the novel but also on Israeli television.

After a lecture I give at a midwestern university, a student confronts me: "You who do so much for so many oppressed people, what are you doing for the Palestinians?" Elsewhere another student asks me the same question, but more directly: "I am Palestinian; what do you have to say to me?" In both cases, a productive dialogue ensues.

A Palestinian whose open letter, published in *Le Monde*, remained unanswered was Mahmoud Derwich. His poem, addressed to the Israelis, incites hate: "Take your graves and go!" Even the Intifada cannot excuse such language. But years earlier, another Palestinian poet affected me deeply.

I remember: The telephone rings. There is a man's voice, speaking Hebrew: "My name is Rashid Hussein. I'd like to meet you. It is urgent." I wait. Surely he guesses the reason for my silence, for he adds: "Don't be concerned, I am not PLO, I am Israeli. An Israeli poet. An Israeli poet writing in Arabic." I invite him to come the next day. "Couldn't you see me today? It really is urgent." Fine, let him come.

Right away he makes a good impression. Serious, sensitive, full of passion, he comes straight to the point, describing the intolerable situation of Arabs in Israel and particularly in the West Bank. From time to time I interrupt him to confess my skepticism. He must be inventing, embroidering, exaggerating. He elaborates, speaking of censorship, restrictions, arbitrary arrests. My response? Impossible, inconceivable; he exaggerates, he invents. "Either you are ill-informed or utterly naive," Rashid mutters. He proceeds to read me a long list of names of Arabs in preventive detention, imprisoned without trial. Impulsively I grab the phone, waking up a well-known journalist in Tel Aviv. "I have in my office a Palestinian poet who is telling me outrageous things. Is he lying? Is he being manipulated?"

The journalist confirms everything Rashid has told me. I must look agitated because he feels compelled to apologize: "I am sorry to be bothering you like this." What does he want me to do? Sign a petition on behalf of his friends in "administrative" detention? Other writers and intellectuals have already done so. I tell him: "I never sign anything against Israel." He replies: "I thought so. When it comes to us, you remain silent," and he stands. I ask him to sit down again: "I have a proposition: Stop circulating your petition and I shall go to Israel. I shall do my best to help your friends." He accepts.

A few days later I am knocking on Golda Meir's door. I tell her why I have come. A motherly smile lights up her face: "Stay out of this," she says. "This is not for you. These things are so complex, you wouldn't begin to understand. Leave it to the experts." It's not easy to contradict a prime minister, but I must. "Golda," I say. "You cannot do this to us, all of us in the Diaspora who try to defend human rights. You should not force us to choose between our conscience and our loyalty to Israel." She would rather not discuss this further, but we do. In the end, she says: "In the West Bank such matters are settled by the military authorities; why don't you go see them?"

And so I meet the commander in chief of the army. He, too, would rather not discuss the topic, but we do anyway. His response: "No arrest is arbitrary; it must be authorized by a commission that always includes a civil judge." I run to the president of the Supreme Court. With him there is no need for discussion: The law is the law. His role is to safeguard every citizen, every individual, from abuses of power. But then what about the preventive arrests? How are they to be explained? The judge reassures me: This only happens when the security services detain a suspect whose guilt is established but the evidence would be dangerous to display before a tribunal, thus before the lawyers for the defense. Why dangerous? Because the evidence is provided by informers, covert agents. What is the solution, to allow the saboteurs to go free and risk the lives and security of peaceful Israelis? I understand but I am troubled.

I see Golda again. I bother so many people, and I annoy them so many times, that finally, to get rid of me, a few prisoners are freed. I fly back to New York, triumphant. I call Rashid Hussein to give him the good news. He already knows. I ask to see him right away, to celebrate the success of our common efforts. He makes excuses: He has no time, some other time. Never mind, it will wait. When we finally meet for coffee, the young Palestinian seems embarrassed. What is the matter? Why isn't he happier? He looks away as he confesses that while I was in Jerusalem, he continued to circulate his petition. "I had no choice," he says. "Thinking of my friends in prison, I couldn't wait. Patience is for happy people, not for us, not yet."

Soon after this episode, Marion and I go to hear him read at the Village Vanguard. He recites poems charged with violence and bitterness. Poor uprooted Rashid: He sinks deeper and deeper into despair. He drinks a lot, I am told. To each his refuge. His is in the bottle. I don't judge him. Rather it is he who, swallowing glass after glass, seems to be judging . . . whom?

When he dies alone and forsaken in his room downtown, I wonder whether his friends are still—or again—in Israeli prisons, and whether the poets among them sing with any less anger or despair.

Let us turn the page. What about my Jewish opponents?

After the *Ani Maamin* performance at Carnegie Hall, friends gather backstage to congratulate the artists and musicians. Among them is a broad-shouldered man with a mustache and darting eyes in a massive face. He introduces himself: Simon Wiesenthal. I shake his hand warmly. We embrace. I know him by name and admire his work. After all, he was in the death camps. He was also the first Nazi hunter of the postwar period. I hold him in great esteem. I know that he resides in Vienna and ask him to visit us next time he is in New York.

A few years go by. Then one day he calls. We speak of this and that: Israel, anti-Semitism, the SS executioners hidden in South America. He talks about his books, but I prefer to listen to his exploits hunting down war criminals on the run. I mention the name Adolf Eichmann. I know how much we owe Wiesenthal in this affair. And so I tell him of my indignation about an article published in an Israeli newspaper in which a former member of the Mossad accuses him of lying when he claims to have played a key role in the kidnapping of this Nazi criminal. Wiesenthal replies that the Israeli secret services hate him, that they are jealous of his successes.

And Josef Mengele, the doctor-assassin responsible for the "selections" at Birkenau, does anyone know *his* hiding place? In his conversations with me, Wiesenthal claims to know and gives me precise details: his false identities, the names of his accomplices and protectors. But then why don't they arrest him? My guest places the responsibility on others. He again complains about the Mossad and the Israeli secret services in general, who, he says, do all they can to smear him. Later I read in an as-yet-unpublished manuscript by Issar Harel, the legendary former chief of the Mossad, a very unflattering portrait of Wiesenthal. He criticizes his boasting, his preoccupation with public relations; he even accuses him of having jeopardized an Israeli operation intended to capture Mengele.

Before leaving, Wiesenthal asks me for a favor: to review his latest book—which I haven't yet read—in the *Times*. It is the story of a dying SS officer who, inside a concentration camp, begs him, Wiesenthal, to forgive him. It sounds preposterous to me, but how do I know? I haven't read it yet. As for the favor he is requesting, I explain to him that things do not work this way in the United States. Book review editors are extremely touchy about anything that smacks of cronyism. But I promise to do my best.

He visits my home on two more occasions. Both times he comes directly from seeing Kurt Waldheim, then secretary-general of the U.N., and his close friend. "Can you imagine?" he tells me, beaming: "He insisted on escorting me all the way to the elevator." At that time the dark past of the future president of Austria was not yet known.

Our last meeting took place in the early eighties. At first, of course, I heard a detailed account of his visit to Waldheim, who, this time, escorted him all the way to the lobby. Again we discuss Mengele. He then tells me all about his current whereabouts, in Paraguay, when in fact the killer doctor had died in Brazil some time before.

We move to a more serious topic: Whom should we remember? He preaches the universality of suffering. More precisely: Since Hitler exterminated not six but eleven million human beings in his death camps—Poles, Ukrainians, Russians, Germans, and others—my guest considers it our duty not to forget any of them. And here Wiesenthal uses a striking image: Since Jewish blood was mingled with their blood in Auschwitz, all victims should be "reunited" within the same remembrance.

I answer him that I don't know where he obtained the figure of eleven million. To my knowledge, no historian has ever cited such a figure. Indeed, the only place I can remember seeing that figure was in Eichmann's report on the Wannsee Conference, where leaders of the Third Reich decided on the Final Solution. But even there, Eichmann referred to eleven million *Jews*, only *Jews*—those of Europe and elsewhere—all of whom were targeted. Moreover, did he, Wiesenthal, really believe that there were five million non-Jews brutalized, killed, and burned in the camps? If that is what he believes, let him bring proof . . . whereupon he accuses me of Judeocentrism: "You think only of Jews. . . . For you they were all saints. . . . As for me, I can prove to you that among them there were the worst kind of scoundrels, worse than the non-Jews. . . ." I am stunned by this outburst, and saddened. His face is red; he apologizes. He didn't express himself properly, he didn't mean it. In fact he wanted to say something else, but . . . So be it. I explain my position to him, the very same I set forth before President Carter and Congress: Not all the victims of the Holocaust were Jews, but all the Jews were victims.

Still, I address him courteously. After all, he is a man who has inspired fear in the archenemies of the Jewish people. To dispel the tension I change the subject. Just then, my son, a small boy at the time, comes running into my study. I introduce him to our visitor. Is it because my son does not show much interest that Wiesenthal becomes angry? "Leave us," he says. "We have important matters to discuss!" Elisha leaves the room. I admit: I did not appreciate this. I don't like to see children humiliated, and certainly not my own. There is no further contact between Wiesenthal and me.

During the years that follow—and that precede my Nobel Prize, which he covets—Wiesenthal makes derisive, derogatory public comments about my "nationalism" and "chauvinism," my alleged contempt for the Gypsies, the Poles, and the others, all the others. He repeats these remarks tirelessly to Jewish visitors to Vienna, to Jewish leaders in America, in interviews, and even in *Penthouse.*

In *Penthouse,* Wiesenthal says: "He [Elie Wiesel] is the greatest opponent of my position, namely, that there should be true brotherhood between the victims, all the victims." To a journalist's question: "Why does Elie Wiesel not agree with you?" he answers: "Because he is a chauvinist and I'm not." In 1980 his diatribes reach the point where the journalist Herb Brin, who is actually an admirer of his, writes an editorial urging him to halt his injurious attacks. "Wiesenthal," he writes, "has a fixation on Elie Wiesel and by it, he dishonors himself." It seems Wiesenthal has two obsessions: the World Jewish Congress (which he hates) and me (whom he detests).

Later I see Wiesenthal on Larry King's show discussing Eli Rosenbaum's book *Betrayal.* The director of the Office of Special Investigations has bluntly criticized Wiesenthal for his friendship with Waldheim. I am astounded to hear Wiesenthal's outrage; he can't understand how a Jew could attack a survivor. I feel like sending him a note: Am I not, like you, a survivor? Why do you, a Jew, persist in slandering me? But I don't. As Saul Lieberman used to say: "To begin a friendship, it takes two. To end a quarrel, it takes only one." I choose to end the quarrel because I have simply lost all respect for the man.

I react only once, with a detailed refutation, in an American-Jewish weekly, of his distortion of facts. Accusation: I did not invite him to a survivors' gathering. Fact: I was not one of the organizers. Accusation: I participated in a boycott against him. Fact: To my knowledge there never was one. Accusation: I prevented the nomination of a Gypsy to the Holocaust Memorial Council. Fact: The White House retains this privilege; my various recommendations frequently went unheeded. Beyond this response, I swallowed hard and kept silent. But I wondered: Why did Albert Speer, the last Nazi minister in charge of arms production, call him his "best friend" in a PBS program televised in the United States? Why did Helmut Kohl suppress a rather unfavorable Austrian documentary on Wiesenthal?

Ever since I was awarded the Nobel Prize for which he campaigned by denigrating me, he has gone further: He frequently states in his books as well as in his private conversations that the prize was his by right and that I am his enemy. When reporters query me on the motives of my alleged hate for him, I always refuse to engage in polemics. Let his advocates and public relations men show me a single newspaper, a single publication, containing a single derogatory remark about him. Until now.

Poor Wiesenthal. How is one to comprehend his rage and hate? Our sages have an explanation: ambition, jealousy. In *The Ethics of Our Fathers* we read that jealousy "excludes man from this world." Let us say that, in Wiesenthal's case, it blinds him.

I feel sorry for him.

Open letters . . . I have written a few: to a young Palestinian, to a young German. I have also received quite a few. Almost all deal with Israel and the Palestinians. Some ask me to support the hawks; others express a wish to include me among the doves. A crude open letter by the owner of the German magazine *Der Spiegel* attacks me because I dared articulate some concerns about German reunification. I am urged to issue statements against one or another policy of one or another Israeli government. I seldom respond.

In July 1967 I entrust an article to Jean-Martin Chauffier, editor in chief of *Figaro Littéraire* and a former comrade from Buchenwald. In it I say that we should have expected that people would be envious of Israel's victory, resent it for having carried out in too spectacular a manner its lightning campaigns against four armies and some twenty Arab nations, or perhaps simply for having waged these battles at all. Israel victorious does not correspond to the image some people like to have of its destiny among the nations. They prefer to see it defeated, on its knees, which permits them to come to its aid and console it afterward. But a Jew triumphant over death? That is a difficult concept, even for some who are not the Jew's enemies, and surely for those who resent the Jew for having cheated the world: The promised second holocaust did not take place. The lamb dared to refuse the slaughter. And worst of all, the Jew, not content with escaping the enemy, even found a way to humiliate him. That was going too far. The most virulent among the critics are the very same who just yesterday were ready to forget their commitment to come to Israel's defense.

In that same article I mention another disappointment: A great Catholic writer whom I admire and respect and to whom I owe much also criticizes Israel, not from a political but from a theological point of view. For him, the nation "evolves in a universe devoid of God" and uses its genius "for purposes of possession and domination that are purely material and to satisfy its craving for power."

Does he really believe that the Jews have chased God from their land, which is also His? Does he earnestly believe that the Holy Land has lost its holiness since the Jews returned to it? My response:

I have seen Israel at war; therefore I can bear witness. I have seen, in the Old City of Jerusalem, barely reconquered, hardened paratroopers pray and weep for the first time in their lives; I have seen them, in the midst of battle, over-whelmed by a collective and ancient fervor, kiss the stones of the Wall and commune in a silence as unbelievable as it was pure. I have seen them, as in a dream, jump back two thousand years to renew a bond with memory and the God of Israel. Don't tell me that they were moved by a will for power or material domination; their will was drawn from the spirituality of their past. Their experience was mystical. Even the nonbelievers felt transcended by their own acts and by the accounts they gave of them later. Their words, on their lips, render a strangely fiery and faraway sound. Their "will to dominate" seems to target only their own pride. And they did succeed in muting their pride. Mankind has never known less arrogant victors. You begrudge them their victory, you are wrong. They needed it not to live but to survive.

I wrote this plea for Israel not in 1988 during the Intifada, but in 1967 just a few weeks after the potentially fatal threats that Egyptian and Syrian armies had posed to the Jewish state.

Less than three years later I felt compelled to publish, once again in *Figaro Littéraire*, a new plea: *To a Concerned Friend*. A few excerpts follow:

You are concerned. That is what you told me when last we met. Worried about the Middle East, of course. I told you that I, too, am worried and frequently depressed. I look at Israel's future with foreboding. Cease-fire violations, exchanges of artillery fire, sabotages and reprisals, assaults and bombings. Too many mothers, on both sides, are mourning. Too many young people, on both sides, are sac-rificing their lives before living them. Will this curse never be revoked? I thought that since you and I are friends, and share the same belief in friendship, we undoubtedly share the same fears.

Only you went on to say: "I would not like for Israel to become a power defining itself through its conquests—yet that is what will happen." And you added, "I would not like the Jewish youth, over there, to develop the mentality of an occupying force—yet if things continue as they have, it will inevitably acquire such a mentality, if it hasn't already."

And so, since we are friends, I want to reassure you. You are wrong to worry. A Jew will not disappoint you in victory: The change in his condition will not change him ontologically. Though no longer the victim, he will not be the torturer. In the Jewish tradition, victory is not linked to the adversary's defeat; above all, it is a victory over oneself. That is another reason why Jews have never been executioners and almost always victims.

. . . You fear that what you call the Jewish soul, molded by suffering and used to persecution, might cease to be Jewish. You fear that it might become evil. Just like the world it confronts. Well, rest assured. The Jewish soul has been able to resist so many onslaughts of hatred, an ageless and multifaceted hatred, that it surely will resist the ephemeral fascination with military glory. Give it your trust; it has given its measure. One's soul does not change so quickly. One does not acquire an occupier's mentality, a conqueror's instinct in a few months, or even in a few years. That requires the work of generations and implies a tradition the Jews do not have. The Jew has not changed in the course of his millennia-old history. Do you believe that he will deny himself, or change because of a few military exploits? . . .

The "concerned friend" was my great and wonderful friend and benefactor François Mauriac, who surely was an ally and defender of the state of Israel and even more so of the people of Israel. How is one to explain his skeptical attitude after 1967? Perhaps it was the good Christian in him, the ideal and idealized Christian feeling tenderness and compassion toward a victim but not toward a victor. This does not mean that the church, at various periods, has not preached respect for power, or has not quite often succumbed to its attraction.

Mauriac remains for me a great humanist, a great conscience, a loyal friend of my people. And I have quoted from these two articles only to confirm a thesis, namely, that Israel has needed to be defended for a long time.

Does this mean that I consider it my duty to plead the Jewish state's cause unconditionally, and in every circumstance, even when its policies appear to transgress certain boundaries?

Question: Does a Diaspora Jew have the right to criticize what goes on in Israel? My answer is an unequivocal yes, on condition that this person has previously demonstrated his or her attachment to Israel. In other words, someone who has been on Israel's side when it was at risk and alone has unquestionably the right, or even the duty, to say what is on his or her mind when Israel forgets its own ethical imperatives. But those who have never loved Israel, never uttered a word on its behalf, never spoken out in its defense, do not have this prerogative.

After the Gulf War, I asked a Jewish activist for peace in the Middle East whether he still believed that he did the right thing when he went to see Arafat in Tunisia. "Yes," he replied, "after all, Moses went to see Pharaoh in Egypt." His response made me smile. Arafat may well have thought of himself as Pharaoh. "The problem is," I told my interlocutor, "you are not Moses."

Does this mean that I do nothing without Jerusalem's approval? Let's say that I will do nothing that might harm Jerusalem. When I feel that I must raise my voice, I do it in Israel. During the Intifada, I told the Israeli authorities that I wished to meet with the Palestinians and went to Gaza. The government did not oppose it. The Palestinians I met were known to have ties to the PLO; one of them was close to Yasir Arafat. At that time I also met the young Israeli soldiers who were battling the rebellious Arab adolescents. I asked both sides direct questions about hate and its consequences, about the legitimacy and efficacy of violence. I then published my impressions in the *New York Times*. But I must confess that at that time, I did not tell everything I had learned. At one point, Israeli soldiers had used deplorable psychological punishments; they would catch one of the stone-throwing young Arabs, take him to his home, and . . . beat his father. By humiliating the father, they hoped to teach the son discipline and respect. True, this reprehensible method was used by only a small number of soldiers, and only briefly. Of course, I reported it, but not publicly. I should have. But I was ashamed.

When I discussed these deplorable incidents with military and political leaders, I was given to understand in no uncertain terms that, as a Jew from the Diaspora, I had better mind my own business.

Nonetheless, I declare openly that the collective punishments meted out routinely under both governments leave me aghast. The sight of an Arab house demolished by the army just because a young Palestinian has been caught carrying a weapon does not leave me indifferent. And I consider all fanatical groups dangerous and evil. Less than a week after the massacre of some thirty Palestinians as they prayed in the Patriarchs' cave in Hebron, I voiced my outrage in a speech given before the European Council in Strasbourg.

There can be no justification for the murderous act of a religious man, a physician whose calling it was to save lives. What was it in Israel's political climate that made this criminal act possible?

And what can one say about Yigal Amir, Yitzhak Rabin's assassin? I think of the reproaches Israelis used to heap, and still do sometimes, on Diaspora Jews disinclined to make aliyah, to immigrate to Israel. Baruch Goldstein made aliyah. And Yigal Amir was born in Israel. And yet . . .

How often have I been on the receiving end of friendly and not-so-friendly advice to come and settle in Israel? There are those who resent my living in the Diaspora and "loving Israel from afar." Since I have written on the Holocaust, they claim, I should have drawn the only possible conclusion and declared publicly that the place of every Jew, and especially of every Holocaust survivor, is in Israel. Had Israel existed in 1939, they say, there would have been no Holocaust. For them, Israel constitutes the unique answer to Auschwitz. For me, Auschwitz remains a question mark.

The real problem? I think it is one of human relations, first between Jews in Israel and then between Israelis and Diaspora Jews. I only realized this during the Gulf War and then again during the international conference titled "The Anatomy of Hate" that our foundation convened in 1990 together with Haifa University, on Mount Carmel. I remember flying home with a heavy heart, with an anxiety that has never left me.

I know that what I am about to say will displease many in Israel. There will be those who say: "Why is he meddling in our affairs? He doesn't live here, he is not a citizen of our country. If he wants to be heard, to take part in our national debates, let him come and live among us, share our fears and our goals, our mistakes and our successes."

Oh yes, I know the formula, having used it myself at times: A person who does not live Israel's ordeals and challenges has no right to criticize its decisions. Never mind. I shall speak out, because the situation is too serious and the stakes too high for me to remain silent. An ancient philosopher said: When truth is in danger, silence equals guilt.

As for me, I may well be guilty of idealizing the land of Israel, which is now the State of Israel, a human laboratory of dreams and nostalgia that successfully turned itself into a structured and pragmatic nation. For many years, moved by a love older than I am, I have been going to Israel. Granted, it has always been as a visitor. I have delighted in walking through the narrow streets of Jerusalem, meeting colleagues and friends. I instantly felt at home in places I had never set foot in. For me, the people of Israel and the land of Israel were one and a Jew could be loyal to Israel even from outside its borders. I still believe that. But . . . what has changed? I'm not sure. I feel that the mood in the country is charged with rancor and hostility toward us, the Diaspora Jews. And let no one tell me that it was always so. Sure of their superiority, some Israelis' attitude toward Diaspora Jews is that they, the Israelis, are entitled to everything. They demand money and then deride those who have collected and offered it.

Ezer Weizman, the former defense minister and proponent of peace with the Arabs, now president of Israel, once asked me publicly why I did not move to Israel. The only answer I could think of was: "What is more important for a Jew: to be a Jew or to be Israeli?" I was wrong; I should not have opposed "Jew" to "Israeli." But as far as certain Israelis are concerned, one can be Jewish *only* in Israel. According to them, the most creative Jews in the Diaspora are less Jewish than a Jewish scoundrel in Tel Aviv.

So be it. I shall be a second-class Jew.

And so, while in times of crisis Israelis ask the Diaspora for support, as soon as they no longer feel threatened, their behavior changes abruptly. Some of their voices get too shrill; they get angry too fast. Among the more obtuse and egocentric commentators, lacking even a modicum of culture, there are a sculptor notorious for his vulgarity and a humorist known for his obscenity. They envy and hate us and each other. Such behavior may well occur in other countries, but in Israel it takes unusual proportions. The saying goes that it is impossible to meet someone who does not hate someone. The fanatic secularists hate the religious; the fanatic religious hate those who are less religious. The hate of one Jew for another sometimes seems greater than that reserved for enemies of the state. It is the main topic of magazines, newspapers, and radio. Political discourse is rarely on a high level; derision substitutes for humor, snickering for laughter, insults for wit. Malice replaces intelligence; rudeness covers subtlety. Debates are simplistic and reductive, discussions no longer about ideas but about material gains. And then there are the rumors. Nowhere else are they as vile, as poisonous. And they are everywhere. What is lacking is a sense of history. The debates in the Knesset often attain a frightening level of violence.

These feelings date from before the cowardly assassination of Rabin. I have lived in fear of the consequences of the hatred that has befallen the country for a long time.

True, other societies experience quarrels and antagonisms. The right to criticize, to oppose, to contradict, and even to denounce is the price of democracy. What would become of a political, economic, or literary system without rivalries? In civilized countries there are limitations to that right, but, for better or worse, Israel refuses limitations. Why, asks the Talmud, did God compare the people of Israel both to the stars and to dust? When Israel wants to attain the summits, none ascends as high; but when it allows itself to slide toward the abyss, it plunges to unprecedented lows.

How can I reconcile these images of Israel with the love I feel for it? I love Israel in times of joy and in times of mourning, in its hours of glory and in its periods of doubt and anguish. And when I feel saddened by it I think of Israel's young people, who will soon be summoned by the army. I think of the dreamers in front of the Wall. I think of all those mothers and fathers who lost their sons in combat. In times of doubt it is their faces that represent the eternal image of Israel.

On Becoming a Speaker

*A*ND THIS IS HOW one beautiful day I became a speaker. Dov Judkowski, the head of *Yedioth Ahronoth,* who in 1956 named me New York correspondent, was right: To give lectures in the United States is, as everybody knows, big business. With a little luck, lecturing can generate considerable income; not as substantial as that of a rock singer or a baseball champion, of course, but who can compare to a rock star or a stadium god?

I remember my first experience. It was 1960. *Night* had just been published in the United States. A few weeks later the Eichmann trial was headline news. I get a call from the president of a Jewish club on Long Island who invites me to come speak about my book to an audience of some five hundred couples. My honorarium? One hundred dollars, almost half my monthly salary. As I hesitate, she adds: "We have all read your work; we are totally enchanted by it. Come, we need to learn, and you are the one who can teach us." She has such a lovely voice. Am I going to fall in love? Again? I accept. The engagement is for two or three months hence. Too bad. I am lonely, but let me be patient. At least I'll have time to prepare myself. We agree on a date. My topic? Literature, philosophy. I devote many hours to perfecting my speech in English, the first I shall deliver in America. In my European frame of mind, a lecture demands serious research, reflection, structure.

In the taxi that takes me to Long Island that Sunday, I reread my thirty typed pages; I add notes in the margins; I am almost ready: I should be able to keep going one hour, perhaps one and a half. Suddenly a wild thought crosses my mind: The woman with the beautiful, voluptuous voice surely mistook me for someone else. Why would she invite me, a novice writer, a total unknown? Mile after mile, my doubts get stronger, and when I finally arrive at my destination I am convinced that the audience is expecting someone else.

The woman with the voice does not disappoint me: She is even more beautiful than I imagined. Graceful, smiling, warm, she thanks me for coming. I could fall in love with her very quickly, even more quickly than usual, but she introduces me to her husband, an accountant for an important electronics firm. They accompany me into the hall: All the women are dazzling and, as expected, all have escorts. I am seated at the head table to the right of my hostess.

In time I follow her to the podium. She presents me to the public with effusive praise in the American way. She proclaims that I am a great writer, then corrects herself immediately: Great? The greatest of this generation. Not only that, of all generations. In other words, I am a genius. If one were to believe my presenter, one might conclude that the deaths of Shakespeare and Dostoyevsky were occasioned by sheer envy over my accomplishments. "All of us have read and urged others to read your magnificent book!" she exclaims. "Future generations will echo what I am saying here, on behalf of all of us: We admire your talent and we love you for sharing it with us." I decide to test them.

Now it is my turn to speak. I thank her awkwardly and launch into a tale, improvising as I go along, that has no connection whatsoever with *Night.* I set the action in nineteenth-century France, where a Jewish seminarian becomes infatuated with a Christian "Mademoiselle" Bovary. I stress the ethical problems involved. The situation is reminiscent of Corneille's dramas. Duty and passion, religion and heresy. I mix quotations from Seneca and Kant and Spinoza, my favorite, why not? I wait for one member of the audience to stop me, to tell me that this is not the book he read. Nothing happens. I speak for three-quarters of an hour; even I have no idea where I'm going. The seminarian is on the brink of suicide when he learns that his beloved has fled from a convent somewhere in the countryside.

The time has come to conclude, for if I don't, I might be tempted to call upon the Bible and assorted medieval mystics and even upon texts that have come down to us from "the night of time"—hence the title of my book. My discourse is rewarded with thunderous applause. I don't know what to make of it. Clearly my intuition had been correct. There was in this hall not a single person who had read my poor little book, the only book that bore my name. Still, I urge myself not to be too hasty. They may be shy, or they don't want to offend me, embarrass me. During the question-and-answer period they will surely express their astonishment at the difference between my reading of my book and theirs.

Well, the question-and-answer period is upon us and everybody refers to the outrageous and incoherent tale I have just invented. Why did the seminarian wait so long before renouncing his love? Why did the young woman not consider conversion to the Jewish faith? As I stammer, my hostess accepts three more questions and concludes the session. I follow her into an office where she hands me my due. We are alone and I use the opportunity to tell her a Hasidic story:

Invited by a disciple from a neighboring village to attend a circumcision ceremony, a rabbi hires the only coach in the village to take him there. He and the coachman begin the journey in high spirits: the rabbi because he is about to perform a *mitzvah*, a good deed, and the coachman because he will earn a few zlotys. At the bottom of the first hill the horse halts, exhausted. The coachman dismounts and begins to push the carriage. Of course the rabbi, too, leaves the carriage and helps push. They push and push until they finally arrive at the Hasid's doorstep. That is when the rabbi tells the coachman: "There is something I don't understand. I understand why *I* am here; the Hasid wishes me to participate in his ceremony. I also understand why *you* are here; this is how you make your living. But the horse, this poor horse, why did we bring it along?"

My hostess with the beautiful voice is speechless for a moment. Then she confesses: Neither she nor any member of her group has read my book. But then why did she invite me? It was a simple mistake: She was confused by a *New York Times* review of two books, mine and another, in the same issue.

Another lesson in humility, this one administered in a Catskill resort: A Jewish group awards me some kind of prize. Some fifty people queue up to shake my hand and congratulate me. I hear whispers: "It doesn't look like him. He looks different in the movies." They had mistaken me for Eli Wallach.

Flattered, I tell myself: At least we share the same initials.

For years, I roam the continents to the point of total exhaustion. I speak so much that I begin to loathe the sound of my voice. After every lecture I emerge with a sense of frustration and loss. I feel as if I have given three lectures in one: the one I meant to give, the one I gave, and the one the public heard. And then, too, how is one to prevent repeating oneself, and how is one to avoid clichés? And yet one must improvise, for if one confines oneself to reading the text, one ends up boring one's audience and even oneself. And what if someone in the room has heard what I have to say, if in a different form? Oh well, he or she has probably forgotten by now.

I accept the topics that are suggested to me with the exception of the Holocaust. I worry lest it become routine. There was a time when few spoke of it, and it was important to lead the way. That is no longer the case. Of course my reticence is frequently misunderstood: I speak about the Bible, the Talmud, the Hasidic movement, yet the questions I am asked nevertheless refer to the Event.

Sometimes I seem to unleash demons. In San Antonio, Texas, a man stands up to confront me: "How can you write about the Holocaust when in fact that is nothing but a Jewish invention?" In St. Petersburg, Florida, a wild man launches into a similar declaration and manages to elude authorities for a while before being removed from the hall.

In a Washington, D.C., university, a group of African Americans charge into the lecture hall. Security people are about to oust them, but I ask them not to: "Since these young men wish to be heard, let them come forward." I invite them to the podium and tell their leader: "The mike is all yours." Taken aback, he stammers a few words about racial intolerance. "Perfect," I say, "that is my subject as well." He sits down, as do his comrades.

In the town of Iasi, Romania, during a commemoration of the 1941 massacre of the Jews, a hysterical woman interrupts my speech: "Lies, lies! No Jew was ever killed here! Nor anywhere else!" Her cohorts applaud. She is asked to leave. The many officials present are embarrassed. The governor apologizes, as does the mayor, the prime minister, the president. Later I am told that the woman was the daughter of the Fascist general Antonescu's former chief of police.

It sometimes happens that before taking the floor I must listen to three, four, five speakers. They don't all recognize the virtue of brevity. They remind me of a story told to me by Meyer Weisgal, Chaim Weizmann's close associate: During a charity dinner a speaker launched into a riverlike discourse, giving no hint of exhaustion. Eventually, Weisgal tugged at his arm and whispered without undue discretion: "But, sir, that's enough, please stop!" The speaker's pitiful reply: "I'd like to. . . . I just don't know how."

In the course of my public lectures I sometimes am interrupted by listeners impatient to express their disagreement. At the Centre Rachi, in Paris, during a presentation on Rabbi Akiba's troubling adventure in the *Pardes,* the orchard of forbidden knowledge, a woman yelled incoherently. She came up to me at the end and explained the reason for her anger. It seems I should have condemned Rabbi Akiba. And why would I condemn the founder of the Talmud? "Because he cheated on his wife with the governor's spouse."

Another kind of incident occurred in Washington, where the Kennedy Foundation organized an international "Science and Conscience" conference. The inaugural session was followed by several roundtable discussions. Participating in mine were the Nobel laureate biochemist Jacques Monod, Mother Teresa, and a few academics. I spoke of Jewish attitudes toward living beings: To save a human life one has the right—even the duty—to violate the laws of Shabbat. The moderator, an assimilated Jew who was evidently uncomfortable at hearing a Jew speak of his Jewishness in front of such an elite public, pulled the microphone away from me in the middle of my speech. I was too shocked to react, but a priest seated in the rear rose to protest.

In Moscow, things didn't go so well either. As I began to speak—this was in January 1990—during a conference entitled "Global Survival," I stressed the role of memory in education. Again, I was expressing my views as a Jew. I asked Mikhail Gorbachev for a firmer stance against racism and anti-Semitism. Quoting Soviet radio, which described the "pogroms" in Armenia, I chose to demonstrate that all hatreds are linked. I asked that Stalin's crimes be recognized as crimes against humanity. And that investigators, policemen, torturers, judges, and executioners be denied leniency. I asked the president of the Soviet Union to open the archives of the infamous Stalin-era trials. We have the right, I insisted, to know details of the imprisonment and execution of Yiddish writers such as Peretz Markish and Der Nister. A Jordanian delegate expressed his displeasure. He was furious with me and said so openly. Yet I had not even mentioned the Middle East; I had not pled for Israel. He took exception because, apparently, my discourse was . . . too Jewish. He then evoked Yitzhak Shamir, whom he called a hawk. I was Jewish, he was Jewish, therefore we were all hawks. And all guilty. Guilty of dwelling on our past. After all, the Jordanian delegate proudly concluded, he, too, had been in Auschwitz. He omitted to say that he had been there . . . as a tourist.

In Madrid during a Young Presidents Organization conference, I am constantly reminded of the 1492 expulsion of the Jews and therefore deal with the theme of exile. In the beginning was exile. The child is exiled from his mother's womb. Then he is exiled from his home to attend school, and from his family to get married. I note that in our time we experienced the ultimate exile: The victim ceased being a person and became an object. To general surprise, a German businessman rises, red with indignation: He has had enough of feeling guilty, he says. He has had enough of hearing about the past. It is time to . . . That is when I put him in his place by asking a series of questions, each one beginning with the words: "How dare you. . . ."

This confrontation becomes the topic of subsequent conversations. The German delegation requests a meeting with me. I ask whether the delegate had spoken on their behalf. After consulting briefly they express their disapproval of their fellow delegate, who promptly asks to be heard again. I refuse to listen unless he first apologizes. He finally does.

In all my lectures on Jewish themes, I emphasize Judaism's ethics, which, by definition, decry racism. A Jew must not be racist; Jews are committed to fighting any system that sees in the other an inferior being. That is why anyone—regardless of his or her color, ethnicity, or social standing—can become a Jew; all he or she has to do is accept the Law. On the other hand, every person is entitled to dignity and respect; no need to espouse Judaism for that.

Invited to address a prestigious South African university, I set a condition: Black students must be allowed to attend. The university agrees. People commend my "courageous attitude." But it was not a matter of courage—it was simply a matter of not giving in to a system I abhor. As a rule I like to speak to mixed audiences: young and less young, Jews and Christians, believers and nonbelievers.

During a conference of Catholic intellectuals a speaker declares that the Holocaust presents as serious a problem for Jews as it does for Christians. I feel the need to correct him. And I remember the shock I provoked when I said: "Just a moment, my friends. The situation is not the same: The victims may be my problem; the killers are yours."

Speaking in Stockholm's cathedral, I say: "You must understand that the Jew that I am cannot look upon the cross as you do. For you, it represents mercy and love. For us, it evokes terror and persecution."

On the occasion of a visit to the U.S. Military Academy at West Point, the school's commander, General Palmer, organizes a parade in my honor: "The parade is yours," he says saluting. I am astounded: This whole parade is mine? What am I to do with it? Four thousand cadets, their sparkling uniforms and banners flapping in the wind, salute me as if I were a head of state. The Jewish child in me thinks he is dreaming. Never in my life have I been a soldier. And suddenly these future officers—perhaps generals—looking grave and solemn, do me the honors reserved for a president.

That evening my topic is "The Meaning of Freedom":

Man is free, for God wants him to be free. All things are foreseen by God, we are told by our Masters, and yet we are free, free to choose every moment of our life. We are free to choose between life and death, between the next instant and death, between good and evil, laughter and tears, free to choose compassion over cruelty, memory over oblivion, beauty over ugliness, morality over immorality, and we are free to choose between freedom and absence of freedom.

. . . Though chosen by God to be the first believer, Abraham was free to reject that mission. He could have said no, but he didn't. Does it seem like a paradox? I am free not to be afraid of paradoxes.

The idea, I believe, is simply not to confuse divine freedom and human freedom. The two are connected but not identical. God is free, and man must be free. . . . Now what is freedom? Freedom to the slave is not the same as freedom to the owner of the slave. . . . Freedom is not a given; it is something one must constantly fight for. Freedom is not even given by God. Freedom belongs to the human domain. It is up to us to shape and nourish it.

Other moments come to mind, special moments. On a visit to the Ghetto Fighters Kibbutz in the north of Israel, I finally meet "Antek," Yitzhak Zuckerman, the former deputy commander of the Warsaw Ghetto. We have known each other for twenty years—from afar. Every time we made plans to meet, one of us had to cancel. This time, no matter what, the meeting will take place.

We withdraw to the privacy of his office. There is instant camaraderie, no need for preambles. We understand each other. We exchange views, memories, impressions. Survivors from abroad, who are in the country to participate in a conference in Jerusalem, are visiting the kibbutz. I am asked to say a few words to them. I insist that Antek accompany me. But he is sick; he can hardly stand up. They carry him outside and seat him on a bench. I dedicate my speech to him: "Antek, my friend, I am your guest here. . . . From you and your comrades we have learned humanism and the meaning of a Jewish fighter's responsibility. . . . You have taught us a new language. . . . You have taught us the strength of the individual."

I compare our experiences. What were the Jews of Sighet doing in 1943 while he and his comrades were fighting against the Germans? My days were spent at the yeshiva. We studied, we ate, and we celebrated our holidays, while in the Warsaw Ghetto young fighters entered the heroic legend of Israel. And now?

I continue:

What are we doing with our books, with your words? We try to educate our children and all the children of the world. We tell them that man is capable of tumbling into inhumanity; of falling as he loses sight of the divine image of which he bears the imprint. That in those days, the Jew clung to his Jewishness and, thus, to his humanity. . . . Antek, my dear Antek, when I go home, I shall close my eyes and see you with nostalgia, respect, and infinite tenderness.

As I leave, we embrace. He is weeping and inside me someone is weeping as well. He dies the next day.

Standing before the Wall, thousands of survivors are praying. Prime Minister Menachem Begin has just delivered a rousing speech. He has spoken of the Jewish people's need to be strong, to be armed. As far as he is concerned, that is the lesson to be drawn from the Tragedy. But then he said that it was God who wanted Hiroshima . . . going so far as to imply that the atomic bomb was a divine gift, for it allowed the Allies to win the war. As I follow him to the microphone I cannot help but express my disagreement: God and Hiroshima don't go together in my way of thinking. And his comments about strength pose a problem for me: Could this be *the* lesson the Tragedy has bequeathed to us, to choose strength and celebrate it? I think it important to add: "Here in this city of eternity, where every dream is eternal, we must ask ourselves a painful question: Have we, the survivors, done our duty? Have we acted as honest witnesses should?" And I conclude:

> What do we carry away with us from this invincible city, this indestructible city of peace and humanity? We carry with us a spark of its light, a fragment of its song. True, some part of us has remained back there, in Auschwitz and Belsen, Majdanek and Treblinka. But, from today on, something of us will remain linked to this site in Jerusalem, forever. . . . Just as Auschwitz signifies the end of human hope, Jerusalem symbolizes eternal beginnings.

Another speech remains in my memory. Not that it was particularly remarkable, but it was delivered before several hundred "hidden children" whom compassionate Christian families had sheltered in occupied Europe:

> Of all the crimes conceived in fanaticism and hatred, the war against the Jewish children will remain the worst, the most vicious, and the most implacable in recorded history.
>   . . . We now know that Hitler's Germany made the Jewish child its principal target. In condemning our people's children to death, it sought to deprive us, as a people, of a future. For the children who did survive Hitler's Germany, laughter and joy were largely eliminated from their lives.
>   The children who were "hidden" especially have never ceased asking themselves the question: Where is our childhood? So powerful was the enemy's criminal intent that it succeeded in changing their childhood, in replacing it with another one, a false one, a childhood that did not belong to them, a childhood that was not meant for them. In fact, because of the enemy, the "hidden" children have had to live someone else's childhood. But in most cases the enemy did not succeed in changing their memory.
>   Will I ever—as a novelist, as a teacher, as a person, as a Jew, as a father, who loves both to tell stories and to listen to them—will I ever acquire the necessary imagination to describe what goes on in the heart of a father who, moved by a sudden impulse of insane hope, hands his infant child

to an unknown passerby, praying that this final fatherly gesture might save the infant's life? Or will I be able to describe a mother who, on the threshold of muted madness, throws her baby outside the cattle car, hoping that a merciful peasant will catch it? And keep it? Will I ever be able to read in her pain the meaning of her gesture?

I think of the hidden children who survived, and I wonder how they felt at the moment their father or their mother left them. What took place in their still fragile but already wounded subconscious? A rejection? A betrayal, perhaps? How long did it take before they grasped the full meaning of what their parents had to do on their behalf? How long has it taken to overcome the anger some of them might have felt toward their parents as they held them responsible for their separation? When exactly did they understand the fathomless strength their parents needed to give up their children to a stranger in order to spare them their own fatal destiny? On the brink of death, their parents pulled themselves away from their children so as to shield them from death.

Compared with these parents, Abraham seems less heroic. Summoned to sacrifice his son Isaac on the altar, he obeyed a divine commandment. But these parents had to give up a child, sometimes an only child, to an unknown person who, at best, would make of that child a living Christian rather than a dead Jew. Where could they find the faith they needed to offer them some measure of consolation? I have tried to imagine the life and death of a hidden Jewish child in one of my tales.

Taken in and shielded by an old Christian housekeeper, the little boy, named Gregor, must pretend to be mute or retarded so as not to arouse suspicion in the village where he has found shelter with a Christian woman. At the school, he attends a Passion play that is being produced for Easter. The boy is given the part of Judas. As such he is ridiculed, humiliated, and tormented to the point that, unable to bear it any longer, he breaks his silence and begins to talk.

Who among the hidden survivors has not known such trials whose outcome meant life or death? One careless word, one wrong gesture, and it was the end. One frightened look, one sigh poorly suppressed, one prayer poorly remembered, one cloud of sadness on the face, and one could be discovered, and torn away again, and separated again, this time for good. So I wonder, how did they manage? How did they manage not to be sad? How did those who were very young—one or two years old—know that to be sad meant to appear Jewish and to be Jewish meant to die? How did they manage to grow up so fast? How did they manage so quickly to learn terrible and rare ways of keeping alive? How did they manage to hide and/or forget so many things in order to hide the Jewish child in themselves? How did they manage to vanquish fear and loneliness resulting from their parents being absent from their lives? How did they manage to overcome suspicion and not see an enemy in every passerby? How did they manage to remember not to respond to their Jewish names when called? How did they manage all of a sudden to behave as if they were someone else? How did they manage to fall asleep without weeping, without being caressed by a mother and reassured by a father?

A young woman I know told me that she spent eighteen months in silence and solitude in a shelter. She was forbidden to make noise. Once a day the landlord would bring her food. She had to watch herself constantly, not to move, not to snore, not to sigh, not to cry in her sleep. For eighteen months, she lived in total darkness. Not once did she glimpse the stars. How did she manage to stifle her pain and her anguish?

Another young woman I know hid in an attic. A chicken was her only companion. In the beginning, she told me, all was well. Then their relationship deteriorated. The chicken grew arrogant. The chicken felt it could do anything to the Jewish woman. With impunity. She would not shout or hit back. It's incredible, said the young woman; the chicken had become an anti-Semite.

But what about those who were too young to understand what was happening to them? What about those who were still infants? At what point did the truth reveal itself to them? When did they comprehend that they belonged to

other parents, to other places, to another people? And what
did they then feel toward the women who had agreed to
take care of them and their needs? And their true mothers,
those who seemed not to want them, what did they feel
toward them? Whom did they love more? Their absent parents who were dead, or their rescuer parents who were not?
Later when they thought of their dead parents, how did
they think about them? With joy? With remorse?

. . . In allowing a million and more Jewish children to
die, humankind inflicted suffering and punishment on itself.
We may find solace in the emerging role of the survivors,
the rescuers, and especially the hidden children. I look at
them and feel rewarded. They have done something with
their orphaned memories, something of which they can
and should be proud. They have kept their childhood
intact, and they have built on it a temple for future children
and parents to worship in, live in, for the sake of one
another.

At the Reichstag in Berlin during a Kristallnacht commemoration, I choose to tell Germans of the Hitler generation that their past
unfolded under the sign of malediction. I tell young Germans not to
despair of us, whereas they have every reason to despair of their
elders.

I emphasize that I do not believe in collective guilt. The children
of killers are children, not killers. We must never blame them for what
their elders did. But we can hold them responsible for what they do
with the memory of their elders' crimes.

An official pilgrimage to Sighet. At the entrance to the cemetery,
before the local population, I deliberately speak Yiddish. Chief Rabbi
Moses Rosen translates: "How could a human community such as
yours show such inhumanity to my people? What happened to our
friends? Where were they hiding? What happened to Sighet's human
heart?"

In Warsaw, on Tisha b'Av eve, in the last synagogue to remain open,
some ten men mournfully intone Jeremiah's Lamentations: "Ei'ha
yashva badad. . . ." Oh how lonely and solitary she was, the city where,
long ago, our people dwelled. . . .

As I reread the text, something troubles me: The Old City of David does not fill me with sadness. Today Jerusalem is neither desolate nor abandoned. In fact, it is vibrant and exuberant. Its sons are strong, its daughters radiant. But then, what city does Jeremiah's text bring to mind? Suddenly it is clear: The city is Warsaw, the Jewish Warsaw of long ago.

Washington. A few steps from the White House, where Mikhail Gorbachev will be received the next day by President Reagan for the first time. Two hundred thousand demonstrators shout their solidarity with Soviet Jewry. I am exhilarated. Finally my friends and I have succeeded in awakening our people, in jolting them out of their lethargy. Anatoly Shcharansky, Masha and Vladimir Slepak, and many other refuseniks march with us. Did my article in the *New York Times* help? I hope so. On the Op-Ed page of that paper I had issued an appeal for a march for human rights in the eighties to succeed the march for civil rights of the sixties. This appeal generated considerable response. People wrote offering financial and material help; organizations and activists became involved. American Jewry experienced a groundswell of solidarity. And as I march, I cannot help but wonder: Had there been similar demonstrations in the forties, how many European Jews could have been saved?

Kielce, July 7, 1996. It is the fiftieth anniversary of the pogrom that had outraged the world. Forty-two Jews had been assassinated by a mob in broad daylight. The title of my address: "How Could They?" I give vent to my pain and anger about the past but also about the crosses erected more recently in Birkenau. They thought they were justified by also installing a few Stars of David.

My words arouse violent controversy in the Polish press and in Catholic circles. Simon Wiesenthal takes advantage of this tension and, in his usual spiteful manner, criticizes me in Adam Michnic's daily *Gazeta Wyborska*. I do not respond.

There are conferences against hunger, fanaticism, and hatred. A speech on cancer and Alzheimer's disease during a symposium organized by Professor Claude Jasmin at UNESCO. Remarks made at the opening of the Auschwitz exhibition at the U.N. A talk on ethics at CIA headquarters (in order to stay off its payroll, I decline my honorarium, which is contrary to CIA "rules"). A lecture on Job in front of—yes!—six thousand priests, nuns, and professors of Catholic theology. Professor Irving Abrahamson of Chicago devotes ten years of his life to gathering a large number of these speeches and publishes them under the title *Against Silence*.

I speak and speak. There is always a text in front of me, but I prefer to improvise, which of course is fraught with risk; it is easy to err and often impossible to correct. Once uttered, words go their own way; it is impossible to take them back. And so sometimes all that remains after a speech is a sense of remorse. What I have said no longer belongs to me.

Most of my speeches are not transcribed—only those with biblical, talmudic, or Hasidic themes; they are my favorites. I devote weeks, months of research to them. The lectures I have given at the Centre Rachi and the Centre Universitaire d'Études Juives at the Sorbonne in Paris, at the 92nd Street "Y" in Manhattan, and at Boston University are eventually published.

On the other hand, speeches delivered on "occasions" are the ones I give reluctantly. It is impossible to deal meaningfully with any subject in the course of a dinner. And then there is the problem that words, no sooner uttered, tend to age and fade. The orally transmitted thought meanders and dissipates. Sometimes I think the best speeches are those I never gave.

Besides, I still suffer from stage fright, an accursed companion who never lets go. I remember in Sighet, one Shabbat afternoon, I had chosen to explain a text from *The Ethics of Our Fathers* to a group of fellow students. I suffered pangs of hell. Butterflies in my stomach. The expression is apt. As I ascended the podium, my body was seized by a trembling that threatened to paralyze my brain.

I am never sure of myself. Will I be able to communicate, to stimulate, to hold the listener's attention, to logically articulate my ideas? And what if I forget the necessary quotation or the critical point? Once the last sentence has been uttered, I ache to escape.

I no longer have the strength or the desire to travel. There was a time when I liked being on the road; I was ready to give up everything to go somewhere, anywhere, by any means. No longer.

A journey I did not undertake: December 31, 1991. Bernard Kouchner, a founder of Doctors Without Borders and deputy health minister of France, and now U.N. civil administrator of Kosovo, asks me to join him on a mission to Dubrovnik, which is being bombed by the Serbs. I hesitate. The Belgrade Jewish community is fiercely opposed, fearing the consequences. And then, how is one to ignore the anti-Semitic book written by the Croatian president Franjo Tudjman? As it happens, my body decides for me: I come down with a virus, running a high fever.

Now, as I consider invitations to speak, I think of the words of Rabbi Israel of Rizhin: "Sometimes we speak before a crowd so that one individual will understand, and, sometimes, for the sake of one individual, we remain silent."

Of Madmen and Visionaries ──○

I HAVE NOT AS YET SPOKEN of my madmen: Like my father in Sighet, I seem to attract them. Aren't we all a little mad, each of us in his own way? Mad to wish to live and to refuse to live, mad to believe in the future and also to negate it, mad to think that we have eluded death and the dead?

The ones that pursue me belong to a different species. Not all are Jewish. There are among them Christians, Buddhists, agnostics; former musicians and future geniuses; authors of works not yet written and as-yet-unrevealed saviors. In truth I don't really dislike meeting with them. I would even say that their imagination enriches mine. However, the problem is that one does not choose them, and some of them are burdensome and difficult to shake. Each has something "urgent" to communicate to you, a solution to offer. You speak to them for an hour, and they will come back ten times. And don't try to avoid them; they will find the trail that leads to you. Don't bother to hide; they will outsmart you.

A man calls me and insults me: Every obscenity in the English language pours out. "But who are you?" I ask. His name is Marx, "like Karl." "Do I know you, dear Mr. Marx?" Yes. No. Another avalanche of insults and curses follows. I hang up. He calls back. I hang up again. The next day it starts all over. When I'm away he leaves messages: "Mr. Marx called." How to get rid of him? The police claim to be helpless. Never mind. As a matter of fact, he stops calling. Three days and three nights of respite. But on the fourth day, he is back: "Aha, you thought you could escape?" And he spills out his dose of horrors. Oddly, he appears to be informed of all my activities; he "knows" with whom I dined the night before, what play I've seen. One afternoon I have a visitor, a woman friend from Paris. The telephone rings. It is

he: "I don't know her," says Mr. Marx. "Who is she?" I feel as though
I'm going mad myself.

A few months later I leave for Europe. When I return, no more
Mr. Marx. No letter, no message. A great relief. Could he have disappeared for good?

Of course he reappears. But I have learned my lesson. I shout:
"Mr. Marx, whatever happened to you? Were you sick? I was worried
about you. What can I do to help you?" Taken aback, he chokes with
annoyance. Then he unleashes on me a last stream of obscenities and
goes on to look for more vulnerable, more nervous victims, before
returning, perhaps, to his insane asylum.

A "romantic" persecution: A young waitress from New Jersey gravely
informs me that I am her husband. She knows it, even if I don't. She
knows that I married her, evidently in another life. Hence her solemn
warning: If she sees me with another woman, she'll make me pay
dearly. She has connections, she tells me, in the most influential circles. In other words, I would be well advised to be careful, to behave
like a faithful husband. Otherwise . . . Once again the police refuse
to intervene. "Let her kill you first and we'll be right there to arrest
her," is what I am told by a police officer with a macabre sense of
humor.

This "romance" goes on for months. Day after day I receive
interminable letters. She tells me what she does with her free time,
her dreams, and even her infidelities with famous actors, infamous bil-
lionaires, mafiosi. . . .

You never know with crazies of her kind. And you don't play
with the Mafia. So I return to the police station, and there is the same
police officer. I confess my fears and ask his advice. A psychologist in
his spare time, he shrugs his shoulders: "Good grief," says he "why
don't you 'divorce' her?" Fortunately the waitress has a father who is
aware of her illness and makes sure she returns to her psychiatrist.

And then there is the doctor who calls me from Canada: He must
come to speak to me at once; it is urgent. Very urgent. A matter of life
and death. Who and what is this about? It's about the whole world.
Could he be more specific? I try to make him talk. In vain. "Not on the
telephone," he says, "it's too risky." The slightest leak could make the
project fail. "You understand, don't you? All this is confidential. Top

secret." Suspicious, I lower my voice: "Are you sure it's me that . . . ?"
He gets angry: "I know what I'm doing." I ask him to call me back that
afternoon: time enough to cancel a few appointments. And, of course,
to call Canadian friends, have them check if this fellow really is a doctor. Yes, he is. His name is in the directory. All right, let him come.

That particular Sunday it snows. The airports are paralyzed, the
train stations deserted, the streets empty. I'm optimistic: He won't
come. But here he is. The doorman calls to announce him. Curious, I
welcome him. He hands me his calling card. Impressive titles. I invite
him to sit down; I offer him coffee; he refuses. "Time is short; you
must accompany me," he says resolutely. Where to? Canada? "To
Nepal," he replies unblinking. I ask him to please say that again. "Yes,
to Nepal. I have prepared everything; it is all arranged. Look." He
hands me an airline ticket for that very evening and a sum of money. I
stammer like an idiot: "But today is Sunday. What am I going to do in
Nepal on a Sunday?" He does not flinch: "We'll arrive tomorrow.
Tomorrow is Monday." I continue my inane interrogation: "And what
would you have me do in Nepal on a Monday?" His answer is instantaneous: "Meditate." I don't understand: He must be mad, but he
doesn't look it. I ask him: "Meditate? On what?" He replies: "The
world is in danger. To save it we must go to Nepal. I don't know how
we'll do it, but once we are there we'll know." I insist: "Why there?
Why not here?" He says: "It's not the same. There we will be heard."
"By whom?" I ask. "I don't know. There we will know."

I observe him carefully. He looks normal, sincere, and gentle.
How can I send him away without offending him? "I have no visa," I
say, trying to look sorry. Never mind, he says, a visa is waiting for us at
our destination. He has answers to everything, this Canadian savior. I
come back to the weather: There is no car to take us to the airport,
and, anyway, no planes are taking off. I show him, through the window, the empty and icy avenue. He is stubborn: If the weather is bad,
then it's because of me, because of my skepticism. As soon as I accept
his invitation, the sun will shine over New York. The weather will be
perfect and we will leave. How does he know? He knows because in
Nepal the weather is very beautiful. Where does he get this knowledge of world weather? "Easy," he says. "I close my eyes and I see."
"See what?" I ask. "Nepal." Now I've got him. "But then, since you can
see Nepal by closing your eyes, why must we go there?" His answer is
simple: "I can, but you can't."

In the end, I show him my calendar: "I have important engagements this week. I cannot possibly cancel them." At that he goes into a cold fury: "The world is lost, or almost, and all you can think of is your cursed calendar." To calm him I suggest that he leave for Nepal before me to prepare everything; I shall come later.

He flew off the next day. Evidently he managed without me. The proof: He did not come back. And the world is still around.

As I evoke the mystical madmen, or the common variety madmen, how could I omit the visionary perturber from Colorado? Right in the middle of a lecture I am delivering at a university in Denver, someone begins to howl like a wounded beast. The security guards scrutinize the rows unsuccessfully. Vaguely anxious, I pick up the thread of my talk. And it happens again: a long sharp cry. But who is it? And what can he possibly want? I make a new effort to concentrate. I shorten my talk. As soon as it is over, ignoring the students waiting for me, the security guards surround me and push me into their car, which has been waiting at a side door, and we take off for the airport, where I am to take the midnight flight to New York. On the way they explain that they have been caught unprepared; nothing like this has ever happened to them. Better to be careful. "What about the students? They'll be disappointed." Never mind, answer my guardian angels. Better they be angry with you alive than that they mourn your death. Their logic is irrefutable. I have no further comment. Times being what they are, it is unwise to disobey fellows who are so sure of themselves. I receive enough threatening letters to be aware of that; anti-Semites, pro-Palestinians, deniers: Surely they don't wish me well. And so the word "security" deserves respect and silence.

At the ticket counter all is quiet. There are few passengers. I shall have a good seat. I'll be able to nap on the plane. I thank my escorts, so concerned with my well-being, and enter the long twisting corridor leading to the boarding gate. I sigh; at last I am alone. But suddenly a young man emerges from the shadows and whispers under his breath: "Forgive me for screaming. You understand? When God orders me to scream, I have no right to remain silent." I glimpse a telephone booth; in a panic I jump into it. My heart beats wildly. I feign to be dialing a number, to have a conversation, to be interested in what my imaginary interlocutor has to say. The young man waits patiently for me to finish. I leave the booth only when other passengers appear. Then I follow them, with the young messenger from the

Lord in hot pursuit. Thank God he does not have a ticket. "Take this,"
he says as he hands me a small notebook. "You'll read it on the plane.
You'll understand many things." In his message he claims to be the
Savior, the real one, the last, the only one; he is but waiting for the
prophet Elijah to announce his coming. If he yells, it is to be heard by
the prophet, so that he may know that the Savior has come and is
waiting for him. Feeling sorry for the prophet, I fall asleep.

Many months later, I stumble upon humanity's Savior; he is waiting for me at the entrance to my office at Boston University. What
else does he want from me? He has no problem letting me know: "Be
my associate. My messenger. Together we shall save the planet and its
inhabitants." I explain to him that while waiting for the Messiah I
must teach Kafka and the *Epic of Gilgamesh* to my students. The following week, there he is again. Skinny, head buried between his shoulders, he dares not look at me but shyly drops this question: "Would
you have some time for me today?" I tell him: "I have my class. You
know that." "Whom are you going to speak about this morning?" "The
prophet Jeremiah." Looking disappointed, he says: "What a pity. I am
waiting for the prophet Elijah."

For weeks on end he comes to my office. How does he live in
Boston? Where does he sleep? Nobody knows. Cindy Margulies, a
student who works in my office, has a good idea: She advises him to
go to Israel. Since he wishes to bring deliverance to the world, he
should be in Jerusalem: "If the Messenger is waiting for you somewhere, surely that's where he is."

I never saw him again, and I wonder where he is, this young mad
visionary from Colorado who lived so intensely in the expectation of
a stranger.

And the others, where are they? Each had a solution to insoluble
problems, a key to unfathomable mysteries, a message from a heavenly angel. It was my practice to answer every letter; I was curious to
meet people. It became a problem when they answered my answer
and subsequently demanded appointments or, at the least, answers to
their answers. The problem was time—there never is enough time. I
often think of Nikos Kazantzakis, who wished to stand outside
churches to ask the faithful: "In lieu of alms, give me the time you are
not using."

And then there are the madmen of Hollywood: They wish, at all
costs, to "discover" me; not as a star, thank God, but as a screenwriter.

In the face of my bewilderment, they admonish me: Do I realize that William Faulkner practiced that very craft? Did I know that the world's greatest novelists work for the movie moguls? I know, I don't know, what does it matter? At more or less regular intervals ever since the sixties, a person connected to Hollywood appears, seeking to seduce me. But then as soon as I am almost ready to succumb, he disappears.

Someone wants to make a film of *Night*. I refuse: There are topics around which one may not create spectacles. I receive a proposal from the great Orson Welles. I answer that I am flattered but . . . He finally takes an option, which he renews again and again. Eric Rohmer likes *The Accident*. Samy Halfon fancies *The Gates of the Forest*. Several directors wish to acquire the rights to *A Beggar in Jerusalem*. Eventually, film adaptations of *Dawn* and *The Testament* are made. I feel sorry for the directors; neither was received favorably by the public.

My idiom remains the word, not the image.

Cardinal Lustiger, My Friend —

*I*N 1980 THE FRENCH PRESS publishes and discusses at great length a sensational news item. No doubt to underline his philosophy, rather than his theology, of openness, Pope John Paul II has appointed a converted Jew of Polish origin as archbishop of Paris. Jean-Marie Lustiger rapidly becomes one of the most mediatized and popular personalities of France. Charming but sincere, endowed with a rare gift of communication, he has a knack for finding the right tone, not just from the heights of his cathedral pulpit but also on television, in the newspapers, and in addressing varied communities.

Interviews, declarations, commentaries—his stands on issues are well received in all kinds of circles. Academics and ministers praise his erudition; his words are quoted; the depth of his convictions is recognized and his tolerance appreciated. His trajectory is transparent, his speeches without a false note. The new prelate does not conceal his Jewish roots: On the contrary, he never fails to claim them. He repeats that his Jewish name is Aaron, that he is of the Jewish people. A proud Christian, he assumes his Jewishness, and does so without the slightest complex. In fact, he describes himself as a "fulfilled Jew," which arouses in me—understandably—a certain uneasiness. If he, a Jew-turned-Christian, is "fulfilled," does that mean that he is a better Jew than those who have remained Jews?

I think of the tensions and conflicts that over centuries have marked the relations between our two religions: the hateful writings of the church fathers, the massacres during the Crusades, the Inquisition, the pogroms, the public humiliations. I think of the silences of Pius XII; his intercessions with Third Reich authorities were restricted to converted Jews. Only they mattered to him. I cannot forget this deplorable aspect of Holocaust history.

I try to imagine a conversation with the archbishop. What could

I tell him? What can I say to a converted Jew? And how would he respond? Sure, I know some Catholic priests. But none claims to be a Jew. I also recall my Master, Saul Lieberman, telling me about his resolve never to shake the hand of a *meshumad*, a renegade. On the other hand, the Talmud states that *"Israel af al pi shekhata, Israel hu."* A Jew, even a sinner, remains a Jew. How is one to classify Aaron Lustiger?

"Try to meet him," is Marion's advice. "Then perhaps you will know." I decide, for this special occasion, to revert to my former profession. I ask my French publisher's press person to inform the archbishop's secretariat that I wish to write a piece about him, perhaps for the *New York Times*. His reply reaches me within the hour: He will receive me, but only "off the record," meaning not for an article. Just to meet; two Jews who wish to make acquaintance, what could be more natural? A date in March 1981 is set, since I plan to be in Paris to participate in a colloquium organized by Jack Lang for François Mitterrand, the Socialist candidate in the presidential elections.

I owe it to my Christian friends to say how I really feel. It is complex and not likely to arouse religious hope. In the past, both distant and recent, their ancestors inflicted suffering on ours because of our faith. That is a fact. But there is more. The master killers of the twentieth century, were they not all, or almost all, born in and baptized by the church? True, there were Christians who sacrificed themselves to save Jewish lives, in Italy as well as in France, Poland, and Holland. But they were so few. Then, of course, there was John XXIII, but doesn't his humanism represent a moment of exception rather than a prevailing tendency in the Vatican's recent history?

My own relationship to the Catholic Church? As a child, I feared it. As an adolescent, I had no reason to give it my attention. Still, I could not disregard it, for it was a time when between the Christian world and my own there existed only ties of violence and exclusion. For me, a Christian was the hostile stranger, the false avenger. "You killed Christ" was one of the insults hurled at me by my schoolmates. I didn't understand: I hadn't killed anyone; throughout history, Jews have been victims and not assassins. The Christians that surrounded me were wrong in believing in anti-Jewish stereotypes, and I was wrong in oversimplifying.

After the war, I discovered the complicity of the Catholic and Protestant churches, both German and Austrian, with Hitler's regime.

The documents I read about Pius XII only reinforced my distrust. François Mauriac was the first to denounce his silence. Historians were providing mostly devastating evidence. I still can't understand why Adolf Hitler was not excommunicated. And why the Vatican or one of its agents helped Adolf Eichmann, Stangel, and Mengele escape from justice. I cannot forget that 22 percent of the SS were Catholics and that some of them regularly went to confession.

It is only when I reached adulthood that I understood the importance of dialogue between people of different religions. I understood the danger of living in a world made of stereotypes. During the war there *were* devout Christians who helped. I overcame my inhibitions and suspicions. Diversity—the word of the moment is pluralism—is part of the Creator's design. If all human beings spoke the same language, dreamed of the same happiness, belonged to the same tribe practicing the same religion, the history of mankind would have been short-lived. Adam was neither Jew nor Christian, and yet he is the father of us all.

Today's Christian is not responsible for what his ancestors did long ago. I believe that a synergy of religions is both possible and necessary, but only in total honesty. My Master, Saul Lieberman, often warned me against the adverse impact of comfort, spiritual as well as material: "Remember," he would say, "that our people has lost many more souls through seduction than through persecution." Our sages quote Scripture: When Esau embraced his brother Jacob, the latter began to weep. Why did he weep? Because, they answer, Jacob understood that Esau's embrace was a trap more dangerous than his hate.

In accordance with my tradition, I wish to convert no one, just as I don't wish anyone to convert me. A Jew's aim is not to convert another to his faith, but to help him become more fully who he is.

Those were my thoughts on the way to the archbishop's residence. The debate I hoped to open was at once simple and painful: Can one be Jewish and Christian at the same time? Can one continue to belong to the Jewish people while opting for another religion?

The archbishop is waiting for me. His welcome is warm but tense. What am I to him, a reminder, a reproach? And he to me? A lost, estranged brother?

He speaks kindly of my work. The encounter makes me think of the disputations of medieval times, when Jews and Christians debated the merits of their religions. Except that our meeting takes place with no audience or constraints. In medieval times the rabbi fasted on the day he went to meet the prelate, and the entire community fasted as well, as a token of solidarity.

We are alone in the drawing room, alone in the house. I dispense with preambles and go straight to the heart of the matter: "Who are you? Are you our emissary to the Christians, or theirs to us?" It is not in my nature to wound or provoke, but the tone is set. It seems to me that the archbishop has blushed. He does not respond. He speaks to me of his childhood, his secular parents, his meeting in the Latin Quarter with a student chaplain at a moment when he was yearning for spirituality, religiosity. Had he met instead with a rabbi, I might have found myself today face to face with a rabbi. I ask him searching questions on his relationship with his new faith. His evident sincerity makes him seem vulnerable and profoundly disarming. I question him about his attitude toward his people, which judges severely those who abandon their religion. I ask about his father's reaction in March (his mother died in Auschwitz), when he attended his investiture in the crowded, illuminated cathedral. That last question elicits a smile: "He was happy . . . he who was not a believer was proud that his son had succeeded in his chosen religion." I persist: "But what about your great-grandfather, who surely would have chosen death rather than kiss the cross, what would he have thought as he saw you wearing the silver cross on your chest?" Again it appears to me that he has blushed. He lowers his voice: "To me, what matters is grace; it is the only thing that matters."

Around 1 p.m. he stands and says: "Let's have lunch, shall we?" In truth, neither one of us feels like eating. We continue the conversation, talking about current events as well as the past. Owing to its nature, much of our exchange shall remain confidential. Again and again we come back to his ambiguous, not to say ambivalent, attitude toward Judaism. Who are the "real Jews"? Could they really be those for whom faithfulness to Moses, Isaiah, and Rabbi Yehuda Ha-Nasi is obsolete and the laws of Torah are abolished?

True, the archbishop is not the first to have converted to Christianity, but those who preceded him never claimed to be good Jews, "fulfilled" Jews. But he insists that having been born a Jew, he will die a Jew. I try to explain to him why this stand seems untenable to us; I cite laws and customs. Then I use a concrete argument: His example may well encourage those who call themselves "Jews for Jesus" and whose proselytizing takes advantage of many young people who, in the absence of any spiritual bonds, have lost their way.

Abraham had already understood that Judaism means separation and choice. One cannot belong to two religions. True, it is the same God who governs our lives, but the paths that lead to Him are different.

"And yet I feel Jewish," the archbishop responds. "I refuse to renounce my roots, my Jewishness. How could I betray my mother's memory? It would be cowardly. And humiliating." He goes on to make the point that his Jewishness annoys anti-Semites and that this does not displease him. Why should he make them happy by turning his back on the people they execrate?

There is something about him that moves me. Is it his yearning for purity? Or his need to unite his Jewish past with his Christian future? I plead with him: "At least, cease defining yourself as a 'fulfilled Jew.'"

We resolve to remain in touch, to continue our discussions. And in fact we meet often, and the friendship that binds us has become deeper. He no longer uses the formula "fulfilled Jew" but is determined to remain a son of the Jewish people. He acts accordingly; anyone who requests his assistance in defending a Jewish cause can count on his support. In fact he participates in all the battles for human rights. He is an ally of all those who militate against fanaticism and injustice wherever they are found. No matter what the risk, he raises his voice in defense of the weak, the dispossessed, the victims. With his elevation to the rank of prince of the church, his influence continues to grow.

We sometimes smile as we evoke this extraordinary trajectory. "Admit," I say to him, "that Jewish history has a rare power of imagination." He admits it. But does he, as I do, have a sense of the surreal when we come face to face—he, the son of Polish immigrant Jews revered by millions of Catholics, and I, the talmudic student, the Jewish chronicler? One day he may be called to assume yet greater responsibilities. He is certain that he will not. I am not so sure.

How do his peers feel about him? I know many who greatly admire him and are devoted to him. But I am told that at the annual gatherings of French bishops he appears to be something of a loner. Though he is close to the Pope, he is sometimes at odds with one or another stance of the Curia. During the scandalous affair of the

Carmelite convent at Auschwitz, for example, his interventions must have raised a few eyebrows in Rome. As must his sympathy for the State of Israel, of which he is the most devoted defender inside the Catholic Church. He is a courageous, loyal man, profoundly bound to his faith but respectful of that of his father.

Our friendship will endure.

Upon publication of a book by the archbishop, I am asked to review it for *Le Monde*. I accept on condition that the archbishop agrees. Concerned about his reaction, I show him my article in advance. I am not prepared to modify it, but I am willing to withdraw it, if that is what he wishes. Although the article is not uncritical, he voices no objection. In the piece I speak of my great affection for him, but also of my sadness at his conversion, which has deprived the Jewish people of a great spiritual figure. I reaffirm my conviction that a Jew can only fulfill himself from within his Jewishness. Some Catholic readers found my attitude disrespectful and did not hesitate to insult and curse me in their letters, both private and public.

In the article I said:

> Cardinal Lustiger disturbs. That is no secret for anyone. He disturbs the Christian extremists because he still considers himself Jewish, and he disturbs the Jews because he became a Christian. He also worries and perturbs the secularists by preaching humanism through the faith and tolerance that are part of him. Whoever heard of a priest who is both a humanist and a liberal?

And I concluded:

> . . . And so, Cardinal Jean-Marie Lustiger and I continue to be friends and allies. He has chosen, or "God has chosen" for him, a path different from my own, but both deserve to be illuminated by the same light, for they lead to the same truth, whatever that truth may be.
>
> What matters is that like myself, Cardinal Lustiger proclaims that God alone is alone and that God alone is God and that He is everywhere, in what unites men but also in what keeps them apart. And also that even after the coming of the Messiah, son of David, mankind will not

become Jewish, but simply more human, more generous, more tolerant with one another.

In an old volume of midrashic commentaries and tales, I discovered a strange story that is said to have taken place in the Middle Ages. It is the tale of a Jewish child from Mainz, the son of Rabbi Shmuel, a wise man whose star had shone in faraway places. The boy was a prodigy, and when he was very young a priest took him from his parents and baptized him so that the church might benefit from his extraordinary intelligence. The child grew up in an atmosphere of piety and prayer and chose to become a priest and devote his life to God. Before long he was appointed bishop and was summoned to Rome, where he became secretary to the Pope and eventually succeeded him.

That is when he received a touching letter from the old priest in Mainz, requesting, at the end of a long life of devotion, to be appointed bishop. He argued that, after all, it was he, the humble country priest, who was ultimately responsible for his having risen to wear the papal tiara. He also told him the truth about his origins.

The Pope answered immediately: Yes, he would name him bishop. But first he was requested to inform the Jewish community that beginning immediately, all circumcisions and observances of Shabbat would be prohibited except if a delegation of scholars were to come to Rome to convince him, the Pope, that his decrees were unjust. And he insisted that Rabbi Shmuel be part of that delegation.

Rabbi Shmuel and his colleagues remained at the Vatican three days. They explained certain biblical laws to the Pope, who declared himself satisfied and immediately voided his decrees. When the time came for the delegates to take their leave, the Pope asked Rabbi Shmuel to postpone his departure by a few days so that they might discuss a topic related to the Kabbalah. Once they were alone, the Pope revealed his true identity to the visitor. Father and son embraced, never to leave each other.

I tell the Jewish cardinal this legend. He listens intently, without comment. I add that there are several versions circulating regarding the end of this strange Pope. Some say that he returned to Mainz, where he lived out his life as a good Jew. Others say that, fearing reprisal from the Christians, he had to go underground. Yet another story has it that he was assassinated.

One day on the telephone, my friend the cardinal addresses me

with the familiar *tu*. I wonder if I've heard right. And I don't know how
to respond. That a prince of the church should address me in this
manner strikes me as strange; but for a Jew like me to answer him in
kind seems even more so. Using caution, I speak indirectly in a
sequence of awkward circumlocutions. In the end I confess my embarrassment; he insists this is how he wants it. And so, during a television
program moderated by Frédéric Mitterrand (the president's nephew),
we both eschew the formal *vous*, something that is not customary on
television. "It would not be natural," is the cardinal's answer to my
expressions of doubt. Repeated several times, the program reaches a
sizable audience. The most beautiful compliment on it came from the
philosopher Emmanuel Levinas, first by way of the journalist Shlomo
Malka, then in person: "It was *kiddush hashem*—you sanctified the Lord's
name." In friendship, too, all is mystery for those who believe.

Our friendship endures. When fanatics in Israel insult him, I call
to tell him how much it pains me. We often consult each other when
confronted with problems related to Judeo-Christian relations.

One morning in 1987, I receive an invitation from the Vatican to
meet the Pope. It comes at a time when the Jewish world is in an
uproar over the Waldheim affair. It is my position that the leader of
the Catholic Church should not have received the Austrian president,
a former Nazi—in any case, not with such warmth.

Still, the cardinal encourages me to accept: "The Holy Father
knows your work." John Cardinal O'Connor of New York shares his
view: A conversation between the Pope and me could be useful. The
Vatican's influential Cardinal Casaroli, whom I meet "somewhere" in
Manhattan to avoid media attention, also agrees. I tell him that I am
ready to go to the Vatican, but for a conversation, not an audience.
Also, I would like it to be totally private and without strict time limits.
My most important condition is that there be no publicity. Cardinal
Casaroli tells me that he must consult Rome.

Eventually, I receive an affirmative response. I begin to prepare,
which for me means reviewing as much as I can of all that is known of
Judeo-Christian dialogue since the birth of Christianity and the first
debates between talmudic sages and members of the new sect. I study
the arguments of Flavius Josephus against Apion and those, in the
twelfth century, of Rabbi Joseph Kamhi of Narbonne, the disputations
between Nahmanides and a supposedly erudite convert in the cathedral
of Barcelona. The sources are rich and varied. I uncover corroborations
as I compare ancient and modern texts. Finally, in August, I am ready.

That is when the *New York Times* announces my upcoming meeting with the head of the Catholic Church. Who is responsible for the leak? I am told that someone at the Vatican wanted to sabotage the encounter. True or not, the meeting that was intended to be private loses all meaning as it risks turning into a media spectacle. Journalists start calling, asking for interviews. Many of them insist on accompanying me to Rome. I begin to have serious doubts; better to give up the project or at least postpone it.

And all during this time, a number of rabbis are calling me frantically. It seems they have obtained an "audience" with the Pope, to take place one week after my "conversation"; the nuance is significant, and they worry that for the press my visit will overshadow theirs. When I inform them of my decision not to go to the Vatican, they are overjoyed.

In truth, the Pope has troubled me for a long time. I reproached him for his first speech at Auschwitz, in which he never once used the word "Jew." He then went on to celebrate a mass for the victims, all victims. Why did he not invite a rabbi and nine more Jews to recite Kaddish for the murdered Jews? Did he really believe that a Christian mass was the appropriate prayer to honor their memory?

Soon thereafter he came to the U.N. Once again he disappointed me. Israel was not mentioned in his address.

And yet.

As I record these memories I must admit that recently I have been pleasantly surprised by the Pope. Has he changed, or have I? I see him as more open, more tolerant. His visit to the synagogue in Rome, the concert in the Vatican commemorating the Holocaust, his warnings against anti-Semitism and, most important, his decision, however belated, to open diplomatic relations with Israel. It may well be that Jewish history will remember him as a benevolent and merciful Pope.

Sometimes it seems astonishing, not to say miraculous, when non-Jews understand the nature and intensity of Jewish anguish of the past and Jewish hope for the future. Some would like to understand. Some actually do.

The question is: Can one erase two thousand years of suspicion and persecution endured under the shadow of the cross? The answer is no, one cannot; nor should one. Only if we forget nothing shall we succeed in abolishing what divides us. Cardinal Lustiger knows this.

And I am his friend.

A Museum in Washington

WASHINGTON, D.C., January 1979. On this icy winter day the White House looks whiter than ever, a calm, sleepy citadel. One of its stately drawing rooms is filled with excitement. Elated Holocaust survivors greet each other, shake each other's hands, embrace. It's the first time they have met in this historic place. A woman with numbers tattooed on her arm is whispering: "It's like a dream. . . . I'm afraid to wake up." And another: "Never could I have imagined this."

Nor could I.

"We have gathered here in this hall which echoes with history—the Declaration of Independence has been hanging on these walls for generations—to try to find appropriate ways to remember what it meant to live and die in the age of darkness." With these words I open the inaugural session of the President's Commission on the Holocaust, created by Jimmy Carter a few months earlier.

House Speaker "Tip" O'Neill has come to swear us in. Members of Congress, Jewish leaders, rabbis, priests, scholars, and journalists are in the audience. Discreetly, Marion reviews the text of a talk I am about to give. She knows it well for having edited it. Sigmund Strochlitz smiles, visibly moved. Benjamin Meed, a Warsaw survivor, doesn't bother to hide his tears. "This is the crowning moment of my life," he tells me, "the most joyous." This is his favorite expression. He will repeat it at every stage of this undertaking. I try to conceal my feelings. As always, I fear disappointment.

Today we are soaring. At last the American government, on the highest level, is showing interest in our past. At last our past is free to emerge from the depths to which it has been consigned. But I am ill at ease; though an agenda has been prepared for me, this is the first time I am chairing a session of this magnitude. And not surprisingly, at this moment, as always, I see myself back in Sighet. How far away it seems, this little town where a Jewish boy begged God to teach him to pray better, study better.

My friend Justice Arthur Goldberg had given me some good advice on how to preside. To me, my opening remarks to the members of the commission are like the preface to a book. Some excerpts:

> It is with a deep sense of duty, privilege, and humility that I agreed to serve as chairman of this uniquely distinguished group of civic, religious, and political leaders.
>
> Some of you, I know, are worthier than I, and most of you are surely more experienced in this kind of endeavor. With your help and cooperation, I hope we shall fulfill our task.
>
> The problems facing us may seem insurmountable. We are supposed to remember, and to move others to remember. But how does one remember, individually and collectively, an event that was intended to erase memory?
>
> By its scope and immeasurable magnitude, its sheer weight of numbers, by its mystery and silence, the Holocaust defies anything the human being can conceive of or aspire to.
>
> All the documents, all the testimony, all the eyewitness accounts, all the history books notwithstanding, we know that we have not yet begun to tell the tale.
>
> How does one reconcile—this is another question that we shall have to face—the purely Jewish aspects of the tragedy with its inevitable universal connotations? True, all Jews were victims; but not all victims were Jewish.
>
> How are they to be remembered? Specifically? Collectively? Individually? Personally? Through monuments? Education? Special liturgy? Ceremonies of remembrance?
>
> We lack a reference point. We don't know what to do because of the uniqueness of the event. We cannot even go back into history and learn that this is what people used to do to commemorate such events, because there was no such event.
>
> Also, whatever our purposes will be—and I hope they will be lofty and daring—we must remember at least this:

that we must think boldly. Let the scope and magnitude of our endeavor not frighten us.

Whatever we do, let it strike the imagination of people everywhere, of all faiths, of all creeds, of all nationalities, of all nations, and perhaps of all centuries.

Let people know that our generation—probably the last that still has something to remember—does indeed remember.

. . . We around this table represent a noble quest for memory and justice. We are all committed to truth. And though we come from different horizons, we shall respect one another's beliefs.

The Holocaust was possible because the enemy—the enemy of the Jewish people and of mankind, and it is always the same enemy—succeeded in dividing, in separating, in splitting the human society: nation against nation, Christian against Jew, young against old.

. . . Forgive me for introducing into this session a note of melancholy. While we are grateful to President Carter and his advisers for being so deeply concerned with the Holocaust now, I cannot but wonder what would have happened had the president of the United States then, and his advisers then, demonstrated the same concern.

If a presidential commission had been appointed in 1942 or 1943 to prevent the Holocaust, how many victims—Jews and non-Jews—would have been saved?

Well, they were forgotten while they were alive. They are dead now. Let us at least remember them and include their memory in our own. . . .

It all began one summer day in 1978, at the Sharon Hotel in Herzliyya. The head of the Israeli opposition, Shimon Peres, is in my room telling me about his new book, when the phone rings. It is Stu Eizenstat, President Carter's youthful adviser for internal affairs. He wants to know why I have not returned his calls. I laugh: For several days the concierge has been handing me messages asking me to call the White House. I honestly thought it was a prank. "Is that you, Professor?" He goes on to tell me that the president wants me to chair the "commission charged with proposing the manner in which to erect a monument to the memory of Holocaust victims." I remember my journalist's reaction, immediate but unvoiced: "The name is too long." What I did say was: "Please thank the president for the honor he wishes to bestow on me, but . . ." The White House official cannot imagine that there could be a "but."

I tell him that I don't think this position is for me; I'm not a political person; I have no desire to become one; all I want is time to write and study. Eizenstat's last words: "Please reconsider." He calls back the next day. When I tell him I haven't changed my mind, he informs me that the president wishes to see me. This I cannot refuse. The appointment is set for the following week.

An hour later I receive urgent calls from Yitz Greenberg— my former colleague at City College—and Sigmund Strochlitz. Both are aware of my conversation with the White House. Each, separately, tells me the genesis of the president's invitation. The president had invited a thousand rabbis to the Rose Garden as a gesture of conciliation—his relations with Begin were tense, and he wanted to appease Jewish public opinion. The idea of the monument had come from Eizenstat.

It is impossible not to see the public relations game involved. I tell my friends: "This confirms my doubts: We must never use the Holocaust for political purposes." Still, they beg me to accept. Sigmund tries to win me over by sentiment; Yitz by logic. I stand fast: My time is limited; I need it for my writing and my students. "But this is a unique opportunity to work on the highest level to ensure remembrance," says Yitz. "It would be a pity to let it slip by or to allow some opportunist to take advantage of it." Sigmund: "If you refuse, some politician or other will be nominated. Who knows what he'll do with our memories." To settle the discussion I suggest we wait for my meeting with President Carter. I'll make the decision afterward. Marion's view: "I know how much this means to you, but if you accept, turn this project into a living memorial, not just a monument."

At the appointed hour I present myself at the White House gate. I'm always afraid of policemen, but these are polite, smiling; diplomats in uniform. Ed Sanders, the president's adviser for Jewish affairs, is waiting for me. "Will it bother you if I'm present?" On the contrary, I'm pleased. This way, if I say something foolish he can intervene. He says, "I'll leave you alone with him toward the end. In case you have confidential matters to discuss."

I am nervous, but the president's smile reassures me and instantly restores my confidence. We sit down opposite each other. Sanders takes a chair slightly off to the side. The president tells me he's read some of my writings and quotes some short passages from memory. The skeptic in me whispers that an aide must have prepared some appropriate quotations. I thank the president, who proceeds to quote another sentence from another work of mine. And, with his famous smile, he adds: "I have something for you. I asked my CIA director, Stan Turner, to go through our archives for material on the places where you were held prisoner. This is what he found." He holds out to me a file stuffed with photos, and we look at them together. (Later I will offer copies of them to the Yad Vashem museum in Jerusalem.) Taken by an American bomber flying over Auschwitz in 1944, they show the camp in broad daylight. I learn later that the navigator forgot to stop the camera that was filming the dropping of the bombs.

"I remember that day," I say to the president. "American planes had been bombing the factories surrounding the camp. Germans were holing up in their shelters. As for us, the inmates, we were praying for the Americans to reserve some bombs for our barbed-wire fences, our watchtowers, our barracks. Since we were going to die, let it be for something."

Bent over the photos, the president follows my finger, which moves from Auschwitz to Birkenau, from block to block. "Here is the ramp, the chimneys." He listens to my commentary with an intensity that touches me. I ask: "Were these photos available to the president in 1944?" "Yes, they were." "Then President Roosevelt couldn't help but know what was going on in Auschwitz?" "That is correct." "And nevertheless he did nothing. Why? Why did he refuse to bomb the railways leading to Birkenau?" The president seems uneasy, lost in thought. He doesn't answer. When he looks at me, his smile is gone. He asks: "What can be done now?" I remain silent; does he expect an answer? He already knows the answer, for he continues: "We must fight oblivion. Isn't that the purpose of all your work?"

Which brings us back to the question: Am I going to accept the nomination? I say yes, but . . . but what? "I'm against the idea of a monument." I tell him that Jewish tradition is opposed to monuments. After all, when Jews left a country, they had to leave all they had built. What do I propose in its place? I suggest a teaching project, a national Day of Remembrance, preferably in Congress—in the form of a solemn joint session of Senate and House—or perhaps at the White House, with the president's participation. The president gives his consent. Will he come to the first ceremony? Yes, he will.

I have one more request. I would like his permission to take a fact-finding mission to Eastern Europe to revisit the sites: Treblinka, Auschwitz, Babi-Yar. "Why not," says the president, "that is only normal." I glance toward Sanders: He's in tears. As I leave, I say to the president: "If this project succeeds, Jewish history will never forget you."

The president's willingness to place his administration in the service of memory touched me. For I am painfully aware of the real, constant threat of forgetting. The Talmud says of Moses that by night he forgot what he had learned during the day. Elsewhere our sages insist on the fact that sometimes the Torah was forgotten. We do not even remember God's own ineffable Name. How then can we hope that our own experiences will be preserved?

I leave the Oval Office with a title. From now on, by the grace and authority of the president, I may speak on his behalf, having assumed responsibility for what, in my own head, I have already named the "President's Commission on the Holocaust." Yitz Greenberg will be its director. He chooses as his assistant Michael Berenbaum, a young rabbi from Wesleyan University whose doctoral thesis deals with my writings. Marian Craig, a former White House employee, a young woman as lovely as she is efficient, will be the soul and the professional organizer of the team. I call Marion: "I hope you like Washington. . . . We'll be coming here often."

All at once I'm besieged by requests, congratulations, suggestions, insinuations; suddenly I am surrounded by people who seem to have only one purpose in life—to become members of the commission. Senators, members of the House, business tycoons all telephone to intercede on behalf of their donors or protégés. This one was at Mauthausen, that one makes speeches about Majdanek. There is no end to the pressures. I never thought that this project would generate so much interest. My problem is that I don't know how to say no. Luckily the White House people know how, but their criteria are not always mine. Theirs are mostly political. Mine are simple: I would like to gather as many survivors as possible. Sigmund, who has become my right hand, advises me. As does Yitz, of course. So they, too, become targets of pressure. Mark Talisman, a former associate of Congressman Charles Vanik, and Hyman Bookbinder, of the American Jewish Committee, know best who is most important in the capital; they help us with the recruiting. We choose Bayard Rustin, human rights activist and organizer of the Martin Luther King, Jr., march on Washington; Theodore Hesburgh, president of Notre Dame University; former Supreme Court Justice and Ambassador to the U.N. Arthur Goldberg; and also historians, theologians, philosophers, and teachers who have devoted years to studying, exploring, and interpreting the Holocaust. Among the survivors, Yossel Rosensaft is sadly missing. But his widow, Hadassah, joins my team. Some survivors are rejected by the White House. I protest in vain. So I create a board of advisers and make them members.

There is much work to do. Arthur gives me the benefit of his experience. Having presided over many commissions, he knows how to survive them. He knows when to be tolerant and when to be inflexible, when to encourage and when to call firmly and tactfully to order. Arthur is one of this country's most respected men. The fact that he is a member of my commission surrounds us with a protective zone.

I had first met him with Yitzhak Rabin, who had just been appointed Israel's ambassador to the United States. Arthur had told me about his war years, and how as an officer of the OSS he had occasion to converse with Arthur Zygelbojm, the Jewish Socialist leader, member of the Polish Parliament in exile in London. He described to me how Zygelbojm, in tears, pleaded the cause of Jews in occupied Poland. He was convinced that if only America knew what was happening, it would force the Germans to halt the massacres. Goldberg felt that it was his obligation to tell him the truth. Soon after, Zygelbojm killed himself. Surely this was one reason why Goldberg, after the war, became a fierce defender of Jewish memory and human rights.

The inaugural session begins with a solemn ceremony. After the traditional minute of silence, I invite every member of the commission to introduce himself or herself. Each expresses his or her gratitude to the American people and its leaders for this initiative. My friend Senator Henry "Scoop" Jackson from Washington State comes by to demonstrate his support. He thanks President Carter for choosing me to lead this commission. Senators and representatives of both parties are enthusiastic. Sigmund speaks of Bendin and Rabbi Gottschalk of Berlin. There is a special dimension to their speeches, which seem to be drawn from the most secret zone of their being. Some are sentimental, others matter-of-fact. All are solemn.

After the morning session I ask Yitz to gather nine men in a private room. For that day, the 18th day of Sh'vat, is the anniversary of my father's death, and I must recite the Kaddish. The impromptu minyan attracts more than the requisite quorum. Even non-Jews attend. In accordance with tradition, I officiate. I repeat the *Amidah*, with its eighteen benedictions. Suddenly, my voice breaks. I cannot suppress the sob that rises and chokes me. I see my father's face, his many faces: the one I saw on Shabbat; the one at the Sighet railway station; the one I saw in camp, during the first few days; and finally, the one of the end. I look at him, and he looks at me, as if to ask me what I am doing here, at the White House. This has never happened before, but I cannot go on. I try to hold back my tears as I implore my father not to go away, not to abandon me among all these strangers. Did I shout the Kaddish? Did I whisper it? It stays with me when the session resumes that afternoon.

We appoint the special committees: education, finance, international relations, and a "committee of conscience," which could just as well have been named "human rights commission." To Sigmund, I assign the task of organizing the annual "Remembrance Week" ceremonies. I share my thoughts: Since it is forbidden to remain silent and impossible to speak, how does one commemorate a community massacred a thousand times? What prayer must one recite, what forms must one invent?

From the very beginning, the meetings are dominated by the question of the specificity or universality of the Holocaust. Does our mandate apply only to the Jewish victims? What about the Gypsies? The Poles? The Ukrainians? And the homosexuals? After all, other nations, other ethnic and social groups, also endured the horrors of the Nazi regime. For instance: I am haunted by the tragedy of the Armenians, which inspired Hitler to remark, speaking of the Jews: "Who will remember them? Who still remembers the massacre of the Armenians?" But if we included the Armenians, why then would we exclude the Cambodians? We have passionate discussions, stormy sessions. Arthur Goldberg maintains that since our mandate contains a specific name, the Holocaust, it refers exclusively to the tragic fate of the Jews. Other members of the commission, Americans of Polish, Ukrainian, or Lithuanian descent, don't agree. My position is that the Holocaust is a Jewish tragedy with universal implications. Any attempt to dilute or extrapolate it can only distort its meaning. As a

Jew, my duty is to evoke the Jewish tragedy. But in so doing, I incite other groups to commemorate their own.

Behind the scenes, I rely on Saul Lieberman, Yossi Ciechanover, Bernie Fischman. And, of course, Marion. I do nothing without asking her advice.

I have already referred to Dr. Lieberman and to Yossi. Bernie is a lawyer, a humanist: I don't know anyone as concerned with human rights as Bernie. As soon as he has knowledge of a violation committed anywhere, of any injustice that strikes any human being, there he is, sounding the alarm. I believe him to be the best informed, most passionate man in the world. He and his colleague Arnie Forster have provided me with the information that has allowed me to become involved in more than one fight on behalf of prisoners and victims.

Three months after its inauguration, the commission organizes its first ceremony of remembrance. It takes place in the Rotunda, the great hall of the Capitol. This is where the nation honors the memory of its heroes. It is where, in 1963, its leaders came to pay their final homage to JFK.

Of course all Washington is present. President Carter has kept his promise. He participates in the ceremony. From that day on, thanks to Sigmund's efforts, similar ceremonies will take place in all fifty states of the country.

As we begin, President Carter notices a small boy sitting opposite us, next to his mother. "Who is that?" he asks me. "My son, Elisha." "How old is he?" "Seven." The President motions him to come forward. Bewildered but poised, Elisha leaves Marion and joins us. He will watch the program sitting on the President's knee, a photo that will make the front pages. When asked, he sums up his reaction: "It was pretty uncomfortable—the president's knees are kind of hard."

President Carter speaks movingly and conveys a strong sense of history. But I am troubled by his reference to "eleven million victims." In the car that takes us back to the White House, I ask him where he obtained this figure. The source: the writings and speeches of Simon Wiesenthal. He insists on including all victims: six million Jews and five million non-Jews. I tell the president that this figure does not reflect the facts. The president is astonished: "Are you saying that there were no non-Jews in the camps?" I explain to him that yes, there were, and some of them were heroes of the Resistance and brave humanists, but that they did not number five million; they were a fraction of that figure. Among the others there were fierce anti-Semites and sadistic criminals whom the Germans released from their prisons in order to supervise the camps. "Would it be just, Mr. President, to honor their memory together with that of my parents?" The president never cited this figure again.

The ceremonies of remembrance, established by act of Congress, become annual events. I claim paternity, but their exemplary execution is assured by Sigmund, who invests in them his time, talent, and passion. We owe him our gratitude. I am also deeply grateful to President Carter for spontaneously accepting, at our first meeting, the idea of an annual commemorative session. Of all the projects related to my work in Washington, this is the one that has given me a genuine sense of accomplishment.

Meanwhile we are actively preparing our official trip to Eastern Europe. There is no problem with pre-Jaruzelski Poland. All the visas are granted, all requests agreed to. Not so with the USSR. The Soviet Embassy here informs us that all decisions will be made in Moscow. To avoid the looming difficulties, Arthur Goldberg accompanies me to the Soviet Embassy. He knows Ambassador Anatoly Dobrynin well, and we enjoy a cordial, friendly conversation. Though this is before the Russian intervention in Afghanistan, there is plenty of distrust. What might be the purpose of a commission of inquiry in the USSR, if in fact that is what it is, the Ambassador asks. He understands that we might want to conduct an investigation in Poland, but what might we be looking for in Moscow? I mention Babi-Yar. Well, yes, he can possibly understand Babi-Yar, but Babi-Yar is in Ukraine. How to tell him something he surely guesses, that my wish to go back to Moscow is only vaguely connected with our declared mission? Since 1966, I have been dreaming of returning to "my" Jews of silence. On the pretext that hotels were overbooked, I have been systematically refused a visa. Now, as head of a presidential delegation, I shall get it. Dobrynin confirms this to me.

Still, I don't obtain everything I request. Until August 1979, almost to the eve of our departure, the Soviets stubbornly refuse to issue visas to two members of my party, Yitz Greenberg and Miles Lerman. I learn of this in France, where, with Marion and Elisha, I am spending a few weeks completing *The Testament*. There follows a flurry of transatlantic conversations. My own feeling is that we must show solidarity and inform the Soviet authorities that, because we don't have visas for everyone, we are canceling our trip. Sigmund Strochlitz alone supports me. Hyman Bookbinder counsels moderation. Yitz's assistant, Michael Berenbaum, urges us to go forward. In his view, our mission should proceed as planned, never mind the "undesirables." Clearly we are not on the same wavelength.

Another incident interferes with our preparations. The Union of Soviet Writers offers to give a dinner in our honor. I accept. This will be the first time I shall be able to converse with people likely to have known the Jewish writers Der Nister and Peretz Markish. But I ask to see the guest list. Evidently displeased, the Union directors politely answer that the guest list is their business. I don't remember what made me do it, but I remain firm: In that case, no dinner. The list arrives a day later. The Yiddish poet Aaron Vergelis is on it. An unrepentant Stalinist, he is unacceptable to me. Russian Jewish writers in both Israel and the United States have proffered serious charges against him. I myself heard him telling New York reporters in the midsixties that Russian Jews were living very well, that they enjoyed full freedom, and that campaigns on their behalf were based on lies. In his monthly magazine he went so far as to accuse me of being a CIA agent—why else would I fight so hard against the Soviet Union and Communism? And so, while I have no wish to judge him, I also have no desire to shake his hand. The Writers Union reacts angrily: It is their privilege to decide which of their members will attend their dinner. I respond that, in that case, we too will decide with whom we dine. A new list arrives: Vergelis's name has disappeared. Finally, everything appears settled.

The delegation includes several members of the commission, members of the advisory board, and representatives of various Jewish organizations, among them Judy and Irving Bernstein, of UJA, and the Miami art collectors Irma and Norman Braman.

A native of Poland, Benjamin Meed insists on my sending him to Warsaw ahead of the delegation, as a kind of scout. He implores me to entrust him with the mission of making sure that our program is set by us and not by our hosts. "I know the Poles," he says. "We had better be careful." My instructions to him are simple and precise. From the airport we shall go first to the Ghetto to pay homage at the Monument to the Ghetto Fighters. Only then shall we go wherever our hosts wish to take us.

Surrounded by a welcoming committee from the Veterans' Ministry, Meed is waiting for us at the airport. He looks undone, forlorn. I never would have guessed he could behave so submissively. He tells me it has been decided that we will be taken directly to the Polish monument, the one in the capital. His manner is pathetic. Evidently, for him, our hosts are not much different from the authorities he knew and feared long ago. "I tried to explain to them," he says, his face crimson with embarrassment, "I really tried."

In a VIP lounge, sitting around a table with the officials, we try to find a solution to this first crisis. Not being a diplomat, I take a firm stand that surprises even me. (Whatever happened to the shy Talmud student from Sighet?) I tell our hosts that we are here on behalf of the president of the United States for reasons not of foreign policy but of moral conscience linked to the memory of the Holocaust. Therefore either they will take us at once to the Ghetto, or else we shall, however regretfully, leave on the first plane out. The Polish officials stare in amazement and give in. Surely they did not realize what it meant to us, Jewish survivors, to walk on the Ghetto's hallowed ground. They cannot understand why we insist so much on the Jewishness of the Jewish victims. After all, they lament, Poland lost six million citizens, of which only three million were Jews. They ask: "Weren't we also victims of the Germans?" I reply: "Yes, you were. But we were the victims' victims as well."

This is my first visit to Warsaw, a city I learned to know and love from books. In fact, since Auschwitz, I have not been back to Poland. Is this how I had imagined my return? We move from frustration to frustration. The atmosphere is oppressive. Vanished is the Jewish Warsaw of Roman Vishniac, with its hungry students and their unfulfilled dreams. Aharon Zeitlin's Tlomacki 13, Isaac Bashevis Singer's poverty-stricken Nalevki, all these places immortalized by Jewish writers gone up in smoke. Warsaw, the most Jewish of all Jewish cities in the Diaspora, will not be Jewish again. Ever.

Most of the officials we encounter are courteous, even friendly, but I cannot help feeling that we are in inhospitable territory. People are not used to seeing so many Jews here. Are they afraid that we have come to claim what was stolen from us? I have heard too often of survivors being chased away from their former homes by their new occupants: "What are you doing here? Weren't you killed?"

It is difficult to rid ourselves of the malaise that weighs on us. There is constant tension. The minister of justice, Mr. Buffa, is another disappointment. I expected more from a man entrusted with safeguarding justice. I speak to him of the "deniers," those who on five continents deny the Holocaust. The discussions are exhausting, endless. There's a sense of having to fight for every scrap of truth. Exasperated, I finally cry out: "To whom can we turn for justice if not to the minister of justice?" I don't know why, but at last there is a reaction. He suddenly becomes conciliatory and agrees to most of our requests: the opening of the archives, the exchange of documents, the creation of a joint commission to handle pending problems and unresolved matters.

We leave for Cracow.

Auschwitz. The watchtowers. The barbed wire.

Our guides are waiting for us at the camp entrance. They talk and talk. Marion makes them understand that we don't need explanations. This is the first time I am back.

Auschwitz a museum! That is what is left—a museum. The plaque is offensive, deceitful. Evidently there have never been any Jews here, or if there were, they arrived here by accident, visitors who lost their way. To satisfy the curiosity and appease the feelings of foreign visitors, especially Americans, a Jewish block has been created. And it is closed, most of the time, "for repairs." Schiller's question, "History will judge society, but who will judge History?" comes to mind.

Surely it will be judged by its victims.

I walk past "my" block. The memories rush back: the first days, the first nights at Auschwitz; the apprenticeship of hunger, of death. The terrifying block 11: the prison inside prison. A place one left only for the scaffold or the firing squad. And where is Yossel Rosensaft's dark cell? They all look alike. Dark. Stifling.

We continue on to Birkenau. Here too, it is the first time I am back in this cursed place. A steel fist is pounding at my lungs. It is daylight, but we are enveloped by night.

The silence of Birkenau is a silence unlike any other. It contains the screams, the strangled prayers of thousands of human beings condemned to vanish into the darkness of nameless, endless ashes. Human silence at the core of inhumanity. Deadly silence at the core of death. Eternal silence under a moribund sky.

As I return to Birkenau, centuries after leaving it, I leave reality behind and find myself face to face with the adolescent I was then. Only now it all seems calm, almost peaceful. I close my eyes, and from the depths of time, hallucinating images appear. The thick smoke, the small heaps of ashes. Blank-faced men running in all directions. In Birkenau, no one moved slowly, especially not Death, which after all must be everywhere at once.

Life, death: a frantic race from one to the other. Here the future was reduced to the instant preceding the selection and departure. "I'll remember you all my life," someone said to his neighbor. In an hour he was no more. Here one had to pursue the present before it vanished into nothingness. You ran to wash, you ran to dress, you ran to get your portion of bread, margarine, soup. You ran for roll call, you ran to work, you ran from one block to another, from one man to another, in search of a familiar face, yearning for a word of consolation.

The barking of the dogs—I remember it with painful precision. The howling of the killers. The noise truncheons make when they crack people's necks. The silent pain of the starving prisoners, weak, defeated, humiliated. I'll remember all this forever.

Moshe-Chaim Berkowitz, my childhood friend, a generous and deeply religious man, points to something on our left. What is he remembering? He had arrived with the first transport, a week before me. He may well be showing me the Chief Rabbi, the Rebbe of Bor-she, or the Rebbe of Kretchenev, all gone without leaving a trace. I watch his lips moving. He is reciting a psalm. So am I.

How peaceful it all looks now, on this sunny day in August. The wind ruffles the gray-white clouds above us. And I remember.

The third week of May. It was cold. Hilda and Bea were silent. Jumping down from the cattle car, a small golden-haired girl put on her coat. "Button up," said her mother. The little golden-haired girl, so beautiful, so calm, obeyed. My eyes followed her. I see her still, through my tears, I see her carried away by the crowd, disappearing into the distance, a well-behaved little girl, so very well behaved, with a poignantly beautiful smile, a little Jewish girl with a dreamy but worried face, a shining light high above a shipwreck. It is enough to close your eyes a second for time to grab you and sweep you back to the past. There, nothing has changed. There is a level of existence where nothing ever changes.

Birkenau: I had not realized that the camp was quite small; could this really be the black hole of time, like the one scientists situate in space? It has swallowed an entire people, with its princes and its beggars, its old people and its children, a people with hopes and memories.

Between Birkenau and Auschwitz, it is Birkenau that continues to resonate most strongly in my memory; Auschwitz today is too well tended, too well maintained. And the reality of Auschwitz surpassed anything a museum could display. As the years go by, I have less and less confidence in museums as sanctuaries of memory. That is not the case with Birkenau. Birkenau today resembles the Birkenau of long ago. You only have to bend down to the ground to find the ashes that fell from the sky long ago, dispersing to the four winds the pitiful remains of Jewish children.

We walk through the camp. Here too, a guide wishes to be helpful by providing explanations and commentaries. We pretend to be listening. Here is the ramp, and the railroad tracks that linked this place to every Jewish center of the Continent, ultimately converging on the immense altar of fire whose flames touched, must have touched, the celestial throne. The night of our arrival, in May, we had no way of understanding the meaning of that ramp. We were stunned; we thought we had blundered into a nightmare. So this was where the ramp was. The crossroads. The turning point. Josef Mengele. With a flick of his wrist he showed the way to death. By dawn there was little left of our convoy.

I believe I've read all that has been written about this supreme site of evil. I believe I know everything, can guess everything, about the victims' final hours. I shall say nothing. As we get closer to the place where the killers built their gas chambers and their crematories, we clench our teeth and repress the desire to scream, to yell, to sob. As we stand in what was once the antechamber of death those of us who had been there hold each other's arms. Time is suspended. We remain silent, each with his or her own thoughts. And then, softly at first, then louder and louder, I recite the prayer of the Jewish martyrs; the others join in. "Shma Yisrael. . . ." Hear, O Israel, the Lord is our God, the Lord is One. Once, five times. . . . Why? Because back then, the victims, knowing the end was near, recited that prayer. We needed to show our solidarity with those we loved and still love. And then because, on the threshold of death, all words become prayers, and all prayers become one.

In the open railroad cars that transported us, in a violent snowstorm, in January 1945, from Auschwitz to Buchenwald, we had also shouted that same prayer. With our last breath we wanted to proclaim our faith in Him Who is the source of all faith. Yes, in spite of Auschwitz, God is unique; yes, in spite of the killers, God is our God.

Once again a heavy silence envelops us. I imagine it is not unlike the one that preceded the Revelation at Sinai. The Talmud has this poetic description: "the silence was such that the cattle stopped bellowing, the dogs stopped barking, the wind stopped blowing, the sea stopped heaving, and the birds gave up chattering. . . . The universe held its breath, in expectation of the Divine word. . . ."

Sixteen years later, during the ceremonies of the fiftieth anniversary of the liberation of Auschwitz and Birkenau, I say these words, which will offend some Christians:

> God of forgiveness, do not forgive those who created this place. God of mercy, have no mercy on those who killed Jewish children here. Do not forgive the murderers or their accomplices whose work was to kill. . . . Remember the nocturnal processions of children, so many children, all so wise, so frightened, so beautiful. . . .
>
> God of compassion, have no compassion for those who had none. . . .

I spoke without hatred. With anger? Yes. And grief. It was at Birkenau that I had discovered the kind of evil that saps all joy.

When I return to Cracow on February 6, 1995, I am welcomed at the airport by the American ambassador, Nicholas Rey, and several Polish officials. I get the full VIP treatment, no police formalities. Three bodyguards are assigned to me full-time. Cars with gyroscopes and sirens rush me through seemingly empty streets. In short, much noise and solemnity. This time I represent President Bill Clinton. Together with Undersecretary of State Richard Holbrooke, I lead the U.S. delegation to the fiftieth-anniversary celebration of the liberation of Auschwitz.

My heart is heavy with anguish. I wonder if I did the right thing in coming. I have attended a great many ceremonies of remembrance. This time it's different. The number fifty has special meaning and symbolism. That is why heads of state, dignitaries, and survivors have gathered here, invited by Lech Walesa, president of the Polish Republic.

But this event has provoked many polemics, and the world media have a time of it for several weeks. There are two sides: on the one, the Warsaw authorities; on the other, the Jewish organizations, and in particular, the World Jewish Congress. Until November, the International Auschwitz Committee—presided over by a former Belgian deportee, Baron Maurice Goldstein—had been in charge of the program. Then the chancery of the president took over. Weighed down by bureaucracy, it seems to have gone from misstep to misstep: invitations sent out too late or not at all, ambiguous statements and decisions that offend Jewish sensitivities.

For example, the official program that was sent to me in New York included the Jewish prayers for the dead in a manner that was disconcerting, not to say insolent. Scheduled to start off the event were sirens and the welcoming of crowned heads and dignitaries, followed by accolades and speeches, and then, after all the dignitaries had left, those who wished to recite the prayers for the dead could do so. In other words: the Kaddish and the *El Maleh Rakhamim* were to be kind of optional appendices. In response to a question from a *New York Times* reporter, I said that if no change were made, I would not make my speech and instead would recite the Kaddish myself.

Faced with the scandalous attitude of the organizers, I even considered staying away altogether. Why should I go to Poland to participate in a media operation that could only dishonor the Jewish memory of the victims?

One thing was clear: The Polish officials meant to de-Judaize the tragedy of Auschwitz. This is not new. Beginning in 1945 and under the Communist regime until the nineties, every effort was made to remove or at least curtail the intrinsic Jewish aspect of that tragedy. There was talk only about anti-Fascist and anti-Nazi victims, of Polish citizens and political prisoners. They forgot—or at least wanted other people to forget—that even non-Jewish historians had postulated that 90 percent of the murdered victims in this death factory had been Jews. And all this was still going on under the administration of Solidarity's founder, Lech Walesa, whom I had taken with me to Birkenau and Auschwitz in 1988. Had he understood nothing of what I had said to him then?

In fact, the problem transcends individuals. It must be posed in psychohistorical terms: Why, when it came to the Jewish past, did the Polish people, in its collective conscience, seek to forget? Because it felt guilty? Because it envied the Jews' martyrdom? Or was it merely convenient to remove the Jewish component from the general suffering under the German Occupation?

It may seem paradoxical, but if in the end I decided to accept President Walesa's invitation, it was precisely because of the controversies surrounding this fiftieth anniversary. I convinced myself that I did not have the right to evade the issues. Perhaps in my dual role of Nobel laureate and representative of the American president, and with a little luck, I might succeed in building some kind of consensus.

I miss Marion: I need her advice, her support. But she refused to join me. She has never liked ceremonies.

Two friends accompany me: Sigmund Strochlitz, himself a survivor of Auschwitz, and Pierre Huth, a Paris dentist whose father was the *Schreiber*, the scribe, of the infamous block 11, the punishment block, at Auschwitz.

The Forum Hotel in Cracow is a real anthill, its atmosphere that of a huge international convention. Polish security agents and bodyguards are whispering into tiny microphones. Delegates and journalists are calling out to one another in every European language. Everyone is busy, rushing here or there. All the foreign delegations are expected at the ancient Jagiellonian University for a solemn session to be addressed by President Walesa. I'm not going. My empty chair—between Polish President Walesa's and German President Herzog's—will raise eyebrows. It will be interpreted, rightly, as a protest against the official policy of de-Judaization.

Moreover, at the same time, the Jewish representatives are organizing an entirely Jewish ceremony at Birkenau. I choose to join them.

The day before, Marion had transmitted to me from New York an invitation to a private luncheon with Walesa at Wawel Palace. I would have accepted, of course, if only to try to resolve the conflict. But there is no way for me to return from Birkenau in time. After some negotiation, U.S. Ambassador Nicholas Rey informs me that the meeting has been changed to that evening.

I feel better. Surely Walesa will realize that if he maintains his stand on the prayers, his country's image will be tarnished. After all, what am I asking for? A few minutes to recite a few prayers. Is that too much? No. I'm no longer concerned: This unique commemoration will take place with dignity after all.

I leave for Birkenau.

The ceremony there is moving. The speaker of the Israeli Parliament, Shevah Weiss, who is of Polish origin, speaks in both Hebrew and Polish. I begin in Yiddish and continue in English. I speak at length on a topic that has haunted me since 1945: the children. I keep seeing them, that first night. And I keep seeing a beautiful little girl with blue eyes and golden hair. I keep seeing my little sister whom my father made laugh, my little sister who makes me weep every time I think of her and her smile.

Later that day, at Wawel Palace, there is a meeting of Nobel laureates, representatives from several international organizations, and heads of foreign delegations. The purpose is to compose and adopt an "Appeal from Auschwitz" aimed at mobilizing peoples and nations to work toward preventing another Auschwitz. Walesa chairs the session. He reads us a proposed text prepared by his staff. And—I cannot believe my ears—the word "Jew" is not mentioned. Already that morning, in his speech at Jagiellonian University, he had startled the Jewish participants by omitting all reference to the Jewish tragedy. How to explain his insensitivity? Surely he must know that his behavior can only make matters worse?

On Holbrooke's advice, I ask for the floor the moment Walesa finishes speaking. Politely, I point out the omissions in the text proposed to us. I particularly emphasize the fact that it seems unthinkable to adopt an appeal to mankind on the lessons of Auschwitz without mentioning the Jewishness of the great majority of its victims. I do not deny—I have never denied—that there were other peoples in the accursed realm that was Auschwitz; but I state that, however much against their will, Jews constituted the overwhelming majority there. Shevah Weiss supports me. So do other delegates. The first battle is won. The wretched victory leaves me feeling nauseous.

During that session a diplomatic incident occurs that goes almost unnoticed. Seated at the same table the Serb and Bosnian representatives avoid looking at each other. Normal. But when the Serb begins to speak, the Bosnian leaves the hall. Between the two men there is an abyss of blood and death. Here and there a few delegates comment in whispers. That is all. A moment later everybody is speaking of other things.

"I'll see you tonight," Walesa tells me on his way out. The American ambassador, who never leaves my side, specifies "after the concert."

Finally, in a small room next to the stage, I find myself face to face with the president of the Polish Republic.

To my astonishment, he is the one who attacks: "We've known each other for years. We were friends. But ever since I was elected president, we have had no contact."

I answer that I don't like to disturb him. "Before, it was different. . . ."

Should I tell him I did not appreciate the anti-Semitic overtones
of his last electoral campaign? This is not the time. Right now we
need to resolve the crisis that could well jeopardize the spirit and content of tomorrow's ceremony. I convey this to him cautiously. He
responds, punctuating his thoughts by gesturing with his hands.

"Since you perceived a crisis, why didn't you pick up the phone
and talk to me? Friends talk to each other. Between friends problems
can be settled quickly."

Should I answer that he too could have called me? Instead, I
explain that I called his minister in charge of the commemoration,
called him five or six times, and each time was told to speak in Polish
for he understood neither English nor French nor German. Walesa
nods and listens.

I convey to him the grievances of the Jewish organizations. I
explain to him why we feel offended. I ask him whether he remembers
our visit—our very first—to Birkenau and Auschwitz. Yes, he remembers. And at that moment his attitude changes; even the room suddenly appears lighter, more cheerful. The situation is defused. From
that moment, everything goes quickly, very quickly. Walesa asks
me what I want. I answer: "The Kaddish, and all the customary
prayers. . . ." Before I even finish, he agrees. What else? I would like
him to say what we Jews never stop repeating in every language on
earth, that the Holocaust is, above all, a Jewish tragedy, unique of its
kind. Again, he agrees. And he adds: "And then we'll be friends again,
promise?"

The next day he keeps his word. First at Auschwitz, then at
Birkenau, he mentions the singularity of Jewish destiny in these
places. Opening the general ceremony, a rabbi recites the Kaddish,
chants the El Maleh Rakhamim, and then intones the credos of the martyrs. Centuries ago, those were the affirmations made by pious Jews
who, rather than convert, went to their death by fire and by sword.

Of course the organizers had also invited clergy: Eastern Orthodox, Catholic, Protestant, and a Muslim qadi. Some found that
strange: Had there been Muslims in Auschwitz? Were we not forgetting the SS Muslim divisions? And the Mufti Hajj Amin el-Husseini of
Jerusalem, Heinrich Himmler's friend? In 1942 Himmler acted as his
guide to this very place. Better to let it go.

Journalists, delegates, and survivors congratulate me on a victory. What a victory. . . . I think of those whose cemetery is the sky, and I feel not at all victorious.

Let us return to the fact-finding mission in 1979. Back in Warsaw, the president of Parliament and a few influential members of government invite us to a farewell cocktail. They never knew, they never bothered to find out, that for us it is Tisha b'Av, a day of fasting. A journey that had begun in an atmosphere of little understanding ends in embarrassment.

Next stop is Kiev, the beautiful Ukrainian capital and its gardens, the city and its anti-Semitic past. Kiev means Babi-Yar. Babi-Yar means Jewish suffering, Jewish memory, Jewish anger. I still remember fragments of images of my first visit, in 1965: the cowering old men in the synagogue; the mute woman, her memories sealed—a survivor from the ravine of death, she had lost the use of speech. I could not understand: The massacre had lasted ten days; people could hear the crackling of the machine guns; and yet the Jews made no effort to flee or hide. No, I could not understand: Day after day Jews were being murdered, and the population had done nothing to save their neighbors.

A narrow street was used as the assembly area. At its end was a ravine. There the victims were lined up in rows and machine-gunned point-blank. As the shots rang out, the victims toppled into the ravine, the dead and the living. Kiev means forgetting legitimized. Kiev means outrage. How could a Jew not feel uncomfortable here?

The program is a full one. We are harangued, we watch documentaries never seen by the general public, showing roundups and tortures, humiliations and executions. We see villages set on fire, corpses mutilated. I am constantly nauseous.

The worst is still to come: in front of the Babi-Yar monument, a military orchestra and wreaths of every color. Red carpet and all the rest. It seems as if every official in Ukraine is here. Evidently these political leaders of Kiev are proud of themselves. One can no longer criticize them for the absence of a monument in Babi-Yar. There it is, the monument. Now, they seem to be asking, are you satisfied at last?

The huge Stalin-style monument is grandiose, pompous, banal, and outright vulgar. It is so large and ugly that it has a crushing effect. Never mind, I tell myself, that's their business. It is not up to me to judge their lack of taste. But I can and must reproach them for their lack of decency and honesty, their distortion of historical truth, for the word "Jew" does not appear on the monument. The inscription describes the victims as Soviet citizens assassinated by the Fascists.

I am overcome by rage. I tell the Ukrainian officials that while I had been pained and outraged in 1965, when there was nothing here but emptiness to obscure the only thing that remained of the victims—their memory—that was nothing compared with what I was feeling now.

I ask them how they dare deal so shabbily with the truth. I ask who gave them permission, who ordered them to commit this sacrilege? Those Jews who were killed, were they killed because they were Ukrainians, or Soviets, or Communists?

Rarely have I felt such fury. I remind myself that I am representing the president of the United States, that I have no right to involve him in this way, possibly provoking a diplomatic incident. But I cannot think of that now. I shall think of it tomorrow.

The ceremony ends abruptly. We get into our bus and start off toward the airport. But why are we stopping on the way? The guides and chauffeurs respond that it is all in the program; a light lunch to show us Ukrainian hospitality. But who can eat or drink?

In Moscow, in 1979, we had two purposes: first, to secure the liberation of the "prisoners of Zion"; second, to negotiate the opening of the secret Soviet archives to American and Israeli scholars.

On the second point, we obtain polite promises and assurances. On the first, not even that. Are the Soviet authorities familiar with the State Department's directives to us not to raise political problems? The situation is delicate. We may evoke the past, the persecutions, the racism, the anti-Fascist struggle, and the Holocaust, but not the fate of the refuseniks and dissidents, for fear of jeopardizing relations between the two powers. Hence our dilemma: to follow the rules and do nothing, or disobey and possibly embarrass the president, to whom Brezhnev, known to be touchy, would be sure to complain. The others defer to my judgment. What do the Talmud and our beloved Rashi say about this kind of problem?

These are my thoughts as we wait in a spacious drawing room in the Ministry of Justice to be received by Attorney General Roman Rudenko, former Soviet prosecutor at the Nuremberg trials. I have a list in my pocket. The list, compiled by the special team dealing with Soviet Jews in the Israeli prime minister's office, includes four names, among them those of Anatoly Shcharansky and Iosif Mendelovich. I know that Rudenko has personally taken part in their trials. Can I speak to him without risking an explosion?

The attorney general, in full dress uniform, covered with medals, invites us to take our places around a long table—the Russians adore long tables. In accordance with protocol—the Russians are mad about protocol, too—I face our host. Everything about him suggests authority and strength. His stature, his shoulders, the epaulets shining on his dark jacket, and especially his face. He is not someone you could oppose with impunity.

The discussion starts with a review of the aims of our mission. I say to him: "I am familiar with your role at Nuremberg." He answers: "You may know a part of my life, whereas I know your whole life. I know about your literary activities and the others." He stresses "others." A bad omen? He promises that his department will cooperate with us. He wishes to be given a list of our requests. My colleagues seem pleased, but I am preoccupied by another list, a list of a different sort. After all, I cannot hand it to him in front of everyone, especially not in front of his own people; if he gets angry, I'll be to blame. But then how will I manage to communicate the four names to him? I am determined not to go back to my room with the famous list, and so, after the session ends, I say to Rudenko: "Mr. Attorney General, I should be grateful if we could talk alone." He wants to know why. Courtesy of the Talmud, I have an answer ready: "In order to explain to you why we need to be alone." A fleeting smile crosses his stony face: All right, come along.

The three of us—he and I and his interpreter—walk into his huge office. I am ill at ease: I am moving onto dangerous terrain; if I make a mistake, others will suffer. I beg the god of amateurs to help me, and I launch into my plea: "You said a moment ago, Mr. Attorney General, that you know all about me; therefore you know I'm not a political person. . . ." He interrupts me: "Not a political person, *you?* Do you, perhaps, think that you'll be able to deceive me? Do you, perhaps, think I am not aware of what you are doing against my country?"

I must have changed color. I open my mouth for air. He is still talking: "I know you came here in 1965 to write a defamatory book against the fatherland of Socialism. You came back a year later to write a play, also directed against us. Don't bother to deny it; I know all about it. I also know the rest. Your articles, your speeches, your statements, I know them all. So don't tell me that you're not a political person!"

The verbal avalanche makes me feel as though I am literally shrinking. I am annoyed with myself for having pushed too hard. How am I going to get out of this? I must try: "I repeat, Mr. Attorney General, I am not a political person. If what I write sometimes has political connotations and repercussions, it is not my fault." He does not seem convinced. He counters with a shrug: "Very well, let's get on with it. You wanted to see me, you're seeing me. Is there anything else? I am a busy man, you know."

It is now or never. I hand him my list. He glances at it and tries to give it back. I refuse to take it. His face, his voice, his whole body stiffen: "I have no idea what or whom you're talking about." He is lying. I know it. I am sure of my Israeli friends; it was he who prosecuted the four refuseniks. "I can explain it to you," I say. He is close to losing his temper: "I haven't the time. . . . Your explanations don't interest me. . . . Write me a letter through normal channels. . . ." I tell him that he is holding that letter in his hand; it contains all the facts concerning the four cases that he should resolve on purely humanitarian grounds. He persists: "I've just told you—I don't know them!" I answer that he undoubtedly knows someone who does. Now he sees red; his face is turning purple: "None of this pertains to me or my department."

Our conversation has lasted some twenty minutes. Outside, Sigmund and Marion must be worried. Maybe they already picture me in a cell in the Lyubianka. As for me, I know that at most I am risking expulsion and a reprimand from the State Department. I can deal with those. And then, a small miracle: Abruptly his tone changes: "I'll make a deal with you. Two of the four. Tell them to write me directly."

So he knows that we have ways of contacting the prisoners in the Gulag.

The letters were sent. And he kept his word.

Saturday we make our way to Arkhipova Street. The huge synagogue is packed. How did these Jews learn of our presence in Moscow? As always, word of mouth functions here with tested efficiency. The rabbi is absent. "Well-informed" people speculate that he must have been advised to spend Shabbat elsewhere. But his assistants treat us with great respect. "Personal" messages are whispered to us: refused visas, separated families, official humiliations. Nevertheless these Jews do not give up hope. A man pushes his small son in front of me: "Take him to Jerusalem!" An old woman: "I don't mind living here, but I want to die in Israel." Young people tell me about their secret meetings in the cemeteries of all the large urban centers; they've been studying Jewish history and Hebrew. These Jews will never cease surprising me. They are amazing.

As I sit in synagogue, I scrutinize them, these people, so near and yet so distant, whom since 1965, in one way or another, I have never left. Do they recognize me? Some of them tell me they do, no doubt to please me. What matters is that I recognize them. I even recognize those I am meeting for the first time. Though impoverished, they do not seem unhappy. The spirituality they seek within their defiance confers on them an air of exaltation. Young and old, I admire, I love them all; I almost define myself in terms of the love that binds me to them. It is clear they have not come to pray—do they even know how to read the siddur?—but to communicate.

I am given the *maftir,* the privilege of reading the chapter from Isaiah in which the prophet consoles his people; generous, poignant words that in their simplicity are so appropriate to the situation. Forming a semicircle around the *bimah,* the faithful silently repeat the words after me, word for word, hardly moving their lips. How many understand their symbolic meaning? But every one of them longs for consolation. And in my address, I tell them of my joy at being with them. If President Carter had created this commission just for these encounters, *dayyenu*—it would have been enough.

But our visit to the Soviet Union was about to produce a more concrete effect, one I believe is worth reporting.

Among the personalities whom the authorities have us meet there is a heavyset man, with an open, smiling face—General Vassily Petrenko, the liberator of Auschwitz. Upon meeting my young son, he removes one of his many medals and pins it to Elisha's jacket. I instantly find him even more appealing. We isolate ourselves in a corner and exchange reminiscences. He describes to me the atmosphere in his unit as it prepared for the assault, and I describe to him the last day, the final hours inside the camp, the urgent discussions between fathers and sons, friends and comrades: What to do? Hide? In which barracks? And would the SS not clean out the death factory before retreating? To the general I say: "The Red Army was so close, so close; we were all praying for you and your men. No believer ever implored God with more fervor." Petrenko answers that his soldiers had an idea of what they might discover in the camp, but that they could never have imagined the reality they found.

I say: "You could have advanced your attack by one day, by a few hours. You could have saved a great many prisoners, Jews and Russians." He explains: "It wasn't easy. There were logistical problems, strategic considerations. And then, I had to get the order from the Stavka, the High Command. . . ."

And suddenly, as we chat, the general and I, as we exchange stories about courage and despair, an idea flashes through my mind: We must bring together the other liberators of camps—to listen to them, to thank them, and to ask for their support. Our testimony has been questioned, even refuted by Nazis and moral perverts. The voice of the liberators would make them hold their tongues. That was the genesis, in my mind, of the Liberators' Conference that was to convene in Washington in 1981.

In the plane that takes us from Moscow to Copenhagen, where we go to express our gratitude to the Danish people for having demonstrated to the world that it was possible to save Jews, my Elisha, who until then had never complained about being hauled around the world, exclaims: "That's enough! I'm resigning from the commission!"

From Europe, that commission continues to pursue its fact-finding mission in Israel, the place where memory has been preserved better than anywhere else. We have endless meetings with the directors of Yad Vashem, Israel's Holocaust museum. How can we put their concerns to rest? They are worried that the museum project we are planning will relegate theirs to second place. I believe they are wrong. Yad Vashem will remain the essential site of remembrance. It deserves absolute priority.

In the report we are about to submit to the president, we are proposing the creation of a museum. Such is the wish of most members of the commission. They feel that having entered into the era of the audiovisual, books alone no longer suffice. My position is that we Jews have never assigned much importance to museums. How are we going to "show" the Tragedy, when it is almost impossible even to speak of it? Could images be more eloquent, more effective? And what images? Those taken by the enemy? In the end I go along with the concept of a "living museum," as long as the accent is on "living." Now that the concept has been accepted by the commission, there remains the matter of drafting the report to the president.

With the exception of my introduction, it is written by an aide to the director. Unfortunately, it is badly written. In the end, our friend Lily Edelman undertakes a rewrite. It takes her a full three days.

Another ceremony: We deliver the report to the president in the Rose Garden in the presence of many dignitaries and congressmen. The president seems satisfied. We have proposed that a new organization be created to succeed the commission. The proposal has been accepted. What shall it be called? Just as they had for the commission, the White House suggests a name as long as a stifling summer day without water. Once again I invoke my authority to shorten it. It will be inscribed in various legal documents as the United States Holocaust Memorial Council, or just the Council. I summarize its purpose in a sentence to be engraved on the museum wall: "For the dead *and* the living, we must bear witness."

Words of Remembrance

*W*HEN PRESIDENT CARTER appoints me to head the newly created Holocaust Memorial Council, I foresee the difficulties awaiting us. By now I am no longer a novice. My most urgent task is to establish a list—once more. It seems as though one does nothing else in Washington. I ask Arthur Goldberg to stay on with me. He declines; he does not believe in the museum: "You'll see, it will be created at the expense of Jewish remembrance." He feels that it would be better not to embark on a project that he thinks can only end in compromise. "I am your friend," he tells me. "I know Washington. This is not for us." I beg him to change his mind, to trust me, without success. I am deeply sorry.

Still, there is no shortage of candidates. As during the establishment of the President's Holocaust Commission, we must take into account the religious and geographical considerations that influence all decisions on the federal level. But even that is not enough, and the White House calls us to account. It seems we have forgotten a factor that politically weighs more heavily than the others—the ethnic factor. After all, we are on the eve of an electoral campaign.

We have the first alerts, the first disagreements. The Council membership list evidently displeases the White House; "too many Jews," the President is rumored to have said. His adviser Stu Eizenstat exerts pressure on us along those lines. The new Council director, the eminent law professor and civil rights activist Monroe Freedman, acts as our liaison to the administration. A distinguished-looking man who has returned to traditional Judaism thanks to his wife, Audrey, a convert, Freedman impresses people with his graciousness and precision of thought. Unlike many others, he is not in awe of Washington or power, and his integrity prevents him from getting involved in political maneuvers. He expresses a pessimism that events eventually confirm. Example: We are asked politely but insistently to accept a Pole, that is, a non-Jewish American of Polish origin. His connection to the Tragedy? None. He is to represent the Polish nation, which, undeniably, has suffered as well.

So my friend Arthur had been right. I call an urgent meeting with my close collaborators and ask for their advice: Should we resist the pressures? For Frank Lautenberg, industrialist and future senator from New Jersey, compromise is unavoidable; he thinks that a rejection would signify the end of the project, the end of the memorial. "Sometimes," he says, "if it is for a just cause, one may sell one's soul to the devil." Siggi Wilzig, a Jew from Berlin and a survivor of Auschwitz, flies into a rage and—fortunately—puts him in his place. In Miles Lerman's view, if it were a Ukrainian he would say no, but a Pole, that's something else, less serious. How is it less serious? The discussion leads nowhere. As for me, had the White House asked us to nominate a Pole who had been a deportee or had fought in the resistance, I would have said yes without hesitation; but I am opposed to the political argument that imposes on us the representative of one ethnic group or another. If we went along, tomorrow we could be pressured to accept a representative of any minority, be it Ukrainian, Lithuanian, Hungarian, or even German. More discussions follow, all just as sterile. Pressures from my fellow survivors weigh on my judgment. Finally, a majority favoring compromise takes shape. We shall have to trust the White House; after all, a council with minor political motivation is better than no council. And of course we can always resign later. I report the situation to Arthur. Predictably, he says: "I knew it; this is only the beginning. You can't win with these people." His predictions came true: After the Pole, a Ukrainian was recommended—I mean imposed on us—then a Hungarian, then a Lithuanian . . . all perfectly honorable men, worthy of our trust, but we have become part of the machine.

My displeasure is no secret. Neither is the administration's. As a result, our relations with the White House deteriorate. As everywhere in a bureaucracy, there is no end to the intrigues. Cliques form and there is an attempt to pit me against some official or other; I no longer recall whom. Eizenstat is annoyed, and I am disappointed. It becomes more and more difficult to make decisions, even important ones. To be sure, Congress offers us unconditional support, but since Congress is dependent on the executive branch, for all practical purposes it is impossible to function.

The first internal crisis breaks out: Monroe Freedman feels compelled to dismiss his assistant. The latter, taking advantage of the fact that I was out of the country, allegedly engineered the hiring of a candidate with a questionable past. Monroe derailed the maneuver immediately. But because the assistant falsely informed the White House that I had approved the candidate, the administration concluded that I had gone back on my word—and was furious.

As a consequence of our tense relations with the White House, it becomes impossible to get the president to attend the second annual Day of Remembrance, and so it does not take place. Monroe and I exchange bitter letters with Eizenstat. We feel that he is politicizing the Council, and that our not having a ceremony that year is his fault.

The second conflict: One of our Council members is an American of Armenian origin; Set Momjian is among my closest collaborators. He is helping us commemorate the tragedy endured by his people during World War I. This, of course, angers the Turkish government, which threatens to revise its policy toward the United States and NATO. So here I am, to my great chagrin, mixed up in international politics. What a joke: If NATO falls apart, will it be our fault? But that's Washington; there is no way to escape politics or comedy. Personally, I am pleased that an Armenian has a seat on the Council. I would be even more pleased if a Gypsy were there too.

But the business of nominations is not finished. Just as for the presidential commission, people are soliciting appointments from senators and congressmen who, in turn, exert pressure on us. Notables of both parties intervene. To be a Democrat is an advantage, to be a millionaire a trump card. Political connections are more important than personal merit. My proposals are rarely accepted. My points of view and those of the administration are too divergent. In the end, the Council will have sixty-five members, ten congressmen among them.

Eizenstat attends the inaugural session, which is less moving, less "historic," than that of the Commission a year earlier. Our friend in Congress, John Brademas from Michigan, the Democratic whip of the House, administers the oath. My speech does not deal gently with the administration. I aim at members of Eizenstat's staff without naming them; I make it clear that I find their manipulations deplorable. Colleagues try to calm me: They tell me that once the mechanism is in place, everything will be all right. I am not convinced.

So far, little is settled. For the moment, the White House has other worries, what with the hostage crisis in Teheran and the failure of the military action to free them. In Madrid for a conference, I am with Henry Kissinger as we witness the live broadcast of Jimmy Carter's melancholy speech. He is clearly devastated, which is understandable: All those helicopters unable to take off, all those helpless military men. And those Iranian "students" tormenting their American prisoners, all the while mocking America. How can the Democrats hope to win the presidential elections after months and months of waiting and wallowing in indecision?

Was it true that at the start of the crisis an Israeli emissary had been dispatched to Washington to offer the president the good services of the Israeli army and the Mossad? Was it true that Israel, strategically well placed, had been ready to undertake a rescue operation in Teheran? And that Carter had refused? A thousand rumors are circulating in "well-informed" quarters. All, of course, quite unconfirmable.

If Carter had said yes he might well have been reelected. And so many things might have taken a different course.

The arrival of President Ronald Reagan brings about a change in our relations with the White House. During a visit to Los Angeles, I meet with Ted Cummings, adviser to the new president on Jewish affairs and future ambassador to Austria, who tells me in no uncertain terms that the composition of the Council will have to be altered. He suggests a collective resignation in order to reconstitute the Council on a new political foundation. "You must admit," he says, "that not one member of the present Council is Republican!" He is right. And I am the only independent. "It is only fair," Cummings continues, "for the Republican party to be represented." Eventually he proposes a compromise—a partial resignation of the Council. I oppose it: "You can have my resignation right now. As for the others, you must handle that yourself."

Legally, the administration cannot divest us of our functions before our five-year mandate expires. In practice, though, it is inconceivable that anyone would stay on against the president's wishes. That is the tradition: Every president must have the privilege of naming his collaborators and representatives on every level of the administration down to the most insignificant, such as ours. But I am stubborn: If the Council is touched, I'll leave. It will not be touched, but in the upper echelons of the White House a resentment of me will linger for some time. From that moment on, Monroe Freedman's counterpart will no longer be a high official but a subordinate.

Many of us feel that we are progressing too slowly. At the session of December 10, 1980, I express my position:

> . . . The Event we are dealing with is unique, and our atti-
> tude toward it must be too. Not being a governmental
> agency like the others, we cannot follow their example. We
> lack experience. What seems clear and effective for the
> existing official commissions is not so for us. We are dealing
> with the most burning subject of our lives, and in our work
> we are establishing a precedent for History. Future genera-
> tions will wish to learn what we, the witnesses and sur-
> vivors, have done with our memories. . . . Our words and
> our acts will await the judgment of our children and of
> theirs. . . . That is why the rhythm of our efforts will be
> feverish but not foolhardy, passionate but prudent. Let us
> adopt the adage of the great French poet Boileau: "Let us
> make haste slowly."

The Council must also deal with problems not directly connected with the creation of a museum. We meet to condemn the
resurgence of anti-Semitism or to denounce the attacks on Jews in
Europe. In fact, it is our "committee of conscience" that, according to
our charter, should be in charge, but it is not working well. The committee may not be to blame; the Senate distrusts it because it fears we
might make declarations and take initiatives that might be embarrassing to the executive branch.

Meanwhile, surprisingly, on a personal level, I develop a friendly
relationship with the new president.

Our second annual Day of Remembrance, the first during President Reagan's initial term, takes place not in the Rotunda but at the
White House, for Ronald Reagan has just left the hospital. It is his
first public appearance since the assassination attempt against him.
The East Room is packed. The entire Washington who's who is there.
Six survivors light the six traditional candles. Cantor Isaac Goodfriend of Atlanta intones the customary prayers in memory of the victims. When my turn comes, I begin by giving thanks to God for
sparing the president's life. Then I read, in Yiddish (it is, I believe, the
first time Yiddish has been heard in the White House), a poem that
evokes the massacred Jewish children. I also speak of Israel, that people with a long history, which is also a modern people that should not

be judged on isolated incidents. I conclude by addressing the president directly: "In our tradition, when a human being dies, we designate him our messenger on high to intercede in our favor. Is it possible, Mr. President, that the six million Jewish victims have become our messengers?"

The president is visibly moved. It seems that tears prevent his reading the speech that has been prepared for him. I watch him as, behind the lectern, he rearranges pages and goes on to improvise a magnificent speech against racism, anti-Semitism, and all forms of discrimination.

That same evening television commentators report: "Political circles in Washington were astonished today to hear President Reagan deliver a speech on human rights. But if one is to believe his closest advisers, he did not mean it. It was but an emotional reaction that . . ."

Marion and I look at each other, stunned. How dare these advisers disparage the president in this way? In politics, say my friends in the capital, anything goes.

Two weeks later, the telephone rings in my office. A well-modulated voice says: "Please wait a moment; the president of the United States would like to speak with you." I am convinced it is a prank, until I hear the familiar warm voice. He says hello, and I am so taken aback that I can't think of anything more intelligent to say than: "Mr. President, how did you find my phone number?" He bursts out laughing and keeps me on the line a good quarter of an hour. He begins by saying some nice things about my work. At the end he chuckles: "By the way, just so you know, I meant every single word in my speech." Rumors about this conversation make the rounds of Washington dinner parties. After all, who but me would think of asking the president of the United States how he obtained a simple telephone number. This funny incident is followed by another, which has to do with France of the eighties.

A month later I attend the investiture of François Mitterrand as president of France. During the luncheon at the Élysée Palace, he voices a concern to me: He doesn't know the Americans well, and they don't know him either; they are bound to mistrust him and his political philosophy. On the flight home I ponder this. I wonder how, in some small way, I could be of assistance to the new president. A wild idea goes through my mind: Why not write a note to President Reagan? Through the Council office I send him a brief personal mes-

With son Elisha
and President
Jimmy Carter
the first Day of
Remembrance
ceremony,
April 24, 1979.

At a commemoration
of Holocaust victims
in the East Room of
the White House
with President
Reagan,
April 30, 1981.

Receiving François Mitterrand
at the Wiesel home in
New York, March 24, 1984.
At left, Leonard Bernstein.

With Mikhail Gorbachev.

With wife Marion
and Lech Walesa
in Auschwitz,
January 17, 1988

With Marion and the
Russian Jewish singer
Nehama Lifschitz after
her arrival in the West
in 1970

With Egil Aarvik,
chairman of the
Nobel committee.
In background,
)n and Elisha. Oslo,
)ecember 10, 1986.

With a friend, Dr. Leo (Sjua) Eitinger, Oslo, 1987

With the Dalai Lama (far left), 1991.

With Bosnia Serbian leader Radovan Karadzic, November 1992.

With Gordana Dukovic (Bosnia and Herzegovina) and Ronlad Fox (U.S.A.) at the
"Tomorrow's Leaders Conference" in Venice, May 1995.

Discussing Bosnia with President Bill Clinton in the Oval Office, December 1995.

In class at Boston University, 1982.

With Yitzhak Rabin.

With a friend, Sigmund Strochlitz, April 1984.

With a friend, Joseph (Yossi) Ciechanover (*far left*), and Professor Saul Lieberman

With Elisa (*left*) and nephew Steve in Paris, 1995

Sister Hilda and her s⊙ Sidney, in the south o⊙ France.

sage in which I tell him that I consider it my duty as an American citizen to offer him a psychological sketch of his French counterpart. And I add this suggestion: "If you could ring him directly, simply to say hello and congratulate him, as you did with me, I am sure that will facilitate your future relations." Did he receive my letter? The fact is I received no answer. Oh well, I thought, surely it vanished into one of the proverbial White House wastebaskets. From the Élysée too, silence. Never mind. So what if I made myself look ridiculous. Luckily no one knows.

Years later, a high official tells me that a secretary had indeed transmitted my letter to the president. And he had liked my suggestion. Call President Mitterrand? Why not. Only I had failed to mention that Mitterrand did not speak English. And Reagan has only a little French. An interpreter should have been called in. No matter: The two presidents succeeded in understanding each other. And during the meeting of the seven major economic powers that followed, their easy relationship surprised quite a few people.

When it comes to the affairs of my own Council, I am less lucky. My requests to meet with the president run into insurmountable obstacles, despite the fact that after every one of our conversations he expresses his wish to see me again: Strangely, Reagan's aides have much power. But why would the prospect of my speaking with their boss bother them? Why would it worry them? I have no idea, but the door to the Oval Office remains firmly closed to me. It opens only four long years later, during the Bitburg affair.

End of October 1981: The international Liberators' Conference—the need for which had become evident to me two years earlier in Moscow—takes place in the State Department with the participation of the secretary of state, General Alexander Haig, and the assistant secretary for human rights, Elliott Abrams. The opening session is both solemn and original: When American soldiers bring out German flags taken from the enemy and throw them at our feet, on the stage, even the toughest among the participants shiver. Present are representatives of some twenty countries, from both sides of the Iron Curtain, and this is the statement I make to them:

> . . . Some thirty-six years ago, we lived together a moment
> marked by destiny, a moment without parallel, never to be

measured or repeated; a moment that stood on the other side of time, on the other side of existence.

When we first met, on the threshold of a universe struck by a curse, we spoke different languages, we were strangers to one another, we might as well have descended from different planets. And yet a link was created between us, a bond was established. We became not only comrades, not only brothers; we became each other's witnesses.

I remember, I shall always remember, the day I was liberated: April 11, 1945. Buchenwald. The terrifying silence broken by abrupt yelling. The first American soldiers. Their ashen faces. Their eyes—I shall never forget their eyes, your eyes. You looked and looked, you could not move your gaze away from us; it was as though you sought to alter reality with your eyes. They reflected astonishment, bewilderment, endless pain, and anger—yes, anger above all. Rarely have I seen such anger, such rage—contained, mute, yet ready to burst with frustration, humiliation, and utter helplessness. Then you broke down. You wept. You wept and wept uncontrollably, unashamedly; you were our children then, for we, the twelve-year-old, the sixteen-year-old boys in Buchenwald and Theresienstadt and Mauthausen, knew so much more than you about life and death. You wept; we could not. We had no more tears left; we had nothing left. In a way we were dead, and we knew it. What did we feel? Only sadness.

And also gratitude. And ultimately it was gratitude that brought us back to normalcy and to society. Do you remember, my friends? In Lublin and Dachau, Struthof and Nordhausen, Ravensbrück and Majdanek, Belsen and Auschwitz, you were surrounded by sick and wounded and hungry wretches, barely alive, pathetic in their futile attempts to touch you, to smile at you, to reassure you, to console you, and most of all, to carry you in triumph on their frail shoulders; you were our heroes, our idols. Tell me, friends: In your whole lives have you ever felt such love, such admiration?

One thing we did not do: We did not try to explain; explanations were neither needed nor possible. Liberators and survivors looked at one another—and what each of us experienced then, we shall try to recapture together, now, at this reunion, which, for me, represents a miracle in itself.

After describing the goals and the functioning of the Council, I go on:

> . . . What we all have in common is an obsession: not to betray the dead we left behind or who left us behind. They were killed once; they must not be killed again. . . . You were the first free men to discover the abyss, just as we were its last inhabitants. What we symbolized to one another then was so special that it remained part of our very being. . . .
>
> . . . It would have been so easy for us to slide into melancholy and resignation. We made a different choice. We chose to become spokesmen for man's quest for generosity and his need and capacity to turn his or her suffering into something productive, something creative.
>
> We had hoped then that out of so much torment and grief and mourning, a new message would be handed down to future generations—a warning against the dangers inherent in discrimination in all its forms, fanaticism, poverty, deprivation, ignorance, oppression, humiliation, injustice, and war—the ultimate injustice, the ultimate humiliation. Yes, friends; we were naive. And perhaps we still are. . . .
>
> . . . If we do not raise our voice against war—who will? We speak with the authority of men and women who have seen war; we know what it is. We have seen the burnt villages, the devastated cities, the deserted homes; we still see the demented mothers whose children are being massacred before their eyes, we still follow the endless nocturnal processions to the flames rising up to the seventh heaven—if not higher. . . .
>
> We are gathered here to testify—together. Our tale is a tale of solitude and fear and anonymous death—but also of compassion, generosity, bravery, and solidarity. Together, you the liberators and we the survivors, represent a commitment to memory whose intensity will remain. In

its name we shall continue to voice our concerns and our hopes, not for our own sake, but for the sake of humankind. Its very survival may depend on its ability and willingness to listen.

And to remember.

I have reproduced certain excerpts from this speech because I feel strongly about the circumstances that motivated it. I shall never forget the tears of the American soldier who, in what was called "the little camp," discovered the result of absolute evil. My gratitude to him and all the other liberators of the camps remains deep and eternal. When I draw up the balance sheet of my life, the memory that binds me to them is paramount.

Yet even they pose a problem. There is one question, always the same, I ask American or Soviet officers: Did they ever modify a plan, or decide to launch an attack a day or an hour earlier, in order to liberate a concentration camp? The answer is always the same: no. Military operations were decided by headquarters; no one else could change orders.

How can one forget the liberators' kindness, their warmth, the bewilderment, the horror reflected in their eyes, their sadness? Since our Washington conference, their acts of kindness have been commemorated in many communities—they have been congratulated; they have been urged to testify, to speak, to write; they have been the subjects of newspaper accounts, films. They have been honored and involved in the survivors' effort to safeguard memory. I am proud to have been the one to initiate the process.

There is another international conference I like to recall: "The Courage to Care." The idea had been Dr. Carol Rittner's. This nun, who belongs to the order of the Sisters of Mercy, is one of the most dynamic women I have met. After Monroe Freedman's departure, for political reasons—he was not from the "right" party—I proposed that she take over the direction of the Memorial Council. She agreed, but the White House refused. Because she was not a Republican? Nonetheless, we collaborated for many years, and she became the first director of the foundation I created with Marion after I received the Nobel Prize.

Her obsession is the Holocaust. It is the major topic of the courses she teaches in the university run by her order. Harsh in her judgment of the Catholic Church's attitude during the war, she has great admiration and affection for those Yad Vashem calls "the righteous among the nations," the non-Jews who risked their lives to save Jews. "Why not have the Council organize an important colloquium in their honor?" she asked one day. I liked the proposal, for not enough has been said about these men and women whose spirit of sacrifice saved mankind's honor.

Seventy-five guests, Jews and Christians, from diverse backgrounds arrive to take part in this gathering. Like the Liberators' Conference, it takes place at the State Department. This time it is Secretary George Shultz who participates in the opening ceremony. We witness the reunions of several "saviors" and those they saved. People are embracing, and there is much weeping in the corridors.

Gaby Cohen—we called her Niny long ago, in the Ambloy children's home—has come to speak to us of the Jewish children hidden in France, and those who were helped to cross clandestinely into Switzerland. Madame Trocmé retells the glorious saga of her French village, Le Chambon, whose inhabitants risked their lives to save Jews. The widow of Pastor Martin Niemöller recalls the courageous deeds of her husband. His words about the dangers of indifference are famous:

> When they came to look for the Catholics, I said nothing, since I am not a Catholic. Then they came to look for the trade-unionists; I said nothing since I am not a trade-unionist; then they came for the Jews, and not being a Jew, I said nothing. In the end, when they came to take me away, there was no one left to raise his voice.

Poles, Dutchmen, Belgians, Danes, Frenchmen, men and women of great courage, how could one not be moved in their presence?

And how could I forget the person who, on the eve of the first transport, had tapped on the window of our house, no doubt to warn us? I never succeeded in learning his identity: I would have so wished to invite him or her to this conference.

In my town, and throughout occupied Europe, such brave people were a tiny minority. Why were they so few, these just men and women who took the side of the victim?

I question them in every language I know. For me they are a

unique species. They dared resist the oppressor, interfere with his misdeeds. They proved that it *was* possible to wrest the frightened prey from the killer, to encroach into the Kingdom of Death. Two questions are on my lips: What made you choose danger and heroism over resignation and waiting? And why were you so few? It is impossible to elicit any reasonable answers from them. Heroes, *they?* Why are we pestering them with these questions about heroism when they have done nothing extraordinary, nothing any other human being would not have done?

This reminds me of the marvelous story of a woman from Berlin whom Yad Vashem had honored for having risked her own life to save Jews. Turning to the journalists who were nagging her with questions about her motives, she said simply: "You want to know why I did it? Well, I'll tell you: out of self-respect."

Had I been there, I would have kissed her.

I confess: Of all the activities of the Memorial Council, except for the annual Days of Remembrance, the part I relish most is these personal meetings, discussions, conferences, the exchanges of ideas and recollections. The role of "soul matchmaker" suits me. I find it exciting to watch men and women of every background gathered around a table exchanging ideas, learning from one another just what it is that makes each of us unique. And sharing one goal: to make people understand why and how they must live together on this bedeviled planet. Dialogue: philosophical debates, religious discussions—if the Council had served only that purpose, *dayyenu*—it would have been enough.

On the other hand, some projects I've been involved in turned out badly. Among them, the 1982 colloquium on genocide (see p. 92) and the journey to Bosnia (see p. 389). As for the American-German Commission, regretfully, it was short-lived. The Council had put together a sort of study committee that brought together American and German intellectuals. I had been assured that all of the Germans had impeccable pasts. Two annual meetings had been scheduled, one in New York and one in Berlin. The first took on a confessional tone; we had former deportees on one side and five German academicians and politicians on the other. True and painful words were spoken by Klaus Schutz, ex-mayor of Berlin and German ambassador to Israel, and Peter Petersen, a member of the Bonn parliament who admitted that he was once a member of the Hitler

Youth. A philosopher spoke of his concern for truth. The atmosphere was one of confidence, sympathy.

As I arrive in Berlin with my delegation for the second session, I am keenly aware of the date: January 20. I mention this to our official hosts. They seem not to understand: "Oh that's fine . . . ," they say. I repeat: "Today is January 20th, isn't that symbolic?" Again, they nod: That's fine. Does the date mean nothing to them? What about the Wannsee Conference? Don't they know about the conference that took place not far from here on January 20, 1942? Oh yes, finally the Germans understand, make the connection. Can we see the site that holds such a notorious place in contemporary history? Impossible, they reply. Too complicated. The program is too full. Too many people to see, too many official meetings. And there is so little time.

Never mind; we go anyway. Is there a plaque at the entrance? I seem to remember that it makes no reference to the past. Long ago, before it was confiscated by the Gestapo, the villa had belonged to a Jewish family. It was here that, chaired by Reinhard Heydrich himself, and with the active collaboration of Adolf Eichmann, the infamous meeting of the high officials representing all the ministries of the Reich took place. Its purpose? To set down the principle and devise the strategy for the "Final Solution."

I walk around the villa. I interrogate the walls, the ceilings: Let *them* testify, since the people remain mute. I mention our visit to Wannsee in my public speeches. The embarrassed officials promise to transform the villa into a museum of remembrance. I am told that they have kept their word.

Meanwhile, back in Washington, things are progressing slowly, much too slowly. There is no end to the intrigues and quarrels: overt and covert conflicts and clashes between personalities and ambitions, thirst for the pitiful power that supposedly is ours to give. Early on, to make everyone happy, I had authorized—on a provisional basis—the creation of some twenty committees. They are now a mess. While the plenary sessions continue to provoke worthwhile debates and analyses, petty skirmishes abound in the corridors. Nothing is forgiven. More and more often I find myself in the role of mediator, and I spend hours on the phone soothing angry factions. I am beginning to feel I am wasting my time.

And the problem of specificity versus universality in the Council is getting worse. It surfaces at every session. The theologian Robert McAfee Brown and other Christian philosophers understand the sensitivity of the issue. Others do not. And, of course, one must not expect unanimity from the Jews. To demonstrate to the Council his predilection for universality, a Warsaw survivor tells us one day that while he does not observe his mother's *yahrzeit*, he does light a candle on the anniversary of the death of the Christian woman who hid him during the Occupation.

Every day the problem of finances becomes more acute. Session after session is devoted to it. Should we accept German contributions if Bonn offers them? The majority is against. Should we hire professional fund-raisers? Marion warns me against it. But the majority decides: yes. Everyone has a different opinion. This is not my area of competence. Let others handle that—Miles Lerman, for instance. He has been helping Israel Bonds for years. And of course there is Sigmund Strochlitz, who has successfully raised funds for Haifa University. As it happens, the two are friends. Together they call on wealthy and less wealthy potential donors. I accompany them when they go to see Henry Ford III and to a dinner with the governor of Texas. Optimistic expectations and rude disappointments follow one another. But what about the Jewish survivors? They should be among the first to contribute. Many, including some in New Jersey, could easily help. We organize a working lunch for them. Fifteen people attend. As a group they pledge $600,000, spread over several years. But we need tens of millions of dollars for architects, builders, engineers, librarians, all kinds of specialists. They all cost money that we don't have.

Council Vice President Mark Talisman and Hyman Bookbinder have succeeded in persuading Congress to assign to us a building that is close to the Mall, not far from the Lincoln Memorial, a most prestigious site. The site has a redbrick building, which seems appropriate because of its simplicity and the way it fits perfectly into the surrounding area. The interior will have to be redone, and it will require other repairs. Never mind; we'll surely manage to raise the needed funds.

One night Miles and Sigmund wake me up at three in the morning; they are jubilant. They have good news that couldn't wait. Miles has found the rara avis—a generous multimillionaire who is ready to finance everything. Everything? Absolutely. He knows what to do. All he wants is for us to trust him. In exchange he will deliver a building worthy of our hopes. Now that I am awake, Miles and Sigmund tell me I can sleep peacefully. But . . . it's important that I meet him.

The next day I do meet him, as I have met other would-be saviors of the museum. They all love to talk, to listen to their own voices. The alleged savior has a wish: to make a speech in the course of a planned Evening of Remembrance at the Kennedy Center. And if not? Better not to upset him, say Miles and Sigmund. Well, all right, since the fate of the museum depends on it, let him say a few words. In the end, while he delivered a long-winded speech, our expectations that he might be our savior came to naught.

It doesn't take long before Miles and Sigmund proudly announce their discovery of a new patron to replace the doctor/tycoon: Sonny Abramson, a well-known Washington entrepreneur. He is the image of success—silvery hair, eyes of steel. He wishes to help us. According to Miles and Sigmund, I "must" lunch with him. If things go well, our worries are over.

Sonny makes rather a good impression. His common sense is evident. Even though he is not a member of the Council, he offers us his total support. He speaks like the doctor-promoter, only his voice is deeper. Like the other one, he says that he wants nothing, he simply has faith in us and in our mission. If we just tell him what to do, he'll take care of everything having to do with the renovation. We are told that he has connections in high places and can put them to work. His best friend is an influential member of Congress.

An alliance is forged, and at first it's a honeymoon. God is great and the work goes forward. Everybody is happy. Miles, Sigmund, Sonny—the perfect trio. Miles attends to fundraising, Sigmund watches over programming, Sonny deals with the technical research and preparatory work for the building. Finally, we have peace. Rather than six, I spend only two hours a day on the telephone, settling problems that are really outside my sphere of competence.

One day, in the usual manner—Sonny tells Miles, who alerts Sigmund, who rings me—I receive a shattering piece of news: The building is worthless; it is so rotten inside that it is in danger of collapse. Repairs would cost a fortune; better to demolish it and start thinking in terms of a new building.

I see it as a tragedy. I liked this simple brick building. In fact, we all liked it. It is interesting to read what my colleagues on the Council said about it in plenary session. Some thought it reminded them of the blocks at Auschwitz. Others praised its simplicity: What could be more ordinary than red brick? They thought it efficient. Harmonious. A group of specialists devise a detailed plan, a "Red Book" for the museum. The plan is impressive in its precision, its details, and its creative imagination. Everything is ready; construction could begin. But now, if Sonny is right, we'll have to start from scratch. We discuss the matter with him and his congressman friend. We talk with numerous building contractors and architects. I feel sad about abandoning the building. If we could have used it, the museum could have been ready soon, in two years at the most. And it would have been financially manageable. But Sonny is stubborn; he insists on the need to demolish it. After all, he is the expert. Finally the ritual resumes: Sonny puts pressure on Miles, who persuades Sigmund, who succeeds in convincing me. The building will be demolished. The page is turned.

From that moment on, Sonny's position becomes ever more important. He seems irreplaceable when it comes to the construction of a new building. He introduces us to one of his friends, Harvey "Bud" Meyerhoff, a wealthy businessman from Baltimore. The two form a pair just as Miles and Sigmund do, though the chemistry between them is not always good. We run into problems of authority: Who has the power to decide? Theoretically it is Sigmund, since he is chair of the development committee. Sonny objects, arguing that he lives in Washington, Sigmund does not, and there are decisions to be made every day, decisions that cannot wait, certainly not for the next meeting. We swim in discussions, debates, countless crises. I establish new infrastructures, new committees and subcommittees. Our emissaries travel around the country in search of donors, museum specialists, educators, and archivists. We go from meeting to meeting, from ceremony to ceremony. They all begin to seem alike. And time passes.

To my friends I confide my ever more serious doubts. Should I resign? Had I made a mistake when I opposed President Carter, who wanted only a monument?

Sonny is charged with finding the best possible architect to prepare a design. He falls back on architects working for him. For my part, I invite an Israeli architect, Zalman Einav, to submit plans.

It is now 1985. The year of the Bitburg affair.

The Bitburg Affair

*I*T ALL BEGINS with an innocent enough statement by a White House spokesman at the beginning of 1985. President Reagan will be traveling to West Germany. There is specific reference to the fact that the official program does not include visits to former concentration camps. At once, voices are heard: Some wonder; others are indignant. Had the spokesman not mentioned this detail, it never would have occurred to the reporters to turn it into an issue. But now they view it as a challenge, as though Ronald Reagan wanted to show the country and the world his new attitude toward Helmut Kohl's Germany. It was to be a "normal" attitude based on relations between two peoples that were now allies and friends. The past was buried. Or, as Chancellor Kohl would say, normalized.

Then the other shoe falls. The White House spokesman announces that in the course of his trip to Germany, the president will visit a German military cemetery. No one knows which one. It will be revealed later: Bitburg. The name means nothing to the reporters. It will soon be famous.

People will long remember the tempest aroused by this news, not only among Jews, but also among veterans of the two wars. The editorials are harsh, the commentaries ferocious. Former soldiers send back their military medals, won on the battlefields of Europe. For the first time since his election, Reagan does not have the support of the people. The Great Communicator is having trouble communicating. The White House tries to justify itself—reasons of state, the duty of reconciliation, NATO, the defense of Europe. Most Americans reject these arguments. Yet, at the start of the polemic, everyone thinks the cemetery in question is reserved exclusively for soldiers and officers of the Wehrmacht. The country soon learns that the cemetery at Bitburg also shelters tombs of the SS.

Now the entire nation is outraged. Public opinion unanimously decries the decision. The past is recalled, specifically the atrocities carried out by the SS. The letters "SS" project terror. When Bitburg is mentioned, Auschwitz comes to mind. The White House is besieged. It defends itself as best it can, that is, badly. The drop in the polls is telling; the myth of Reagan's invulnerability has been shattered.

In truth, even if it had been just a Wehrmacht cemetery, it did not deserve a visit from an American president. I know that Germans like to stress the difference between the "good" soldiers of the Wehrmacht and the "bad" SS, and that to earn Germany's goodwill the West played along. Yes, there is a difference. But from that to whitewashing the Wehrmacht is a big step. One cannot forget that it was the Wehrmacht that gave logistical support to the SS units raging against the Jews. Historical documents confirm this, and they are irrefutable. The deadly *Einsatzkommandos* could not have operated at Babi-Yar, Minsk, and elsewhere—in Ukraine, White Russia, and Warsaw—had they not had the active cooperation of the Wehrmacht. The SS were more guilty, that is true. In fact, the Nuremberg tribunal declared *all* the SS formations collectively guilty. And here is the president of the United States preparing to officially, solemnly, bestow on them the honors of our nation by placing a wreath on their tombs!

Telegrams by the thousands pile up in the White House mailroom. Petitions and appeals pour in from all corners of the country. The Senate and the House are unanimous: A visit to Bitburg is a grave error, a gratuitous provocation. Republican officeholders are tearing their hair out. Reagan is moving heaven and earth to get some support. Henry Kissinger telephones me: He understands my position, but the president himself has called, so he cannot help but support him. Too bad, but his support doesn't change things one iota.

To placate irate tempers, at least irate Jewish tempers, the president's chief of staff, Donald Regan, invites a few Jewish Republican leaders for a briefing. Though I am not in that category, I am also invited. Ex officio, as president of the Memorial Council? Perhaps.

Around the table are gathered Max Fisher, the wealthy philanthropist and dean of Jewish lobbyists to the Republican administration; his political friends Gordon Zaks and Richard Fox; and Kenneth Bialkin, the New York lawyer and Jewish community leader.

The administration is represented by Chief of Staff Donald Regan, Patrick Buchanan, and Ed Rollins. Buchanan, a journalist, is the president's adviser for communications, Rollins his political adviser. Of the three, Regan is the only one I know—we met at Colgate University a year or two ago. I had given the commencement address, and he had made the speech welcoming the new students. My words had been tinged with pessimism, while his had been strikingly optimistic. Pleasantly, he reminds me of our dialogue: "Shall we continue it today?"

Some of the Jews present express their opposition to the Bitburg visit: Zaks firmly, Bialkin diplomatically. Fisher is reluctant to criticize the president's decision openly; he recognizes the administration's concern with the possible consequences of a diplomatic incident. Why, he argues, aggravate the tensions between Americans and Germans? Why place the pro-American Kohl in a delicate position? We need to think in terms of air bases and the short-range tactical nuclear weapons the United States maintains in Germany.

I sit there thinking to myself that this is doubtless how things happened during the Holocaust; the Jewish leaders came here to plead for European Jews but wound up saying the same things as their hosts. Probably there was much talk about the situation at the front, but little or nothing about the massacres in Poland.

Among the high American officials, only Rollins speaks against the visit to Bitburg. For what he claims are political as well as moral reasons, Buchanan is in favor of the trip. He argues that, above all, we must avoid giving the impression that the president is yielding to pressures from the Jewish community. I ask him: "But you don't care if he yields to German pressures?" Regan proposes what he considers a fair solution: The president will also go to Bergen-Belsen. He insists on the "also." Does this mean that Bitburg remains on the program? Yes. I respond with a plea: "Give up Bitburg *and* Bergen-Belsen." In vain.

As we leave the White House, Bialkin turns to me and asks: "Did you notice that during the discussion Patrick Buchanan was constantly doodling, scribbling on the yellow pad in front of him? Since I was sitting on his right, I glanced over. Would you believe me if I tell you that he was scrawling two words over and over: 'Jewish pressure, Jewish pressure.' That is what obsessed him in this whole affair, that is what he is afraid of." In Max's plane that takes us back to New York, Bialkin repeats this several times, always with the same bewilderment.

By coincidence, an event that had been decided upon much earlier, a ceremony awarding me the Congressional Gold Medal, is about to be scheduled. This medal represents a rare and prestigious distinction—it has been awarded to no more than one hundred or so individuals in all of American history.

In the spring of 1984, the U.S. Mint is authorized to strike a gold medal in my likeness. We have to choose the artist. For once the decision is easy: the talented artist Mark Podwal. We have already collaborated on a book about the Golem and on a Haggadah. The front of the medal will show my likeness taken from a photo by the legendary photographer Roman Vishniac. Above it, three words: AUTHOR—TEACHER—WITNESS. For the back, Mark draws an open book: Jerusalem and the shtetl, facing each other. On the page representing the City of David, Mark inscribes, in letters barely visible to the naked eye, a verse from the Psalms, "If I forget thee, O Jerusalem . . ."

The White House has been in touch with Congress and me to set a date for the award ceremony. Though the medal is offered by Congress, tradition calls for the president to bestow it. Congressional aides suggest October, then January, then April. The president's aides say yes, then maybe, and change their minds and the date several times. In the end they settle on April 19, 1985. That suits me perfectly. For us it is an unforgettable and historic date: The Warsaw uprising started on April 19, 1943. The technical details remain to be settled, but the White House decides to hold the ceremony in the East Room. Three hundred seats have been set aside for Cabinet members, guests of the president and myself, members of the Memorial Council, and representatives of the media.

Once the Bitburg affair becomes public, however, the White House decides to change the venue. We are now told that the award ceremony will take place in the Roosevelt Room, which can barely accommodate forty people. I am now entitled to a total of four invitations. Obviously the president's staff is trying to scuttle the ceremony, fearful that I might use the occasion to evoke the controversial trip. Everything is arranged to ensure its taking place very quickly, almost secretly. It puts me in the unpleasant position of having to cancel invitations sent to friends in Congress, members of the Council, and friends from abroad. Several senators call the White House asking it to reverse its decision. My own intervention with Reagan fails as well.

Meanwhile the Council holds an extraordinary meeting. There is only one item on the agenda: Bitburg. There are words of resentment, anger. After privately consulting with me, Sigmund, so emotional that he is on the verge of tears, proposes that the entire Council resign in protest if the president really chooses to go to Bitburg. Most members consider that "solution" premature. Let us wait: There are still three weeks before the scheduled trip. Yet something must be done, if only to register our disagreement. I consider refusing the medal. But it is not a presidential award, rather one given by Congress on behalf of the American people. How can I refuse such an honor?

Finally a short and solemn resolution expressing our concern, our anguish, is passed unanimously. We appeal to the president's humanism, to his understanding of history; we shower him with praise even as we ask him to cancel his visit to the SS cemetery.

After our meeting we hold an improvised press conference. I say improvised because, since 1978, we have never used that particular form of communication. Most probably we are the only governmental agency that has never used the services of a press attaché. To my mind, the Holocaust and public relations do not go together. We are doing our duty; let the press do what it is supposed to do. Only this time it's different. As we face the television cameras, the microphones, the flashing lights, we must try to reconcile firmness and discretion, opposition and respect. To a reporter asking me whether I intend to resign, I reply: "I don't believe that will be necessary; I don't believe the president will be going to Bitburg." He wants to know whether I know something they don't. I assure him that I do not. I know the president; he is a man of dignity; he will not ignore the wishes of the American people; he will not pay homage to the SS. Actually I am not so sure, but I tell myself there is nothing to be lost by seeming optimistic.

The country is in a state of upheaval. People are talking about nothing but Bitburg. Why is Reagan being so stubborn? Chancellor Kohl has painted him into a corner. Why doesn't he try to get out?

Back in New York I call another special meeting of the Council. Sigmund reintroduces his resolution asking the Council to submit its collective resignation to the president. I am for it, and this time I say so openly. Nevertheless a majority is against resignation. I fail to understand them; why are they so afraid of opposing the president's decision? And why are my fellow survivors so attached to their official titles? "Resigning would be a premature act," they say. "The trip is more than two weeks off. Why rush?"

The day of the ceremony is getting closer. The journalists are harassing me day and night. How many times must I repeat that the president's visit would be a mistake, both morally and politically? And that there is no way the president will whitewash the SS, whose crimes continue to haunt our generation?

From Washington, I am told to expect a call from Marshall Breger, Jewish affairs adviser to the White House. I am also told that Breger is a practicing Orthodox Jew and that surely he will understand our position. When he calls I tell him what I think of the presidential trip. He does not agree with me. I guess that is his job, but I cannot fathom how a devout Jew can concur in an anti-Jewish policy. He should resign. But few low-level officials ever do. They need to earn a living; they need to feel important. Well, it's his problem.

Abe Rosenthal and Arthur Gelb, the powerful editors of the *New York Times*, are with us, not only in their professional capacity but as friends. As Jews. They are men of conscience, and they are an ideal team. There are those who fear them, and others who swear by them, but all agree that they are superb professionals. Marion and I keep them informed of developments. Sigmund acts as liaison with Capitol Hill. The atmosphere becomes more and more tense. The ceremony is scheduled for the following Friday. We still don't know anything, including whether we will be allowed additional guests. And most important: Will we succeed, at the last hour, in persuading the president's advisers? Or will the visit to Bitburg take place?

Suddenly there is a new question from the reporters trailing me: Will I attend the ceremony, or will I boycott it? To maintain the suspense I do not give a definite answer. But my speech is ready. Well, almost. Abe and Arthur are positive about it. Its tone is respectful but firm and uncompromising. As always, since I rarely write in English, Marion offers precious, indispensable suggestions.

On Wednesday, April 17, we take the shuttle to Washington. Elisha accompanies us. He will celebrate his bar mitzvah in June. I see that he looks a little troubled. Is it his bar mitzvah or our nervousness?

Per Ahlmark, former deputy prime minister of Sweden, outspoken foe of anti-Semitism, and talented poet and writer known for his moral courage, has come from Stockholm. We meet for lunch. He gives us sad news: Our friend Tim Greve, editor in chief of the Norwegian newspaper *VG*, has been diagnosed with cancer. None of us touches the food.

Marian Craig calls from the Council offices to inform me that Michael Deaver has been trying to reach me. I consider Deaver *the* adversary. More than just an adviser to Ronald Reagan, he is the one who, on the American side, bears responsibility for Bitburg. He is reputed to be wily, arrogant, and self-satisfied, and he beats all records for unpopularity among the president's staff. He led the group that months earlier had gone to Germany to prepare the presidential trip. He was the one to whom they showed the Bitburg cemetery. Did the Germans tell him of the SS graves? They swear they did. I have no desire to speak to him, but, then again, perhaps he has good news. I call him back. He can no longer be reached, but Arthur Burns, U.S. ambassador to Germany, comes on the line. I know him. We met in Newport, Rhode Island, during a conference about the first Jews who came to America. A Jew who has no problem with his Jewishness, he tells me that "he has been asked" to speak to me. "Since the president is going to Bergen-Belsen, I consider Bitburg acceptable," he tells me. I do not agree. He goes over the same geopolitical and diplomatic arguments. To those he adds the necessity of not letting down Kohl, Washington's great ally. I let him have his say, but my response is still no. I tell him: "To me it's a question of Jewish memory. Bitburg will taint that memory. That must be avoided." He has done his best to convince me. He too has failed.

Thursday morning we attend the annual Day of Remembrance. It takes place in the Rotunda. There is a procession of flags of the particular army units that liberated the camps. We go through the ritual: the songs, the lighting of the six candles. Feelings are running high because of Bitburg, as is to be expected.

Most congressional leaders are present along with personalities from the worlds of politics and religion. Secretary of State George Shultz represents the administration. His speech, delivered in his slow and dignified style, is not just eloquent—it is moving. I am not surprised. Shultz is the humanist on Ronald Reagan's team.

In my speech, only partly devoted to the subject that is on our minds, I evoke the inhumanity that the SS symbolizes. At one point I speak directly to Shultz and ask him to "be our intercessor."

He understands me. His spokesman, Bernie Kalb, confirms it later. The secretary of state calls his ambassador in Bonn several times, hoping to convince Kohl not to insist on Bitburg. But to Kohl, this visit to the military cemetery is too important. He needs the image of Reagan bowing before the graves of German soldiers, including the SS. Shultz personally expresses his reservations to the president, but Reagan feels committed to Kohl. Even a partial rehabilitation of the SS will reinforce Kohl's popularity, and not only in the nationalist circles of the German right.

Peter Petersen, an old parliamentarian too close to Kohl for my taste, tries to reason with me: "You are wrong to condemn all the SS. There were bad ones, but there were also decent ones: Not all of them were running concentration camps; many of them fought at the front."

But for me there were no "good" SS. The German tactic is obvious: to whitewash the SS. It is the final step in a carefully conceived plan. To begin with, Germany rehabilitated the "gentle," "innocent" Wehrmacht. And now, thanks to Kohl, it was the turn of the SS. First of all, the "good" ones. And then would come the turn of the others. And once the door was open, the torturers and the murderers would be allowed in as well. Bitburg is meant to open that door. From Kohl's point of view it makes sense, but it is difficult to understand Reagan. Why is he so intent on compromising himself in this affair? He has nothing to gain. Deaver and Buchanan are harming him, can't he see that? Officials in the State Department tell me that Kohl bears full responsibility for this debacle; he convinced Reagan that if the visit were canceled it would be his, Kohl's, defeat, and hence that of the alliance between the United States and Germany.

Following tradition, the Council gathers in full session after the ceremony of remembrance. The schedule for the day includes an urgent matter dealing with the future museum. We must choose between two designs, Zalman Einav's and the one proposed by Sonny Abramson's architect. The first is sober, modest. I prefer it to the other, which reminds me of a glorified supermarket. But we are on the eve of the White House ceremony. Everyone is more preoccupied by Bitburg than by architectural models. People come and go constantly. The vote is taken while I am outside giving an interview on television. Abramson's banal proposal wins. I listen to Benjamin Meed's panegyric praise: He loves this design; he believes in it; he knows now that the museum will be built; therefore, it's the greatest day in his life. Someone tells me that the rules were not followed; there was no quorum. We'll see about that later.

In the corridors it is impossible to move without running into a photographer or a reporter. Everybody wants to know whether I'll go to the White House. The suspense continues for another few hours.

In my hotel room with Marion, Elisha, Sigmund, and Per, I review my acceptance "response" to Reagan. Later I have a copy dropped off at the White House. No one had asked for it; I consider it a matter of courtesy. I want the president to know in advance what I intend to say to him tomorrow. Who knows; a miracle is still possible.

A journalist calls: Am I aware of the secret meeting being held at this very moment, in my hotel, on a lower floor? Breger has brought together a group of Jewish leaders to discuss Bitburg and to exert pressure on them in the hope that they might put pressure on me.

There's nothing surprising about this. Most of the Jewish leaders refuse to support me. They tell me of the importance of conciliating ethics and politics. Senator Lautenberg of New Jersey advises me to keep a low profile. Don't make waves, he says, don't rock the boat. Why be in conflict with the president? Other Jewish personalities also preach moderation, appeasement. After all, Bitburg is but one episode in the Jewish community's relationship with the president. It is better to compromise. There will be other crises; we shall need the president's goodwill. Amazingly, these are the same leaders who after the ceremony hasten to congratulate me and applaud my courage, adding: "You know that I was on your side, believe me, I was."

The evening is hectic, interrupted by "urgent" calls. Insiders pass on the latest piece of information from "reliable sources," or a last piece of advice. Elisha acts as switchboard operator, secretary, and spokesman. I am told that some reporters are spending the night downstairs, near the elevators, waiting for a scoop. It all reminds me of the old days, when I was a reporter.

Friday morning a limousine takes me to the studios of CBS, NBC, and ABC. It has been ages since I worked as a journalist, but today especially I would have preferred the role of interviewer to that of interviewee, perhaps because I know in advance the questions that will be put to me: Am I going to accept the medal from the president? (Yes—a refusal would mean offending the American people.) What am I going to say to him? (That he should change his mind.) What is my stand on collective guilt? (I don't believe in it.)

At almost 10 o'clock we go to the White House. At the gate we run into the Israeli ambassador, my old friend Meir Rosenne, whom I have invited. Breger walks over; there is instant antagonism between us. Breger tells me I know his in-laws. To get into my good graces, he mentions the Talmud. Since I don't react, he comes to the point: He feels my speech is somewhat long. In other words, he'd like me to shorten it. In other words, he'd like me to remove the critical passages.

I don't react. In the antechamber I glimpse Rosenthal and Gelb. Marion joins us. The four of us retreat to a corner for a brief, last-minute consultation. I tell them of my hurried, unpleasant conversation with Breger and that I'm going to try to see the president before the ceremony. I want to try one last time to convince him. They're skeptical, and so am I. I ask them what I should do if an attempt is made to cut my speech. "In that case," Rosenthal says, "you don't make a speech. You say thanks for the medal and you read your text in front of the cameras and the press, outside, on the lawn."

Just then Breger comes running. Breathlessly he tells me that Donald Regan is waiting for me in his office. On our way there, Breger resumes the attack. I still don't react. Regan greets me warmly. I ask him if he has read my speech. Yes, he has read it. No objections? Absolutely none. And the president? No objections. So it was only Breger who wanted to censor me. Why such zeal from a man whose roots, if not his emotional ties, are in Jewish Eastern Europe? Why would a Jew—an Orthodox Jew, to boot—behave so contemptibly? To win points from his superiors? His punishment follows almost instantly.

Regan escorts us into the Oval Office. With us is Peggy Tishman, an intelligent, elegant lady devoted to various Jewish causes who heads a cultural group that organizes an annual "Week of Jewish Heritage" event, which this year is under the president's auspices. Why have the two ceremonies been linked? Probably an idea of Breger's intended to minimize the importance accorded the event honoring me. Regan presents Peggy to the president, who politely says he knows who she is; then he presents me. The president interrupts him: "There's no need; we know each other."

Now comes Breger's turn. Clearly, the president has no idea who he is. Regan has to explain to him that Breger deals with Jewish affairs at the White House. Poor Breger, who has been boasting everywhere about his personal relations with the president, who has been speaking on his behalf, supposedly expressing his wishes—I watch him turn pale: The president has treated him as one would a stranger.

After we sit down, Peggy and I speak of our concerns, of what is troubling us. I say: "Mr. President, it's not too late. Imagine for a moment the following scenario: You deliver your remarks, you hand me the medal, I respond, you already know my response. When I finish speaking, you return to the microphone and simply say: 'Very well, I shan't go.' Do that, Mr. President, and people everywhere, Jews and non-Jews, young and old, Republicans and Democrats alike, will applaud your decision. They will say: 'The president of the United States doesn't really need advisers; he decides.' "

"Too late," he says to me with a grave, sad smile. He has just spoken to Chancellor Kohl on the telephone. The German leader has told him that if the visit to Bitburg is canceled now, it will be a "national catastrophe" for his country. The president is committed. Break his promise? Unthinkable. I feel sorry for him. I know he feels trapped, and that if it depended solely on him, he would decide differently. The threesome of Regan, Deaver, and Buchanan have in fact made the decision in his place.

It's almost 11 o'clock. We take our leave of the president and walk in the direction of the Roosevelt Room. Squeezed together like passengers in a subway during rush hour, the guests are already there. There are about forty people, fifty at most. Vice President George Bush is there, as are the president's chief advisers, the four congressmen who had introduced the bill proposing me for the medal, and the press pool. NBC is broadcasting the ceremony live, as is CNN. Elisha and Marion are seated in the first row. Just behind them, Sigmund, Abe Rosenthal and his wife, Shirley, Arthur Gelb and his wife, Barbara. The president enters at precisely 11 o'clock. The audience stands, waiting for him to sit down. As always, images from long ago flash through my mind. I see myself back home, in my little town. It is morning. I'm going to shul. It's winter. It's snowing. I am alone in the street. No—not quite. I hear footsteps. Someone is following me. To assault me? To protect me? How does one measure the road from Sighet to the White House? The president speaks well, of Jewish history, Judaism, the weight of heritage, ethics and culture, Jewish suffering—no one can read a text as he does. But he is tense, as I am, and, evidently, as is the audience. There is a sense of history unfolding.

The president covers me with praise. He appears to be attributing to me everything that is good in the world at this moment in time. Do I feel flattered? No, not really. Embarrassed? Not that either. It's something else. There is this sense of the unreal I have whenever I listen to people talking about me. This time it's even stronger, as though I were somewhere else, centuries ago. I hear my name. I get up and approach the president, who, with a smile, offers me the pen with which he has just signed the Jewish Heritage Proclamation. Then he hands me the gold medal. There is applause. Who is being applauded here? The Jewish child from Sighet? Out of the corner of my eye I see Marion, and I look at Elisha. I feel emotion gripping me. That's how it is; it is enough for me to look at my son to feel a lump in my throat.

Has he any idea of what he represents for his father? I had not planned this, but as I leave the podium I walk over to him and place the medal in his hands.

In fifteen or twenty minutes I try to cover the entire problem, my entire life. With the respect due the leader of the world, with the affection I feel for the man who has always shown me friendship and understanding for Jewish concerns, I feel it is important to tell him that "it is not a question of politics but of good and evil." I stress that it seems to be the opinion of a majority of Americans that "that place is not your place, Mr. President. Your place is with the victims of the SS." I say: "When the decision was taken to go there, you were unaware of the presence there of SS tombs. But now you know." Therefore he should cancel. I tell him why. I dwell briefly on the immensity of the crimes committed by the SS. "I have seen them at work. I have known their victims. They were my friends. They were my parents. . . ." I remind him that on another April 19, in 1943, the fighters of the Warsaw Ghetto found themselves abandoned by the Allies; all the clandestine networks in occupied Europe received arms and money from London, Washington, even Moscow, all except the Jewish resistance fighters of the ghettos. I speak of their feelings of isolation, abandonment, of the hostility they had to face, and of the behavior of the free world's leaders: Though they knew what was happening, they did little. In fact they did nothing to save the endangered Jewish children. A million Jewish children perished, I say; if I spent my whole life reciting their names I would die before I finished. "The Jewish children, Mr. President, I saw them, I saw them being thrown into the flames, alive." Did I convince him? Television images show him overwhelmed, his face reflecting pain. Did I succeed in making him realize how deep a wound he was inflicting on countless victims, their families, their friends?

After the ceremony I am literally pulled out to the lawn, where I find myself facing the media. I never thought there were so many reporters accredited at the White House. Questions are flying from every corner. The coverage is live. How does one come up with ten original answers to ten journalists all asking the same thing?

My speech makes headlines everywhere. The *New York Times*, the *Washington Post*, most American newspapers reprint it in full. *Newsweek* magazine writes that my "impassioned plea was surely one of the remarkable moments in the annals of the White House." Chris Wallace of NBC: "It was one of the most extraordinary scenes I've ever watched in my three years at the White House. Like a professor addressing a pupil, Elie Wiesel told the president that . . ."

Inside, champagne is being served. A marine officer hands me a sealed envelope; I withdraw to a corner to open it. It is a hastily scribbled note: "I'm in the office next door. I'm here on a mission, so I cannot show myself. I saw you on the screen just now; I'm proud of you." I recognize the handwriting; it is that of Jacques Attali, at that time President Mitterrand's special adviser.

The marine officer returns: Chief of Staff Donald Regan wishes me to join him in his office. To criticize me, to tell me of his displeasure? No: He congratulates me. And, interestingly, on the president's behalf, he thanks me for my courteous and respectful tone. After all, I could have said anything I chose. I could have, with the whole country listening, flaunted my disappointment. We appreciate your moderation, Regan tells me. To show our appreciation we wish to propose the following: Come with us to Europe on Air Force One. Together you and the president have made history today, and that way you'll continue what you started. I listen to him, thinking naively that I have prevailed. If I am invited to join them on the trip, it must mean that I have persuaded them. I instantly think of a problem: How am I going to come back? If I go to Europe with the president, how am I going to be back in time for my class at Boston University? After all, they won't be giving me another plane, presidential or not, for the trip home. While these thoughts go through my mind, Regan keeps on describing our future exploits—a stop here, a reception there, the president will speak, I'll respond. . . . The dialogue begun today will thus be continued for the greater glory of men of goodwill. Whenever he stops to take a breath, I ask: "And then?" Meaning: How am I going to get back to the United States? Regan, in full swing, can't be interrupted. And then, he says, we'll go here, there. . . . I insist: "And then?" "Then," says Regan, "we'll quickly dash to this place of damnation, Bitburg and. . . ." This time I manage to interrupt him: "Mr. Regan, I don't understand what you're saying: I desperately don't want the president to go there, and you want me to go there with him?"

(Regan later wrote in his memoirs that I had promised him beforehand not to make a speech when the medal was given me. My lawyers immediately demanded a retraction and an apology. Under the threat of legal action, he gave us both.)

• • •

During the weeks that still separate us from the fateful trip, people from throughout the country continue to exert pressure on the White House. Jesse Jackson comes to tell us that he is leading a delegation to Dachau, to see and to testify. Articles and letters from readers abound in the press.

To the end I cling to the conviction that somehow, at the last minute, the president will not proceed with the scheduled visit. I say so to all the reporters: He won't go, you'll see, he won't go. I was mistaken. In the end, President Reagan did go to Bitburg. That day, I was in New Jersey for a conference. There was a television crew on-site, and I was asked to comment on the presidential visit live. I chose to dwell on the symbolic significance of his act: "With these few steps taken by the president, forty years of history have been wiped out."

When the president and Kohl arrive in the former concentration camp Bergen-Belsen, Menachem Rosensaft (son of Yossel and Hadassah) and other survivors from this camp offer them a "welcome" that respectfully takes issue with the trip. The German police attempt to manhandle some of them, but, aware that the eyes of the world are on them, they decide to be more polite.

Bitburg is a turning point. Kohl knows it, and we know it. Relations with Germany are changed forever. The SS, former or current, will no longer be considered outside the law. Bitburg will remain a "response" to Nuremberg.

Never before and only rarely afterward did I receive so much mail, extraordinary not only by its volume but by its content. By standing up to the most powerful man in the world, the former refugee in me had in just a few minutes touched a thousand times more people than I had with all my previous writings and speeches.

One evening, dining at a restaurant with Marion and friends, I notice at the other end of the room an admiral in full uniform celebrating a birthday with his family. Suddenly he sees me. He gets up and walks over to our table, salutes me, and thunders: "I am Admiral ———. And I must tell you: Though the president is my commander in chief, it is you I am proud of."

A news commentator later said to me: "In fact, Bitburg did do some good; it allowed you to teach America something about history and remembrance."

Perhaps, but I could have done without it.

• • •

Just as sin begets sin, so shame begets shame.

The spectacle of the cemetery visit will be accompanied by presidential statements that many consider more offensive, more outrageous than the visit itself. To justify his decision Reagan declares that the SS buried in Bitburg were victims in the same way and to the same degree as the prisoners murdered in the concentration camps. The angry reaction of the survivors surprises no one. Never before had anyone dared push blasphemy as far as in this odious comparison. To thus link the SS to their victims transcended the limits of decency.

Hadassah Rosensaft, a survivor of Auschwitz and Bergen-Belsen, whose candidacy I had presented to the commission and later to the Council, calls me in despair: "How could he, how dare he say what he said?" She tells me that she is now sorry for not having voted for the collective resignation of the Council. I try to calm her: "In two days we'll have another session. If a new proposal to resign collectively comes before us, will you vote for it?" Her answer is instantaneous: "Absolutely. You may count on me."

This session is as tense, as agitated as the last. The president's ill-chosen words weigh on us. It is impossible to ignore them, brush them aside—or, as they say, "live with them." What line of conduct are we to adopt? Sigmund renews his motion to resign as a group. I note with sadness that he and I are still in the minority. In the end, only Irving Bernstein, Bob McAfee Brown, Siggi Wilzig, and Norman Braman vote with us. Most of our colleagues—including the survivors—oppose the motion. I am the last to take the floor. I say:

> There comes a moment in the lives of every one of us when we must justify our presence. For us, this is the moment. I cannot quite see how we can continue to serve a president who has just insulted the memory of our dead. Since we have been appointed by him, we have only one option: to signify our disagreement by resigning. Otherwise we lose the moral right to defend that memory. Our resignation will leave only a small trace, but a trace nevertheless: Two or three phrases in this document will recall that we were able to resist the temptations of cowardice.

I slowly look around the table. The uneasiness is tangible. Many eyes are cast down. The meeting is still in session when I am asked to step outside for an urgent call. New Jersey Senator Frank Lautenberg is on the phone. He seems beside himself with fury. He has learned that some of us are thinking of resigning. He warns me and asks me to warn the others on his behalf that if they resign, he will take steps, he will denounce them to the media, and then we shall learn what he's capable of. I don't argue. What's the point?

That day, the day of the shameful vote against collective resignation, I decide that I have had enough. At the first opportunity I shall hand in my resignation to the president. Marion agrees. In fact it has been months, if not years, that she has been urging me to quit. Washington is taking too much of my time. I am forced to spend hours and hours on the telephone. And then things are not right with the Council: too many intrigues, too many jealousies; endless ideological and ethnic quarrels; requests from one side, recriminations from the other; Washington millionaires who are grumbling, philanthropists who have other priorities, money that's not coming in fast enough. I had stated from the start that collecting money was not my forte. With Sigmund's help, Miles is doing the best he can, but it is going slowly. We have hired professional fund-raisers, but their advice costs us more money than they bring in. I use my lecture tours to support Miles's efforts. There is no lack of promises. I try to motivate some of the Hollywood moguls. Steven Spielberg sets the example. One of the moguls will install an electronic system in the future museum, another will take care of the video systems. But there is little progress. I no longer have any "influence" on nominations. The signals are anything but ambiguous: I am not to expect any cooperation from the administration.

Sigmund is against my quitting. So is Irving Bernstein. They urge me to wait—a few weeks, a few months. They say my resignation might be interpreted as an attempt to politicize the Council and its mission. In the meantime, Sonny and Bud have become more active, and they are clamoring for more authority, obviously at Sigmund's expense. The feeling between the two factions is evidently one of animosity. I have to intervene more often, too often. How can I escape this atmosphere of arguments, of quarrels? I spend hours appeasing one side or the other—a waste of time. I don't show it, but I'm losing patience, especially since I continue to have doubts about the very mission that has been entrusted to us. Who knows, perhaps the museum had been a mistake after all. And what if Jimmy Carter had been right? Jewish memory has survived without museums; it has survived thanks to writing, thanks to books, thanks to schools. In addition to the Day of Remembrance, we could have created archives and educational programs. All our problems, all our difficulties stem from the creation of the museum. Without it we would have been spared all these grandiose and expensive traps. Or we could have renovated the brick building that had been offered us. The Holocaust and luxury are incompatible. Now it's too late; impossible to go back.

So we persevere. Sonny insists that we hire his friend Shaike Weinberg, former director of Beit Hatefutsot, the Diaspora Museum in Tel Aviv, who is now living in Washington. I hesitate. I know that museum. Young Israelis like it for its technical novelties. Here we call them "gimmicks"—gadgets, tricks, special effects. I worry that while this approach may be useful for children in secondary schools, it might not be right for a museum dedicated to the Holocaust.

In Washington, the administrative team is going through its own series of crises. Monroe Freedman has decided to return to academia. I propose to the White House to replace him with Leon Jick, professor of contemporary Jewish history at Brandeis University. He is turned down. I suggest Sister Carol Rittner. Suggestion rejected. Finally, an active Jewish Republican, Richard Krieger, succeeds Monroe Freedman.

Sonny and Bud are getting impatient. They're having difficulty getting along with Sigmund, but toward Krieger they soon become downright aggressive. He refuses to be manipulated, which, in turn, exasperates them. As he is responsible for the implementation of the Council's decisions, he insists on checking all expenses. Sonny has fits of anger. He wants nothing to do with either Sigmund or Krieger. He acknowledges my authority but not theirs. In fact, he would like to replace Sigmund as chair of the committee handling the construction of the museum. I am against it: I don't wish to humiliate a survivor and a friend. Thereafter, Sonny turns openly hostile. Bud, of course, takes his side. In a way I understand them: Building is their business. Why do we get involved with it? If only we would leave him alone—that's all Sonny asks. What does this museum mean to him? Just another building project? Nothing but a pile of bricks and cash? I refuse to believe that.

On July 2, 1986, I go to Washington one more time, hoping to restore peace between the adversaries. My notes from that day reflect my mood:

I cannot believe what I read and hear. What is happening to them? Why such antagonism? Why such hostility and suspicion? I once thought that our team would be inspired by the grandeur of its mission; I thought we would be happy working together, that the time between our meetings would seem long. . . . Instead, what do I see? Absurd rivalries, petty intrigues. . . .

Once more I try to convince them. But peace lasts only until the next argument—especially since Sonny now has a new reason for being unhappy. The architectural design that had been approved in my absence has been demolished by an article in the *Washington Post*. We shall have to find a new architect. Arthur Rosenblat, a fine-arts specialist brought in by Sonny, suggests James Ingo Freed, a noted associate of I. M. Pei. I meet with Rosenblat and Freed separately. Both impress me favorably. But I wonder why, though both are Jewish, neither has ever felt the need to visit Israel. And what concerns me even more: Freed confesses to me that even though he's a refugee from Germany, he has never been interested in the Holocaust. He has repressed his past. Should we hold this against him? I don't think so; I like him and his work. I spend many hours with Freed, who wants me to share with him my vision for the museum. He listens silently. Occasionally he asks a question. Then another. He stays with me until he is sure he understands. I like his approach. I consult I. M. Pei. He confirms that Freed is excellent. I decide to hire him. I write the Council: ". . . By its magnitude, the Holocaust defies language and art: and yet one and the other are necessary to tell the history that must be told. In James Freed we have found an architect capable of mastering this unique challenge. . . ."

Sonny and Bud favor his candidacy but remain on the offensive about everything else. Sonny has the support of his friend in Congress. Through his wife, an influential member of the Republican party, Bud has access to the White House. They are determined to reduce Sigmund's influence. To my great surprise and chagrin, Miles Lerman rallies to their support. Not only has he become their defender, but their accomplice as well. He comes to see me to "confide" that if Sigmund is not removed from the museum committee, Bud and Sonny may well withdraw from the project. My instinct tells me this is so. In fact, I shall have proof of it a few days later. Bud comes to see me at home. After the usual banter, he comes to the point, an ultimatum: If I keep Sigmund, Sonny and he will call it quits.

Though Sigmund is unhappy when I tell him of the conversation, he agrees, though reluctantly, to give in. But I am not ready. There is another reason besides loyalty. Again, the same one—I refuse to humiliate anyone, especially a friend.

To Miles, who tries to overcome my resistance in the name of a ruthless pragmatism—which I understand but reject—I respond that I cannot sanction publicly humiliating a man as devoted as Sigmund. "Moreover," I tell Miles, "he is your best friend." He replies that if I don't submit to their ultimatum—he doesn't use this word, but the sense is there—it means the end of the project. And, he insists, the project is more important than any individual.

This whole business upsets me terribly. What about friendship? How does one sacrifice—worse, betray—a close friend? It was Sigmund who gave him his first chance and supported him inside the Council. He would not have been nominated if Sigmund hadn't begged me to do it. And then hadn't he learned yet that one human being is more important than all of man's endeavors?

I feel exhausted and dangerously close to a red line that I am not ready to cross. On the one hand, I refuse to hurt a friend; on the other, I don't want to harm a project that at this point has little chance of succeeding without Sonny and Bud. There is only one solution. Resign. I shall announce my resignation at the beginning of December, at the regular Council meeting.

En route for Washington one December evening, Sigmund and I stop off in New Jersey, where I am to give a lecture at a local university. Afterward, we have dinner with Sam Halperin, a survivor and a successful businessman, in the company of his associates. I don't tell them of my decision; Sigmund and Marion are the only ones who know. Siggi Wilzig, bubbling over with energy, promises me that things would work better without Sonny and Bud. He guarantees that twenty-four hours after their resignation a new builder will put himself at our disposal. "I want to speak to him," I say. He immediately puts me in contact with a famous builder, Bill Zeckendorf, who confirms what Wilzig has said. Only I am tired of all the promises of all these people, the ones I know and the ones I don't. Whom can I trust? Nevertheless I try one more time. I say to Halperin: "You are in real estate and construction; why don't you take over the project?" He answers that he cannot, that the moment is not right; he's too busy with too many things.

That settles it. My absolutely final effort has failed. The next day I hand in my resignation to the White House. Everyone is astounded. Donald Regan's reaction is: "What? You're resigning? But the president has just reappointed you for another five years! Is it something we did?" He is worried about possible political consequences. I reassure him: "It has nothing to do with you." My reasons are personal. This is not quite true, but almost. Since the Bitburg affair I have not felt right. How can I "serve" under a president who "objectively" (using Marxist terminology; once is not a habit) has whitewashed the SS by comparing them to their victims? But that is not the only reason.

Back from the White House, I know that word has leaked out. Sigmund is sad, but there is nothing he can say to make me go back on my decision. Marion is happy; Marian Craig, my loyal assistant, is unhappy. Miles suggests that I take a year's leave. I shrug my shoulders. Yitz Greenberg and Alfred Gottschalk, president of Hebrew Union College, beg me not to abandon the project. I tell them that it's too late. Technically that is not true: A simple call to Regan and everything could be as before. But that's just it—I don't want things as they were before.

The Council meeting is pathetic. There is a series of sentimental appeals imploring me not to go. With the exception of Bud and Sonny, almost all the members ask to speak. I would be too embarrassed to repeat what was said—yes, embarrassed, not flattered. They question me, plead with me, make me promises. Some use emotional arguments, others prefer logic. They are not unlike children fearful of becoming orphans.

As always, I listen to them attentively, just like at the university, where from the start I have always tried to set an example. I owe it to my students and to my colleagues not to let myself be distracted. I concentrate on what each one has to say. My personal opinion, or any comment I have, is given only at the end.

I look out over the assembled Council members with a mixed feeling of accomplishment and failure. All things considered, we did some good work. Sworn to preserve memory, we had all been resolute in fighting defamation and oblivion. We reached certain goals, fought certain battles, and obtained victories of which we can be proud. Not many. So what? I refuse to judge my colleagues, those who fell short. We all have our own way of doing what we consider to be our duty.

As far as I am concerned, I consider it my duty to relinquish the reins. I acknowledge my shortcomings: I am a poor manager, a bad administrator. I have problems giving orders, and I am incapable of hurting anyone, even in the name of supposedly sacred aims. I don't like firing people. I abhor reprimanding, punishing. I would rather write, study, and teach than "preside." In my letter to President Reagan, which I read to the plenary session, I suggest that since the project has now entered the practical, concrete phase, my successor ought to have the qualities required of a C.E.O., someone able to administer, organize, and navigate through budgetary labyrinths.

A few weeks later the White House appoints Bud Meyerhoff. Together with his friend Sonny Abramson, he will monitor the work of the Council. They bring back Berenbaum and Weinberg, take revenge on Sigmund (who will no longer be a member of the executive committee and will not even be reappointed as a member of the Council), and dismiss Richard Krieger and then Professor Eli Pfefferkorn—in short, all those who were close and devoted to me are removed.

From that time on, whenever a survivor comes to see me to tell me about what is going on in Washington during the meetings and behind the scenes, I stop him or her; I would rather not know. With my resignation I gave up the right to criticize. I want my successors to do their work without criticism from me. Once the project is realized and the museum is built, I'll speak my mind—not before.

What really hurt and disappointed me? That when Sigmund was excluded from the executive committee, of which he had been a part since the beginning, not one survivor rallied to his support. A comrade, a colleague had been humiliated, and they all looked away. The same was true for Pfefferkorn. No one spoke up to save the job of this Holocaust survivor.

How can these people labor for remembrance of the past when in the present they flout the dignity of living people? But then, perhaps, I expect too much of them. They are human, hence capable of anything. Just like everyone else.

This said, the new team deserves praise. Miles and Bud excel in the art of collecting funds. People who refused to help earlier now show themselves more generous. The New Jersey group's gift comes to several million dollars. The project is taking shape. Hundreds of specialists are at work.

. . .

January 1993: I visit the essential part of the museum, and my first impression of the building itself is positive. But paradoxically, the museum, by trying to say everything, does not say enough. Yes, there are the ghettos, the yellow stars, the terrified men, the starving children, the corpses in the street, the cruelty of the torturers, the misery of the victims. You enter through the cattle car imported from Poland. You walk on the cobblestones of the Warsaw Ghetto. "Identity cards" are distributed at the entrance. These things are designed to make things look authentic, to give the visitor the impression, if not the feeling, that he or she is *there*. Upon leaving, the visitor will be able to say: "Now I know everything; I understand." Later he or she will say: "I was there." I had a different vision of the museum. I should have liked the visitor to leave saying: "Now I know how little I know."

And then: There is this huge bas-relief that shows—yes, shows—the process of annihilation. The Polish sculptor has depicted the inmates upon arrival, upon assembling at the ramp. He "shows" the selection, the march to the "showers"; he "shows" the members of the *Sonderkommandos* pushing the victims into the antechamber to undress and then into the gas chamber; then you "see" the corpses being "treated" by the "dentists" before being sent to the furnaces. You "see" it all. You "see" too much.

That is how it is: By trying to illustrate too much, reveal too much by contrived means, it all becomes too facile.

The men and women who have gone through concentration camps and try to speak of it know the boundaries of language. They speak in order to tell us that no words can possibly communicate the unspeakable. In trying to show everything, you conceal the essential. It is not by "seeing" the ramp in Birkenau that the visitor will feel what those newly arrived Jews felt as they moved toward the selection. In this case the saying "less is more" is apt.

Also, though the building is powerful, you become aware of the magnitude of the ambition and the means expended. As though it had been decided that this museum had to be "the best, the greatest in the world." All these computers, all these videos, all these ultramodern technical and electronic effects, all those buttons to press, all those photographs accumulated to shock you, make you weep. It is an enormous enterprise worthy of our capital. James Freed has produced an excellent piece of work. If there is fault, it lies with those who conceived and shaped its content.

Publicly I have said nothing until now, but in truth I would have preferred a more sober, more humble edifice, one that would suggest the unspoken, the silence, the secret. I think of a talmudic saying: The children of Israel deserved to be delivered from Egypt because they had safeguarded their mystery. Here, the sense of mystery is missing.

And yet. . . . Upon revisiting the museum sometime later, I change my mind to some degree. It is undeniably impressive. The first section, which covers the rise of Nazism in Hitler's Germany, is excellent. The maps, the statistics, the photographs are magnificent. The same is true for the way the lack of any "response" from the Allies and the neutral countries is presented. The builders' devotion is so evident that I silence any impulse to criticize. In fact I often praise the museum in public.

I take part in the official opening, together with Presidents Bill Clinton and Chaim Herzog, on April 19, 1993. Once again, it is that symbolic date: the fiftieth anniversary of the Warsaw Ghetto uprising.

It is raining that day and it is cold. I am soaked, and so is my text. I had worked on it until three in the morning and now it is illegible. I have no choice but to improvise. I evoke the genesis of the project under President Carter, the deep reasons that impelled me to give it form with the words: "For the dead *and* the living—we must bear witness." I tell the story of a woman in her kitchen, preparing for Passover in 1943, discussing the news from Warsaw. She wonders: "Why did the young Jews there think it necessary to rebel? Couldn't they have waited quietly for the end of the war?" My speech ends with this small sentence: "That woman was my mother. . . ."

Three weeks before the opening, Bud Meyerhoff, my successor as chairman of the Council, is suddenly stripped of his functions. Why? There are bizarre rumors. Some say that, together with his deputy, William Loewenberg, he refused to invite Chaim Herzog to speak at the inauguration.

Now and then, members of Congress and members of the Jewish community call, asking me to return to my old post, which Miles has been coveting for a long time. Sigmund is for it, but Marion is dead set against it. Friends point out that now that the museum exists, I would no longer be burdened by administrative tasks. I refuse. Having been gone for almost seven years, I don't feel I should take up the reins again. Though the idea of launching a project never fails to seduce me, once a project is realized I tend to lose interest.

Besides, the museum does very well without me. The public is lining up outside, people from all over the world, Jews and Christians, young and old—altogether more than two million visitors in a year. It is impossible to get tickets without waiting days, weeks.

And, more important, those who have seen the exhibition leave overwhelmed, full of enthusiasm and admiration. It seems the museum is playing a pedagogical role of the first order. I help as much as I can. After all, this museum is not meant for people such as myself who know and who remember, but for the others, the multitude who know nothing and for whom the Holocaust is not unlike all the other episodes of the war. I am pleased to see that so many people have finally become interested in learning the dark history of the twentieth century. After all, that was the purpose of all my work on this project and that of my fellow survivors. Yes, I am grateful for having been allowed to contribute. And I thank the American people and all those who have helped.

Having said this, I repeat: For my generation, nothing is completed. Just like knowledge, this achievement is tinged with anxiety. I cannot help but think: "All this is good and well. And yet. . . ."

Indeed, and yet.

From Sighet to Oslo ——

*I*N MY DREAM *I ask my father, in Yiddish of course: How are things up there? Did you meet . . . ? What do they talk about? What do they know about us, about me? Strange: We are walking around a house I've never seen before . . . going through empty rooms.*

I am used to following him. Now he follows me. Can he hear me? Is he pleased with me? I hear him breathing heavily. I'm afraid of his opinion. I'm afraid of leading him where I shouldn't.

We come to an empty room. Nothing on the walls. Or on the ceiling. Three doors with shattered panes. Outside it's snowing. Dirty reddish flakes. Suddenly they are inside the room; I don't know what they are. Beings? Creatures? Words?

Swirling in the darkness, they come to rest on the walls. There, they light up. They are no longer snowflakes. They are part of the fire that's burning up the room. I begin to scream: "Save me, save me!"

I try to wake up but don't succeed. I struggle, I keep on struggling; but I no longer know against whom.

Perhaps against my father?

Against myself?

☙

Was it Oscar Wilde who was wise enough to say that he who lives more than one life ends up dying more than one death?

I have lived a few lives. How does one relate to the other? I look for the life of the boy from Sighet in that of the orphan abandoned in Buchenwald.

"How do you manage not to be disoriented, to stay your course?" asks a journalist wiser than the others. "Think of the itinerary that has taken you from your forsaken little town to Auschwitz and from Auschwitz to Oslo. . . . Doesn't that drive you mad?"

Yes, it does. I think of it often and always with a feeling of embarrassment and disbelief. Who indeed has traced this strange path for the young Jewish boy who, lost more than once among the dead, found himself, one chilly December day, receiving the greatest honor mankind can bestow on one of its own? Sometimes a wicked thought crosses my mind: Could the Nobel be meant to make up for all the rest? I reject the idea at once. There can be no such thing as making up for the rest, neither individually nor collectively. Not even Israel can be a compensation. The only compensation I might accept, just possibly, would be the arrival of the Messiah.

In truth, many survivors feel this same astonishment in recalling the past. Can this be me walking around freely, with my wife or a friend, along the Champs-Élysées? Can this be me wearing these fine clothes as I look up at the skyscrapers of Fifth Avenue? And can this be me eating all I can eat? Is it really me sending back a dish because it's too cold or not cooked enough? Can it be me laughing or making others laugh? But here I am, feeling at a loss, as I get closer to happiness.

In truth we have not left the Kingdom of Night. Or rather: It refuses to let us go. It is inside us. The dead are inside us. They observe us, guide us. They wait for us. They help us by forcing us to appreciate things and sensations at their just value. They are judging us.

One cannot cheat the dead. They are not to be appeased with lies nor with triumphs. Their truth is not that of the living. But the truth of the living, where is it to be found? In the happiness of others, perhaps.

Not in my own?

Yom Kippur, 1986. I have been at the synagogue since early morning. I like the solemn litanies of this Day of Atonement, in which one reminds God of His promise to remember us. The fasting has been easy, as always. Only I have a frightful headache. As usual, it tears at my brain as though meaning to shred it. Around 4 p.m., after the *Musaf* service, I go home to rest. It's only a ten-minute walk. "A gentleman is waiting for you," the doorman tells me. I wonder who it could be. Who would disturb me on a day that is devoted to meditation and prayer? A smiling man introduces himself: He is the New York correspondent of the Norwegian daily *Dagbladet*. He has something urgent to tell me. I interrupt him: "Please sir, not now, not today; come back some other day, tomorrow perhaps." But not only is this fellow stubborn, he doesn't want anything from me; all he wants is for me to listen to him; what he has to tell me can't wait. I ask patiently: "Don't you know today is Yom Kippur?" He knows, he knows, but there is something he *must* tell me, something *very* important. He asks to come up to the apartment with me. It will just take one minute, no more. He swears: just one minute. Riding up in the elevator, I rack my brain: What could be important enough for him to track me down on Yom Kippur? I don't know, it must be this damned headache of mine that prevents me from seeing clearly, from guessing, from catching on.

Marion is surprised to see my companion. To her unspoken question I respond by introducing him, adding: "He'll explain it all to us." At that point the journalist hands Marion a bouquet of flowers. I hadn't noticed them before. Where had he hidden them? "You should know," he says, "that tomorrow my newspaper's headline will be about you." I begin to understand. I don't know why, but I'm frightened. I stammer: "You're mad . . . this is impossible." But he shakes his head, sure of himself. I beg him to phone his editor, to change the headline. Tomorrow we'll all look ridiculous, and I most of all. It must be stopped. . . . "Too late," the journalist answers, unmoved. I beg him to try, at least to try. Nothing doing. And all the time he doesn't stop smiling. "I'm not asking you for anything just now," he says before leaving. "But tomorrow you will give me an exclusive interview, won't you?" I promise him; I would promise anything as long as he leaves me in peace. I must hurry back to synagogue, where *Neilah*, the majestic, sorrowful service of the closing of the celestial gates, is about to begin.

On the way I think it useful to warn Elisha that something interesting may happen tomorrow. As usual he is "cool." "Is it the Nobel?" How did he guess? At fourteen he already knows many things, my son. How is he reacting to the possibility of this distinction? He shrugs his shoulders as if to say: We'll see.

At the synagogue the congregants are just finishing the *Minha* prayer. One can almost feel them waiting for *Neilah*. They seem to be meditating, turning inward. *Neilah* is the last chance before the closing of the gates of heaven, the gates of prayer. For another forty minutes they remain ajar. Quickly now, the words that can revoke the verdict; quickly, the entreaties, the pleas before it is sealed. And suddenly one forgets hunger, thirst, fatigue; even my headache is gone. With the rest of the congregation I pray for a year of good health and prosperity, a year of peace, particularly for the people of Israel, and for all the peoples on Earth. Still, I admit, from time to time I cannot help but think of the Norwegian journalist. I improvise a silent prayer: Lord, let me not be humiliated tomorrow morning. I don't say "disappointed"; I say "humiliated." But almost instantly I reprimand myself: What would my grandfather say if he knew the object of my concern during the sacred service of *Neilah*? I see him, I see myself with my grandfather visiting the Rebbe of Borshe. The shiver that runs down my spine links me again to a happy and less ambitious world.

As is our custom, we break the fast with friends. There is the usual table talk. I take part absentmindedly. My mind is in Oslo. Tomorrow's *Dagbladet* is already printed. Will everyone be laughing at me tomorrow? Or worse: Will they feel sorry for me?

Back home, we decide to call two or three close friends. Sigmund and Yossi cut short their dinners and hurry over. Per Ahlmark, who is in New York, meets them in the elevator. Unabashedly optimistic, they are preparing for tomorrow: What to say to whom. Should we call my sister Hilda in Nice? Wake her up? But to tell her what? That maybe . . . First of all, I'll have to forewarn John Silber. I need to locate a place for a possible press conference. Yossi, the eternal pragmatist, insists on a general rehearsal: What am I to say if I'm asked "delicate" questions about Israel and the Palestinians?

Yossi thinks of everything. That's his nature. It's no accident that David Ben-Gurion, Moshe Dayan, Menachem Begin, and Yitzhak Shamir all asked him to join their teams. His judgment is uncanny.

I try to calm his excitement and my own. I try to reason with the others, with myself. We all know about rumors; all this may end up as a punishment for giving credence to other people's certainties and wishful thinking. So superstitious am I that I fear that at the last moment the Nobel committee will change its mind, if only to punish *Dagbladet* for its indiscretion. My friends, stubbornly optimistic, deride my eternal skepticism. Marion is thoughtful, silent. Per suggests we call Rabbi Michael Melchior in Oslo. There it is now three in the morning; we can't wake him up after a day of fasting. But it is he who calls us. He's even more confident than Sigmund, Per, and Yossi. "It's you who should go to bed," says the Chief Rabbi of Norway. "They're going to wake you early tomorrow morning." In fact, the traditional press conference of the Nobel committee has been called for late morning in Oslo, 5 a.m. New York time. From then on it will be chaos, he says. I whisper: What if nothing happens? Sigmund admonishes: "Bite your tongue before you say anything else."

I'm afraid of falling asleep, of dreaming, of waking up. At four o'clock Marion suggests that we might as well get up, just in case. Orange juice, hot coffee. The night porter announces that Sigmund, then Yossi, then Per are coming up. His voice betrays his astonishment: Four-thirty in the morning is a strange time for social calls.

"So?" I shrug; still no news. I am praying silently: Please don't let them have gone to all this trouble for nothing. Nobody is speaking. Suddenly, the telephone rings in the living room. I force myself not to rush; it could be another reporter, a neighbor, anyone at all. But it's not. It's Jakub Sverdrup, the director of the Nobel committee and the Nobel Institute: "Excuse us for calling you so early . . . and so late," he says, using his words carefully, the Norwegian way: "But we didn't have your telephone number; it took us an incredible time to get it." Around me everyone looks tense. Sverdrup is in no hurry: "So as you understand, to find the number—your private number—was far from easy, as you are unlisted. And when we finally found it, your number, we thought it was still too early in New York, surely you were still sleeping, so we hesitated, you understand." At last Sverdrup comes to the point: "I have the honor, on behalf of Chairman Egil Aarvik, to inform you that . . . The vote was unanimous. Congratulations. Technical details are on their way."

Why are my eyes blurring? I am overcome by emotion. *We* are overcome by emotion. Marion clutches my hand. Yossi and Sigmund for once seem at a loss for words. Per is smiling. All have tears in their eyes. And then we hold out our arms to each other and embrace. How long did we remain like that, motionless? The telephone breaks the silence. One of the first calls comes from my childhood friend Haim-Hersh, from Sighet, who now lives in Oslo. He is in tears, saying: "I'm looking at television. Nobel Chairman Aarvik is reading a statement. . . . Can you hear, do you understand?" Aarvik is speaking in Norwegian, Haim-Hersh is translating into Yiddish. From the lobby, the doorman, beside himself, is shouting into the intercom. There is a commotion, he says, reporters, photographers, television cameras. The poor fellow is trying to keep calm. Overwhelmed, he doesn't understand what is happening. If only he had known, he keeps saying, he would have requested an assistant, a security guard. And then he tells us that there is a Norwegian journalist waiting. He came before the crowd. He's been waiting for three hours. He is the first to come upstairs, with another bouquet of roses for Marion. He happily reminds me that I promised him an exclusive interview. Then Norwegian television arrives: Jan Otto Johansen from Washington and special correspondent Erik Bö. We are connected live to Norway. The Oslo journalists tell me that in Norway the announcement of the prize is being magnificently received. I call Hilda. She is so excited she can't speak. Around six o'clock the doorman calls again: "What shall I do with NBC?" Then: "And ABC? And CBS?" The *New York Times*, Agence France-Presse, TF1, and Antenne 2 from France. The apartment now looks like a battlefield. Around me are technicians, sound engineers, lighting people, reporters, and producers who seem to be walking over each other. The telephone doesn't stop ringing. From Tel Aviv, Dov and Eliyahu tell me that they expect statements from Chaim Herzog, Yitzhak Shamir, and Shimon Peres. For once there's strange unanimity in the Holy Land. Jacques Attali calls to tell me that President Mitterrand is going to call me at any moment. In Paris, too, the unanimity is striking: Prime Minister Jacques Chirac, whom at that time I had not yet met, sends a message that moves me by its warmth and eloquence. Henry Kissinger: "I was not proud of my Nobel, but I am of yours." The Lubavitcher Rebbe: "You have consistently devoted your life to our people's welfare; from now on you'll do so even better." From all over, my publishers send congratulations and flowers. At eleven o'clock there are still reporters waiting in the hallway. Suddenly I remember: I haven't yet said my morning prayers. I shut myself in an empty room and put on my tefillin.

Elisha takes advantage of the tumult to skip school. I ask him what he feels about all this commotion. Deadpan, he says: "Oh, not much. But . . ." But what? "Well, wouldn't this be a good time for . . . you to increase my allowance? What do you think?"

An urgent, very urgent call from Jerusalem: Dan Shilon, director of broadcasting, insists on interviewing me immediately. We've known each other from the time he was correspondent of Kol Israël— the Voice of Israel—in the United States. I tell him that I first must go to a press conference. He gets upset—I understand his feeling that surely Israel should have priority. I mumble some answers while people pull at me from all sides—we're late. I feel awful that Dan is angry. But today I am not the master of my time.

The press conference, conducted by John Silber, takes place in the Kaufmann Concert Hall of the 92nd Street "Y," where since 1967 I have been giving four annual lectures. Preempting some of the questions the press may be getting ready to toss at me, I point out that the Nobel Prize does not magically transform laureates into experts on politics, the economy, or sociology. I don't expect that I know more today than I did yesterday.

That evening we plan dinner in a French restaurant. To my amazement, on the way to dinner as we pass people standing in line at the entrance to a movie house, they suddenly burst into applause— just like that, in the street, in the heart of Manhattan. At the restaurant, the maître d' comes over to tell me that the corner table is offering us a bottle of wine. Then it's another table . . . and another.

When we get home, we find journalists and photographers waiting: "one last interview" for the 11 o'clock newscasts and "one more shot" for the first morning edition. As I answer the questions I hear the door open: It's the Norwegian consul general and his wife, who give Marion, on behalf of Jo Benkow, president of the Norwegian Parliament, the most magnificent bouquet of roses we've ever seen. The doorman comes up with a package of telegrams, most of them addressed simply to ELIE WIESEL—NEW YORK.

Ed Koch, New York's mayor, informs me that in light of all this attention, the police department has decided it must protect me with "close security." I have the right to two plainclothesmen, who will scrutinize anyone who comes close to me. They accompany me even when I go to synagogue for Sukkoth. It all seems surreal.

A funny episode: The telephone rings. A pleasant voice asks me whether I am ready to accept a call from the commissioner. The refugee in me still trembles—commissioner to me means commissioner of police. Is it a crime to become a Nobel laureate? I take the phone: "This is Peter . . . Peter Ueberroth. We met in Madrid a few years ago." The knot in my throat loosens: "What can I do for you?" Solemnly he announces: "We have decided to bestow a great honor on you, the greatest that . . . Very few people are given this honor." I feel a tug at my heart: So the Nobel is not the "greatest" honor after all? "We invite you to throw out the first ball in the first game of the World Series." I think quickly. Should I tell him I know nothing about baseball? No point in offending him. I ask: "Why me?" He laughs. "Because . . . ," and he says some nice things. I fall back on the calendar; with a little luck I'll be busy that day. "And this big game, when is it?" He tells me the date, and I thank the Lord: Thank you, God, for commanding us to celebrate our festivals. "I'm terribly sorry," I say, "but it's the second day of Sukkoth." He doesn't know what that is or how it could be connected to baseball. I give him his first lesson in Judaism: "A practicing Jew is not allowed to travel or play any sport on a religious holiday." "What a shame," he says. Then he asks whether I couldn't get some kind of exemption from a rabbi.

Elisha comes home from school just as I'm saying good-bye to Ueberroth. His eyes open wide: "You were talking to Ueberroth? Peter Ueberroth?" I confirm this. "The baseball commissioner?" Yes. Himself. "What did he want?" I make a report. "What? You refused to throw out the first ball of the World Series? You turned it down?" He can't stand still. He seems to be personally stung in his honor as an American adolescent. "Do you realize what my friends will say if they hear of your blunder?" He wants me to call back Ueberroth, tell him I've changed my mind, that I've found a way of sidestepping the traditional laws. I stand firm. Thank God, Ueberroth calls back: "In consideration of your religious constraints, which we respect . . . here is a new proposition, which we hope you will accept. This year, exceptionally, no one will be invited to throw out the first ball of the first game, but you could throw out the first ball of the second." Elisha is still in my study. He follows my end of the conversation. He begs me, orders me to accept: "Yes, yes, say yes!" I ask: "So there's a second game?" Ueberroth chokes with laughter. I say: "This second game, when is it?" He tells me the date. I glance at my calendar, and I mumble: "It's the Sabbath." "What does that have to do with baseball?" asks Ueberroth, slightly irritated. He now gets his second unexpected lesson in Judaism. Elisha is devastated. He makes it clear that he'll never forgive me. I explain to him that though I have the right to violate all the laws of the Sabbath in order to save one life, any life, I do not have the right to violate the law for the—for me, dubious—pleasure of throwing a ball in front of a crowd of baseball fans.

Ueberroth saves me by calling a third time: "I've checked with an Orthodox rabbi. After nightfall you have the right to travel, so you can come to the stadium. With a police escort you'll get there in time. . . ." Elisha is jubilant. Many of his friends and classmates are invited. Suddenly his jaw drops: "Do you even know *how* to throw a ball?" No, I don't; they never taught me that in Sighet. Never mind—he'll teach me. Still, some 75,000 paying spectators will be watching me, plus all the television viewers whose number will exceed 30 or 40 million; I must not bring shame on my son. Am I a good pupil? Suffice it to say that the team that receives my first ball amid deafening roars loses the game. And the following day, for the first—and surely the last—time in my life, my picture adorns the first page of the *New York Times* sports section.

At the synagogue, people are mercifully discreet. I am grateful. I am given an aliyah, the honor of reading from the Torah. Cantor Joseph Malovany chants a special blessing. Rabbi Sol Roth contents himself with wishing me *mazel tov*. In the face of God, we are all His creatures. Evidently the Nobel doesn't count for much in heaven.

With a Nobel Prize come quite a few lessons. For one, you learn who is a friend and who is not. Contrary to popular wisdom, a friend is not one who shares your suffering, but one who knows how to share your joy. I was pleasantly surprised by some and sadly disappointed by others.

There are envious and jealous people everywhere; they are part of the human landscape. Some who praised my writings when I was poor and unknown now resent me for being "rich" and "famous." Others were faithful to me as long as I wrote for a limited public; now it bothers them to see my name on pages other than literary. Sadly, some "admirers" turned against me after the Nobel, as though to punish me for a success some of them had actually helped me achieve. These betrayals hurt me the most. I cannot explain them.

In my first volume of memoirs I told of I. B. Singer's account of the offensive and heinous jealousies he endured after he was awarded the Nobel. Singer laughed as he spoke of them; it made him happy that these people were not. I also think of Camus's years of depression after the Nobel. Olivier Todd, his biographer, describes that period with tact and honesty.* Intellectuals from the left and from the right constantly made him feel that he owed them something. As for me, I try to follow Spinoza's advice: not to laugh or weep, but to understand. Of course, I endured instances of sheer malice I shall never understand.

Never mind. I can take it. At this point in my life a few petty personal attacks in the press will not change anything for me.

• • •

***Albert Camus: Une Vie* (Paris: Gallimard), 1996.

During the intermediate days of Sukkoth, Marion and I fly to Moscow, invited by the Soviet authorities. Sigmund Strochlitz and Michael Melchior accompany us. The official purpose of the trip is to prepare for Soviet participation in an upcoming international Holocaust Memorial Council conference in Washington. Also, thanks to the Prize, I hope to be able to help Ida Nadel, Andrei Sakharov, Vladimir Slepak, and other dissidents.

To the journalists welcoming us at Moscow Airport, I speak of my total solidarity with Andrei Sakharov and announce my intention of visiting him in Gorki. Yes, my main concern is for the refuseniks, but the Soviet Nobel Prize winner's exile to me epitomizes injustice. I return to this theme two or three times a day, at every opportunity, at every meeting with officials and the foreign correspondents posted in Moscow.

My official hosts are unhappy. They can accept my pleading on behalf of "my" Jews but not my associating Sakharov with them. "Sakharov is a scientist," they tell me with irritation. "He was sent away from Moscow for reasons of state: He's in possession of nuclear secrets that the government must protect. In short, this is not your business." Stubbornly I argue: "He is your only Nobel Peace laureate. It's normal for me to want to meet him." They refuse my request.

Everybody tells me that the final decision is Gorbachev's. With her usual logic, Marion advises me to take a direct approach: "Why don't you ask to meet him?" I stare at her; did I hear her right? "Meet him? To whom, do you think, should I submit such a request?" As always her answer is clear and simple. "Write him." Fine—I'll write him a letter. And then what? "Then you give it to Andrei [the young official in charge of our security]. He'll know what to do." It sounds so simple when Marion says it that I feel disarmed. Anyway, I have nothing to lose. On a piece of hotel stationery I write a note to the secretary-general of the Communist party. Handing it to Andrei, who has just arrived to take us to a meeting, I say: "This is for your boss." He looks incredulous as he glances at the envelope. "Stay here. Wait for me," he tells us, "I have to leave for a few minutes." He returns an hour later. I ask him: "Well?" He answers only that we're late for our appointment at the Veterans' Ministry. I understand; he can tell me nothing.

In the evening he whispers to me that my letter has been delivered to the Kremlin; it is being dealt with at the highest level. To Marion, I say: "You'll see; nothing's going to come of this."

The next day, while we're having breakfast, Andrei asks me to step into the corridor: "I have the answer. It is positive." I can't hold back a cry of surprise. Andrei puts his finger to his lips; best to keep quiet.

We go to the synagogue on Arkhipova Street. It's Simhat Torah. Let's forget our dealings with the authorities. Let's celebrate.

The huge synagogue is brightly lit. It is also packed. Thousands of faithful jostle one another. Tradition has it that we must celebrate to the point of ecstasy. What if one is not in the mood? Force yourself, says the Law. Simhat Torah—the celebration of Torah—is different from other festivals; it is the essence of joy. We are commanded to dance, sing, get drunk on hope and nostalgia. One pleads with one's soul to rise to heaven, and the soul, docile and gentle, is happy to obey.

And so am I happy. Yes, really happy. Vladimir "Volodia" Slepak, the oldest of the refuseniks, is with me. I've kept the promise I made to him years earlier; I've returned to "my" Russian Jews.

The congregants are pushing forward and backward while they observe the procession of the Torah as it slowly makes its way around the synagogue. Clutching the scrolls to my chest, I greet people— here and there I recognize a face. One is that of an old man who, as on an earlier visit, stuffs a piece of paper into my pocket. It is hot; I have trouble breathing. I am afraid to slip, to fall. I am afraid I shall wake up far from these Jews yearning for freedom and tradition.

This is my fourth trip to the Soviet Union. It was during the first, in 1965, that I discovered the "Jews of Silence." They talked to me with their eyes. In them I read the history of their suffering, their solitude. Even on that Simhat Torah eve long ago, they did not seem afraid. They were the first—and let us never forget that—to reject the reign of terror; the first to defy the Kremlin; the first to openly demand their right to be different, to be free, and to remember.

Since then things have changed. The Kremlin has had to open its gates, thanks to pressure from abroad, and thousands of Jews have emigrated to Israel. And ever since 1965, these young people who fill the streets and declare their pride in belonging to the Jewish people have modified the character and the mentality of their elders by showing them their example of defiance and hope.

My admiration and affection for these youngsters are constantly renewed. Seventy years of Communist education and dictatorship have not stifled their Jewish identity. Without schools or cultural centers, without formal infrastructures, the kind that have long been offered to other ethnic minorities, how do they manage to safeguard their Jewish particularity, to educate their children? There are courses in Jewish history, Hebrew lessons, biblical commentaries, circles for talmudic study, religious initiation, lectures on literature. If these exist today, it is largely thanks to these people.

They never cease to surprise me. Take Volodia Slepak. In a way he is freer than people in the free world. I ask him: "Aren't you afraid? Afraid of prison?" He shrugs. No, he's no longer afraid; he knows prisons. And forced exile. And brutality. And threats. Not easy? Who says being a Jew, and particularly a Jew in the USSR, is easy?

Nevertheless, the strength radiated by my friend Volodia is surprising. I call him the moment I arrive at the hotel. We embrace. We have been waiting for this moment a long time—seventeen years. Seventeen years of a "relationship" interrupted only by forced silences on his part. Seventeen years of anguish, and of hope. Marion and I adopt him and his wife, Masha. We take them along everywhere. Never mind that the officials and our guides don't like it.

A political dissident and human rights activist, Volodia was an example to a great many young Jews whom he urged to return to Judaism. Anatoly Shcharansky, who owes his Jewish involvement to him, was actually apprehended as he was leaving the Slepaks' apartment. Slepak, too, was arrested. Despite imprisonment, five years of Siberian exile, persecution of every kind, Volodia did not give in.

Every day I request permission to visit Sakharov. Again and again I am refused. Why? Nobody knows. Many years later, when I was introduced to Sakharov, he held my hand in his for a very long moment; he told me he knew how hard I had tried to see him.

How have all these people—perhaps a hundred of them—succeeded in losing their "shadows" and coming together in this Moscow apartment? And who has been in touch with every one of them? I ask no questions. I am too happy to meet, at last, these refuseniks whom until this moment I have known only by name or photo: a famous professor whose visa has been refused for the past ten years and a well-known chemist whose visa has been refused for more than twelve years. We chat freely, but the same question keeps coming back: "How long are we going to live like outcasts?"

There are some old acquaintances in the crowd. A teacher accosts me in Hebrew: "I saw you in 1966, but I didn't dare speak to you." A woman breaks in: "Do you remember me? In 1979. . . ." Yes, I remember. "It was at the doctor's house." She smiles: "Imagine, he's here now. . . ." I start: "Here? Dr. Kogan is here?" Someone calls him, and he hurries over; he looks older, but I would have recognized him anywhere. "I promised you we'd meet again," I tell him. "Promise me our next meeting will be somewhere else," he says. I promise him. I would promise him anything.

A shy-looking, youngish man pulls me into a corner. He wants to tell me a secret: "Look," he says in a husky, excited voice, "a few years ago I translated your first book—in samizdat, of course—I've kept a copy for you. . . . I knew that one day we'd meet." How do you thank a man who has risked his freedom to let others know your work? I'm still thinking this over when he hands me an envelope—and then he's gone.

An hour later, in another room of the same apartment, an old man, tall and thin, gives me an envelope: "I translated your first book," he says with a smile. "In samizdat. Here's the first copy. It's yours."

They don't know each other. Each in his own circle carried out his solitary task without knowing that someone else was doing the same thing for the same reasons. Suddenly I know how to thank them. Without a word, I take one translator by the arm and lead him to the other. After a brief moment of bewilderment, they embrace as only Russians embrace. And they burst out laughing. I feel like reciting a prayer of gratitude. Had I come to the USSR for nothing else but this laughter I would be satisfied.

I take their names and put them on one of my lists. And I pray to heaven: Lord, You who read everything, look at these names, look at these men and protect them.

Let's get back to Gorbachev. During the procession with the Torah a stranger whispers in my ear: "When you see the boss—[in Yiddish] the *balebos*—tell him that . . ." How did he know that I was going to meet the *balebos*? Marion and I have told no one. Andrei? Impossible. He's with us, but he is not speaking to anyone. To all the mysteries of life in the USSR, one more has been added. We return to the hotel.

Around three o'clock I grab my raincoat and get ready to go to the American Embassy. A meeting has been scheduled there with dissidents and refuseniks. I'm already at the door when the telephone rings. A man in less-than-perfect English says he wants to see me, but he does not give his name. No doubt a dissident. "Come in two hours," I tell him. "No," says the anonymous caller, "I have to see you at once." In that case, I suggest, meet me at the U.S. Embassy. "No," he says, "I cannot go to the United States Embassy." He's afraid, I say to myself, afraid of being followed. He goes on: "Nor do I think you should go there." He lowers his voice and adds: "I've got a message for you, a message," he goes on, "from the man you want to meet." A message from Mikhail Gorbachev? That changes everything. "Come at once!" I tell him. He'll come in twenty minutes. I look at Marion: "You were right—all we had to do was write a few words to penetrate the impenetrable Kremlin." Then I think of something: What if this is a KGB trap to punish me for having insisted so much on Sakharov's plight?

I call the American ambassador, sum up the situation, and ask him to send me someone to be present at the interview. He tells me I'm right to be wary, he'll send me his number one adviser. I hope the adviser will come in time; he does. The Soviet arrives a few minutes later: squat and with a dour face, he greets us without bothering to mention his name. He's accompanied by two men; one will be his interpreter. The other, bald with a moon face, remains silent. After the customary polite words, the mysterious emissary asks to speak to me alone. I insist on Marion's being present. No problem. I invite the emissary and his interpreter to follow us to the other room. Without asking permission the bald man comes along. We sit down, but the emissary gets up immediately. He clears his throat and delivers a long message in Russian, and then he sits down again. The interpreter stands up: "I have a communication from Mikhail Sergeyevich Gorbachev," he says solemnly. "He greets you in the name of the Soviet Union and congratulates you. . . ." There follow a series of compliments delivered in a monotone. "And therefore . . . he would be happy to meet with you Tuesday afternoon to discuss certain subjects that mean a great deal to us." The interpreter sits down. There is a rather long silence. I break it in order to respond: "Tell the secretary-general how touched I am by the warmth of his message, but to my deep regret I cannot accept his invitation, since I must return to Paris on Sunday. . . ." The emissary does not even wait for the translation; he leaps to his feet as though stung by a snake: "Impossible, impossible I tell you. You cannot! The day before yesterday you wrote your letter; we are answering it today. Admit that we have responded quickly. And you . . ." He doesn't finish his sentence. He is beside himself. How can I calm him down? I say to him: "When you explain to the secretary-general why I cannot stay, he will understand: My wife and I have promised President Mitterrand to celebrate his seventieth birthday with him and his family." He leaves shaking his head.

I see him again the following day, at the airport. This time he is without his interpreter. He whips out a little notebook and asks me for my "wish list." I recite the names of certain refuseniks, I stress the cultural needs of the Jewish communities, and, of course, I speak of Sakharov. He promises to see what he can do and to contact me in New York.

He keeps his word.

As for Gorbachev, I saw him five years later, in far more dramatic circumstances. And Mitterrand had something to do with it.

As for the Soviet emissary, he remains mysterious to the end. Though I eventually discover his name, I never learn where he fits into the scheme of things. After Moscow we have a number of phone conversations. The latest deals with Andrei Sakharov. I tell him that if the scientist is not freed from his forced residence in Gorki, I will most certainly speak of him and his plight in my Nobel address. Interestingly, the Soviet authorities seem to fear the impact of criticism in that address. A member of the French Communist party's Politburo contacts me to persuade me not to mention Sakharov. What is it about the Nobel Prize that worries them? Back in Moscow, Gorbachev's emissary had made quite a few promises. I want deeds. When I arrive in Oslo, one of the first calls is from him: Sakharov will be freed; he gives his word. I am not convinced. And in my acceptance speech I speak of Sakharov.

Oslo, December 9, 1986. After the official reception at the airport we go on to the Grand Hotel. In the Nobel Suite, there are flowers, chocolates. We quickly take a shower and change our clothes. We meet our Israeli, American, and French guests, and then we are taken to the press conference.

The room is packed with reporters. One of the first questions strikes me as bizarre: "How do you explain that the security detail assigned to you is larger than the one protecting the king of Norway?" I have no idea what the reporter is referring to; I haven't been told as yet that the police had intercepted information about threats against me, or that the Holocaust deniers were planning a demonstration. And so it is the top official of the foreign affairs ministry, who is chairing the press conference, who answers: "That is because the king of Norway is protected by four million of his subjects." The other questions, for the most part, have to do with the Middle East: the Palestinians' right to self-determination, the Shamir government's policies, the chances of peace with the Arabs. I don't understand why these reporters are trying to trap me by insisting on a discussion of this problem. Surely they know my views on the subject. One question on Israel, even two or three, make sense. But ten? Did they ask these questions of previous laureates? For me, this is not a new phenomenon. For years, every time I find myself confronting the media, the Israel-Arab problem is waved at me. And each time the journalist in me cautions: Never lose your patience with the press.

In accordance with custom, the chairman of the Nobel committee, Egil Aarvik, accompanies me to the Royal Palace for a private audience with King Olav V. Well-informed on international current events, the old monarch reminisces about the war years, which he spent in Great Britain and the United States. He is loved by his people for his wisdom and courage, and I find his simplicity, his humanity, moving. And I am confounded by the warmth he shows me. At one point, smiling shyly, he says: "In my position I don't have the right to suggest candidates to the Nobel committee; otherwise I would personally have proposed you." Of course he will attend the ceremony, surrounded by his family, members of the government, Parliament, and the diplomatic corps.

Outside, though I was to learn of this only later, Holocaust "deniers" from France and other European countries are distributing pamphlets attacking Jewish memory. For them it's the ideal occasion to disseminate their "thesis": There never was a Holocaust; it is nothing but a myth invented by the Jews in order to collect money. The street demonstration explains the worries of the police and the tight security.

The ceremony is incredibly impressive, and I know that it will leave a profound mark on me. It also is a time when the eyes of the whole world are on you.

As I enter the brightly lit, crowded Aula—the great hall of Oslo University—and walk through the tense and silent crowd, I think of all those who are not present. The emotion that overcomes me is so powerful that I have difficulty moving forward. I feel choked, and there is a heavy weight on my chest. I glimpse smiling, familiar faces as I take my seat next to Elisha, who is sitting beside his mother.

The Oslo Philharmonic Orchestra is playing Grieg, but I barely hear the music. Next comes Aarvik, who speaks in Norwegian. I don't understand a word, but he has the audience in the palm of his hand. He seems moved and happy. Later, much later, he tells us: "Last August, when the decision was made in your favor, I felt like singing. Then, in the train that took me home that night, it seemed to me the very trees were singing."

An English translation of his speech has been distributed to foreign visitors along with a biographical sketch of me, a literary analysis, quotations from my novels and essays, a philosophical and ethical interpretation of my writings. He speaks of my role as "a witness for truth and justice" and "a messenger to mankind whose message is not one of hate and revenge, but of brotherhood and atonement. . . . In him we see a man who has gone from utter humiliation to become one of our most important spiritual leaders and guides."

Here are some more excerpts from his speech:

> . . . His aim is not to gain the world's sympathy for the victims or the survivors. His aim is to awaken our conscience because our indifference to evil makes us partners in the crime. . . .
>
> . . . Naturally, it was his own people's fate which formed the starting point for his work. Through the years, however, his message has attained a universal character, standing as a communication from one human being to humankind. Its involvement is limitless and encompasses all who suffer, wherever they might be. . . .
>
> . . . his vision is not characterized by a passive obsession with a tragic history; rather it is a reconstructed belief in God, humanity and the future.
>
> . . . I doubt whether any other individual, through the use of such quiet speech, has achieved more or been more widely heard. The words he uses are simple, and the voice that speaks them is gentle. It is a voice of peace. But its power is intense.
>
> . . . It is in recognition of this particular human spirit's victory over the powers of death and degradation, and to support the struggle of good against evil in the world, that the Norwegian Nobel Committee today presents the Nobel Peace Prize to Elie Wiesel. We do this on behalf of millions—from all peoples and all races. . . .

As Aarvik speaks, I read the translation. I listen and read at the same time, but the words hover in the air; they do not come to rest inside me. Is he really talking about me? About my life, my destiny? Once again I see myself in my parents' house; I see my father and mother, and my two sisters who are gone, and all I can think of is how much I wish they could have known my son; I so long to tell them that I go on loving them, that I have remained faithful to them. Aarvik is talking, and I am far away, on the other side, with Elisha, with Marion, strolling through the town of my childhood, where my Masters, my friends, my dreams are waiting for me.

Suddenly I sit up. Aarvik is no longer speaking in Norwegian; he is addressing me in English. He says: "When your father was dying you were at his side; it was the darkest day of your life. This day, for you and for ourselves, is a glorious day; I would like your son to stand next to you as the greatest prize that mankind is able to grant is bestowed on you. . . ." And because he has made this unexpected connection, because in a few simple words he has created a link between my father and my son, I feel overwhelmed with sadness.

Elisha steps up to the podium, and I follow him. I don't hear the applause; I hear nothing, and then all I hear are the invisible tears flowing into my soul, I hear the prayers my dead parents are chanting on high, I hear the call of my little sister Tsipouka whose suffering should have extinguished the sun for all eternity.

I am standing alone. Aarvik has sat down. Elisha, too. And the public, too. I am expected to deliver my speech. It is ready—I have it in front of me, a few typed pages. But I cannot read them; I try—and fail. Later, Danielle Mitterrand will tell me that she was afraid for me. Perhaps she thought I would never again be able to open my mouth. I look at my wife, my sister, my son. And then, behind my son, as though to protect him, I see my father. That's why it is so difficult, almost impossible, for me to speak. Out of respect I never said a word in his presence without asking his permission.

But before I ask his permission, I must ask his forgiveness. For Aarvik was mistaken. I see myself once again with my father on the last day of his life, the last night. I was near him as he agonized, but not at the hour of his death. I speak of it in *Night*. He called me. My father called me, gently, weakly. I heard him moaning. I heard him calling. His cries tore me apart; they tear me apart still. In spite of the danger I should have gone to him, run to him. I should have said to him: I'm here, Father. Your son will never leave you. I should have told him something, anything. But we were forbidden to speak. I would have been beaten, beaten to death. I would have been killed. I was afraid then. And I am afraid now.

How much time has passed since I approached the podium? Forty-one years? Forty-one centuries. And then . . . I shake myself and wake facing a king and a kingdom that wish me well.

Back at the hotel we lunch with Aarvik and his family. Then I spend several hours calling refuseniks in the Soviet Union. I want them to know that they are in our thoughts, that their courage has been spoken of and celebrated today. Rabbi Melchior does not leave my side; he knows these phone numbers by heart. It's not easy; the calls must go through the switchboard. Some of the people are not at home. Never mind, we shall call back; twenty times, if necessary.

In the evening there is the traditional torchlight parade in honor of the laureate. It is a dazzling, breathtaking spectacle, an unforgettable sight: young people and old, from every corner of the country, students and workers, teachers and pupils, representatives of political parties and of humanitarian associations sweeping down like a flaming stream from very far away until they pass under my window. Cries in every language and shouts of "Shalom, Shalom!" rise up to me. Thank you, thank you a thousand times. Behind me a reporter says: "Since Schweitzer, there hasn't been anything like it."

The last of the flame-bearers are passing before us. We still have a little time before dressing for the official dinner. Aarvik says: "Mother Teresa turned down this dinner. She asked us to give her the price of the dinner for her charitable works." The idea is admirable, but the Norwegians would rather not see it repeated too often; tradition must be continued. Still, "my" dinner has caused them problems since it has to be kosher. New dishes, new silverware. The sumptuous menu is personally supervised by Rabbi Melchior, the wines specially imported from Israel and France. Too excited and exhausted, I hardly touch them: My mind is elsewhere; I am not hungry. But the dinner, I am told, is a success. The novelist Gieske Anderson, vice chairman of the Nobel committee, gives a brilliant, inspired speech. Leo (Sjua) Eitinger, sensitive, forceful, speaks from the survivor's point of view. In my improvised remarks I stress the importance of gratitude as a human and social virtue. The dinner goes on far into the night. The guests are reluctant to leave. They do not want the day to end. Some of them accompany us to our room, just to talk. Each evokes an incident in his or her life in which I was involved. Amusing remarks, memories of all kinds of occasions, make up a biography spoken in many voices. We part before dawn.

Just a few hours later we meet again in the same Aula where, following tradition, I am to give the "Nobel Address." This time it is another committee member, Professor Francis Sejersted, who presides over the ceremony. His speech is a model of academic excellence. In spare prose it develops the theme of peace as the supreme ethical imperative and explores and compares ancient and modern ideas on violence and its remedies. I startle everyone as I begin my speech by singing the prayer *Ani Maamin*—I believe in the coming of the Messiah. If anyone in Sighet had asked me which announcement would come first, that I won the Nobel Prize or that the Messiah is finally on his way, I certainly would have bet on the coming of the Messiah. I invite those who know the melody to join in with me. It was the song of the martyrs in the ghettos, and this is my way of paying homage to them. Another first: No laureate before me has ever sung on this formal occasion.

We go on to Stockholm and its glitter, and a dinner with community leaders. Also present is Gunnel Vallquist of the Nobel Academy; her translation of Proust, I am told, is a masterpiece that equals the original. I converse with Lars Gyllensten, another academician, who listens to me gravely and speaks carefully. I deliver an address in the cathedral: I make the point that in times gone by, a Jew like myself was usually invited to church only in order to come out a convert.

In Copenhagen, Chief Rabbi Bent Melchior, Michael's father, embarrasses me by opening the evening at the city's largest hall by pronouncing the blessing one recites upon meeting a sage. Then Liv Ullmann introduces me to the audience. Since sharing the 1980 International Rescue Committee trip to the Cambodian border we have taken part—sometimes together—in many human rights struggles. Among her many accomplishments is her ambassadorship for UNICEF, helping disadvantaged children. Like the beloved Audrey Hepburn, she has done much for them.

Upon our arrival in Israel, we are welcomed by our friend Yossi Ciechanover and a group of officials from the Ministry of Foreign Affairs. A young radio reporter pushes her microphone in front of my face: "What do you think of the criticism your prize has aroused in Israel?" I answer her: "And what do you think would happen if, first of all, you said 'shalom' or good evening? Is politeness out of fashion in Israeli journalism schools these days?" And so I learn that Israel is the only non-Arab country where, along with the praise, there were negative articles on the Nobel committee's decision—not many, but enough to make me sad. A journalist from the extreme right scolds me for not living in Israel; one from the extreme left is angry because I have not sufficiently espoused the Palestinian cause. Once again I am told that by choosing to live in the Diaspora, I have sinned against Israel.

To be sure, most of the articles are favorable. But everybody knows that in Israel no consensus or unanimity exists, not even in the sacred books. So when Dov Judkowski, the editor in chief of *Yedioth Ahronoth*, asks the reporter Shaike Ben Porat to do three interviews with me covering all aspects of my life, a remark of Saul Lieberman's comes to mind: "A man must choose between inspiring pity or envy."

Mostly I encounter affection and friendship. I am covered with medals and parchments and feted like a conqueror. Rabbis and professors come to congratulate me. Anatoly Shcharansky comes to see me. Ever pragmatic, his first question is: "How are you adapting to your new status?" I must confess I was a little disappointed. A few words of thanks for what I had done to obtain his freedom, in all modesty, would have made me happy. Many former Soviet citizens come. A woman brings me a box of chocolates; she knows I helped her father leave Russia. Another offers me a *mezuza* her husband has brought from Lithuania.

The government treats me as a VIP. Marion and I are guests of honor at a dinner given by President Chaim Herzog and at a luncheon with Prime Minister Yitzhak Shamir. And there is yet another lunch, this one tendered by Shimon Peres, Minister of Foreign Affairs. The mood is friendly, the speeches warm, even with traces of pride.

Rabbi Menashe Klein, my friend since Buna, Buchenwald, and Ambloy, announces the creation of a Beit Hamidrash, a house of study and prayer, that will bear my father's name. Rabbis, Hasidic Masters, deputies, and school directors, as well as the mayor of Jerusalem, Teddy Kollek, are among the guests. This house of study and prayer means more to me than any laurels I could receive, for my parents' dream had been for me to become a *rosh yeshiva* (head of a yeshiva).

Reb Menashe recounts: "In the camp, one Yom Kippur, an SS man came into our block. After beating some inmates he shouted triumphantly: 'Jews, so where is your God now?' At that time we were too terrified to answer. But here is our answer now, and we give it to him in Jerusalem: 'God of Israel, our God is God. And He is where His people is.' "

Encounters⟶

*I*N OCTOBER 1986, back from Moscow, I mention to François Mitterrand that all the reporters ask how I intend to spend the Nobel Prize money. Rather than posing questions about my political, philosophical, or religious views, most of them seem preoccupied by my financial situation and future.

Mitterrand smiles roguishly. "Is that so? Well, tell me—what *do* you intend to do with the money?" I shrug and answer: "Oh, I don't know. . . . Marion and I have spoken about it—we're thinking of starting a foundation." "Oh, really, a foundation? And what will it do?" "I don't know yet. I think we may organize conferences, special colloquia on burning issues. . . . " As I speak a mad—impractical—idea goes through my head: "What I'd really like to do is organize a conference bringing together all the Nobel Prize laureates, from all disciplines. It has not been done before. For the first time, Nobel Prize winners from the world over would join together in large numbers to discuss mankind's fears and hopes for the coming century."

I tell him about my adventures in the USSR. Thanks to the Nobel, I have been able to help several refuseniks get exit visas, and to assist several other dissidents. I also hope to have been instrumental in breaking down official attitudes toward Sakharov, still in exile in Gorki. Imagine, I said, ten or twenty laureates combining their efforts and mobilizing their networks of friends for humanitarian causes.

Mitterrand is interested. He urges me to research the project, to look into the details. I am only too happy to comply. I know what is involved in conferences, and I like them. For me the word "dialogue" is one of the most inspired. For that matter, at Culture Minister Jack Lang's suggestion, the French president and I had by then already decided on a joint project: to write a book of dialogues. In a dialogue, the other loses his otherness. I also like the word "colloquium." As long as people talk and listen to one another, everything remains possible.

And so it happens that I tell the president: "If you like this idea, let us do it together." In other words, my foundation (to-be) would participate in its financing.

Mitterrand agrees, and that is how I become a "partner" of the French Republic. Procedures and technical details are to be worked out with Jacques Attali. No problem there—we understand each other and work together perfectly. We had met during a conference at the Sorbonne organized by Lang in 1982. Possibly mistaking me for a fellow member of the Socialist party, he said *tu* to me immediately. I was flattered. I knew his work, and I admired the brilliance of his ambitious intelligence. Also, he is interested in things Jewish—mysticism, the Talmud; he wants to learn. And then, in many areas—economics, international politics, the philosophy of science—he knows much more than I. We see each other every time Mitterrand receives me simply because, in order to reach the presidential office, I must go through his. That office is important to him. One day, he told me half-seriously that he wouldn't have accepted the post of special adviser if he couldn't have had that particular office. There are those who resent his arrogance, his obvious taste for power. It's said that he treats his subordinates badly. But people say so many things about so many people. My relations with him are excellent, professionally and personally. There is mutual confidence. We exchange manuscripts, seek each other's advice. I write a review of his book on Sigmund Warburg for a Paris daily. In short, there is a friendship. I visit his home, he visits mine. Because he usually answered my calls immediately, once, when I could not reach him after several calls, I wrote him an angry letter. Before sending it, on Marion's always-wise counsel, I telephoned his office once more, then his home. And I found out that he had had an accident and was in the hospital. To redeem myself in my own eyes for having been unjustly angry with him, I dedicated my novel *Le crépuscule au loin* (*Twilight*) to him.

Jacques finds the idea of a Nobel conference excellent. We discuss it over a few lunches, a few dinners. He will create a group at the Élysée Palace to collaborate with our foundation's small New York team.

Our first task is to make up a list of the more or less two hundred laureates. No problem there. The dominant theme will be the twenty-first century. Next we must establish the program and settle on a date. That is where things get a little complicated.

We are at the end of 1986. We must allow six to eight months for the preliminaries, on the condition that we start work immediately. And at the Élysée things are dragging. Is it because of *la cohabitation* between the parties of the left and right in the government? That's what's insinuated here and there. Weeks go by; I'm beginning to feel uneasy. If the Élysée now faces other priorities, I should be told. If Mitterrand is no longer interested in the project, that's fine, too, but someone should deign to inform me.

Now it's 1987 and we still don't have the green light. From a purely practical point of view, that should please me: The more we keep postponing things, the fewer laureates will come and the less expensive it will be. That would be better for our foundation, which, though financially linked to the Élysée for this project, is not rich. However, objectively, not being able to gather a large group of laureates would have a negative effect on a conference that might otherwise have considerable impact. As for the financing, Mutual of America, a prestigious insurance company whose president, Bill Flynn, is a friend, offers us very generous support.

Spring is here; Paris is alive with the joy of its lovers, but as I leave the Élysée I'm depressed. I don't dare discuss my worries with Mitterrand; I would appear to be complaining. Rather I speak to Jacques, who counsels patience. It's all a matter of scheduling, of calendars, but the decision will be made in a few days. By the time it is made, it is summer. The conference is to convene the third week of January 1988. The presidential election is to take place the following May but, naive as I am, I do not make the connection. Can everything be ready in time? Yes, if the Élysée machinery starts to move. How will we reach everyone? And how will we convince those who hesitate? The French embassies do their best. Joshua Lederberg helps. His wisdom and generosity are indispensable to me. President of Rockefeller University, this Nobel laureate (in biology) is adept at smoothing edges. Bishop Tutu offers his regrets, and so does Saul Bellow. Solzhenitsyn *never* leaves Vermont. Henry Kissinger hesitates: "I'm not too popular in scientific circles," he says. He may not be wrong. There is anger because of his Southeast Asia policy in general and with respect to Cambodia in particular. At Harvard he is decried as a hawk. He's afraid of embarrassing himself and me by being booed. I insist; he gives in. In the end he'll be grateful to me.

Time is running out. The Élysée team is overwhelmed by technical and logistical problems. Everyone had forgotten that Americans must obtain French visas. Instructions go out to all passport-control stations: Nobel laureates are to enter without a visa.

But where can they all be lodged? Kissinger will stay in the U.S. Embassy. Special arrangements are made for Willy Brandt. The others will stay at the Méridien and Bristol hotels. Special buses with motorcycle escorts will shuttle back and forth between the hotels and the Élysée and Marigny Palaces, where the regular sessions are to be held and meals are to be taken.

We spend hours fine-tuning the program, the composition of the various commissions. Who will preside? How and according to what criteria will one laureate rather than another be accorded certain privileges? The solution: We shall invite the presidents of the various Nobel committees to direct the debates. On the French side, François Gros of the Collège de France, and Hélène Ahrweiler, the rector and chancellor of the Universities of Paris, agree to perform the same duties. François Mitterrand and I decide that I shall chair the plenary sessions. It may seem funny—it did to me—but as far as protocol is concerned, I represent, in the same way as the president of the French Republic, an "inviting power." Yes, I know—the word "power" fits me as a tuxedo might a kangaroo. But then I'm not responsible for protocol.

Meanwhile, as cosponsor of the conference, I feel responsible for everything else. And "everything else" is immense. For example, one problem, a serious one: Should Prime Minister Jacques Chirac, head of the opposition, be invited? I am in favor of it. We must not offend him by leaving him off the program. I suggest we ask him to participate in the opening session. After all, he's also mayor of Paris. A high Élysée official vetoes the idea. I insist: Let Chirac extend greetings at a plenary session. Veto. Why not ask him to offer a toast at one of the dinners? Veto. The problem is political, I'm told. I wouldn't have guessed. I keep arguing: If Chirac is not invited, surely we'll be accused of politicizing the conference. Nothing doing.

With hindsight I realize, of course, that even though conceived outside any political considerations, by me anyway, the conference proved extremely useful to Mitterrand in the May election.

As for Chirac, I refuse to admit defeat. Without consulting anyone I go to see him at Matignon, his official realm. I tell him that, as co-chair of this conference, I would be honored by his presence at its inaugural session. He is as charming and as friendly as when I met him in 1987 at the Paris Town Hall. The man who years later will become president of the republic tells me he appreciates my gesture but prefers to abstain.

One essential question remains unanswered: How many of our invitations will be accepted? Ten? Twenty? We hope it will be fifty. We are astounded when we learn that seventy-nine writers, scientists, and statesmen have accepted. Still, there are some refusals that sadden us. Lech Walesa would like to come but is not allowed a visa; General Jaruzelski has turned him down. Our response is immediate: Since our colleague is being prevented from joining us in Paris, we shall go to see him in his own country.

To go to Poland we shall need a plane. We have an urgent meeting at Jacques Attali's office: Would the government let us have a so-called *Glam*, government airplane? Not likely; we're in a period of *cohabitation*. Should we charter a commercial plane? Jacques knows the president of Air Inter, but Air Inter's planes are not permitted to leave French airspace. So we have to fall back on Air France. But who will cover expenses? It will have to be our foundation. Jacques takes charge of the visas; he has already discussed the matter with the Polish ambassador. Everything is arranged. A collective visa will allow us to make the Paris-Cracow-Paris trip. It is now Thursday, and departure is scheduled for Sunday. Around three in the afternoon Attali calls. He is beside himself: The Polish ambassador has just informed him that the collective visa has been refused. Why? Evidently Jaruzelski is not enchanted by the interest shown Walesa by the Nobel laureates. We don't want to give up the trip. So we decide to play the American card: Ronald Lauder, a Republican, former United States ambassador to Austria, calls the vice president of the United States, George Bush, and tells him of our predicament. Bush asks that I call his chief of staff. I call and in a few sentences inform him of the situation. "Stop worrying. Everything will be taken care of," the chief of staff assures me. I insist that it's urgent. "Come now, calm down. When we do something, we do it quickly." The vice president has indeed acted swiftly. He has summoned the Polish ambassador in Washington to come to his office on Friday morning. I don't know what he said to him, but that same day, around 4 p.m. (10 a.m. in Washington), Attali informs me that the Polish ambassador in Paris is desperately trying to reach me. He wishes to tell me the good news in person. The visa problem has been settled. The visas will be issued on the spot. The White House has been more efficient than the Élysée.

Walesa is waiting for us at the Cracow airport, surrounded by his close advisers: Bronislav Geremek, Tadeusz Mazowiecki, and the priest Henryk Jankowski. Under the watchful eyes of Jaruzelski's secret service, we tell them of our admiration and it feels good to see them reassured, happy.

Particularly moving is the meeting between Walesa and Egil Aarvik, who says to him: "Do you know, Mr. Walesa, that we are still holding your check?" "I know," Walesa answers, "I don't think about it. What would I do with that money here?" Suddenly he has an idea: "Give it to Elie, he'll know how to use it." Aarvik asks me: "Would you accept his check?" Out of the question.

We make a pilgrimage to Birkenau and Auschwitz, to recite the Kaddish and to open symbolically the Paris conference: One cannot reflect on the future without casting a glance backward on the waning century for which Auschwitz will remain a monument. Walesa does not hide his emotion, and I'm surprised to learn that this is his first visit here. In my brief speech I speak directly to him: "We shall be the emissaries of *Solidarnosc* [Solidarity] throughout the world, I promise you. But promise us to be our representative here to protect the memory of the Jewish victims as well as their cemeteries, both visible and invisible." He promises. I shall be bitterly disappointed, years later, when he makes certain remarks with anti-Semitic overtones in order to win an election. Another disappointment: In his second autobiographical book he quotes my speech but forgets to mention my request—and his promise. A third: At the time of the fiftieth anniversary of the liberation of Auschwitz, he delivers a solemn speech without ever mentioning that Jews were assassinated and annihilated there.

Bernie Fischman, a director of our foundation, observes *Yahrzeit* for one of his parents on that day. He recites the Kaddish at the old synagogue that bears the name of Rabbi Moshe Isserlis. Again it is the first time that Walesa, a fervent Catholic, sets foot in a Jewish place of worship.

I didn't know it then—I discover it only in the early nineties—but facing the ruins of the gas chambers and crematoria where, among all the others, the Hungarian Jews were exterminated, a dozen crosses were erected. Some of them were glued to stars of David.

How can this sacrilege be explained? Who dared put these Christian symbols on the invisible tombs of the most pious among our Jews? We are told that some young Poles planted them there as a token of reconciliation. Though the intentions may have been honorable, the result is no less offensive.

I am appalled by the insensitivity of the Catholic Church of Poland, and the indifference of European and American Jewish leaders. There is no place for religious symbols, Jewish or Christian, in Birkenau. Its ruins are the strongest symbols of what was perpetrated and destroyed in that camp.

We return to Paris, and the conference opens the next day, in the Great Salon of the Élysée Palace. For me the date is significant: January 18, the day of the evacuation of Auschwitz.

Transmitted live by France's premier television station, TF1, the opening session is impressive. No one has ever seen so many laureates from so many countries in one place, discussing problems concerning the future of mankind. What has motivated them to come from so far away, surely disrupting their overloaded schedules? I ask the question of my friend Joshua Lederberg. Wisely, he answers: "At this point, what else can we hope to obtain? A Nobel Prize? We already have one. Now we must give something back."

The mood is solemn, as this extraordinary gathering of extraordinary minds listens to the president of the republic bidding them welcome:

> . . . When—it will soon be two years ago—Elie Wiesel and I elaborated the project that has brought all of you to Paris, we never thought so many of you would be able to come. Elie Wiesel is a great writer in the French language and a universalist; he is also a man of faith: his own faith is contagious. He likes to move mountains, and, as we see, does so successfully. For, not content to juggle concepts, to link dreams and symbols, he affects reality. Thus we went from idea to project, then from project to event. . . .
>
> . . . You are going to reflect together on the "threats and promises of the twenty-first century." . . . What have all of you in common? A title, perhaps the loftiest, in each of your domains. You are "the Nobels." It is an aspect of glory. It is a challenge. It carries with it a kind of moral obligation.

Your presence here bears witness to that. By "obligation" I mean a certain responsibility toward universal conscience. . . . You are the bearers of an immemorial hope . . . but we have learned, to our cost, that science, which has brought so many benefits to mankind, can also cause disaster. . . .

Of all the conferences I had participated in up to that moment, this was the most spectacular—and the most stimulating. It taught me a lot: about peace and justice; the challenge of intelligence, and the challenge to knowledge; the duties and limits of science; the Third World and the rich countries; biological research and genetic temptations. How rewarding it was to watch these great minds meet, become friends, and combine their talents and determination to move history in positive and constructive directions. To see them, involved in general discussion, disagreeing, laughing, listening to Slava Rostropovitch, and visiting the newly opened Musée d'Orsay.

I observe Betty Williams, an Irish laureate, as she accosts Henry Kissinger and tells him in a loud voice, for everyone to hear, how much she once hated him. "Yes, Dr. Kissinger, there was a time when I not only hated you, I cursed you; I told everyone how evil I thought your policy was in Cambodia and in Vietnam. . . . Well, I've just heard you speak. And I beg your forgiveness."

Kissinger is dumbfounded. He blushes. It is one of the very few times I've seen him too embarrassed to respond with humor. She kisses him on both cheeks. Suddenly shy, he just stands there, speechless.

In the end, Kissinger thanks me for having insisted that he take part in the conference. I knew how he feared hostile reactions from the pacifist scientists. As a matter of fact, I had shared his apprehensions. But I had faith in his ability to meet the challenge. And he did. Rather than reading his prepared speech on geopolitical problems, he had improvised a short personal address, a sort of credo: "I am not speaking to you as a former secretary of state, nor in my capacity of political science theoretician; I am speaking to you as a Jew who lost twenty-six members of his family in Auschwitz. . . ."

I like playing the role of matchmaker of souls.

Our conference is going well. There is perfect harmony: People wish to learn, to understand, to venture beyond familiar territory. Surely that is why the scientists choose to participate in debates on culture, and, conversely, the humanists listen to scientific debates. The eternal, timeless questions lead to courteous but dramatic exchanges between optimists and pessimists, pragmatists and utopians. Perhaps all of them are right. If one contemplates the road traveled, one may be proud; and if one looks at the road yet to be traveled, one may well be anguished. All the speeches are remarkable; some are dazzling. We experience some powerful moments.

While we convene in Paris, in the Holy Land the Intifada is taking on devastating dimensions. Did I make a mistake by not placing more emphasis on these events in my opening speech? Should I have launched a firmer appeal to reason? Only three speakers allude—discreetly—to the violent clashes between Israeli soldiers and Palestinian adolescents. Privately, I am asked: "What do you think? What should be done?" I suggest setting up our own commission to visit the area. The arrival of ten Nobel Prize winners would not pass unnoticed. And while I am at it, I propose—still privately—the creation of an association of laureates who, in periods of crisis, would send ad hoc commissions to areas of conflict to bring assistance or, at least, to bear witness. The majority agrees, but a minority is wary of the political power such an association might acquire. In the absence of unanimity and means, it is wiser not to initiate anything.

But during the twice-daily press conferences and television broadcasts we are being asked more questions about the Intifada than about our debates. I have rarely felt so uneasy. How can one tolerate armed soldiers hunting down youngsters, even if they are not only capable but determined to wound and kill? On the other hand, how can one defend the provocative acts of the Intifada fighters determined to shed Jewish blood on the West Bank?

Despite Yitzhak Rabin's prediction that it won't last, the bloodshed continues. How many victims, on one side or the other, will fall before Israelis and Palestinians decide to meet around a table rather than on the battlefield? But that's another story. Let us return to the conference about to close.

The closing ceremony is telecast live. At the Élysée the mood is solemn and festive. The trumpets and drums of the Republican Guard resound. The laureates love it. In each of them a child continues to dream. As for me, I admit I'm satisfied. It is true that nothing concrete has been decided, but the encounter itself was a positive act. In my report I summarize the essential gains of our labors:

. . . So here we are at the conclusion of this conference. It opened under the sign of gratitude; it is culminating under the sign of appreciation. We are being asked what we have learned during these four days. First of all, we have learned to know each other and perhaps recognize ourselves in each other. We have discovered that beyond our specialized disciplines, we share preoccupations and anxieties, of course, but also commitments and hopes concerning the future of our children.

. . . Have we resolved some of the problems that confront our society? Their number is as vast as their complexity. How can one resolve, in four days, what in fifty years or even five thousand years, since Cain and Abel, mankind has simply ignored or barely touched upon? The Nobel Foundation has not yet discovered the secret that would enable it to offer the laureates universal wisdom in addition to worldly glory. . . .

. . . We must seek and situate the success of this conference in the conference itself. The fact that it has taken place is in itself significant and important.

And what is the goal we have set for ourselves? To identify the problems and prioritize them. To name the diseases, the epidemics, the famines, the fanaticism. Torture. Pollution. AIDS. The nuclear threat. The distress of children beaten and killed far from the eyes of men, and perhaps from the eyes of God Himself. Just by enumerating these problems, it would be easy to become discouraged. Every one of the participants is proof of what an individual is capable of undertaking and achieving for the benefit of mankind.

Our conclusions follow, and I admit that none is particularly original. Human rights, priority for education, scientific cooperation, encouragement for research in molecular biology, disarmament, aid to developing countries—they could appear as a collection of clichés. One editorial writer ironically compares them to behavior guidelines for schoolchildren. True, in that sense we have done no better than all other conferences of intellectuals. Their resolutions are frequently futile, if not banal, and have never had the slightest influence on the great of this world, as everyone knows. Sadly, ours fare no better.

There were sixteen "conclusions."

Let us take as an example: the sixteenth—and final—"conclusion" of our labors. "The conference of Nobel laureates will meet again in two years to study these problems. Until then, wherever it is felt that there is urgent need, several Nobels will personally travel to wherever human rights are threatened."

Many times two years have gone by since then and . . . nothing. I brought it up with President Mitterrand on several occasions. I reminded him of "our" promises, our public commitments. Each time he was content to answer, "Oh really?" For that matter, this is not the first public promise he has chosen not to keep. In his speech during the Sorbonne conference in 1982, he entrusted me with the organization of an international conference on hatred. Thereafter, several working sessions with scientists and philosophers ensued. Then came the *cohabitation.* And that was the end of a stimulating project meant to fight the rise of racism and xenophobia in Europe. With hindsight I think I should have protested immediately.

∾

*T*HIS NIGHT AGAIN, *I see my father in a dream. Very close, over there, under a gray sky that is not that of Jerusalem. Behind him I sense my little sister. I sense her because my father is smiling the way he does only for Tsipouka.*

He looks at me but doesn't see me. I call him. He doesn't answer. I try to speak to him, but he doesn't hear me. Suddenly he seems to tremble. I turn around and see an unknown woman. I know she's a widow, for she's dressed in black. I ask her: Since when have you been in mourning? As she remains silent, I pronounce the ritual formula: May God comfort you together with the mourners of Zion and Jerusalem. I see her lips moving, but there is no sound. I say: I can't hear you. She acquiesces with a nod: It's true, you don't hear me. Why this pain that seizes me abruptly? I look behind me for my father to come to my rescue, but he's no longer there.

First he hides the horizon from me. Then he illuminates it. And that is how it should be.

∾

The effect of the Nobel Prize? As Nadine Gordimer described it to me, it is sort of a full-time job. And it makes you travel. Invitations pour in from every corner. The world is yours; it is up to you to enrich it—according to your benefactors—or to amuse it, if you've remained lucid and kept your sense of humor. There is prestige in having a movie star to dinner, or a Nobel Prize winner on one's roster of speakers. It is both chic and serious. You are asked to name your terms. You travel first-class or on the Concorde. You stay in luxury hotels. Rewarded for your activities or your work, you no longer have the time to pursue them.

I accept an offer to deliver a lecture at the Centre Rachi in Paris. While I am in Paris, Mayor Jacques Chirac presents me with the coveted Médaille de Vermeil. Thanks to Hélène Ahrweiler, rector of the universities, the Sorbonne awards me a doctorate *honoris causa*. I confess that the ceremony, in the presence of several ministers and academicians dressed in green, touches me; it brings back memories of my student years. Every morning I had to choose whether to walk from the Porte de Saint-Cloud to the Latin Quarter and buy myself a cheese sandwich, or take the bus and stay hungry. And now here I am, the same person, being told that I am honoring this great and venerable institution. The violinist Ivry Gitlis plays a new composition for us. Hélène Ahrweiler's address is exquisitely intelligent and erudite. She stresses the connection between writer and witness. I, in turn, place the emphasis on the vulnerability of education: How can one forget that many of the *Einsatzkommando*'s commanders had advanced degrees? A university diploma does not constitute a guarantee of morality or humanity. In other words, a little humility would do our intellectuals no harm.

On the personal and professional level I receive a serious lesson in modesty administered by my various publishers. Between celebrity and success there is a bridge I have not yet crossed and probably never shall. The proof is that my books, though quickly reprinted, have only modest sales; some do quite well but rarely become bestsellers. The Prix Médicis, one of France's most prestigious prizes, helped *A Beggar in Jerusalem*. Contrary to popular belief, the Nobel Prize does not influence sales much—at least not the year I won.

As for celebrity, sometimes I am accosted by a smiling person who asks: "You look like a famous person. Who are you?" Or else, "My elderly father adores you." Or again: "My children admire you." It's always someone else who reads me.

Rather than royalties, the Nobel Prize brings you an audience. Egil Aarvik had murmured this in my ear the night of the official dinner in Oslo: "From now on you will have a forum, a tribune; your words will not vanish into a void. I don't promise you will be heard, but people will listen to you."

Invitations continue to pour in. Which should I accept? Seminars, colloquia, conferences: I am invited to speak on all continents, as though it had been discovered suddenly that I had not lost the power of speech.

I return to Oslo to honor Sjua Eitinger. I no longer like all this moving around. I do it anyhow. I don't like facing audiences; I face them anyhow.

I make a lightning trip to Brazil. David Pincus, a director of our foundation, accompanies me. Hardly has he landed in São Paulo than he disappears. He's carrying out his own investigation on disadvantaged children. Children are his "cause," his obsession. He looks for them everywhere; he organizes help for them everywhere, in Rwanda as well as in Bosnia. By the time he leaves Brazil he will leave behind him an organization—financed by him—to assist the children of the impoverished districts, the *favelas*.

March 1987: Aside from India, I hardly know Asia at all; but it is not in order to discover it that I'm going to Japan. I am going in order to research a bizarre and disquieting phenomenon there: the rise of anti-Semitism. Popular books are spreading a hatred of all things Jewish. *The Protocols of the Elders of Zion* and other anti-Jewish writings are on the best-seller lists. I can't understand it. There are hardly any Jews in the country, probably not more than five hundred, all foreigners, so what is to account for the rampant anti-Semitism there? In my lectures, in Tokyo and Osaka, I tell my audience how astounded I am: "Anti-Semitism without Jews? In Japan? Don't you know this is a Western disease? Why are you importing it here?"

The writers and university professors I meet do their best to reassure me: Japanese, they say, do not hate Jews, quite the contrary— they admire them. If they read books about the Jewish people, it's in order to absorb their wisdom, to get to know more about these Jews who seem to dominate the world by virtue of the money they make(!), the solidarity that links them to one another, and the influence they exercise in the press and in international diplomacy(!!). The Japanese want to know them in order to emulate them; it's as simple as that; it has nothing to do with anti-Semitism. I am far from convinced by these "reassurances."

In response to a standing invitation from the Jewish community of Australia, we visit that country in August 1988. Two of our friends, Harriette and Noel Levine, go with us. I find this faraway continent, a haven for the outcasts of Europe, particularly exciting. It has become a lush, vibrant place of freedom and culture. In Sydney, I meet a woman who used to live on my street in Sighet. She and her husband pull me into a corner to tell me their problem: Their daughter is about to marry a non-Jew. He's going to convert, they say, weeping, but . . . but what? I quickly explain to them the rules of conversion: A male convert becomes a son of Abraham, a female convert a daughter of Sarah, and each assumes the duties and privileges of any other Jew.

David Burger, a survivor of Auschwitz, tells me of his experiences in the camp. He should write a book about them. If only I had the time to help him. That is my obsession: to make the survivors talk, to encourage them to testify, to put their recollections on paper.

Marion rushes back to New York with Elisha. Her sister Anny has just died.

In the airplane that brings us from Paris to Kiev on a cold October morning, in 1990, we have a minyan for the *Shaharit* service. Wrapped in *tallitot* and with tefillin ringing our foreheads, we are saying our prayers. A young Bratzlaver Hasid is officiating. He has a melodious, fervent voice, filled with beauty and melancholy. Marion and our traveling companions are watching us in silence. Marion seems taken by these prayers. That is unusual for her.

It all had begun with a surprising question: "Would you like to visit Uman?" Clément Vaturi asked me one day. "I'm going there with a group of Hasidim." We had met Clément through his sister and brother-in-law, Alice and Daniel Morgaine. I knew Daniel from his days as a journalist at *France Soir*.

"Did you say Uman? In Ukraine?" "Yes," Clément answers. "Does that mean something to you?" Does it *mean* something to me? The word is part of my intimate, imaginary landscape. Uman was the last home of Rebbe Nahman of Bratzlav, the marvelous storyteller of the movement founded by his grandfather the Besht. It is the place where the Rebbe is buried.

Rebbe Nahman is close and precious to me on more than one level. He makes me dream. I love everything that touches him, everything that refers to his life, his work. I love everything that is impregnated by his universe—the stories of princes who lose their way and of exalted beggars, his tales of unknown worlds, his biblical ideas and commentaries, even the comments he used to make at table. "Take my stories and turn them into prayers," Rebbe Nahman used to say. Well, as far as I'm concerned, I'll turn his prayers into stories.

An old wreck of a bus is waiting for us at the Kiev airport. The guide is there, the driver is not. The guide is running around looking for the driver. Now the driver is there, but the guide cannot be found. We extract him from a sort of bar. Finally we're all ready. We get to Uman toward the end of the afternoon, after a horrendous drive across fields and villages where peasants and children stare at us blankly.

We see nothing of Uman, a small hamlet where no Jews live anymore. We've come to tell the late Master of our love for his teaching, to meditate and pray on his grave. We plead for his intercession—Rebbe Nahman had promised his followers, "Whosoever will recite psalms on my grave—in the prescribed order—I will help him."

By now, night has fallen. The wind is determined to blow out the candles we're holding to shed light on our psalters. The flames resist. Our shadows dance on the wall behind the grave. In the street a few villagers seem scarcely surprised by our presence. They're accustomed to seeing Bratzlav Hasidim, especially around Rosh Hashana. Such was the Master's wish: to attract to Uman as many followers as possible for the High Holidays. And they came. Even during the Stalin era they crossed the frontier illegally to be with the Rebbe, who, before dying, had promised his disciples that his flame would continue to shine until the coming of the Messiah. Some of the disciples were arrested, thrown into prison.

Rabbi Koenig of Safed, son of the famous Rebbe Gedalia, recites the psalms. We repeat them after him. There is an air of mystery to our gathering around this grave, for, in general, there is no cult of the dead in Judaism. And yet. . . . There comes a moment when Rebbe Nahman's followers stretch out on the tomb of their Master, dead for more than two centuries. And I too stretch out beside them. And deep down I too address my secret requests to Rebbe Nahman.

Then a Hasid starts chanting a Bratzlav melody, and we all join in, repeating the words drawn from a psalm of King David. We repeat

them fervently, our eyes closed, our minds aflame. And we start dancing around the tombstone. It's getting late; all the better—one prays
better at night. It's getting cold; never mind. We dance the way
Hasidim dance, hand in hand, flinging our arms from front to back
and our heads up and down. At first we dance slowly, then faster and
faster, our eyes shut, our hearts open, our souls seared by a burning
wound; we dance as though we were being drawn to the heights of
those prayers that go up all the way to the seventh heaven; we dance
like madmen whose beings stretch out toward *the* Being, whose fire
wills itself to become incandescent. No one will be able to stop us, no
power will be able to muzzle us; we sing as we weep, we weep as we
sing, and from afar, very far, I believe I'm hearing a strange and yet
uncannily familiar voice, and it is telling very beautiful but extremely
disquieting stories, in which princes and beggars meet in enchanted
woods and inflict harm on one another in order to better fight evil and
sadness. Now and then, exhausted and out of breath, one of us tries to
stop the dance or at least to slow its rhythm, but then another begins
to dance with new vigor. And we go on.

We take our leave of Rebbe Nahman with regret. I knew I loved
him, but I only now realize just how deep my attachment is. Though I
am a Hasid of Wizhnitz, I had claimed Bratzlav as my own, never
acknowledging how profoundly I was tied to him.

In the bus we are silent. The young Rabbi Gabbai passes around
almonds and dates brought from Safed. To me they have a special
taste. I think of Rebbe Nahman and of his adventurous journey to the
Holy Land. Hardly had he set foot there when he felt the need to tear
himself away and go back home.

I, too, believe that a part of me has remained in Uman.

Another memorable journey followed, though of a different order.
Invited by Moses Rosen, Chief Rabbi of Romania, I have come to
commemorate the fiftieth anniversary of the murderous pogrom at
Iasi that occurred in June 1941. It seems the Romanian government
considers this visit important. The Romanians are obviously trying to
please the foreign visitors. I am housed in one of the official—and
luxurious—residences of the president. The permanent ambassador
of Romania to the U.N., Aurel Munteanu, escorts us in all our travels.
I tell him how outraged I am by the renewal of anti-Semitism, however traditional it may be, in his country. Two widely circulated week-

lies are fomenting hatred against the fifteen thousand Jews, most of them elderly, who still live in Romania, and against world Jewry, which they accuse of every imaginable and unimaginable sin. Every cliché is used. Among other things, the anti-Semitic propagandists dare to write, without fear of ridicule, that Israel's goal is to colonize Romania. Still, it's not the stupidity of the anti-Semites that embarrasses me; I'm used to it. It's the passivity of those who allow it to flourish, those who don't oppose it, who don't chase the liars from the public arena, who don't say to them that no honest person will believe their senseless lies, that no reasonable person will believe that the Jews have established concentration camps in Romania in order to practice genocide. Nevertheless this is what local anti-Semites are saying and repeating with impunity.

I am received in private audience by President Iliescu and his prime minister, Petru Roman, who are soliciting my help in Washington, especially in economic affairs. I answer that I cannot assist a regime that tolerates hatred. I cite the minute of silence that their Senate has observed in memory of the Fascist dictator Antonescu, the virulent anti-Semitic campaign of a substantial segment of their press, the xenophobic statements of certain officials. . . . "But what about the starving children," Roman interjects, "are you forgetting them? Even if the grown-ups are guilty, why punish the children?" My answer: "Don't make us responsible for their hardships; it is *you* who bear the responsibility! Silence the hatred in your country, and the whole world will come to their aid and yours."

Iliescu seems sincere. He initiates proceedings to bring to justice the editors and writers of the anti-Semitic weeklies. He also invites me to accompany him to Sighet, so that I may show him my birthplace, and then to Rezavlia, the village near Sighet where he was born. Much later, I read in the press that the Romanian government has decided to turn my house into a museum. The people who live there are worried about what will happen to them. I promise them that as long as they are not offered other decent lodgings, they can stay on in their home—or rather in mine.

With Elisha and his cousin Steve, I see Iliescu again, around the end of July 1995. The situation is unchanged. The anti-Semitic papers are still spreading their poison, while Antonescu's memory is more and more widely revered. I try to make Iliescu understand that he must oppose this vigorously, that it is important for the reputation of his country, that his honor is at stake. But he is afraid of upsetting his citizenry: Too many people view Antonescu as the only leader who fought against the Soviets. I rejoin that Hitler, too, was anti-Soviet. Iliescu promises to find an occasion to speak out and to give the people his own low opinion of Antonescu, who was Hitler's ally during the war. Will he find the necessary self-confidence and strength? I hope so, for I believe he is sincere.

Vienna, 1992: a happening. Some sixty or seventy thousand young Austrians have converged on the Heldenplatz (Heroes' Square) to demonstrate against the renascent fascism in their country. Singers and rock musicians, among the most famous, take up the major part of the program. I would not have believed that I would ever willingly attend, let alone participate in, this kind of event, whose very noise would normally make me flee.

Some time earlier I had received a letter from the Austrian minister of culture and education offering to organize an "Elie Wiesel Day," in the course of which my books would be discussed, after having been studied in all the schools. My response had been: "Thanks for the kind invitation; I accept. I shall come to Vienna the day after Kurt Waldheim leaves." The infamous past of the former secretary-general of the U.N. is well known. Declared persona non grata in the United States, he has, for all practical purposes, been banned by the leaders of most civilized countries, the notable exceptions being certain Arab leaders, Helmut Kohl, and, sadly, Pope John Paul II, who all visited or received him.

But now Austria has elected a new president, and I feel free to come and meet the youth of Vienna.

The press is largely favorable to the demonstration. Austria clearly wants to close the regrettable parenthesis opened by Waldheim. But to do so it must reject the Fascist-leaning nationalism of Jorg Haider, who a year earlier had declared that there were some positive aspects to the Third Reich's policies, notably with respect to employment. A demagogic politician, he seems to be a darling of the media. Evidently the Austrians, who have never confronted their Nazi past, easily identified with Haider's xenophobic program. The polls are troubling; the number of anti-Semites in Austria is climbing. A well-known commentator publishes in the *Kronenblatt*, a tabloid with a large circulation, an article denying the gas chambers. I'm told that I'm the target of death threats. The demons are not all gone. For all these reasons Austrian democrats wish to strike a major blow "for Austria." For them this demonstration presents the ideal occasion.

As for the place, it is symbolic: It was here, in this immense square, that half a million Austrians gathered in 1938, the day after the Anschluss, to salute Adolf Hitler as their beloved Führer. Indeed, I'm told proudly, I shall deliver my speech from the very balcony from which he had harangued the ecstatic crowd. It is a tempting prospect, I admit. It seduces me.

Though Marion was just a little girl at the time, she remembers hearing the speech over the radio, as she remembers the change in her neighbors. She lived through the very horror the youth of Vienna are demonstrating against today. Since Hitler, no one had been permitted to speak from that balcony. Strange, but I sense his evil shadow; I feel it enveloping this square, this city, this country. But these young people united in their quest for change merit our setting aside our anger. I have written a text. I decide not to read it. I choose to improvise.

> . . . I am not sure history has a sense of justice, but tonight I am convinced it has a sense of humor! The speaker who preceded me on this balcony, soon after the Anschluss in 1938, decided on death for me, my parents, my family, and my people. . . . Who could have imagined that a Jewish writer would succeed him in this very place in order to speak out against hatred? But note this: The crowd that came to salute him in 1938 was much larger, and its jubilation far greater. . . .

> . . . Remember, young people of Vienna! In 1938, your ancestors, your parents and grandparents, following Adolf Hitler's teaching, looked with indifference or complacency upon those Jews—one of whom was my wife's father, a Viennese—who were arrested, humiliated, and often sent to their deaths. Today, as you close the era of lies and deceit symbolized by Kurt Waldheim, you are free to open a new chapter. Open it without erasing those that preceded it. Do not run toward the future by obliterating the memory of the past. Learn to live without betraying the truth. You must learn to confront, to assume responsibility for, that truth.

An incitement to rebellion? No. An appeal to my listeners to repudiate their parents' and grandparents' generation. Intervention in a country's internal affairs? Never mind. Austria has lived equivocally and hypocritically too long. It must shake itself. I have confidence in its youth. They will do what must be done.

Chronicle of a Deposition ⎯⎯⌒

*S*PRING 1987. Why would I testify at the Klaus Barbie trial? I never even met Barbie. At the time he was terrorizing and torturing his victims in Lyon, I was a long way from France: first in Hungary, then in Auschwitz. And even though I am concerned with this trial, follow it passionately, and consider it of paramount symbolic importance, I prefer keeping up with it through the media—as an observer, not as a witness.

These are the arguments I offer to attorney Alain Jakubowicz, who on behalf of the Jewish community of Lyon has come to ask for my help. Though I had asked some friends for advice, among them Bernard-Henri Lévy, and Marc Kravetz, and several of them urged me to accept, I remain negative.

"You're all crazy," I tell them. "It would be enough for the defense lawyer to ask me some geographical or biographical questions, like, Where were you during the Occupation? Were you in Lyon? Were your parents living in France? for my testimony to become irrelevant. Let his victims depose. That should be enough; that will be enough."

But the lawyers for the plaintiffs, and several historians, insist. To be sure, the deposition of the victims is essential, but . . . I still resist. So then they talk about context, milieu, testimonies in the public interest, until in the end I have to give in. There remains the problem of scheduling. Jakubowicz suggests that I be deposed on June 12, which, because of prior commitments, does not work for me. My preference is for June 3, that is, the eve of Shavuot. Jakubowicz persuades Chief Justice Cerdini to call me as the first witness to enable me to return to Paris before nightfall, before the beginning of the holiday.

So here I am, for the first time in my life, a witness in the trial of one of the killers of my people.

• • •

For weeks I have followed the debates from New York and Japan, which I am visiting, and I have been commenting long-distance on them daily for France-Inter Radio. I read as many newspapers and reviews as possible, familiarize myself with the entire cast of characters, noting Cerdini's solemn demeanor, Barbie's sarcastic smile, his lawyer's hateful vehemence, the plaintiffs' lawyers' earnest determination, and above all the witnesses, the survivors: the mothers who try hard not to weep but do, the men who in a barely audible voice attempt to express the anguish of the underground fighter, and to describe the torture that Barbie and his henchmen inflicted on them. I admire the courage, the selflessness of the resistants: I love, I totally empathize with, the woman who as an adolescent girl saw her father shot before her eyes, as I admire the counselors, men and women, who risked their lives trying to save the Jewish children in their care. I said this before the trial, and I repeat it here: This trial will be remembered above all because of these witnesses; it permitted them, at last, to speak freely, to protect a past that many choose to reject and others deny. This trial is necessary for the world to be able to hear certain words said in a certain tone of voice.

After an initial surge of irritation, I am getting used to Barbie's absence. He will not be able to silence his victims. Too bad that no one has thought of installing a camera in his cell so that he would have to face up to the images, so that he would see and be seen. Of course it wouldn't be the same; I too would prefer to see him in a glass booth facing his victims. Never mind. Just as in the past he failed to make his prisoners talk, so he will not manage to render them mute. Though he may refuse to listen, the world will hear them.

"What is expected of me at the trial?" I ask.

Bernard-Henri Lévy has been following the sessions since the very first day, has experienced all their vagaries. He answers that what is expected of me is a text or a message to remember. "Remembrance and justice?" He responds instantly: "Yes, that is it, that's it without a doubt."

I set to work. Conscious of the significance of the moment, I propose to say in a concise text what, throughout my life, I have tried to convey in my writings: my apprehensions about language, my doubts with regard to the efficacy of education and culture, the anguish involved in confronting the extraordinarily heavy duties that memory imposes on the survivor.

Meanwhile I'm traveling more than ever. There seem to be more and more conferences. Michel Barthélémy of France-Inter calls me in Los Angeles and Hiroshima. He is asking for a sort of meditation on this uncertain era, in which the past keeps coming back to haunt the present. And where the silence of the dead rejoins the murmur of the survivors.

I leave Tokyo and return to Paris via Oslo. A telephone conversation with Jakubowicz. I am astounded to learn that all my work has been for naught: The law prohibits a witness from reading his deposition. But the lawyer is authorized to read it. I give it to Marc Kravetz, who publishes it in *Libération*.

Lyon, June 2. I visit Cardinal Decourtray: fraternal as always. I visit Chief Rabbi Klinger, who is warm and helpful. There is a meeting with Jakubowicz, and one with Beate and Serge Klarsfeld, the tireless Nazi hunters. I visit the memorial. There are photos of children and old men, emaciated bodies, eyes open to the horror.

The courtroom is packed, as it is every day. There are well-known faces and unfamiliar ones. An obscure anxiety comes over me, as it does every time I'm forced to speak of those times. What am I going to say? How can I say it? A prayer goes round and round in my head, the prayer of the *hazzan*, the cantor, who, prior to the *Musaf* service during the High Holidays, declares his apprehension before the task ahead: "See to it, Lord, that my tongue does not falter."

The witnesses are called. We withdraw to an adjacent room. Chief Justice Cerdini publicly notes the defendant's absence. He dispatches court officers to his cell to invite him to attend the hearing. Twenty minutes go by. The officers return with their usual report: the defendant refuses.

As I stand before the court, I am gripped by an emotion that takes me by surprise. I put on my *kipa* to take the oath. I shall articulate those things that, until now, have remained buried within me. I speak of my grandmother; how I admired her silent, radiating sweetness and good nature. She could go for days and nights without opening her mouth. And what if I spoke of her mute litanies before this court? Or of the merry laughter of my little sister whose image never leaves me? And what if I revealed, just once, what I feel every time I recall my mother, every time I see her again, as she moves toward the nocturnal crossroads lit up by gigantic, somber, so somber flames?

That is the dilemma for the witness: What face should be illuminated, what name should be mentioned, what destiny should be included as one shares one's memories? Should I speak of the rabbi who let himself be buried alive rather than violate the Shabbat? Or of the ghetto children who at the risk of their lives slipped back and forth through the holes in the walls to bring bread and potatoes to their starving families? Should I recall the youngsters who, against all odds, defended the burning Warsaw Ghetto to save Jewish honor? Or the Greek Jews who chose to die rather than accept assignment to the Birkenau *Sonderkommando*? Or the countless victims who moved, trance-like, to their mass graves in Babi-Yar and Ponar? They seemed to have little regret leaving a world corrupted by hatred and cowardice.

I shall not repeat here what I said in ten minutes during my deposition. All I remember is trying to stress the incommunicable aspect of our experience, and rejecting the despicable questions of the defense attorney, who did his best to dishonor the United States, France, and Israel by comparing them all to Nazi Germany. I also remember that I refused to look at him—the Talmud forbids looking at the face of an ungodly person—addressing my answers to the chief justice instead. I recall the reactions in the courtroom and how warmly the survivors, Barbie's victims, looked at me. And then, perhaps most important, there were all these young people who seemed to want to catch every word, every sigh, every murmur in the courtroom. Sunshine flooded the city that afternoon, and I remember the packed, noisy railway station; I recall everything except what I may have said to the court. But I remember my tone, that of the thirteen-year-old who, in his remote little town during his bar mitzvah, trembled with fear as he recited the customary prophetic words, the *Haftorah*.

You see, that is how it is, and I can do nothing about it; everything carries me back to my childhood, and to the children of yesterday, and to all the Jewish children of Europe whose existence, in the eyes of Barbie and his accomplices, seemed incompatible with theirs.

The Gulf War

*A*UGUST 1990. Iraq invades Kuwait. The mad Iraqi dictator Saddam Hussein is capable of anything. President Bush and his European and Soviet allies are anxiously monitoring the situation.

The first American soldiers land in the Saudi desert. The U.N. Security Council adopts resolutions demanding the Iraqi army's immediate evacuation of Kuwait. Saddam couldn't care less. For the killer of Baghdad, the chapter is closed.

According to Henry Kissinger, there will be no military intervention; Bush will not make a move. Kissinger knows Washington better than anyone else. Amr Moussa, the Egyptian ambassador to the U.N., disagrees: The war *will* take place, it must. Saddam must be defeated, not only to help Kuwait, but to protect the entire Arab region. If Saddam succeeds, he will emerge as a latter-day Salah el Din, the uncontested leader of Islam.

As yet Saddam has done nothing against the Jewish state, but everybody knows he is capable of the worst. He counts on the world's indifference. If he could gas thousands of Kurds with impunity in 1988, what will prevent him from doing the same to the Israelis?

Fully expecting war, Sigmund Strochlitz and I board an El Al flight to Tel Aviv. It is the evening of January 12, 1991. As we enter the terminal at Ben-Gurion Airport we see droves of people preparing to leave the country. Is it the fear of gas? Israelis are used to danger. In 1956, 1967, and 1973, they rushed back from wherever they were—Europe, the United States, Asia—to rejoin their combat units.

I see Prime Minister Shamir and tell him how traumatic the threat of Scuds is for people haunted by the word "gas." "Have faith," he responds. "Our army can deal with it." The next day I meet with his defense minister, Moshe Arens, who tells me the same thing, though he adds with a straight face: "Of course if a Scud happens to fall on your head, it won't be pleasant."

Arens arranges for me to visit the military zone. A liaison officer drives us "somewhere." We are received by an air force colonel who takes us on a tour of his base. I chat with his colleagues and subordinates. If Israel decides to respond, these are the men—officers, pilots, and technicians—who will be doing the job. They exude confidence. In their presence even I feel invincible.

I board a parked F-16. I am afraid to move. What would happen if, by accident, I were to push the wrong button? "Better you don't know," says one of the officers. Later, in his Jeep, the colonel details some of his responsibilities. "What if there were an alert right now?" I ask. "How long would it take you to reach your command and give the appropriate orders?" He calmly glances at his watch: "Ninety seconds," he says.

We lunch with his staff. Suddenly I hear a loud exchange outside the mess hall. Someone wants to enter, and the M.P. on guard refuses to let him in. This hall is reserved for high-ranking officers. "But," says a voice, "I don't want to eat. I've come to see my uncle." It's my beloved sister Bea's son, Steve, a doctor in the legendary Golani Division. I had called him as soon as I landed, but he explained he couldn't meet me; he was on duty.

We embrace. This kind of miraculous encounter can happen only in Israel. "I saw the television crew," says Steve. "They told me it was for 'some writer.' I thought it might be you." I would have been disappointed if I had had to leave Israel without seeing him.

It has been said of every war, but for Israel the Gulf War is in fact different from the others. Imposed by a cruel and cynical enemy, it seems to take place unilaterally. Israel appears not to be participating, at least not actively or directly. Because the Americans and their allies attack Baghdad, Iraq is now bombing Israel. It is an aggression that is insane, criminal, absurd, but, coming from Saddam Hussein, it surprises no one. We witness a new and incomprehensible phenomenon: The missiles are falling and the Israeli armed forces are not responding. Is it a policy of restraint rather than strength? Let us say, a policy of strength that expresses itself with restraint. For the first time in its history Israel leaves its defense to others. And the people do not protest. The ideological conflicts of yesterday are forgotten; this is not the time to engage in fighting among brothers. With this policy of restraint Israel earns the respect of many nations. Strange: In 1967 Israel was admired because it fought; now people praise it for not fighting. But how long will this current of sympathy last?

I marvel at the friendly and generous behavior of the civilian population during alerts. People are courteous, warm. Nobody is pushing, nobody is losing his temper. There are no tears, no hysteria. One hides one's fears as best one can. One tells funny stories, evokes memories. Radio programs of patriotic and sentimental songs from the time of the Second Aliyah are interrupted by the coded warning "snake viper," to announce an alert. Israelis seem grateful to visitors who choose to be with them. A taxi driver refuses to be paid. At the restaurant we are offered free drinks.

At night one is afraid to fall asleep, afraid to be awakened by the sirens, and afraid of having to head for the sealed rooms; afraid to have to use the gas masks. I don't even know how to use mine; never mind.

My cousin Eli Hollander invites me to his house for dinner. "We'll wait for the Scuds together," he says. A funny thought. An image returns: Our last Sukkoth together, in 1943, in the little town of Khust, in the Czech part of the Carpathians.

I accept my cousin's invitation, but at the last moment I am forced to cancel. That evening I listen to the news. A missile attack has just been launched. Later, I call Marion to reassure her. Then I call Eli to make sure he is all right; no answer. Nor do I reach him the next day. A month later, I hear from him. He thanks God that I canceled our appointment: "Had you come, we would have stayed home. Since you didn't, we spent the night at our children's house. Our house was completely demolished by a Scud."

Miraculously the Scuds caused no fatalities. Even more miraculous, thus far, they have not contained gas. Still, the threat of chemical warfare remains everyone's obsession. "And to think it was German engineers who supplied the gas to Saddam Hussein," whispers an old woman. Someone else notes that Germany sold the gas to Iraq and the masks to Israel.

The old question of Israelis versus Diaspora Jews surfaces again. A *Davar* editorialist lectures foreign Jews who did not experience the missile attacks, practically labeling them bad Jews. Let them stay home, he concludes. Similar odious attacks are published under other bylines. Why didn't the Diaspora Jews come? And those who did, why didn't they stay longer? And those who stayed longer, why aren't they settling in Israel? What are they waiting for to break with the gilded lives they lead in exile? Rarely have I sensed, in the Israeli press, such hatred toward the Diaspora.

I am reminded of an incident that occurred during the Lebanon war. A journalist asks to see me. I receive him at the Hilton in Tel Aviv. His demeanor is unappealing, self-important; what he has to say makes him even more repugnant. Is he trying to provoke me? He gives me a description of what is happening in Lebanon, where the war is in its second week: Israeli soldiers, he tells me, are behaving "like SS." Incensed by this analogy, I get up. He continues: "And it's your fault." Seeing my amazement, he corrects himself: "Of course, I am not speaking of you personally; I am referring to Diaspora Jews, especially Jewish intellectuals. If you were here, our soldiers would not be committing these atrocities. . . ."

He later publishes a pamphlet in which he describes the Jews of the Diaspora, myself included, as more dangerous to Israel than Yasir Arafat.

I try to determine to what extent his opinions are shared in Israel. The results of my investigation scare me. I hear Israelis more intelligent and cultivated than he express, in more elegant terms, more or less similar ideas.

The foreign correspondents have a different point of view. They pelt me with questions: "Why did you come to Israel now?" "Are you attracted to danger?" I try to explain: I love Israel too much to stay away when it is in danger. Having lived what I have lived, having written what I have written, I am compelled to link myself to its destiny.

What about the bombings of the Iraqi military bases? And the punishment inflicted on Baghdad? "You are known as a man of peace," notes an Italian newspaperman. "How can you identify with those who make war?" Normally this kind of question troubles me. But in the context of this conflict the question seems irrelevant. This is a war that Israel endures but does not participate in. It is Saddam Hussein's war. The security of the civilized world is at stake, its right to peace, not just Israel's future. We should have understood and intervened the day he ordered the Kurds gassed. If at that time we had convened an international tribunal to try him for crimes against humanity, the Gulf War could have been avoided.

This is what I say when I testify, for the second time, before the U.S. Senate's Foreign Relations Committee, which is debating the need to establish an international court to bring Saddam to justice. The senators' unanimous vote is yes.

• • •

The pressure exerted on Shamir by Bush was too great for Israel not to take into account. During that entire period Israel did not make a move. The United States showed its gratitude: Its intercepting missiles, called "Patriots," could be seen at strategic locations; they were reassuring. But people didn't think they were the reason why the Iraqi missiles caused so little damage. But then what was the reason? Miracles were a big topic in Israel, not only in religious circles. Even Yitzhak Rabin mentioned them in a speech he gave in the synagogue I attend in Manhattan, which caused one listener to comment: "Now *that* is a miracle—to hear Rabin use that word."

In the Hasidic courts and the yeshivas, every situation is examined in the light of biblical texts. Thus, on Shabbat, one reads the passage: "God will do battle for you and you will remain silent." In Brooklyn the Lubavitcher Rebbe declares to his followers: "You have nothing to fear; the war will be over before Purim." My friend from the camps, Rebbe Menashe Klein, promises me solemnly that "nothing will happen to Israel." I am told that a third rabbi has made a similar promise. Perfect. Three rabbis constitute a tribunal. And a tribunal has the power to issue a verdict. And even the heavens must obey a rabbinical verdict. In that case, why worry?

Only, I have learned to be wary of miracles. They trouble me. They trouble me even in the context of Hasidic tales, to the point that when I tell them I try not to make too much of them. True, I believed in them as a child, like everybody else. They fascinated me. Today they are a problem. They imply God and His selective compassion. If God has at times taken the trouble to save His people, why has He been so sparing in His interventions? He could have intervened more often. Paradoxically, for my generation, there are many miracles to be thankful for.

As a child in Sighet I would repeat my prayers; daily rituals contain their own miracles. I still believe this. But today it is their human dimension that matters to me. "And God in all this?" asks one of my characters in *The Trial of God*. I would answer: The very question contains the miracle. What is a question if not the element that allows a human being to transcend himself? A morning prayer tells us: "Every day the Creator renews His creation." In other words, miracles abound, only man is sometimes blind.

François Mitterrand and
Jewish Memory

*I*T IS TO JOB, and the French minister of culture Jack Lang, that I owe my encounter with François Mitterrand. And it is because of René Bousquet, organizer of the infamous roundup of Jews at the Vélodrome d'Hiver in Paris, that we went our separate ways.

Philippe Nemo, one of the young right-wing "new philosophers" who later reproached me for my friendship with President Mitterrand—who, as everyone knows by now, had a right-wing past and a left-wing future—had written a book on Job. Having also read my own commentaries on that particular biblical figure, he proposes to interview me for the radio station France-Culture.

Nemo is referring to my *Célébration biblique,* published in the United States as *Messengers of God,* and we agree to devote a series of broadcasts to Abraham, Isaac, Jacob, and Moses. And what we imagine happens in fairytales comes to pass. An important political person listening to his car radio hears a few thoughts about Jacob, the weakest, the palest, the most awkward, the most malleable of the Patriarchs, until he became Israel. The future president of France finds it an original way of approaching the Bible. He likes it. He listens to several broadcasts, obtains all the cassettes, then decides to offer another set to his longtime friend Charles Salzman, but is told his supplier has just run out of stock. Of the author, he knows only one book, the witness account *The Jews of Silence.*

During the electoral campaign of 1980, Lang, matchless as an intellectual and artistic impresario, learns of the Socialist candidate's interest in me and invites me to one of his debates, the real purpose of which is to illustrate François Mitterrand's impact on the outside world. I am quite aware that this initiative is not an innocent one: The elections are looming on the political horizon. As an American citizen I should not get involved. But I play the game.

The first meeting takes place at the house of one of his friends. We exchange a few words. There are too many people around us. Never mind; next time.

Next time will be at the Élysée. And I shall return there often.

I welcome François Mitterrand's victory as an act of justice.

There is joy everywhere. The capital is festive, especially the Place de la Bastille. Socialism is being celebrated. There is singing and dancing in the streets. The Socialist victory has turned people's heads. Some go so far as to hiss the outgoing president as he leaves the Élysée—a regrettable lapse of tact.

Celebrations are in progress both at the Arc de Triomphe and at the Pantheon, where Roger Hanin, the actor and President Mitterrand's brother-in-law, is directing the ceremony. The newly elected head of state stands in solitary but regal splendor before the crypt of the heroic *résistant* Jean Moulin.

From outside, the sound of pouring rain. Bareheaded, the new president listens, motionless, to the fourth movement of Beethoven's Ninth Symphony, conducted by Daniel Barenboim. Hoping to please his new boss, a future minister sends a message to the young maestro: Couldn't he conduct a little faster? I go back to the hotel drenched to the bone.

Mitterrand wishes to receive me the following day. I am flattered and tempted, but I cannot delay my return; I am scheduled to spend the weekend at Yale. A pity. It's not every day that one is officially declared to be a "friend of the president." But the people at Yale wouldn't understand. Would there ever be a next time?

Once established, the contact proves solid, fruitful. Mitterrand insists that I come to see him every time I'm in Paris. When I tell him of my hesitation to disturb him, he answers that he always has time for his friends. I see him again a few months later, during a Sorbonne conference. He scolds me: "I know you come to Paris often, but you don't call me." I promise to call the next time. And I do, certain that I shall run into one of those barriers behind which the great and not-so-great of this world hide. But to my surprise, I'm told he will receive me that same day.

The man, as much as his power, intimidates me; I feel ill at ease. At first I answer his questions evasively; I need time to overcome my inhibitions. But little by little I feel free to speak. I like the way he listens and smiles.

We sometimes lunch together in his private quarters at the Élysée. He is interested in the complicated laws of kashrut: Why is one meat ritually pure when another is not? Why are Jews forbidden to mix meat with milk? What is the difference between biblical command- ments and their rabbinical interpretations? And again and again, he asks, what does Jewish tradition say about the immortality of the soul?

Our relationship grows more intense. I have also become fond of his wife, Danielle. Gracious, sincere, she has convictions and knows how to share them with others. Her activities on behalf of human rights have won her admiration and affection. The president often feels he has to explain her absence at the table: "She's off some- where . . . in Latin America," or, "She is in Africa." I'm often too taken by the conversation to eat. So this is how it works: When the presi- dent eats, I speak; when he speaks, I listen. He takes an interest in my activities; he asks about Marion's, too. He invites me to accompany him to Normandy for the fortieth-anniversary celebrations of D-Day. I would give much to go with him, but June 6 falls during the festival of Shavuot. (He will renew his invitation for the fiftieth anniversary, and this time I'll accept.) I explain our festivals. His interest in every- thing that touches the Jewish religion—and religion in general—is genuine. We sometimes spend hours discussing related subjects. He would make an excellent professor of religious studies and of litera- ture, possessing as he does a profound grasp of both the classics and modern works. His quotations are always perceptive. And he's rarely wrong. He knows his biblical texts: Jacob amuses him, Moses intrigues him, and Jeremiah irritates him: "First this prophet demoral- izes his people, then he snivels about its defeat." He calls him a "very ambitious thunderer, ambiguous in his relations with the Babyloni- ans." It so happens that I like the author of Lamentations. This leads to endless discussions that I propose to end by consulting the text, hop- ing thus to rehabilitate in his eyes this man from Anathoth who moves me so. "Some other time," says the president.

Usually, according to a tacit agreement, we avoid touching on French domestic politics. On the other hand, we often discuss Israel. His admiration for David Ben-Gurion and Yigal Allon, the former chief of the Palmah; his respect, with some reservations, for Me- nachem Begin; his affection for Shimon Peres. Though he disagrees with Yitzhak Shamir's policies, which he considers extremist, he nev- ertheless remarks that if he were Israeli he might act similarly. He stresses the fact that he has never referred to the "occupied territories" but to the West Bank; "occupation" for him, too, is a word with specific connotations.

His visits to our home in New York have left unforgettable memories. The first time, he arrives from Washington, where he has been on a state visit to Ronald Reagan. The chairman of the telephone company calls in person to inform us that a special line is to be installed for the exclusive use of our guest of honor. The French later tell me that this line will connect him with the French army's strike force, just in case. Amused and slightly worried, we ask to have the instrument installed in Elisha's room, among his toys. And when I show Mitterrand the supersecret telephone's location, I tell him that if it rings I am thinking of answering: "Sorry, wrong number." I am not looking forward to having World War III start in my apartment. The guests we have invited are happy; the other tenants in our building are not: The security agents have closed the street and taken over one of the elevators.

For every one of his visits, we invite intellectuals—artists, journalists, writers, professors—to meet him. He likes their company more than that of politicians or diplomats, and he, in turn, always impresses them with his eloquence and erudition. People tend to compare him—favorably—to other Western heads of state. His preeminent standing in cultural affairs, in France as well as abroad, is unchallenged.

We rarely, if ever, discuss my writings. When I offer him my most recently published book, the conversation invariably revolves around its implications rather than its theme. If it's a novel, we talk about literature in general. An essay on the Talmud? We discuss the Talmud's complexity, its capacity for synthesis, and the magic of its style. A book on Hasidism? The subject draws him into a comparative analysis of various forms of mysticism.

One evening he invites me to dinner not in his private apartment but in a restaurant. But which one? He reflects a moment and decides: Le Train Bleu. A quarter of an hour later, we're there. Two bodyguards sit at the next table. I ask him whether he isn't worried about security. "What could happen to me here?" he answers. "How could a terrorist prepare an attack here, since I myself didn't know a half hour ago where we would dine?" He didn't realize, I was told later by Pierre Joxe, his interior minister at the time, that some twenty Internal Security agents were scattered among the customers. A fatalist, François Mitterrand?

Here is something that may surprise some who knew him better and longer than I: I never heard him say anything derogatory about his opponents, even in the midst of the electoral campaign or during the first *cohabitation*, which surely was painful for him. Of course, he did not cover them with compliments either, and I could tell when he did not like this or that person—his face would cloud over abruptly. But he rarely used his sharp sense of humor to wound.

Still, I know that he could be severe, unfair, even merciless with anyone stupid enough to annoy or cross him. He had no tolerance for contradiction. He was incapable of ever admitting that he might be wrong on any subject. A saint he was not; far from it.

That he loved gossip, political and other, became evident only when we were not alone. In his entourage, official and private, there were always people whose company he enjoyed because they knew how to entertain him with funny tales about public figures.

I like his simplicity—which is genuine. At the beginning of his seven-year term, he went home every evening to his apartment on the Rue de Bièvre. The Élysée, he explains, is only a workplace for him, an office for dealing with affairs of state.

For many, his most appealing trait is his intelligence. For others, it is his tenacity. For me, it is his loyalty to friends. Those closest to him repeat this to me often enough: Friendship for him is more important than anything else, the only thing that matters. I am told he never lets down a friend, even when the friend is wrong. That pleases and touches me. Of course, that was before . . .

My notes are full of impressions of our encounters. Of course, as is usual for me, every time I walked into the Élysée Palace, I remembered where I came from and wondered in what possible way a former yeshiva student from Sighet could interest the leader of France and one of the world's great men. Probably too respectful and certainly more than awkward, I let him go on indefinitely without ever interrupting him. Even when we had our dialogues—I'll return to that subject a little later—I chose to make him talk rather than to express myself. I liked listening to his confidences, to his analyses of the workings of high international politics. The man intrigued me. I saw in him a living symbol of the Resistance. Whenever I left the Élysée, I felt that I had been close to a leader with great impact on current events, and I would rush to the Bristol to jot down his every word in my diary.

Some of the questions:

God? "I'm an agnostic." A strange agnostic, fascinated by mysticism.

Nuclear peril? It preoccupies him, of course. I say: "Let us imagine the following scenario: Your red phone rings; it is late at night. A general informs you that the Soviets have just launched a nuclear missile in the direction of France; it will hit its target in seven minutes. What will you do? Whom do you call first? On what basis will you decide to give the order to respond?" Silence. I insist: "Do you know now what you would do then?" He says very quietly, "Yes, I know." And he immediately adds: "But I also know that we must do everything to prevent this from happening."

Israel? Israel holds a crucial place in his political philosophy. He knows the country that according to him belongs more to history than to geography. Israel, for him, is the land in which the Bible and its characters still live and communicate with one another. For him it is the place possibly inhabited by God, and certainly by Abraham, David, and Ezekiel.

The Middle East conflict? The historical claim of the Jews on the one hand, and that of the Arabs on the other, the tragedy of two peoples bound to the same—largely arid—soil. "What is evident," says Mitterrand, "is that over these last centuries the Arabs have settled there; therefore it is their country too." That is his view of the "incredibly confused" situation in which we live today: "two peoples, two Gods, two religions, two prophets all crowded into one small land."

Israel, a political challenge? For Mitterrand it transcends politics. Politics deals only with the present, albeit with an opening toward the future; Israel defines itself by its past as well. Israel is Jerusalem, and Jerusalem signifies the ineffable. One day, contemplating what he might do at the end of his mandate (he was then finishing his first seven-year term), he formulates a sort of wish, a hope: "I'll go to Israel, to Jerusalem. . . . I feel like spending some time there . . . perhaps I'll do some writing. . . . It's one of those places that arouses all kinds of aspirations in me. It's not the only one, but it may be the one that brings together the most spiritual, intellectual, historical, and political elements. . . ." I tell him that all my life, since my earliest childhood, I have done nothing, in a way, but sing of Jerusalem, the light, the luminosity of Jerusalem. He responds: "Everything in that region is inten-sity. Not only Jerusalem. One must wonder about all those peoples who, over centuries and centuries, have been burned by faith. . . . As though each stone contained a force, as though there were explo-sive atoms with religious characteristics. . . . It is a land scorched by passion."

What is it that fascinates him the most: the people, the country, or the history of Israel? Perhaps it is the destiny of Israel. Everything Jewish arouses his interest. The Jewish attitude toward death and toward the stranger. What Judaism says about suffering. The role of Exile in our tradition. Is there such a thing as specifically Jewish ethics? Can one be Jewish outside Israel, or against Israel? Can one be a Jew outside the Jewish community? And anyway, what exactly does it mean to be a Jew?

He has his own ideas about all these questions. So do I. Often they are not the same.

In preparing my "dialogues" with François Mitterrand in 1988–1989 and again during the summer of 1993, I plan to keep the theme of memory for the end. Memory in regard to the Holocaust, that is. We had often spoken of World War II and even of the death camps, but not of Vichy and Pétain. That was before the heartbreaking—and for me at the time, incomprehensible—report of the wreath he chose to lay secretly on Pétain's grave. And before the publication of Pierre Péan's revelations about his connections with the Vichy regime. The deportations, the death camps, the Warsaw Ghetto uprising—he told me that he knew about them at the time, through the underground press. But what about Vichy and the complicity of the French author-ities? How was one to understand his measured views of Vichy and his silence about Pétain? I hoped he, a former member of the Resistance, would explain it all to me one day. I still didn't know about his own past at that time. It was well before the Bousquet affair.

Until September 1994, our most serious disagreement had to do with Yasir Arafat's visit to Paris. I had picked up warning signals a few weeks earlier and had confided them to an Israeli friend, who in turn hastened to inform Prime Minister Yitzhak Shamir, who refused to believe him: "How can President Mitterrand receive Arafat when he has just welcomed me so cordially?" Shamir was naive. A more sea-soned diplomat would have understood the connection between the two events, the policy of "evenhandedness." Mitterrand most likely had received him so cordially as part of the groundwork for the invitation to Arafat.

Whose idea was it? Jacques Attali acknowledges that it was his during a painful discussion over dinner, in the presence of Marion; his wife, Elizabeth; and his publisher, Claude Durand. And why? To start things moving in the Middle East, to exert pressure on the Shamir government; for Israel has to be saved in spite of itself. Because, for Attali, Israel embodies the Book, the triumph of the spirit, the power of its ethical message. His brand of logic leads him to say that if he had to choose between the State of Israel and the Book of Israel, his choice would be easy. Out of concern for justice and truth I must specify that all this took place during the Intifada. According to him, Israel was in danger of losing its soul—and I my credibility, if I did not publicly denounce Israel.

Later on, Attali told me that he had had mixed feelings about the visit of the PLO chief, and that he had had trouble coping. He told me that on that day, which happened to be the Day of Remembrance of the Holocaust, he had put on a black tie.

What is certain is that Mitterrand had been encouraged by Jewish (and non-Jewish) intellectuals to reach out to Arafat. They probably told him that since a number of Jews, Americans and others, were meeting with Arafat, why should he continue to boycott him?

As for me, for personal and objective reasons, I do not agree. I feel Mitterrand is making a mistake, which could well harm Israel and the Jewish community and himself as well. To the journalists who try immediately to get my reaction, I do not hide my disappointment: "As far as I can tell, Arafat does not yet deserve to be received at the Élysée. There is still time to cancel the invitation. If the president considers it useful to strengthen the relations between France and the PLO, that is his right. Let the minister of foreign affairs negotiate with Arafat, or the prime minister. But not the president of the republic. . . ." My words, however respectful and cordial, reflect my disenchantment. Nor do I have any illusions: Our friendship is at stake. One of his close aides suggests I come to Paris to speak to Mitterrand, as friend to friend. I ask: "And if I succeed in convincing the president, will he cancel the invitation?" The answer: "No, it's too late. Arafat is coming." I stay in New York.

I write these lines toward the end of 1995. Meanwhile the Rabin-Arafat handshake has altered the image and role of the Palestinian leader. This citizen of Gaza, president of the Palestinian National Authority, is now considered a moderate by public opinion. For the government of Shimon Peres he was the only valid interlocutor. The terrorist of yesterday has become Israel's ally. Fine. I support with all my heart their policy of reconciliation and their aspirations to peace. Nevertheless, I still think that Arafat's visit to the Élysée was a mistake. The head of the PLO, with his bloodstained past, with his charter that stipulates the annihilation of Israel, should not be received by the head of state. I was told to note the difference in certain details of protocol: three motorcycles instead of seven, no red carpet, reception by a deputy rather than by the minister of foreign affairs or the head of protocol. Nonsense. This time it was a matter of image, of symbols, and details were of no importance.

Arafat has scarcely left Paris when I receive a call from the Élysée. Mitterrand wants to see me. Urgently. I drop everything and go to Paris. I come to the appointment tense and frustrated. He wishes to explain his actions to me: "Please understand me. I am not an Israeli, I am not a Zionist; I am responsible for French policy, which, as such, must take the Arab world into account. . . ." He tells me of his meeting with Arafat, who evidently not only knows his lessons well but knows how to present his case to best effect. He tells Mitterrand of his brother's death; he was buried like a thief somewhere in Egypt. What about Arafat the terrorist? He is renouncing terrorism. And the infamous charter of the PLO? Dead. "Null and void." Mitterrand tells me that it was in his office that this phrase was proposed, studied, and adopted.

What Mitterrand did not know at the time (did he find out later?) was that while Arafat was showing him a peaceful if not pacifist face, Faruq Khadumi, his assistant, was chatting in the antechamber with several high French officials and told them, in an astonishing outburst of candor: "The old man is talking nonsense; the Palestinians refuse all compromise. We do not want a part of Palestine; we demand *all* of Palestine."

Mitterrand continues to think—and no one has the right to doubt it—that he was acting for the good of Israel. Hurt by the attacks from Jewish extremists, he keeps repeating: "One day people will know who is the real friend of Israel." He does care about what he considers his privileged relation with the people of Israel. He keeps coming back to it. Wasn't he the first president of France to make a state visit to Jerusalem? Did he not speak out for a Palestinian state before the Knesset? Why are people reproaching him for that now? He informs me in strict confidence of certain actions he has undertaken on behalf of the Jewish state since 1981. And at the time of the terrorist attack at Goldenberg's restaurant, hadn't he gone immediately to the scene of the tragedy? It seems there had been some excited young people who greeted him with cries of "Murderer!" This incident pains him as much as it does me. How can anyone subscribe to the notion that he is not or is no longer Israel's friend? From his point of view, he invited Arafat for the good of Israel. Though I try to refute his argument I feel I have no right to attack his motive: I do believe he wanted to do the right thing and that he is psychologically and morally incapable of wishing to harm Israel.

But . . . what about Arafat and his past? He trusts him. Not totally, but enough to believe in his sincerity. Did his attitude toward him change a little later? After the fall of Nicolae Ceauşescu, wasn't it he who expressed astonishment, speaking of the last spectacular Communist congress organized by the Romanian dictator: "And to think that Arafat was treated there as a sort of guest of honor. . . ." He wanted me to explain that to him. I answered that he was in a better position to explain.

As for his explanations of Arafat's visit to Paris, he didn't convince me, but neither did I judge him. You cannot judge a man on one isolated act. What counts is the totality of the person. From that perspective—we're still long before the Bousquet affair—I continued to declare that Mitterrand had remained a friend and faithful ally of Israel and the Jewish people. I cannot forget his participation in the demonstration that followed the desecration of the Jewish cemetery at Carpentras, and his second trip to Israel, and his decision—a symbolic gesture—to designate July 16 a day of national commemoration of the rounding up of Parisian Jews in the Vélodrome d'Hiver. Nor can I forget his many statements against racism and anti-Semitism.

My friendship with him has earned me criticism and recriminations from Jewish extremists. I have been asked many questions about it, and some of them were painful to hear. I find them unfounded, regrettable.

Around that time, Elizabeth Schemla, one of the best journalists in Paris, asks me on behalf of Le Nouvel Observateur if I still have confidence in Mitterrand. I reply unequivocally: "I have no doubt that for him as a man, the survival of Israel constitutes an imperative. I haven't a moment's doubt of his loyalty. When the chips are down, François Mitterrand is a friend of the Jewish people and of Israel."

And so we continue to see each other. The question remains: Did he manipulate me? Did he use our friendship as an alibi vis-à-vis the Jewish community, as he made use of it when he sent me, after the coup d'état in Moscow, to take a message of support to Gorbachev? That is what people say. I don't believe it.

August 1991: Marion, Elisha, and I are spending the last two weeks of the month at the house of friends on the Riviera. I'm having breakfast when I learn of Mikhail Gorbachev's arrest. It is Monday morning. Has perestroika come to an end? Can history, as proclaimed by Marxism-Leninism, be reversed? Are we going to witness a return to Brezhnevism, perhaps Stalinism? Nervous, I listen to the news, switching from station to station. The rumors are alarming: The life of the Soviet head of state is supposed to be in danger; Boris Yeltsin's as well. The Western capitals are getting worried. Is there to be a politico-military insurrection? How is one to know how it will end? The fact is that when Moscow moves, the whole world trembles.

That afternoon my New York office calls. Jack Lang is trying to reach me, urgently. The situation in the USSR is alarming; the danger is real. The process of democratization is in jeopardy. Though worried, the minister of culture is, as always, bubbling over with ideas. He wants me to come to Paris immediately to cochair with him an international committee to safeguard democracy in the Soviet Union. I agree. We quickly make up a list of personalities whose collaboration we deem necessary. Tomorrow we'll announce it to the press. Then he proposes a second task to me, to take to Gorbachev and Yeltsin a message of support from Mitterrand. Why me? His "logical" explanation: "Gorbachev is a Nobel Prize winner, and so are you. Nothing could be more normal than one laureate coming to the aid of another." No need to think about it; I accept.

Later on, Mitterrand's political opponents claim that both initiatives were designed to make up for his blunder that first Monday evening on television, when he seemed to insinuate that the news from Moscow might be a fait accompli, going so far as to read from a letter he had just received from the chief conspirator, General Yanaiev. Who was manipulating whom? Mitterrand explains to me that from the first he had thought of following a twofold strategy: On the one hand he quoted the promises of the conspirators (without approving them); on the other, keeping in mind their victims, he entrusted me with a message of total support. Did this mean that at first he had believed that the rebels might win, however temporarily? He explains to me that in the beginning the situation had seemed unclear. "The French needed to be reassured," Mitterrand tells me, while giving me instructions as to what I should say to Gorbachev in his name. He also says that "it was necessary to show that France was ready for all eventualities."

I try to help him in a modest way. The press conference, at the Ministry of Culture, has attracted a great many journalists. Yves Montand, Jorge Semprun, and Jack Lang all make political statements. There is much indignation and determination. In a few sentences I explain my own position: "Let us not respond with silence to the man who broke the silence in the Soviet Union. . . ."

I hurry back to the Côte d'Azur to pack a few things. Elisha and Marion are not convinced that my trip to Moscow is reasonable or necessary. But one does not refuse such a mission. Gorbachev deserves to be encouraged by Mitterrand, and Mitterrand deserves that I accept the role of his emissary. My son likes to argue, and he knows how to convince, but this time he does not insist.

As she prepares my bag, Marion asks me questions about the practical aspects of the mission. A government airplane is coming to pick me up tomorrow morning. "Got your passport?" "Yes I have." "Your Soviet visa?" I had forgotten about that. "Do you think they'll let you in without a visa?" By God, she's right. I rush to the telephone and call Jack Lang, who calls the Élysée, which calls the Soviet Embassy, which remains silent. It seems that the ambassador, Yuri Dubinin, prefers to keep a low profile until things become more clear. As do his colleagues. Hours go by before a consular official can be tracked down. He asks me whether I have submitted a visa request to the consulate. The question is absurd; he knows the answer. In that case, no visa. Fortunately there is such a thing as the fax. What about photos? We urgently look for a photographer, find one. But the official at the Soviet Embassy informs me that only Moscow can deliver the visa. And that it will take some time. How long? A few days at least. At the Élysée they're getting nervous, and I am told to leave without a visa. What? Go without a visa? The refugee in me protests: never, hear, never! Even carrying a supernormal visa I quake as I go through passport control. Do you see me landing in Moscow (Moscow!) without the miraculous stamp of an obscure consular clerk? And what about the

Gulag? A product of Solzhenitsyn's imagination? At the Élysée they reassure me: In a government plane there is nothing to be afraid of; nothing can happen to me. I am no hero, and my heart tells me not to yield, not to expose myself to stupid risks. But I'm ashamed to admit my cowardice, and so I fly off to Moscow without a visa.

It turns out that I shall not be traveling alone. Jean Lecanuet and Michel Vauzelle will accompany me. Their situation is more comfortable than mine; their visas wait for them on arrival. The former represents the Senate, the latter the National Assembly. But I am the one charged with transmitting the French president's message—that is, if I'm not turned back or thrown into prison.

Upon landing I finally accept the evidence that my fears were unfounded. In spite of the late hour an impressive welcoming committee has come to greet us. The French ambassador brings us up-to-date on events: The putsch has failed; Gorbachev will be back tomorrow. We spend the rest of the night at the embassy residence. There is comfort, courtesy, friendliness. In spite of the unscheduled nature of our visit everything seems minutely prepared, as if we had been expected after all. Tomorrow, with a little luck and persuasion, we shall get a chance to fulfill our mission.

An embassy staff member has already contacted the Yeltsin team and a high Kremlin official. Thus they are aware, at the highest level, of our visit and its objective.

Another member of the staff takes care of the formalities, which are as simple as they could be. In fact there are none. I don't dare mention that I have no visa; but in fact no one has asked me. I don't even remember anyone opening my passport.

Next morning we're taken to the "White House," the Russian Parliament, where, we're told, Yeltsin will receive us with full honors. In the capital, which we cross at high speed, everything looks normal. With the exception of the district we are about to visit, it all looks peaceful, sleepy, quiet. But where then is the revolutionary atmosphere the media keep talking about? Paris in 1968 was stormier. Here and there some women are standing in line in front of a department store. Taxis are circulating on the main avenues. It is business as usual, a morning like any other. The city does not seem to be living through a "historic" crisis and ordeal or experiencing anything exceptional.

The only place where one perceives unrest is around the Parliament. There are scores of idle soldiers, a multitude of young people. You might think you were in the Latin Quarter with Daniel Cohn-

Bendit and the "sixty-eighters." People stand around in groups; everyone is debating, remaking the world, reinventing humankind.

Parliament is in session. The hall is packed: The deputies have not closed their eyes since the beginning of the putsch. On some of the benches young "revolutionaries" are dozing. Owing to the lack of space in the galleries, we are seated among the deputies. Yeltsin is on stage witnessing a noisy debate. I don't understand what it's about, but the thought flashes through my mind that I could vote, like the deputies next to me, just by pressing one of the three buttons in front of me. Fortunately I see the world-famous Russian-born cellist Mstislav (Slava) Rostropovitch, who sums up for me what is being said by the representatives of the people.

We're all waiting for Gorbachev's arrival, but after several false alarms we give up. In fact, Yeltsin leaves, too. Outside a demonstration is taking place. On the balcony a dozen fiery speakers are haranguing the growing crowd, which keeps applauding.

Suddenly, I notice Edward Shevardnadze. A solitary figure, he keeps aloof from the people and their leaders. He seems remote, thoughtful. The bold minister of foreign affairs of perestroika hardly matters anymore. He is a "has been" who might as well be absent. When our eyes meet, we rush toward each other to embrace. He invites us—the two French parliamentarians and me—to his office in the early afternoon. I tell him: "I was watching you a moment ago. You looked sad, melancholy. Why? After all, things are falling into place. The putsch failed, perestroika is saved. Gorbachev is back in power. You should be happy." He admits he's not. How could he be? He tells us that everything is going badly in the country; it is coming apart. Poverty is so widespread that if the West doesn't help, there will be famine. And anything could happen. We ask him why he is angry with Gorbachev, whom he has just criticized with astounding frankness in an interview. Yes, he is angry: He should never have gone on vacation to the Crimea; he should have foreseen the putsch, taken the necessary measures. No doubt there are other reasons he chooses not to discuss. To cheer him up, I ask as I'm about to leave: "Shall I have to call you Mr. President one of these days?" "Never!" he answers laughing. "I have seen the nature of power; I don't want any part of it."

His later accession to the presidency of his native Georgia confirms to me the popular wisdom that says no political figure should ever use the word "never."

Gorbachev's press conference, the first since his return from the Crimea, is tumultuous. His account of what happened to him is poignant. You listen to him, afraid to breathe, stirred by his courage. He tells of his comrades' treachery, his feeling of isolation, and that of those close to him. One of the two most powerful people on the globe cut off from the outside world: How could it happen? If it hadn't been for the loyalty of a small group of bodyguards, there would have been no way out. But why does he think it necessary to defend Communism? The disappointment in the hall is palpable. People continue to listen but in a different way. Does he realize that, for him, this is the beginning of the end?

The French ambassador takes us over to him. Three sets of security agents, automatic rifles at the ready, guard him. His face shows lines of fatigue, insomnia, perhaps bitterness. I am so moved by his appearance that I don't hear what Vauzelle and Lecanuet tell him or what he says in reply. A French student acts as interpreter. He thanks me for having come from so far away. I transmit Mitterrand's message to him, adding how pleased I am to be here. And that as a Jew, I really owe it to him; after all, he was the one who allowed the "Jews of Silence" to leave for Israel. I may be wrong, but I believe his eyes fill with tears. But all he says to me is: "I know who you are, but I did not know how influential you are." Seeing my astonishment, he explains with a smile: "You must be someone very important; President Mitterrand has called me three times today, always about you." I feel like answering him: I am the same man who for years wrote you letters and letters on behalf of Shcharansky, Sakharov, Slepak, and Nudel, the same man who for years implored you to speak out, preferably on television, against the anti-Semitism that is still rife in your country. But this is not the time. There will be other opportunities to speak of that.

In the plane that takes us back to France, I review everything I've just heard and lived through. Yeltsin's populism. The passivity of the Muscovites. Gorbachev's emotion. He above all is the object of my reflections. Rarely have I seen a man so disillusioned, so solitary. Almost all his friends betrayed him. Almost all his comrades abandoned him. His collaborators—almost all repudiated him. Moreover, he had been convinced that he held great power, when all that remained was illusion and memory. And his religion, Communism, is bankrupt. What is left? Nothing but ruins.

Back in Paris, I demonstrate my total ignorance of foreign policy as I present my report to Mitterrand. Gorbachev is not finished, I say with certainty. He will recover. And Yeltsin? the president inquires. Yeltsin? Not a chance! It would have been difficult to be more wrong.

Mitterrand remains in power, but the people are disenchanted. He drops dramatically in all the polls. His own party seems to be turning its back on him. Certain Socialist leaders tell me: "Before, he helped us; now he is in our way." Others go further: "Before, he was the solution; now he's the problem." And others go even further: "If we lose, it will be his fault."

All that is rather unfair. Few men have as broad a vision of the world. But it seems that the gods have abandoned him. In biblical terms one would say, Grace has left him. Before, people went so far as to like his failings, and now he is blamed even for his virtues.

In 1988, Jack Lang proposed to Mitterrand the creation of an international intellectual body whose purpose would be the exploration of the larger social and cultural themes that confront mankind at the close of the twentieth century. The president authorized the project. Two top advisers on cultural affairs at the Élysée—Laure Adler first, then Bernard Latarget—together with a representative of the culture ministry were to act as liaisons to the government. And that was how the Académie Universelle des Cultures was born. Among its members, many prestigious names of the literary, artistic, and scientific worlds. Ten Nobel laureates, a movie star, novelists, teachers, musicians, architects: Each occupies a singular place in his or her domain. We devise an exciting agenda: annual prizes, various scholarships and projects.

As usual, things drag. The inauguration—at the Louvre, no less—by Mitterrand takes place a few months before the legislative elections. As a result the promises and commitments made on the ministerial level are not fulfilled. The relatively modest annual budget of six million francs (around a million dollars) remains an objective, if not a dream. Nevertheless, the academy functions. Its first conference, held in the main amphitheater of the Sorbonne, deals with the problem of "intervention." In Sienna, as guests of the municipality, academy members gather for a debate on "intolerance." Whatever the academy does, it does well. It could do better—if it were given the means.

There is no doubt that Mitterrand could intervene to release the funds, even during the era of *cohabitation*, especially since this is a project conceived with him. I speak to him about it several times. Each time he replies that he will mention it to the prime minister and to the minister of culture. The last time I bring up the subject, he simply says: "What can I do? I no longer have the power I used to have."

I had never found him so pathetic. That was in 1994.

Until the Bousquet affair, I believed that history would be kind to him. Since then, I no longer believe it. And I say this with sadness. From now on, whenever the name of René Bousquet is spoken, another name will instantly come to mind: that of his friend François Mitterrand.

The Bousquet affair breaks into the news in September 1994 like thunder announcing the days of awe and anguish of the Jewish High Holiday of Rosh Hashana.

I am in Paris for the publication of *Tous les Fleuves vont à la mer* (*All Rivers Run to the Sea*). Invited by France-Inter radio for its 1 p.m. news program, I am waiting for my turn when I hear someone speaking about Pétain and Mitterrand. A staff member tells me the speaker's name: Pierre Péan. The man himself seems pleasant and restrained, but what he says nevertheless upsets me. How can he pronounce the names of Mitterrand and Pétain in one breath? I listen to him unaware that he will be the tangible cause of my estrangement from Mitterrand.

Even before I have a chance to read Péan's *Une jeunesse française,** I must endure the onslaught of the media as his revelations take on proportions reminiscent of the first stages of Watergate.

When I read the book, my first reaction is disbelief. I refuse to believe that a man like François Mitterrand could have concealed his Vichy past, formed intimate relationships with former *cagoulards* (members of La Cagoule, a clandestine right-wing organization), and become the friend of Bousquet, the French chief of police who, always surrounded by SS officers and the Gestapo, had organized the deportation of French Jewry. It couldn't be. None of this fits in with the personality and life of the man I thought I knew so well.

True, from time to time, I had heard rumors, mostly vague. The person telling me this or that would be content to grin at me with an air of complicity or allow a sentence to go unfinished. Like everyone

*Paris: Fayard, 1994.

else I ascribed all this gossip to right-wing propaganda. I would wonder what else they would invent to harm him. I rejected these defamatory reports; I refused to discuss them. Rabbinic law teaches that it is forbidden not only to spread calumnies but even to listen to them.

Péan's book is something else. These are not calumnies. In light of his revelations, and those they lead to, my attitude has become untenable. How can I defend a political figure who praised Bousquet even after he had been indicted and convicted of crimes against humanity? He said he found him *"sympathique"* and saw him "with pleasure"! Was that all he could say about the former accomplice of the SS? To Nicole Leibowitz-Boulanger of *Le Nouvel Observateur,* I admit feeling pained, offended. I say the same on television, and to audiences that come to hear me in Nancy, Lille, and elsewhere. But I refuse to go any further. It is not in my nature to join a mob, especially since Mitterrand is ill, seriously ill. The public's reaction is hostile. Here and there people tell me they cannot understand how I could be the friend of the friend of Bousquet. My answer: "The president honors me with his friendship; I owe it to him to listen to his explanations. The sooner the better." But we are getting close to the Jewish High Holidays, and I must go home for Rosh Hashana.

It is when I come back to New York that I pick up the echoes of Mitterrand's television interview with Jean-Pierre Elkabbach. I experience the same shock and outrage that is expressed by the French press. Some of the comments are offensive, but they come from precisely those who until recently showed him nothing but loyalty and affection. I hear disillusioned remarks from all sides. How is it possible that a man so intelligent, knowledgeable, and informed could not have been aware of the anti-Jewish laws of Vichy? The plundering, the persecutions, the arrests, the roundups—how could he have failed to know about them? And the "Vél d'Hiv"—he claims not to have known about that either, he who always wants to know everything? And if he knew, is it conceivable that he remained indifferent, which would be a thousand times worse? I find it difficult to cope with this affair, which gets more poisonous by the day. Abandoned by many of his political allies and personal friends, Mitterrand balks instead of confronting the problem. Or so I am told by a close female aide who when she dared to suggest to him that a new course of action was necessary, drew his wrath. That same day she handed him her resignation—which the president refused. Will he ever understand what is happening to him?

I call Anne Lauvergeon, who has succeeded Attali as the president's right hand. Anne is discreet, superbly intelligent, and highly effective. She knows the depth of my dismay and appreciates my restraint. An appointment is made with the president for the week of Sukkot.

The welcome is friendly as always. The president's face is marked by his illness, his gaze crossed by somber shadows. His voice is tense, broken. He is tired and speaks to me of the treatment he is undergoing. I wonder how I shall bring myself to ask him the questions that are sure to pain him. But I have no choice. As an opening, I quote to him a saying of Rebbe Nahman of Bratzlav, already reported in the first volume of my memoirs: "The world is mistaken about two things. First, it is wrong in thinking that a great man is incapable of making mistakes; it is also mistaken in thinking that once the mistake has been made, the great man ceases being great." I feel that I have offered him a good way out, but he refuses to take it.

He tells me squarely that he has made no mistake. None? None. Hence no remorse, no regrets. The anti-Jewish laws of Vichy? Never knew about them. But as a civil servant of Vichy, had he not been asked to fill out a questionnaire in which he was required to declare that he was not a Jew? No, he was not a civil servant; he had a contract. And what was the difference? Precisely that he was not required to fill out that questionnaire. In short, he had done nothing wrong. But what about Bousquet? How could he have maintained friendly relations with this high Vichy official, an associate of the SS chiefs Heydrich and Oberg, who had organized the deportation of French Jews to Auschwitz? He shrugs his shoulders and replies that when he made his acquaintance, Bousquet had already been rehabilitated by the courts and was being received by the cream of financial society. In fact, there were in his entourage several very well known and respected Jews. How then could he, Mitterrand, have doubted his innocence? Moreover, they were not friends. They had seen each other only a dozen times and had never addressed each other by the intimate *tu*. As I insist on the strangeness of their relationship, he finally concedes that perhaps he should have shown himself "more vigilant." I suggest to him that he take advantage of a future television interview to make a statement: "I was young and inexperienced; when one is young, one does things that are sometimes foolish; but after all, since then I've done other things." I tell him that if he says that, the public will turn the page. He refuses. I say to him: "Even God admits to having made a mistake; read Genesis. But you have never made a mistake?" Then I suggest to him that we meet once more to record a conversation that would get to the bottom of the matter. I explain to him that I must understand. It is indispensable for me to understand. We shall then publish it somewhere. Mitterrand agrees but asks me to address my questions to him in writing beforehand.

After another hour and a half of discussion he accompanies me to the door, more cordial than ever. Did he know that we would not see each other again? With a heavy heart I linger in Anne Lauvergeon's office before leaving for the airport. I tell her how unhappy I am with the conversation. Why had I not been able to pierce the shadows in which the president has wrapped his past? I tell Anne of my certainty that this affair will leave a black stain on Mitterrand's passage through history; his tendency toward equivocation is doing him harm. I tell her of my suggestion for a recorded interview.

My questions—on Vichy and Pétain, the wreath and Bousquet, his writings for an anti-Semitic magazine, and the Francisque medal (Vichy's highest decoration)—I fax to Anne for transmittal to the president. Did he read them? Certainly. His reaction is negative. Is he annoyed that I am not ready to be his defender? I am sure of it. In any case, he does not think he has to justify himself. In other words, he will not respond to my fax. There will be no further interview. No further dialogue.

I am disappointed. Sometimes I tell myself the word is not strong enough. For suddenly I understand that there's a coherence and a logic in Mitterrand's political course. His refusal to investigate the Nazi past of certain Frenchmen and to bring them to justice, his annual custom of secretly arranging to place a wreath on Pétain's tomb, his links to former members of La Cagoule and other Nazi collaborators, his determination to suppress that part of his life, his habit of surrounding himself with Jews—all this must have an explanation.

I cannot believe that he wanted to deceive me, that I had been both dupe and victim of his genius for manipulation. I want to believe that there must be some other explanation. Would he give it to me, if only to complete our book of conversations that the publisher Odile Jacob is dying to publish? It is a project conceived long ago and that in the end becomes grafted onto the Vichy-Pétain-Bousquet affair, adding a new unpleasant angle.

. . .

Jack Lang had had the idea for the book since 1985, and the president liked and accepted it. Lang used the preparation for the Nobel laureates' conference two years later to broach it again even more forcefully. Were there some ulterior motives connected with the presidential elections in May? Perhaps—but I don't see how a book like that could have been of use to the Socialist candidate. The Jewish vote? It was his to start with. And then a book, especially a book with two authors, isn't written in three months. And Jack knew of my reluctance to intervene in French internal affairs. Anyway, the project didn't tempt me, as though I had a foreboding that, for me, it would become a source of great disappointment. As for the president, he procrastinated. Months went by. He was not in a hurry. Nor was I.

But Jack Lang was impatient: "These dialogues, they must be done; this has been drawn out far too long." In the end, he got his way. In the excitement of the conference that took place in January 1988, I settled down to the task. The idea was to have a dialogue between two men linked by friendship but seemingly separated by everything else: ethnic origin, social position, religious education. It was to be a book of open-ended conversations, discussions on general, timeless themes. After considering the matter for several weeks I drew up a table of contents: power, friendship, war, childhood, death, God, the Bible, Israel, faith, writing. Attali thought it was fine, and the president approved. Our first subject: childhood, of course; comparing his with mine. The childhood of a leader who has reached the summit of power and that of a Jewish writer who will never succeed in tearing himself away from his yeshiva.

Two sound engineers busied themselves behind a screen. And suddenly the tape recorder refused to cooperate. As it happened, Jacques Attali was present—a fact that later on, in 1993, will cause me much sadness and a huge headache. But during this first session for the book I was pleased that he was there, for he made himself useful: It was decided he would take notes on the president's remarks, but not on mine. Anyway, my memory is good. And for our subsequent talks, the tape recorder was repaired.

Our conversations, each from one hour to an hour and a half long, are carried on in an atmosphere of friendship. I ask questions and Mitterrand responds. Only rarely does he ask me questions. I don't feel at ease in my role of interviewer; I gave that up a long time ago.

To be sure, I could be more confrontational, but that's not in my nature. And then, too, I am respectful of the man sitting across from me. I don't dare push him on the points he seeks to avoid. I steer clear of minefields. I don't touch upon embarrassing subjects. Not yet. I tell myself that, in any event, this is just a draft. I'll have a chance to rework it, as he will, too. That will be the time to urge him to review his positions. There's no hurry. His mandate has just been renewed. Seven years is a long time.

In his replies, Mitterrand is open. I like what he says about his childhood: "I had no friends my own age." About his adolescence: "I went from wonder to wonder." About his parents: "They were very available. They hardly spoke. My father would say you don't learn anything from words, only from deeds." About his mother, traveling in a train with people making anti-Dreyfus, anti-Semitic remarks: "My mother's eyes opened wider and wider with surprise." About his discovery of the stranger, who is "welcomed into a closed circle like a thief." He is severe with De Gaulle, skeptical about Mendès-France. His favorite writers: Barrès, Chardonne.

He has a talent for quickly finding answers that suit him. Sometimes he asks me to repeat my questions, saying that he doesn't understand. Then, rather than launch into explanations, I change the subject. The major problem is time—his own, of course, but also mine, since I live in New York and teach in Boston. Months go by between appointments and more than once I consider abandoning the project. But we go back to it again and again. Seven topics have been dealt with; there are three left. Then we'll review the entire text. We have time.

These talks require an effort of concentration on my part. I believe not as much on his. We are rarely disturbed by the telephone. He seems attentive but relaxed, and when he escorts me to the door he asks about Elisha's studies, sends his regards to Marion, and asks me to come back every time I'm in Paris: "You are always welcome in this house, which is yours." I come back, but we speak less and less about the book. Have both of us lost interest? Or perhaps he simply wishes to wait for the end of his second term.

But neither he nor I could foresee an incident provoked by our mutual friend Jacques Attali.

When I think of Attali, I feel sad. I regret the years of our friendship. I thought it beautiful, productive. Adroit, endowed with countless talents, he loved his position at the nerve center of French and international political life. How did he manage to be in so many places at once? And to be part of so many projects? He knew so many things about so many subjects. My trust in him was total. I thought it was mutual: He would tell me about his life and his experiences at the Élysée, the challenges he had met, his struggles, his personal dreams, and his ambitions as a writer. He had no qualms about telling me of the complexity of his relationship with Mitterrand. He understood that I could keep a secret. What spoiled our friendship?

I was familiar with his project for a journal covering the years 1981 to 1986, whose title I did not yet know. And he knew that I was writing a volume of memoirs. I had even mentioned to him on the telephone (he was by then head of the BERD bank in London) that I planned to describe in it my conversations with Mitterrand and the difficulties they presented. The idea that Attali might make use of these same conversations—and quite extensively—never crossed my mind, especially since the first volume of his journal was to end with 1986, long before Mitterrand and I began our "dialogues."

When his journal, *Verbatim*, appears with great fanfare, Marion and I happen to be in Europe. Stopping off in Paris we meet the publisher Odile Jacob, who asks if we have read the article devoted to Attali in *Le Nouvel Observateur.* "You're mentioned," she adds. So we read it and find a rather appealing portrait of Jacques. The article also reproduces, in italics, certain excerpts attributed to Mitterrand that seem familiar. Oh well—I'll read the book to clear up the mystery.

We are in Venice attending the closing session of a meeting of the International Press Institute when, from New York, we learn that Odile Jacob has been desperately trying to find us. She is beside herself: "I've just read *Verbatim.* . . . Your conversations with the president are there in print. . . . It's mind-boggling . . . scandalous . . . unforgivable. . . ." By special courier she sends us a segment of ninety-five pages—photocopies of *Verbatim* excerpts side-by-side with photocopies of our manuscript.

For there does in fact exist a manuscript of my seven conversations with Mitterrand. It is based on the transcript made by the Élysée staff, and notably by Attali's office, of the still-unfinished seven chapters. One copy is in the hands of Odile Jacob, whom Mitterrand had chosen as publisher of the Nobel conference papers and whom he has now also chosen to publish our dialogues. I had, in fact, thought that he would wish to be published by Claude Durand of Fayard, since he was Attali's friend, while I, personally, had leaned toward either Le

Seuil or Grasset. But Mitterrand had decided in favor of Odile Jacob, and it had been with his blessing that I had given her a copy of the manuscript. Evidently, Attali must have not known or forgotten this fact.

Minutely prepared by Odile Jacob, the document is devastating. Marion and I, dumbfounded and hurt, study the file at length. We take it along to Oslo, where, as guests of the president of the Parliament, we attend the official celebration of Norway's national holiday, the most beautiful in the world because it is the children who celebrate it, and are celebrated in turn. On Sunday, May 16, I place a call to Attali in Paris. By chance he's at home. I say to him: "I must show you something. . . . This is urgent, superurgent. . . . If I could jump into a plane now I'd do it, but I cannot. Please come here. I'm at the Grand Hotel. It's something important that concerns you. . . ." He doesn't understand, or pretends not to. He wants to know what it's all about: the president's health, national security? I insist: "This is not something we can discuss on the phone. . . . Believe me: It justifies your coming." I still think that if he had come, we could have settled matters between us. I'm profoundly convinced of it. But for whatever reason, he does not accept my invitation. Subsequently he told me he had no recollection of it.

This incident was painful for me and for him as well. I shall come back to it in another context.

I no longer believe in this book of dialogues. For that matter, I have not seen Mitterrand since the Bousquet affair. Odile Jacob does everything in her power and more, as only she can do, to keep the project alive; but for my part, since the president chooses not to answer my written questions about Bousquet and Vichy, I am less eager. Undeniably, between Mitterrand and myself things are no longer what they were.

People in his entourage now tell me he is displeased with me because I dared criticize him on television about the Bousquet affair. According to him, the laws of friendship required me to be his defender. But in opting for friendship with Bousquet, had he not violated and sacrificed ours, and much more? Did he not make his choice by receiving Bousquet at home, perhaps the same day that he saw me? I thus may have shaken the hand that had shaken that of the SS murderers' accomplice.

In short, my enthusiasm is gone. And happily, our book seems to be deferred to messianic times. So I am surprised when Odile Jacob calls me in March 1995 to tell me that Mitterrand's illness is getting worse, and that he now wishes the book to come out. I can't hold back a cry of astonishment. "He wants it to come out? As it is? But it's not finished! We were supposed to rework it! It's nothing but a draft! Moreover, he hasn't answered my questions about Vichy and Bousquet! Do you really think that I could cosign a book with him without raising these questions?" Odile understands. She will speak to Mitterrand. She calls me back soon after: he also understands. He's asking me to send the questions again. I make up a new list and fax it to Odile. In time he sends his responses directly to her. They express "neither regrets nor remorse" on the subject of his past. Even in September, during our last encounter, he locks himself into this pose of infallibility, too proud, too sure of himself to recognize that to err is human. His aides had often told me that he was incapable of saying "I should not have done this."

So how can I reach him? How can I speak to him without wounding him, listen to him without showing him my disagreement and my disappointment? I am in Paris several times and don't call him; I no longer wish to see him, nor evidently does he want to see me. Looming large between us, the dark ghost of Bousquet eliminates any possibility of direct contact. We had been too close not to seek refuge now in distance. From now on everything goes through Odile Jacob, who is determined to publish the book before the elections. She succeeds in getting it printed in less than a week. She is equally successful, several days *after* the publication of the book, in getting us to exchange a few courteous trivialities on the telephone. I tell Mitterrand he has done good work—meaning he, not I. For I am not proud of my contribution. I would have required at least a month to correct and flesh out my own text. And I would have liked to respond to his responses.

The title for the dialogues was chosen by Mitterrand. I should have preferred something more sober, more discreet—and truer. *A memoir in two voices?* Mine can hardly be heard. For that matter, I have the impression that Mitterrand, too, considers the book not a work by two authors, but something he alone has written. Otherwise would he have dedicated it to a certain Lucia without advising me beforehand, if only out of politeness?

Journalists keep calling me. I manage to elude most of them. But I do respond to Annette Lévy-Willard of *Libération* and to *Info-Matin*. My tone is cautious, respectful; I don't wish to hurt a sick man. But at the same time I want people to know that I have decided to keep my distance from a work I no longer consider mine.

The situation worsens as a result of an interview Mitterrand gives to Bernard Pivot. When the latter questions him on what I say in the book about his, Mitterrand's, relations with the former chief of police, he practically cuts him short: "Take note that it was I who insisted. . . . I said to Elie Wiesel: 'If you don't question me about Bousquet, there will be no book!' "

We are in Israel for Passover and watch Pivot's program at a friend's home. As we listen to Mitterrand, we turn to each other in shock and disbelief. When we return to New York we see a rebroadcast of the program. Marion then records it, and I admit to watching it five or six times. I am stunned by Mitterrand's statement. Rarely have I had so much difficulty in restraining my disappointment and anger. I want to send him a letter and write draft after draft, but all are too harsh, and so they all wind up in a drawer of my desk.

On April 23, 1995, I fax Mitterrand—still via Anne Lauvergeon—a more temperate version:

Mr. President,

I have finally seen the "Bouillon de Culture" of 14 April, which has been broadcast by TV5 on an American station this evening. I don't like to cause you pain. But in your presentation, in all other aspects moving and brilliant, the part concerning our conversations troubled and grieved me. You say that it was you who had insisted, personally, with me that questions regarding Bousquet be included in the book and that otherwise you would never have consented to its publication. Yet since last September until the very day the book was published, we have not spoken.

The impression given by your words is that you had to force my hand for me to ask you questions about Bousquet. And yet. Did I not come specially from New York, precisely in September, to speak to you about this subject? And above all to listen to you? Did I not send you, as agreed, a few days after our meeting, my questions—two pages of questions—which you did not see fit to answer? Do you think, Mr. President, that I would have agreed to have this book published without our exchange on Bousquet? I have asked Anne Lauvergeon to tell you: This is a subject that, for me, is painful and grave. I would like to understand. I ask you, Mr. President, to clarify it for me.

I receive no answer from Mitterrand. I ask Anne Lauvergeon whether I should expect one. She checks. Her reply is negative.

I take my pen and write:

Mr. President,

This letter is the last you will receive from me. I am writing with regret and sadness. It marks the end of a friendship that for fourteen years was a part of my life.

You are ill, you are suffering. It may be wrong of me to add to your pain. But out of respect for the man I admired, and because I believe that lying to him would betray you, I feel it incumbent on me to clarify the reasons for my decision.

This is followed by three pages of explanation . . . that I do not send. Other drafts meet the same fate. Then the *New York Times* asks me for a piece on Mitterrand and how he went wrong. I take up my pen again: "I regret to have to write these lines. I regret above all to have to write them now, at a time when the man in question is old, seriously ill, and at the end of his political career. Yet I cannot, I can no longer be silent. Silence, in my tradition, means approval."

A four-page article follows . . . to be buried in my desk. To the editor of the *Times*, I write that I *cannot* hurt a man so seriously ill. I give the same response to the editor in chief of an important Paris magazine. I do not say that I don't feel like writing such a piece. The fact that Mitterrand does not see fit to answer me upsets me, but I prefer to swallow the pill, and I wait for the present volume to say what is in my heart.

Still, this time Anne was mistaken. I finally do get an answer, two months later. To say it stunned me would be an understatement. In essence, this is what Mitterrand offers in explanation: He acknowledges having received the questions concerning René Bousquet that I wished to see dealt with in the "still possible" book we were to write together and that he, alone, had edited. But when submitted to him "ready to print," our "dialogue on Bousquet" was not in the book. This omission had to be corrected—and that was what he had explained to Pivot.

Well, now there is no longer any ambiguity. There is only contradiction and, I am sorry to note, a distortion of the facts. To Pivot he had said that he had ordered me, personally, to include questions on

Bousquet. In his letter it is no longer to me but to Odile Jacob to whom he gives the instructions. And then there was the tone, the facial expressions, the body language on the screen. His letter is dry, abrupt. I do not respond to his reply. What's the use of restating my position? He obviously refuses to understand. He may, in fact, be incapable of it.

So is this then the end, the break? I'm afraid so. Especially since there was yet another event, in May, that I and others close to me considered an affront: his speech in Berlin. On that occasion, Mitterrand praises not only the Germany of today, but Germany throughout history—hence the Third Reich as well. Standing before Helmut Kohl, who is beaming with pride, he sings the glory of the German army of today and yesterday—thus of Hitler's army. He says that the German soldiers' uniform meant little to him, nor did the ideas that inhabited their minds; "they were brave," that was what mattered then, that is what matters to him today. (The next day, in Moscow, he compares the courage of the Russian soldier with that of the German soldier, and the suffering of the Russian people with that of the German people.)

How is one to explain this kind of reductionism? So the uniform means so little to him? Has he forgotten that the Gestapo too wore that uniform? And that they too harbored certain ideas? What possessed him to whitewash the German military in this way, in this, his next-to-last official speech? A desire to be provocative? To please his hosts, to emphasize the importance of reconciliation in his political philosophy? His plea for peace and reconciliation won him the enthusiasm of some and shocked others. A cartoon in *Le Monde* is terrifying, showing a hefty Yeltsin towering over a tiny Mitterrand, begging him to say something nice about the Russian soldier's courage in Chechnya.

As it happened, I might well have been at his side in both capitals. He had invited me to accompany him. A seat had been reserved for me in his Concorde, and a room in the hotels. I refused. I don't regret it. On the contrary, I believe I made the right decision. Had I been present in Berlin, I would have left the hall in the middle of his speech.

Still, even though I've distanced myself from him and his universe, I feel sad. This was not how I had imagined his exit from my life.

. . .

On January 8, 1996, I am in the South to lecture at a small college. The phone rings in my room at 6 o'clock in the morning. "I have sad news for you," Elisha says. "Your friend Mitterrand is dead." Elisha had been awakened by journalists calling from Paris.

I feel the silence slowly descending on me, leaving a familiar feeling. A whole chapter of my life is ended. The place Mitterrand occupied in my book of friendship covers many pages. There were journeys, discoveries, reunions, luminous moments, glowing images, picturesque episodes. I knew my friend in his glory, I knew him in sickness. How did he enter into death? I imagine him in his small, monastic room alone with his physician, alone with his past. Did he choose the asceticism of solitude before sinking into it for all eternity? Did he finally become reconciled with God at the moment of leaving His creation? The religion he rejected had, in fact, always interested him. The sacred fascinated him both as challenge and as shelter. And what if, in his own way, he had been a lover of God as he followed his fervent desire to conquer history?

I don't respond to most of the requests for interviews. Why add to the verbal deluge sweeping over France? To Christine Pouget, of Agence France-Presse, I point out that Jewish tradition recommends saying nothing but good things about the dead. For *Paris Match* I write an article along those lines: I speak only of the good period. I recall the early days of our friendship, when he thrilled those he loved and made them dream. I have no intention of speaking about René Bousquet, nor of Vichy. No, I will not talk about the last year of his life. Doesn't the Talmud say that death erases all sins?

But then—what happens to memory?

The media report the emotion that has taken hold of France. It is sincere and profound. That is normal: The man left his mark on his era; everyone agrees on that. Some extol his European spirit, others his political genius; still others vow never to forget his passion for freedom.

There are moving scenes of people: the silent crowds. The tears, the roses—the French recognized themselves in Mitterrand's very ambiguities. The funeral at Jarnac. The sorrow on people's faces. The solemn mass at Notre Dame. And thus the end rejoins the beginning.

Lucid to the last, sovereign in everything, but a victim of his body, he freely chose his hour to free himself. In summoning death he, in a way, conquered it. The last word of his book was written by him.

What was on his mind as he took leave of the living shadows before rejoining those that had come before? The great game he had played? Had it been a game?

I glance through my notebooks. How often did we speak of what is awaiting us afterward? Paradise, hell, the Last Judgment, the Apocalypse—he wanted to know. Could human life be nothing but the flutter of an eyelid? But then, what remains of what one has received and what one has given?

Three Suicides

BENNO WERZBERGER in Israel, Tadeusz Borowski in Poland, Paul Celan and Piotr Rawicz in Paris, Bruno Bettelheim in the United States, Primo Levi in Italy—the writers who were part of the shrinking community of Holocaust survivors endured severe hardship. Despairing of the written word's power, some chose silence. The silence of death.

Was it because as guardians of memory they felt misunderstood, unloved, exiles in the present, guilty of having failed in their task? Were they afraid of having spoken too much—or not enough? In light of the tragedies that continue to tear apart society, did they admit defeat?

I knew three of them well. Their final acts continue to haunt me.

Primo Levi, speaking of "experts" on the Holocaust, said: "They are the thieves of Time; they infiltrate themselves through keyholes and cracks and cart off our memories without leaving a trace."

Why did Primo, my friend Primo, fling himself from the top of a staircase, he whose works finally succeeded in shaking public indifference, even outside Italy?

From our first meeting in Milan, during the seventies, we had formed bonds. In a way we were meeting *again*, having already "met." *Over there*, in Buna. I had spent some time in his barracks. I had seen him without seeing him. He had crossed my path without noticing me. Even *over there*, social differences existed.

Now, transcending frontiers, we moved forward side-by-side as we clung to our links to those who had abandoned us. Was it he or I who said: "Maybe I'm dead and don't know it." Like him I was convinced that our experiences isolated us, that people living today or tomorrow could never understand their nature.

When we turned our gaze inward we saw the same universe. The selections, the *kommandos*, the "roll calls" in the icy wind, the hanging of the young boy, a member of the underground—yes, he remembered it all as I did. Sometimes he would question me about a sentence of mine he had read somewhere; I told him I was a bad interpreter of my writings. I did better commenting on his.

Why death, Primo? To tell us what truth about whose life?

Did he want to reach to the very end of his thoughts, his memories? Truly enter death? I don't remember why, but I called him shortly before his death. A premonition? His voice sounded thick, heavy. "Things are not good," he said slowly, "not good at all." "What's not good, Primo?" "Oh, the world, the world's no good." And he doesn't know what he is doing in a world that's going so badly. "Are you having problems, Primo?" No, he has no problems. In Italy and elsewhere he is read, admired, honored, but it's going badly. We speak of mutual friends, of his plans, of his son, Renzo. I suggest he come to New York, spend some time with me. He doesn't say no, he doesn't say yes; he doesn't answer, as though he were already elsewhere, behind other walls. To cheer him up I describe to him the success of his works on American campuses. No reaction. "Are you there, Primo? Do you hear me?" Yes, he hears me—but he's no longer there.

An American novelist publishes an article that shocks quite a few of us. He says that Primo's friends should have urged him to get treatment, and that a good therapist could have cured him. This is a typical banalization: Here we have existential evil, the lifelong incandescent wound of a soul, reduced to a nervous breakdown common among writers whose inspiration becomes blocked, or among men of a certain age.

Is there another explanation? If there is, it has something to do with a Holocaust writer's attitude toward memory and its workings, writing and its pitfalls, language and its limits. Like Kafka's unfortunate messenger, he realizes that his message has been neither received nor transmitted. Or worse, it has been, and nothing has changed. It has produced no effect on society or on human nature. Everything goes on as though the messenger had forgotten the dead whose message he had carried, as though he had misplaced their last testament.

Yes, we had our disagreements. In my own way I'm a believer; he declared himself an atheist. I persist in wanting to work from within our tradition; he kept his distance. I did not share his leftist tendencies, just as he distanced himself from my attachment to Israel. And then, I thought him too severe with survivors: There our disagreement was total; he ascribed too much guilt to them. His theory of a "gray zone" in which every inmate was guilty—some more, some less, directly or indirectly, simply for having survived—well, all this seems to me simplistic and unfair. By speaking of the "relativity" of their innocence, he was attenuating the guilt of the killers. Only the criminals are guilty, I told him; to compare the victims in any way with the torturers was to dilute or even deny the killers' responsibility for their actions.

Primo's theory reminds me of the advice Karl Jaspers is said to have given Hannah Arendt to mistrust the "false innocence of the victims." What false innocence is he talking about? That of the children, the sick, the old? Surely, they were not guilty, nor were the rabbis, the priests, the dying, emaciated men and women. To say that every one of them could have become a killer is to indict the whole world. It is to compare the privileged *kapos* with the moribund *Muselmänner*, "Muslims," as they were called. It is to punish the innocents who have been punished enough.

In my opinion, Primo felt guilty in terms of the present rather than the past: All Holocaust writers are subject to the same feeling of remorse and impotence. Perhaps they think that if things are going so badly it is their fault, because since they have not been able to find the right language to communicate, they have failed to impact the destiny of their contemporaries.

From the first to the last day, I felt his despair. "It's worse today than yesterday, worse than ever," he kept repeating. What did he mean by that? That talking of yesterday was worse than having lived through it, than still living through it? That nothing makes a survivor despair more than knowing that he is useless, that the past will not serve as lesson? Was that why he returned to the land of the dead, because the living would not listen?

He killed himself because he could not go on.

At times I find myself whispering to him: You shouldn't have, Primo. Not that, not that. Death is never a solution, you know that. . . .

And yet, deep down, I understand him.

The first review of Jerzy Kosinski's *Painted Bird* was written by me for the *New York Times*. Poor Jerzy, who entertained so well and lived so badly—misunderstood in his lifetime, will he be better understood after his suicide?

When he first called me, I was still a bachelor, living on Riverside Drive. He was young, nervous, impatient, eager to dazzle and disconcert. I ask him two questions: "Is your book based on fact?" And then: "Are you Jewish?" "I'd like to know," I say, "since your character is presented as a Gypsy. And the word 'Jew' is hardly mentioned." He answers yes to the first question and no to the second. I am amazed: "What? You've lived through all these atrocities and you're not even a Jew?" Thinking that this makes him even more deserving, I add a few compliments to my positive review, which nets me a number of insulting letters from Polish Jews. According to them, I was wrong to be so kind to a Jew who is ashamed of his Jewishness. They knew him in Poland. His book is nothing but a collection of mad rantings. I refuse to believe them. I call him: "I must see you again." "Aha!" is his answer. "So they've contacted you." Who? "My enemies." Who are his enemies? Why does he have any? In any case we need to meet. I invite him for lunch. Again, I ask him the question: "Are you Jewish?" He again answers that he is not. "Then why do these people say that . . ." They are his enemies. This discussion goes on for weeks if not months. When the novel appears in France, my friend Piotr Rawicz writes about it in *Le Monde*. I ask him: "Is Jerzy Jewish?" "Of course he is," Piotr replies. "Did he tell you so?" No, he didn't; on the contrary, he denies it. But then how does Piotr know? "I know," says Piotr. "Why does he conceal his Jewish origins?" I wonder. "Ask him." Piotr asks him; he maintains his position. Piotr wants to know whether he's circumcised. Jerzy refuses to answer. It is only when Piotr, who wouldn't hurt a fly, threatens to call a few friends to help him undress him, that he acknowledges that he is a Jew.

When his second novel appears, I review it for the *Forverts*. I say that the novel is good but that I find the author peculiar; I explain his bizarre behavior as an attempt to elaborate a philosophy of ambiguity. Jerzy is angry. He sends a letter to the newspaper and threatens to start legal proceedings if I don't retract. He denies ever denying his Jewishness. His letter is published, followed by my response: I have Piotr's letter and other evidence. If he insists, I am ready to publish them. I add that I had expected more gratitude from him. I'm greeted by silence, no lawsuit. A few months later Jerzy telephones and says he wants to see me. At once. I demand an apology before seeing him. He apologizes. I pick up our dialogue where we had left off. "Why did you lie about your Jewishness? The war is over, Jerzy. Jews no longer need to hide." He says he doesn't know what happened to him; that he was absentminded, distracted. And anyway it was better that way. For Poland and the Poles, it was better. A Jewish tragedy written by a Jewish writer would have left them cold, whereas if a non-Jew was being persecuted and a non-Jew was telling of his sufferings, that was something else. Arthur Gelb of the *Times* believes that his bizarre behavior was motivated by fear—fear of the anti-Semites, fear of persecution.

The quarrel was over. Jerzy recovered his roots, his identity. And my affection. Others were more severe than I. A long article in the *Village Voice* called him an impostor. A recent biography tries to destroy the myths surrounding him. He went through the war with his parents and thus couldn't possibly have experienced the atrocities described in *The Painted Bird,* and thus couldn't possibly have written his books himself.

The news of his suicide—which was like that of Bruno Bettelheim—shattered me. So this hedonist was unhappy, even unhappier than his own eccentric or tragic characters.

Piotr Rawicz, my comrade, my companion. Why did he withdraw from the world of the living? I can see him now: hunched over, his gaze hopeless, ironic but lucid, so terribly lucid. *Le Sang du Ciel (Blood of the Sky)* will remain one of the masterpieces of the period. In my article about it in the *New Leader,* I wrote:

> It is only with sobbing and blaspheming that one can write about the death of a Jewish community betrayed by heaven and earth. Piotr Rawicz has made his choice. His book is an outcry, not an echo; a challenge, not an act of submission. Facing a grave filled with corpses, he does not recite *Kaddish;* he sheds no tears. . . .
>
> . . . You will need courage and strength to read this novel. But read it, and you will understand that the tragedy of Boris [the central figure of the novel] did not begin with him. You will also understand that, after Auschwitz, there is nothing left to understand, for reason itself has drowned in the blood of the sky. . . .

I remember our long strolls in Paris, his pessimism so lucid and merry that it would have taken little for me to go mad with optimism.

His monologues—I remember his murmured monologues in which philosophic reflection (the Bhagavad Gita and Lao Tzu, Spinoza and Wittgenstein) refused to yield to humor, and conversely. For him, everything had to do with metaphysics, even derision. He liked to evoke Germany as he had known it long ago and as he was then rediscovering it. Its fragmented capital attracted him; he saw it as a huge phantasmagorical farce—Berlin and its noncommitted, detached intellectuals; Berlin and its hard-to-bear snobs; Berlin and its false or real aristocrats turned into true or false cynics; its dangerous but ridiculous spies; Berlin and its friendly, voluptuous, and oh-so-easy women.

During our dinners in a small restaurant in the Latin Quarter, he brought to life the ghetto of Lvov replete with scholars and romantic beggars. Other times he would speak of his experiences in the Leitmeritz camp. What had saved him from death? He attributed his luck in large part to his knowledge of German and Ukrainian. He was taken for a Christian. Nevertheless, he remained more often than not in the company of Jewish prisoners. "And what about fear, Piotr?" I asked him. "How did you experience fear over there?" "Oh, it made me laugh," he answered. And without waiting for my reaction he explained: "The whole thing was just a farce, a farce on a cosmic scale." I reminded him of Rebbe Nahman of Bratzlav's story in which a prince who has lost his way hears laughter at night, an otherworldly laughter. Piotr nodded: he knew Rebbe Nahman. . . . He knew many things, my friend Piotr.

I sometimes took him along to religious services. We spent a Yom Kippur together in a small, improvised synagogue near the Place de la République. The next day he described to me the High Holidays in Lvov. He tried to make it humorous but didn't succeed. Yom Kippur was the only day on which he was incapable of laughter.

Why did he kill himself, he who still had so much to give to life? A rifle bullet through his mouth put an end to a singular destiny.

When I recall Piotr, a knot forms in my chest. Writer, ethnologist, anthropologist, essayist, and poet, he deserved glory and surely happiness (to the extent that these go together) as much as others, more than others. Why did he turn his back on life when he had contributed to raising it to a higher level by making it funnier? Was it the illness and then the death of Anna, his wife and best friend? Was he afraid of solitude? The specter of decline?

Piotr. Often penniless but elegant nevertheless, always generous. Terribly busy but always available. Desperate but pleasure-loving. Our dinners were unforgettable. Endless, too. He loved to talk, and he talked with the clarity of a scientist; a heavy Russian accent, pedantic French, smiles that were alternately melancholy and sarcastic. He pitied the social climbers, celebrated the humble, the beginners, the unknowns. He had written a novel, but what about his childhood memories from Lvov, had he written them down somewhere? And where would one have to look for them? Had he entrusted them to someone?

He drank a lot, smoked a lot, laughed and loved a lot. Why was he no longer writing? Oh yes, he protested vigorously, he was writing; he was writing, but only in his head. (Felipe Alfao, the Spanish author of *Locos*, told me the same thing.) "Come," he said to me once, "I'll show you." He led me to his tiny room, where one couldn't take a step without knocking over messy piles of books and reviews. He showed me manuscripts, let me read a few pages of mystical poems. Yet he called himself an agnostic. Can one be both mystic and infidel, both prophet and heretic? " 'Why,' " he said, "is a word that God gave man by mistake. God is God, can anyone say that God does not believe in Himself? Or that He does not believe in anyone else?"

Why did he choose suicide? What message did he leave us when he opened his lips to welcome death?

Understanding —⟋

WITH THE YEARS the inevitable happens: My extraliterary and academic activities become too demanding and take up too much of my time. How am I to maintain my normal schedule and devote four hours a day to writing, which, after all, remains my priority? I snatch every moment of freedom and impose on myself more and more rigorous discipline. The author of Ecclesiastes does not believe in books, but I cling to them. The day I stop writing, what shall I be? I still have so many stories to tell, so many subjects to explore, so many characters to invent or reveal. I am still tormented by the same anguish: Notwithstanding all the books I have written, I have not yet begun. But then I write them in order to understand as much as to make myself understood.

In the Haggadah, the admirable account that on Passover night relates the Exodus from Egypt and urges the children to ask questions of their elders, we read:

> Blessed be the Lord, blessed be He
> Behold the four sons of whom the Torah speaks;
> One is wise, the other wicked,
> The third incapable of understanding the question
> while the fourth doesn't even know there is a question.

In a new translation of the Passover Haggadah (illustrated by Mark Podwal) I recall the traditional commentaries on this passage. Then one evening I ask myself: Why does the text mention only four sons? I imagine a fifth, the one who has not returned. I open the doors of memory to him by making him into a character in my novel *The Fifth Son.*

It tells the story of a failed existence, of a vengeance gone awry, human and divine truth mutilated. It narrates the tragic destiny of the Tamiroff family. Reuven, the father, a survivor of the Davarowsk ghetto, struggles with the ghost of the "Angel," the SS killer who tortured and exterminated Jews as if to prove that evil would triumph. The mother, who has sunk into a kind of benevolent madness, is elsewhere, a prisoner of oblivion. And Ariel, their only living son, tries to understand them, and above all to understand the reasons that led them to give him life.

They live in Brooklyn, among the Hasidim. Reuven is a librarian: "He chats with Homer and Saul, Jeremiah and Virgil," but his favorite writer is Paritus the One-eyed, whose *Oblique Meditations* had a great impact on medieval philosophy. They are surrounded by a circle of illuminati. Bontchek, who remembers everything; Simha-the-Dark, who calls himself a merchant of shadows. They all come from Davarowsk and gather regularly to evoke their common past. And what about the son in all this? He slowly discovers and absorbs this past: the life before, in the ghetto, with its illusions and nights of waiting; the scenes of horror in which the Angel pulled on the mask of a bloodthirsty god, ally and servant of death.

I forbid myself to imagine what happened inside the gas chambers; my gaze follows the living people who enter them to die of suffocation only as far as the entrance, yet I force myself to see the massacres of Jews in Babi-Yar, Ponar, Romboli, and Kolomyya. Why? Where is the difference? I have no idea. But it is important for me to be there, if only in my imagination, to be there among those who say the Kaddish for the dead and for themselves. I often study the photographs taken by the Germans that show the processions of men and women moving toward the mass grave. What are they thinking? What is the child saying to his grandfather, whose face looks composed? Firsthand accounts and documents are practically unanimous regarding the passivity of the doomed. An SS officer, member of the *Einsatzgruppen*, confesses somewhere that it drove him crazy. He could not understand these people who let themselves be shot, by himself and his soldiers, without putting up the slightest resistance. A Jew lying down on the edge of the trench asked the Germans: "Is this how I should lie down?" Calel Perechodnik, a Jewish policeman in the ghetto of Otwock, not far from Warsaw, describes in his testimony

that some men and women could have fled but chose to wait calmly—
yes, he says "calmly"—the "liberating" bullets. I shall never forget the
episode of a group of runaway Jews accidentally discovered hiding in
a field by a Polish policeman. He begins to kill them one after another
but is forced to stop when he runs out of bullets. He sends a boy to
fetch more ammunition. And there he is, unarmed, facing Jews who
could assault him and render him harmless. Instead they wait for the
boy to return. And the massacre is resumed.

How are we to understand resignation on such a scale? It is possible that these unfortunate Jews, abandoned by everyone but Death,
were tired of hiding, running, hoping, tired of living in this disgusting
world where human beings murder innocent Jewish children without
feeling the slightest remorse.

How many Jews were massacred in this way by the SS with the
logistical support of the Wehrmacht? A million? More? The *Einsatzgruppen* had contests as to who could kill the largest number of Jews
per week. Their statistical reports have been recovered.

In *A Beggar in Jerusalem*, I describe the disappearance of a community. It contains a "dialogue" between an SS officer and the last Talmudist, whom he fails to kill: "You think you'll be able to testify? But
no one will believe you; you think you know the truth? But it's the
truth of a madman."

In *The Fifth Son*, I return to this theme. And Ariel listens to the
confrontation between the Angel and Reuven Tamiroff, the sadism of
the torturers, the suffering of the victims, their despair, the death, in
the ghetto, of the first Ariel, the brother whose name he has inherited.
And what about the soul in all this? And God? Memory is everything.

As in my other novels I try once again to examine more closely
the relationship between father and son. But here the drama of the
son is twice as great, for it is linked to a dead brother. If the first Ariel
had not been murdered, the Tamiroffs' second son might have been
born, but he would surely have had a different name. And what about
justice in all this? And vengeance?

Ariel ultimately will try to write a new page in his father's book.
He will go to Germany to confront the Angel—who is now Richard
Lander, an important industrialist, respected and influential in the
world of finance and politics—and to punish him. But he will not kill
him.

The story includes many letters written by Reuven to his son.
But when he says, "Do you know that I am looking at you, that I

would like so much to hear you," whom is he speaking to, the dead or the living son?

I think back to Job's children, those he was given as a reward after the test God and Satan had made him endure. What did they think of the problems their parents had endured? And of their innocent brothers and sisters who had been sacrificed because, on high, there had been some doubt of Job's piety? Did they try to find out who their elder siblings had been? It was with them that Job and his wife would have lived happily if Satan and God had not made their wager.

At the end of the account Ariel writes:

> I have been waiting years, centuries. I've been waiting to find my father again. I've been waiting to meet my brother. I have tried to live their lives as my own. I've said "I" in their place. In turn, I have been one, and then the other. Yes, we've had our differences, our quarrels, our conflicts; but we have transformed them into renewed bonds. Now, more than ever, my love for my father is whole: as though he were my son; and as though I were his, the one he lost there, far away. The bottom line is disappointing: I have moved heaven and earth, risked failure and madness as I sifted through the memories of the survivors and the dreams of the dead in order to live the life of all these human beings, close and distant, who continue to haunt me. When—yes, when shall I begin, finally, to live my own life?

It is not surprising that so many children of survivors have recognized themselves in this story.

In my play *The Trial of God*, published in 1979, I have Job return so that we may hear his protest. Does faith in God always, invariably, do honor to God? In other words, is religious fanaticism also a path that leads to God, and is that what He desires?

The play was first produced in the Montansier Theater in Versailles, directed sensitively and imaginatively by Marie-Odile Grinwald. It was also done in San Miniato, a beautiful small town in northern Italy, then in Germany, Scandinavia, and in several university playhouses in the United States.

The action takes place on Purim eve 1649, in a tiny Central European village. Three minstrels arrive at the village inn; they have come, in accordance with custom, to entertain the Jewish community. But there are no longer any Jews in Shamgorod—they have recently been massacred during a pogrom. The sole survivors are the hotel-keeper, Berish, and his daughter. Nonetheless, the minstrels will perform a farce whose subject has been imposed on them by the innkeeper. It is to be a trial of God in which Berish means to play the prosecutor. But there is no defense attorney to be found. One of the actors bemoans the situation:

> The misery of it all, the misery. . . . In this vast world, from east to west, from south to north, there is no one—no one—to take on the defense of the Lord!

His two partners chime in:

> That's how it is, brother. No one to testify to His justice. . . . No one to sing His grace, His glory. . . .

The first continues:

> In all of creation, from kingdom to kingdom, from nation to nation, is there no one to justify the ways of God? No one to explain His word? No one to love Him in spite of every-thing, to love Him enough to plead His cause? In this immense universe is there no one to stand beside Him? No one?

At that moment a mysterious stranger who has gone unnoticed until now speaks up:

> There is. I shall take His defense.

And so a real trial takes place. Berish accuses God of hostility, cruelty, and indifference:

> Either He doesn't like His chosen people or He just doesn't care. . . . It's one or the other; either He knows what is hap-pening to us or He doesn't. Either way, He is guilty!

And to the defense attorney who is asking for evidence, he replies:

> Look at us carefully: we are the last Jews to be seen in
> Shamgorod. The others are invisible. Absent. Dead. Look
> at us, I say, and you will remember the absent; look at us
> and you will be convinced.

The attorney:

> I look at you and I see well-fed, fairly well dressed, not-too-
> unhappy living beings. . . .

And once again he demands facts. Berish becomes angry:

> How many times do I have to tell you? The first fact is right
> here, before you, around you. Shamgorod. Shamgorod had
> a Jewish community before . . . a Jewish life, Jewish
> warmth. A Jewish melody on every street, in every shack.
> Go look for them now. Shamgorod is silent. Its silence,
> that's a fact, isn't it?

The prosecutor is making his case with conviction, but the defender is
refuting his arguments with talent and piety:

> What do you know about God to speak of Him with such
> assurance and even arrogance? You turn your back to Him
> and then you describe Him. Why do you turn your back to
> Him? Because of a pogrom? How many times have our
> ancestors had to weep over the death of relatives or over
> homes in ruin, and yet they went on repeating, for cen-
> turies, that God is just. Are we more deserving than they?
> More intelligent? Wiser or more pious than the Rabbis of
> Mainz and York? More virtuous than the dreamers of
> Worms, the Just Men of Prague, the mystics of Saloniki?
> Could the massacre of Shamgorod be more important than
> the burning of the Holiest of the Holies? Could the looting
> of your homes be a more abject crime, a greater abomina-
> tion, than the ransacking of the city of God? Who are you
> to wish to indict or even interrogate the Creator of the
> Universe?

The lawyer for the defense evidently knows his business. If his reasoning is cold, his passion for God is not. So much so that toward the end of the play the minstrels and the innkeeper are convinced that he is a saint or a Just Man in disguise, and that his voice is heard on high. They start to beg him to do something to save them from the next pogrom, of which there are already early warning signals: the hate-filled mob screaming, the church bells tolling. . . . But the lawyer is anything but a saint. The fact that he defends God and even faith in God does not make him a man of faith, a man of compassion; in fact, he is the enemy of God and man. His fanaticism reveals who he is: the devil.

I shall speak of fanaticism later. I have been fighting against it for years, wherever it appears. Be it religious or political, fanaticism is the real danger threatening the twenty-first century. Those who sow it today are provoking tomorrow's catastrophes.

Meanwhile, I am working on a new novel. I feel lost when I don't have a novel in the works. Is that habit or superstition? I never hand a novel in to my publisher before I have started a new one.

Novels take me longer than essays. Why am I, consciously or not, more careful with the imaginary? First of all, I must make sure that the novel I am working on does not tear away and rush back toward the shadows of the Holocaust. The temptation is always there. But I'll say it again: Auschwitz and fiction are incompatible. And so it happens that I write a novel on another subject simply to avoid the theme I have forbidden myself.

When I write, I constantly "see" the Maharal of Prague and the Golem he has created for one purpose: to come to the aid of threatened Jews. Isn't that what the novelist does when he turns words into "living" beings, even though the mission he entrusts to them may be different? At times I am afraid of my own characters. What would I do if they threw off their roles and repudiated me or lifted me to dizzying heights or, worse, pushed me into the abyss inhabited by ghosts?

Who were the writers who influenced me as I wrote my works of fiction? I couldn't say. Surely the great classics I discovered in my youth remain with me—Stendhal and Dostoyevsky, Kafka and Mann, Munthe and Kazantzakis, Dickens and Conrad, Camus and Mauriac. Some taught me the art of liberating the word by pushing it to delirium; others showed me how to restrain language by imposing on it unalterable rules and limits. One can do anything to words except make them into slaves. For some, language is an instrument, for others a vehicle, for others yet it is a song rising to invisible skies. To mutilate language is to destroy man, for he uses it to understand the universe.

But a novel does not live only from words. It also exists thanks to the silence it contains. I have probably said it somewhere, but I repeat: The quality of a novel is measured not by the weight of its words but by that of its silence.

And silence, as well as madness, I sought—and found—in kabbalistic tales.

I am preparing *Twilight*, a novel about madness. Characters in it take themselves for Abraham and Isaac. And the Messiah.

I bring back Pedro from *The Town Beyond the Wall*. Someone is trying to denigrate him in the eyes of his friend whose name, here, is Raphael. The two look for each other, call each other, communicate beyond space, beyond reason. What will save them? What will save their friendship, if not memory? But there is a danger lying in wait. Where is it? In doubt, in madness? What must one do to determine madness? Where is it to be found as it relates to man, to God?

I tackle the disconcerting phenomenon of cults. What is there about them that attracts so many young people, ready to sacrifice everything to be admitted? Is it authority they crave? Is it the strangeness they find irresistible?

As in my earlier novels, I do everything to eliminate from *The Forgotten* all autobiographical reference. I do not recognize myself in any of its characters. Fehérfalu is not Sighet, and Elhanan Rosenbaum did not cross the threshold of the concentration camp universe.

As principal theme I choose the terrifying Alzheimer's disease. Malkiel, whose mother has died, witnesses the mental decline of his father, Elhanan, a retired therapist and melancholic survivor of the ghettos.

Is there a disease worse than Alzheimer's? It is a cancer of identity, of memory. In the novel I compare it to a book whose pages are torn out one by one, until all that remains is the cover.

Elhanan, who has so much to communicate, realizes one morning that he remembers less and less. His native village in the shadow of the Carpathian mountains, his Hasidic childhood, the secret mission, the "Jewish work brigades" that were part of the Hungarian army, the partisans in the woods, the return to the deserted ghetto, the displaced persons camps in Germany, his encounter with beautiful and wondrous Talia, the clandestine emigration to Palestine, the battle for the Old City of Jerusalem—these events, which he alone went through and for which he alone possesses the key, will they all disappear with him, into the darkness of the soul? Tormented and in the grip of a hitherto unknown anguish, he composes this prayer:

God of Abraham, Isaac and Jacob, do not forget their son who calls upon You now.

You who are source of all memory, well know that to forget is to abandon, to forget is to repudiate. Do not abandon me, God of my fathers, for I have never repudiated You.

God of Israel, do not cast out a son of Israel who yearns with all his heart and soul to remain bound to the history of Israel.

God and King of the universe, exile me not from that universe.

As a child I learned to revere You, to love You, to obey You; keep me from forgetting the child that I was.

As an adolescent I chanted the litanies of the martyrs of Mainz and York; erase them not from my memory, You who erase nothing from Your own.

As a man I learned to respect the will of our dead; keep me from forgetting what I learned.

God of my ancestors, let the bond between them and me remain whole, unbroken.

You who have chosen to dwell in Jerusalem, let me not forget Jerusalem. You who wander with Your people in exile, let me remember them.

God of Auschwitz, know that I must remember Auschwitz. And that I must remind You of it. God of Treblinka, let the sound of that name make me, and You, tremble now and always. God of Belzec, let me, and You, weep for the victims of Belzec.

You who share our suffering, You who share our wait, let me never be far from those who have invited You into their hearts.

You who foresee the future of man, let me not cut myself off from my past.

God of justice, be just to me. God of charity, be kind to me. God of mercy, plunge me not into the *kaf-ha-kallah,* the chasm where all life, hope and light are extinguished by oblivion. God of truth, remember that without memory truth becomes only the mask of truth. Remember that only memory leads man back to the source of his longing for You. Remember, God of history, that You created man to remember, You put me into the world, You spared me in time of danger and death, that I might testify. What sort of witness would I be without my memory? Know, God, that I do not wish to forget You. I do not wish to forget anything. Not the living and not the dead. Not the voices and not the silences. I do not wish to forget the moments of abundance that enriched my life, nor the hours of anguish that drove me to despair. Even if You forget me, O Lord, I refuse to forget You.

And yet he will forget: There is no cure for his ailment. But thanks to his son, Malkiel, and to Tamar, the young woman his son loves, a solution is found. The three will proceed with a memory transfusion just as patients are treated with blood transfusions. In the end Malkiel will remember even an episode his father had repressed.

Sages and Dreamers is in its way a celebration of memory. Just as I do when I tell Hasidic tales, I smile as I write about the sages and their disciples of two thousand years ago. All of them fascinate me, and I consider myself their student. From old Shammai, I learn to apply rigor to myself; from Hillel the Elder, I learn moderation toward others. I love Rabbi Akiba's romanticism and Rabbi Shimon bar Yohai's inflexibility. But what about Elisha ben Abouya, considered to be a renegade? Am I his pupil as well? I shall repeat Rabbi Meïr's words: One can savor the juice of a fruit even as one throws away its peel.

Talmud means "study." Studying Talmud means studying how to study. In other words, one never concludes the study of Talmud. Just as the Torah has no beginning, the Talmud has no end. For two thousand years it has been given to us to add a commentary here, an opening or a hypothesis there.

The Talmud or the beauty of dialogue—the entire Talmud is nothing but that, a series of dialogues between a sage and a disciple.

Sometimes they are centuries apart, and yet, as one studies them, one has the impression that they are seated at the same table looking into each other's eyes in order to better understand each other.

How many thinkers know that Talmud also signifies tolerance? The minority always has equal right to be heard; it demands and deserves the same respect as the majority. Both positions are recorded in the same way.

And then, is there another religious text where ancient Masters interrogate God on His actions in history? Of course they do it respectfully, but that makes their arguments neither less strong nor less daring.

To study Talmud is to celebrate it. It is also to be in touch with a memory in which death alone is silent.

And now? A new idea for a novel on judges is on my mind, taking shape, preoccupying me. I have many notes, pages filled with points of reference. Excitement and anguish run high.

The Anatomy of Hate⟶

BEGINNING WITH the Nobel laureate conference in 1988, the Foundation for Humanity that Marion and I created at the end of 1986 has been organizing international conferences on a single theme: "The Anatomy of Hate."

"Hate," the key word, describes the passions, often contradictory and always vile, that have torn and ravaged the twentieth century. Only the twentieth century? In truth, the word contains and illustrates the full recorded memory of human cruelty and suffering. Cain hated his brother and killed him; thus the first death in history was a murder. Since then, hate and death have not ceased to rage.

Hate—racial, tribal, religious, ancestral, national, social, ethical, political, economic, ideological—in itself represents the inexorable defeat of mankind, its absolute defeat. If there is an area in which mankind cannot claim the slightest progress, this surely is it. It does not take much for human beings, collectively or individually, to suddenly one day pit themselves like wild beasts one against the other, their worst instincts laid bare, in a state of deleterious exaltation. One decision, one simple word, and a family or a community will drown in blood or perish in flames.

Why is there so much violence, so much hate? How is it conceived, transmitted, fertilized, nurtured? As we face the disquieting, implacable rise of intolerance and fanaticism on more than one continent, it is our duty to expose the danger. By naming it. By confronting it.

In our own way, with the limited means at our disposal, we do what we can. This goes for me in my writings as well as in my activities inside and outside the framework of the seminars organized by our foundation in the United States, the Middle East, and Europe.

At Boston University, which recently celebrated its 150th anniversary, we specifically explored the religious aspect of hate. Bishop Krister Stendhal of Stockholm, dean of the Faculty of Theology at Harvard; Rabbi Yitz Greenberg, former chairman of the Department of Judaic Studies at City College; Professor Mohammed Arkoun of the Sorbonne, as well as another twenty or so scholars and researchers, participated in this seminar. Chaired by the humanist scholar David Hamburg, president of the Carnegie-Mellon Foundation, the sessions tended to be long, passionate, and mostly tolerant. Looking back, I realize that there were important gaps in this conference: We should have invited representatives of other religions. Neither Buddhism nor Shintoism was represented. In ecumenical circles, the tradition of studying the traditional clashes among the three major monotheistic religions is so strong that one easily forgets all the others.

How is one to explain fanaticism's attraction for so many intellectuals, to this day? And what can be done to immunize religion against its pull? For once it absorbs absolutist trends, religion too becomes aggressive and to the same extent as the nations that flout the right of their neighbors or even that of their own citizens to security and happiness, by means of either ideology or force of arms. Wars between races, religions, political ideologies, economic interests—what they have in common is the faith of the fanatics and the moral power derived from their material superiority.

Fanaticism is dangerous not only for the layperson who fights it, but also for the believer whom it fascinates. The fanatic inspires and breathes fear. It is the only tie that binds him to his fellow-man and God. So afraid is he of doubt that he pushes it outside the law. Whether his dictatorship is intellectual or theocratic, he pretends to possess a unique and eternal truth. Insist on a discussion, and he takes offense. He accepts questions only if he alone has the right to answer them. It comes to this: The fanatic accepts only answers—his own—while his tolerant adversary prefers questions.

Since the beginnings of history, man alone suffers from fanaticism and hate, and he alone can stem it. In all of creation, only man is both capable and guilty of hate.

The last decade of the twentieth century, also the last of the millennium, began rather auspiciously. A contagious current of freedom or desire for freedom electrified oppressed nations. It was as though society wished to purge itself of the phantoms and demons brought to life by the violence of the dictators under both Nazism and Communism. All of a sudden, people were moving toward the twenty-first century with confidence, looking forward to a radiant destiny under the sign of alliance rather than vengeance.

Then came the dawn of disenchantment. Joy had lasted but one summer. Had it, too, fallen victim to fanaticism?

We are back to the question: What is fanaticism? How ought one to deal with it? And at what precise point does a belief become integralist or fundamentalist?

An idea degenerates into a fanatical postulate the moment it excludes those who oppose it. By denying the burgeoning independence of ideas or beliefs, religious or political fanaticism deprives them of their ability to function as well as of their right to exist. One confronts its closed fist in every one of the monotheist religions. Catholic integralism matches that of the Protestants, which matches that of the Muslims, which matches that of the Jews. It repels me in all its forms. Whoever declares that he knows the path leading to God better than others causes me to turn away. If he tries to take me there by force, I resist.

Does this mean that I avoid a debate with him? Usually it is the fanatic who shies away from a real debate, a civilized dialogue. He is convinced that he does not have to fight to win, that he has won before hearing the first word. For him, used as he is to monologue, any exchange is an aberration. His discourse is monolithic, closed to doubt and hesitation, hostile to external influences. He listens to himself in order not to hear you. He evolves in a reductive universe deprived of diversity. He inhabits it alone with himself; he becomes the object of his own passion.

For the fanatic is a zealot, a madman of faith. It is he whom Nietzsche was talking about when he said it was not doubt but certainty that leads to madness. Blinded by passion, he turns divine beauty into human ugliness. For him and because of him, the nostalgia for God degenerates into an irresistible desire to hate. He usurps God's place in Creation. He takes himself for God. Like God he strives to make every man in his own image, but smaller. He wants everyone to resemble him yet remain smaller, humble and humiliated, bowed before his throne. Convinced that he is the sole possessor of the meaning of life, he gags or kills the Other in order not to be challenged in his quest. And finally, the religious fanatic sees God not as his judge and king, but as his prisoner.

Let us not deceive ourselves—fanaticism is not exclusively religious in essence. Secular fanaticism is no less vile. The secular fanatic is sometimes more eloquent but no less evil. Both tend to see in the Other not a subject of pride, but an object of contempt.

Fanaticism is a pernicious cancer that undermines the promise of man and crushes him with the weight of evil. The fanatic is tireless because he is never satisfied. He constantly tries to acquire more power, devoting all his energy to that end—one does not hate in the abstract. A fanatic can feed his hate theoretically, but he will soon put it into practice—sometimes he will not relent until he has turned his country into a jail. Since other people's freedom frightens him, the fanatic does not feel free and alive except when others are not. The more crowded the prisons, the more his own liberty flourishes. Thus the fanatic will do the impossible to prevent others from dreaming, loving, thinking in pursuit of their own quest for identity. His goal? To imprison the ideas of others, to paralyze their imagination. For the fanatic, the Other should remain locked in the present, without memory and without hope.

The aim of our conferences? To combat fanaticism, which is the major component of hate, and vice versa. More precisely, not all fanatics are filled with hate, but all those who are filled with hate are fanatics. Their conduct leads inexorably to the destruction of the Being in being. By the time this becomes evident, it is already too late.

I used to say over and over that the opposite of love is not hate but indifference. There is no reciprocity. Hate is always gratuitous, sterile. It is a powerful, insurmountable barrier that permits no intrusion. In other words, nothing good, nothing great, nothing that is alive, can be born of hate. It denies all possibility of metamorphosis or transcendence. Hate begets only hate. It is urgent and imperative to defeat it before it overwhelms us. How can we achieve this? By attacking its visible form—fanaticism.

Combating fanaticism means denouncing the humiliation of the Other. It means celebrating the freedom of the Other, the freedom of all Others. Ultimately it means freeing man from the humiliating chains the fanatic forces upon him. It means opening the prisons and giving back to men, women, and God Himself the freedom the fanatic has stolen.

The sessions often have recourse to psychology. In Boston, Leo (Sjua) Eitinger, of Oslo University, explores the absence of hate among victims, and Robert Jay Lifton, professor of psychiatry at

CUNY, examines with us the power of hate but also the ethical apathy among the killers. He is elaborating on a theme that we have been trying to explore for years, that the absence of hate in the killer is even worse than the hate. The members of the *Einsatzgruppen* massacred thousands and thousands of Jewish children they did not hate.

And God in all this?

Robert McAfee Brown, the most eminent of Protestant theologians; Harry James Cargas, an audacious Catholic thinker; John Roth, an insightful essayist and inspired teacher, all contribute to the theological debate. Could there be a God of hate? The prophets enumerate what the Lord abhors. But is it conceivable that He has come to hate His own creation?

At Haifa University it is the pedagogic aspect of hate that absorbs the conference participants. At what age can one detect the first signs of hate in a child? There is a discussion of the suggestion that a child is incapable of hate until the age of three, that hate is something that is learned, acquired. But if that is so, can it be unlearned as well?

There are some difficult moments at this same conference in Haifa. The great Israeli novelist A. B. Yehoshua, true to his provocative self, overemphasizes his Israelo-centric line. According to him, the Diaspora should "liquidate" itself. After I received the Nobel, he took into account my work and activities on behalf of Israel and the Jewish people and wrote me a letter in which he deigned to grant me—in jest, of course—a *heter*, a sort of purely personal exemption, authorizing me to stay where I am. How is one to explain such a closed mind in a gifted, generous, inspired writer, someone I am fond of?

On the other hand, the dialogues with Muslim participants provoke little embarrassment. Arab journalists, teachers, and students participate in the debates. They are ready to listen as well as to express themselves in an atmosphere of total freedom, I would almost say comradeship. The same desire is evident on all sides: that of finding a middle road. And all this was happening in 1990, well before the peace process was started between Israelis and Palestinians.

At the reception in honor of the conference, in a splendid Druze mansion, a group of Arab journalists from the Old City of Jerusalem approach me. Among them is a young couple. She is beautiful; he has an open, friendly face. They would like to record an interview for Arab television and Arabic-language magazines. They are familiar, they tell me, with my work on behalf of human rights and express their appreciation. But . . . I know what is about to follow: "Why are you ready to listen to everyone who suffers except us? Why do you refuse to hear us?" They speak without hate or anger, as though they wished only to elucidate a purely philosophical problem. Are they expecting me to justify myself in their eyes? Not even. It seems to be a simple matter of intellectual curiosity. They don't resent me; they are not reproaching me in any way. I owe it to them to be truthful: "First of all, don't think that I am deaf or indifferent to what you are enduring. I am listening to you, and I hear you. But since you say you are familiar with the nature of my testimony, you must also be aware of my attachment to Israel. Now, you cannot deny that Israel is living in fear, for reasons that may or may not be valid, and that it is a fear inspired by you. Help me dissipate that fear, and I promise you that my friends and I will do everything we can not only to hear you but to make others hear you as well." Unlike their Israeli defenders, they take up the challenge. The understanding created between us justifies hope.

The next conference is held in August 1990 in Oslo. The theme is "The Anatomy of Hate and Conflict Resolution." In a historic precedent, the Nobel committee itself is our co-organizer. The Norwegian government, supportive as always, places its infrastructure and its considerable means at our disposal. Everything works magnificently, miraculously, without a hitch. Airplane tickets, hotels, restaurants, programs, transportation, simultaneous interpretation, press relations—more than four hundred accredited journalists ensure an international coverage worthy of a summit conference. Under the direction of Geir Grung of the Ministry of Foreign Affairs, Geir Lundestad of the Nobel Institute, and Chief Rabbi Michael Melchior, the event runs as smoothly as a Swiss watch. From the moment they get off their plane, all participants are taken in hand by a member of the reception committee and a representative of the government. There is no passport check, no customs inspection; no customs officials are to be seen. Every guest is treated like the star of the conference. Of course, the list of participants is impressive: François Mitterrand; Václav Havel; Nelson Mandela; the Lithuanian president, Vytautas Landsbergis; Jo Benkow, speaker of the Norwegian Parliament; Jimmy Carter; John Kenneth Galbraith; Conor Cruise O'Brien; Ehud Olmert, Israeli minister of health; Hanna Siniora, editor in chief of an Arabic daily in Jerusalem; the Cuban poet Armando Valladares; the German novelist Günter Grass, the Hungarian novelist György Konrád; the journalists Herbert Pundik from *Politiken* in Copenhagen and Abe Rosenthal and Arthur Gelb from the *New York Times.* . . . All told, some fifty politicians, intellectuals, scientists, educators, psychiatrists from many different countries have gathered to seek together a response to the hate that continues to haunt and afflict nations.

As for the artistic aspect of the event, Marion heads the special team that has taken on the intricate and subtle preparations of the concert that, traditionally, becomes the highlight of our conferences. Audrey Hepburn, delicate and supremely gracious, and Gregory Peck, grave and regal, act as masters of ceremonies. The orchestra is conducted by Lukas Foss. On the program, some of the most outstanding performers of our time: the flutist James Galway, the soprano Frederica von Stade, the bass Simon Estes.

All sessions are plenary. Gidske Anderson (who will eventually succeed Egil Aarvik as chair of the Nobel Committee) and I chair the meetings. More authoritarian and less sentimental than I, she intervenes whenever I am too timid: She will interrupt a speaker who ignores the flashing red-light signal to stop and exceeds his allotted time. Almost all the speakers obey the light signal, including Jimmy Carter and François Mitterrand. One who does not is Elena Bonner. The stubborn, courageous wife of Andrei Sakharov considers herself free as always—free to speak as she wishes, when she wishes, and as long as she feels like it. Our rules not only displease her, they annoy her. I feel bad, but I am happy Gidske is enforcing the regulations.

A moving scene: Jacques Morillon of the International Red Cross is discussing the Middle East situation. He tells us that he fears for the soul of Israel. Ephraim Urbach, the venerable Talmudist, answers him: "Every time I hear that someone wants to save Israel's soul I am seized with apprehension. . . ." And with a great display of erudition, he firmly cites examples from the present and the past. The next day Morillon offers public apologies.

In another scene, no less moving, Leon Wessels, deputy foreign minister of South Africa, addresses Nelson Mandela: "Nelson, I was born with apartheid; what I wish for now is to attend its funeral." The two men begin a dialogue that surely contributed to the process of democratization in their country.

And François Mitterrand charms everyone with his simplicity. He sits surrounded by intellectuals, some well known, some not so well known, but none who has his rank or power.

And Václav Havel, who tells of how he never felt hate, not even for his jailers.

And the Czech children's choir he has brought in his plane to sing—magnificently—at the concert.

And Nadine Gordimer, not yet a Nobel Prize laureate, who denounces racism with conviction.

And John Galbraith, who demonstrates that humor, too, helps resolve human conflict.

The conference ends with the drafting of an Oslo Declaration, which we wish to be solemn. Here it is:

> This ancient scourge, whose origins remain hidden in darkness, knows neither barriers nor frontiers. It strikes all races and religions, all political systems and social classes, and because hatred is willed by man, God Himself is unable to stop it. No nation may consider itself protected against its poison; no society is safe against its arrows. Both blind and blinding, this hatred is a black sun, which from under an ashen sky, hits and kills all those who forget the greatness of which they are capable and the promises once bestowed upon them. Hatred has no mercy for those who refuse to fight it. It kills whoever will not try to disarm it. Parents, teach your children that to hate is to mutilate their own future. Teachers, tell your pupils that hatred is the negation of every triumph that culture and civilization may achieve. Politicians, tell your constituencies that hatred is, at all levels, your principal enemy, and theirs. Tell all those who listen to you that hatred breeds hatred and can breed nothing else.
>
> To hate is to refuse to accept another person as a human being, to diminish him, to limit your own horizon by narrowing his, to look at him—and also at yourself—not as a subject of pride but as an object of disdain and fear. To hate is to opt for the easiest and most mind-reducing way out by digging a ditch into which the hater and his victim will both fall like broken puppets. To hate is to kindle wars that will turn children into orphans and make old people lose their minds from sorrow and contrition. Religious hatred makes the face of God invisible. Political hatred wipes out people's liberties. In the field of science, hatred

inevitably puts itself at death's service. In literature, it distorts truth, perverts the meaning of the story and hides beauty itself under a thick layer of blood and grime.

Today, at the threshold of the twenty-first century, this is what we must tell all men and women for whom we wish a future as bright and smiling as the faces of our children. If we do nothing, hate will come sneaking perniciously and slyly into their mouths and into their eyes, adulterating the mutual relations between people, nations, societies and races. If we do nothing, we will be passing onto the coming century that message of hatred known to us as racism, fanaticism, xenophobia, and anti-Semitism.

Democracy means dialogue. Without the other, neither is conceivable. Together, they contribute towards that "brotherhood of nations" mentioned by Alfred Nobel in his last will and testament as man's only hope of peace and survival. This then is our appeal: "We appeal to governments, organizations, the media, educational institutions to find measures to follow up the essence of this *Oslo Declaration* in ways which can help lead mankind away from hate and vanquish the indifference to hate."

These words do not only mean that we have decided to oppose the flood of ugly, violent hatred that is still inundating our society. By signing them, we first of all confirm our certitude that humanity is strong enough to stem it and worthy of such a victory.

Some of the participants sign this appeal without reading it; others consider it too philosophical or not enough so; still others call it unsatisfactory for failing to include any reference to feminist aspirations.

Like many documents of this nature, this one may or may not find its place in the archives. But that is not what matters. What matters is that once again links have been forged to fight hate, which is so terrifyingly adept at fanning unholy passions throughout the world.

I am sometimes asked: What is the use of bringing together under one roof great figures of the social and human sciences, philosophy and literature? What benefits can mankind gain from seeing always more or less the same experts around different tables, telling one another more or less the same thing? None, suggest the skeptics.

Many, respond the naive. The point is to combine skepticism and naïveté. And above all, not to give in to cynicism. What is the point? is a worthwhile question on condition that it is not answered even before it is asked. As for all social initiatives, everything depends on what one's expectations are. If you expect too much from such a gathering, you will be disappointed. As for myself, I am not. I am satisfied with little. A handshake that brings two adversaries, two strangers, together is enough for me. A sincere remark, an authentic idea that makes one think, that encourages the mind to open up, whether to accept or to reject, is enough for me.

Yes, there are gratuitous and sterile efforts, I agree, but they are rarely totally without merit. They frequently end in failure—that is incontestable—yet a failure is preferable to not having tried.

An example is the Moscow conference our foundation organized in December 1991 together with *Ogonyok* weekly magazine. Like the Nobel laureate conference in Paris, it produced no concrete results. Neither Gorbachev nor Helmut Schmidt, the former German chancellor, for instance, was in a position to move his country toward more humane, more equitable, more generous policies. Schmidt had long since left government, and Gorbachev was soon to leave power. And yet.

To listen to Adam Michnik of Poland's Solidarity movement, pleading the cause of Nagorno-Karabakh, or to Abe Rosenthal denouncing the police totalitarianism of the KGB, to hear François Léotard's exposé of politics and hate, is to take part in an endeavor initiated by a yearning for brotherhood, an endeavor that does honor to all the participants, intellectuals and political figures alike.

For the opening session, Schmidt and Alexander Yakovlev, Gorbachev's right hand, had been invited to compare their recollections of World War II. They had been selected because Schmidt had been a lieutenant in the tank corps that advanced as far as the suburbs of Moscow, and Yakovlev fought, also as a lieutenant, in the Red Army, defending his country against the invader. "How was it for you?" and "Did hate play a role in your motivations?" we ask each of them. I think they were meeting for the first time. Schmidt speaks of his adolescence, his youth. He did not join the Nazi party; it seems one of his grandparents was a Jew. Everyone is too polite to ask him whether he had not wanted to become a Nazi or hadn't been able to. Like Yakovlev, he prefers to discuss ideology, political doctrine, and the future in general.

The appearance of General Oleg Kalugin produces a moment of high tension. He presents the methods and aims of the KGB system in all their brutality. His delivery is that of an expert, his tone cold, almost scientific. The audience pays rapt attention to every word, every inflection of his voice. Questions are fired at him from all sides: Is it true that the KGB was fomenting anti-Semitism abroad? (Yes.) That the KGB once had a hold, and still did, on Gorbachev? And if so, what was it? (Answer vague.) What does he know about Raoul Wallenberg? (No more than we do.) How did the KGB function in the United States? There follows an explosion provoked by Abe Rosenthal: "When a general of the KGB appears before a group of intellectuals, it is incumbent upon him to be clear and frank." What exactly had he done under Communist dictatorship in the exercise of his functions? Of course Abe is trying to find out whether the general had committed crimes, and, if so, which. Kalugin tries to dodge the questions and finally gets angry: "I'm not here before a tribunal!" And Abe retorts: "When a general of the KGB appears before a group like ours, we *are* his judges."

Aside from this incident, which deeply upsets Abe but brings him honor, the sessions take place in an atmosphere of total respect for one another. There are no interruptions, no challenges, not even an offensive comment. Just as in the previous conferences, links are formed.

I don't know whether as a result of our debates hate diminished throughout the world, but I know that in those days in Moscow, friendship won some victories, not over hate but over indifference.

It was on this occasion that I saw Gorbachev again.

In the capital one could sense the coming crisis. The relations between Gorbachev and Yeltsin were worsening by the hour. There was a rumor that Yeltsin, defying protocol, had by a simple telephone call dismissed Edward Shevardnadze from his post of minister of foreign affairs. When Shevardnadze arrived at the airport to welcome James Baker, the U.S. secretary of state, he was denied access to the VIP lounge. Yeltsin's police actually ordered him to turn around. Moscow was buzzing with rumors. There was talk of a new coup, this time initiated by Yeltsin.

Would Gorbachev attend the conference? He had promised us that he would come, but until the very last session we are not sure. Finally we are told he is keeping his word by inviting us to the Kremlin. All of us? No. He was inviting ten "delegates." But there were forty of us. We were told the room was not large enough. Arthur Gelb and Abe Rosenthal, Vitaly Korotich, editor in chief of *Ogonyok,* and other participants advise me to accept: better a meeting with ten than no meeting. I finally agree but make it clear that, in that case, I myself would remain in the hotel. The Soviet officials alternately cajole and threaten me to make me change my mind, but, not being a diplomat, I dig in my heels—either we shall all go or I shall stay among the uninvited. In the end, all of us go.

Gorbachev greets us affably. In his welcoming remarks he speaks mostly of his political successes, and literary, therefore commercial, ones. His book on perestroika has sold extraordinarily well: five million copies worldwide. In one year it has brought him $800,000, which means that in spite of everything his message is getting through. In my response I try to lighten the tension in the room by asking him three questions:

First, why is it that each time we meet it is always in an atmosphere of drama? (He smiles.)

Second, you are a writer, so am I. You are a Nobel laureate, so am I. Why are your books best-sellers and mine are not? (At last, he laughs.)

Third: First you became president, then you received the Nobel Prize. Would a reverse pattern be conceivable for me? (Here he laughs loudly and says: "I don't advise it.")

I go over the subjects that preoccupy us: ethnic hatred, religious fanaticism, the nuclear menace, the future of the regime, relations with Israel, anti-Semitism. I don't conceal that I have met with Jews from Leningrad, Kiev, and other places who all live in anguish. He tries to reassure us. His answers are frank, unvarnished. Israel? He is happy to have renewed diplomatic relations with the Jewish state. *Pamyat* and anti-Semitism? In the past two years the situation has improved.

We were the last foreign visitors he received in the Kremlin as president of the USSR.

I was to see him a third time, six months later, in Haifa, where he had come to receive a humanitarian prize from the Technion Institute. The Soviet ambassador is to make a speech but excuses himself on Boris Yeltsin's orders, or so we are given to understand.

Gorbachev is now an ordinary citizen without rank or title and no longer represents anything, except perhaps his vision of a liberated world. *Sic transit gloria mundi*. He reminds me of Winston Churchill after his defeat at the polls in 1945. But Churchill was a great orator, and you couldn't say that about Gorbachev. Also, Churchill had saved the world from Fascism. Had Gorbachev saved it from Communism? History will judge. In rereading these notes in 1996, I find myself thinking of the resurgence of the Communist party in Russia and other countries of Central Europe. Still, as we watch the successor of Stalin, Khrushchev, and Brezhnev, surrounded by Israeli flags flapping in the twilight, standing at attention as *Hatikva* is sung, all of us in the crowd cannot help but feel the winds of history. Surprised at first but then visibly pleased to see me again, he falls into my arms and kisses me on both cheeks. To his wife, Raissa, who doesn't understand, he explains: "My last visitor in the Kremlin, do you remember? He's the one."

Other conferences follow.

Spring 1992: New York is in the midst of a full-blown racial crisis. Riots are raging in Brooklyn's Crown Heights, when we hear from the governor of New York State, Mario Cuomo: "You are arranging conferences on hate everywhere except in our city. Do you really think that we don't need one, that our ethnic problems are solved?"

Together with the governor, we organize a seminar to be held in autumn. Its title: "To Save Our Children." To save them from hate, of course. There is little time to prepare it. Marion, who is directing the foundation, and Arnold Thaler, her associate and vice president of the foundation, work tirelessly with the governor's staff. Lists have to be drawn up, invitations sent out. It is imperative that every segment of the community be represented: Jews, Christians, Blacks, Hispanics; sociologists, educators, philosophers, psychologists, psychiatrists, journalists . . . and more.

Two plenary sessions introduce the meetings of the commissions. Everything seems to be under control. Then comes the explosion.

A young man bursts into the hall where participants are dealing with problems of education and the media. He protests against the gay community's lack of representation. He is actually wrong: the executive director of the Gay and Lesbian Anti-Violence Project is a full member of the conference. The intruder considers this inadequate and demands that a homosexual participate in every committee. Boston University President John Silber answers him with great logic and characteristic calm: How does the young man know who around the table is homosexual, and who is not? And what if they all were, without advertising it? I was not present when the incident occurred, but all the participants I question are unanimous: Silber never raised his voice. Nevertheless, the next day the executive director of the Gay and Lesbian Anti-Violence Project declares in plenary session that he feels compelled to withdraw from the conference.

A Long Island newspaper reports the incident, blowing it up out of all proportion. For their part, the Boston dailies, which rarely miss a chance to attack Silber, take up the item, adding additional negative comment. In the end, the ombudsman of the *Boston Globe*, after seeing a videocassette of the session, publicly declares that Silber had acted appropriately.

June 1995: another international conference, this one devoted to young people and entitled: "The Leaders of Tomorrow." This time young people, facing "leaders of today," are participating in the debates that take place in Venice's San Giorgio, the beautiful home of the Cini Foundation. Thirty adolescents between the ages of fifteen and nineteen represent the two sides of several areas of conflict. From the Middle East: Israelis, Egyptians, Jordanians, and Palestinians. From Ireland: Catholics and Protestants. From Yugoslavia: Croats, Serbs, and Bosnians. The others come from various African countries and the United States.

In a short time the frontiers disappear and a moving camaraderie develops. A young African American who has already been in prison seventeen times evokes his experiences; the others show great empathy. Bonds are created between the Israelis and the Palestinians. When a young Bosnian forcefully demands on a direct satellite line that First Lady Hillary Clinton make promises for his people and his country, the entire group gives him its support. As always, Hillary is brilliant as she responds to frequently confrontational questions.

Yossi Beilin, Israeli deputy minister and one of the secret negotiators of the Oslo Peace Plan; Uri Lubrani, the legendary savior of distant Jewish communities, and Itzhak Rager, the mayor of Beersheba converse with the Jordanian ambassador to Italy and the PLO representative in London.

Former Irish terrorists sit, for the first time, on the same stage as their enemies of yesterday. Richard Goldstone, the South African judge who is the United Nations prosecutor, charged with arguing cases of crimes against humanity, is speaking of the relationship between justice and memory. Silber speaks to the role of education. Bernard Kouchner, former and future French minister of human rights, later to be appointed U.N. administrator of Kosovo, pleads for intervention wherever humanity is at risk. Susanna Agnelli, foreign minister of Italy, discusses the problems of individual conscience confronting men and women in power.

We have barely returned to New York when we plunge into preparations for the next conference, scheduled for December in Hiroshima. Its theme is "The Future of Hope," and our cosponsor is *Asahi Shimbun*, the most important Japanese daily. The conference opens with a concert in *Asahi Shimbun's* great concert hall in the presence of Emperor Akihito and Empress Michiko.

Ten Nobel laureates; a former Japanese prime minister; Takako Doi, chairperson of the Japanese Parliament; former Secretary of State Lawrence Eagleburger; French Culture Minister Jack Lang; the Peruvian writer Mario Vargas Llosa; several nuclear experts; economists; important journalists—all participate energetically and passionately in debates that begin at eight o'clock in the morning and end late in the evening. In this place our preoccupations seem urgent.

Yugoslavia recalls us to reality.

The Destiny of Sarajevo

SARAJEVO'S RECENT TRAGEDY began in 1991. A wave of murderous violence and hostility sweeps over former Yugoslavia, now shattered. Democracy was not successful in establishing cooperation among its varied and hostile ethnic groups. On the contrary, all it did was release repressed antagonisms. A bewildering fact: Under Tito the various communities had lived peacefully side-by-side. Could dictatorship, when it is marketed "with a human face," be more beneficial than democracy? With respect to Yugoslavia one might well think so, but I don't believe it; nothing can and nothing should be substituted for a government based on freedom.

Once again bombs are falling on cities, civilians are assassinated, children are massacred. Will it never stop? Will the twentieth century be nothing but a bloodstained itinerary leading from Sarajevo to Sarajevo?

Dubrovnik is buried in ruins. Other cities follow. Homes are abandoned, families uprooted, haggard mothers and exhausted old men are in full flight, driven by an ancestral terror.

God in heaven, what is there to be done?

Most Americans don't even know where some of these places are. Bosnia? Whom does it belong to? And the Krajina, where is it? Other unfamiliar names flood the news: Banja Luka, Srebrenica, Tuzla. The geography lessons we are learning are tragic.

Ministers and diplomats now say with regret that they should never have recognized these states. I hear it at the Élysée, and it is confirmed at the White House. Everyone I speak to blames Helmut Kohl, the German chancellor, the first to recognize Croatia's independence. And it was he who immediately afterward exercised unrelenting pressure on his Western allies to support his policy.

But Bosnia is far from our concerns, too far for most people to pause over its fate. Go there? How? On whose behalf and to do what? So there is Bosnia, abandoned, betrayed, removed from our preoccupations. Later, in August 1995, Croat Serbia shares the same fate.

And time is passing.

I feel guilty that since 1988 we have not been able to overcome the financial difficulties and create an association of Nobel laureates. It could have intervened in Bosnia, sounded the alarm, saved some children, helped their mothers. We could have given the victims human and moral support and testified on their behalf.

And time is passing.

My personal involvement dates from July 1992, when I receive a call from Israel Singer and Elan Steinberg, directors of the World Jewish Congress. They show me a letter from Dobrica Cosic, president of the Federal Yugoslav Republic. Evidently he had written to Boutros Boutros-Ghali, secretary-general of the U.N., asking him to appoint me to head an international commission to investigate the situation in prison camps for Bosnians in Serbia.

The world media are talking about these camps. The televised images arouse indignation everywhere. Systematic humiliations, rapes, arbitrary arrests, deportations, summary executions—all are part of a policy of "ethnic cleansing." Everybody is accusing the Serbs. Some people do not hesitate to use the words "concentration camps," "genocide," and even . . . "Auschwitz." I do not. I have never wavered in my affirmation that Auschwitz is unique and will remain so.

What could be achieved there by a single individual, one who has no power and represents no one but himself? Nonetheless, does one have the right to remain neutral, to stay on the sidelines, to keep silent?

After several conversations with State Department and U.N. officials (Boutros-Ghali claims not to have received the Yugoslav president's letter), Singer, Steinberg, and I decide to fly to London to meet President Cosic and other leaders of the former Yugoslavia, who are there to take part in an international conference. They are Slobodan Milosevic (Serbia), Radovan Karadjic (Serbian Bosnia), Alija Izetbegovic (Bosnia), and Franjo Tudjman (Croatia), the last an author of an anti-Semitic work denying the Holocaust. For obvious reasons I do not wish to meet Tudjman; he will be excluded from the list.

The four leaders insist that we travel to their countries. We demand guarantees and total freedom of movement and action. We must be able to go anywhere and meet anyone at any time. And what about the camps? Cosic, Milosevic, and Karadjic protest vehemently. They all blame the media. So then, there were no atrocities, no rapes? Oh well, here and there a few unfortunate incidents, that's all. As we don't bother to hide our skepticism, Cosic summons Karadjic and appeals to him in our presence to shut down all the camps on his territory in "our honor." Karadjic commits to do this. In writing. I have his signed letter. Why not announce it officially at the conference? Fine, they'll do it.

Of them all, Cosic seems to me the most open, the most understanding, the most human. A seventy-three-year-old novelist, he impresses me favorably. As usual, am I too gullible? I tell myself that if the reports of Serbian atrocities are true, he may not be to blame. The crimes may be perpetrated behind his back.

His opponents send me pamphlets and articles to prove his share of responsibility for the "ethnic cleansing." His friends provide me with the same kind of documents on Alija Izetbegovic and his project for a Greater Islamic Republic in former Yugoslavia. The people in charge of propaganda of every kind are not sitting on their hands.

Meanwhile the violence continues to rage in the Balkans. And what about Cosic's promise and Karadjic's commitment? Null and void, as they say. In November, Ted Koppel of ABC's *Nightline* devotes two programs to the Balkans. David Marash's report is gripping, full of harrowing images, heartrending testimonies. Invited by Koppel to comment on them, I speak of the horror the images arouse and the feelings of helplessness I experience. I plead for a summit meeting in Sarajevo.

That is when I decide to go there.

My principal fear is that of being manipulated by one side or another. I must at all costs avoid being turned into a propaganda instrument. Cosic conveys his assurances in that regard. I refuse all dinners, cocktail parties, receptions. I am not coming to savor the undoubtedly delicious specialties of Yugoslav cuisine, but to see the prisoners, speak to the victims. Belgrade agrees to my terms. Am I right to trust Cosic? For all practical purposes, he is my host. He is the one who sends four airplanes to Geneva to take me and my delegation to Belgrade. The group includes a number of our foundation members as well as several journalists: Abe Rosenthal, Marc Kravetz, David Marash, and others. (An Italian journalist has joined us. His pro-Serb

sympathies render him suspect to certain correspondents based in
Belgrade, where, I was told later, he falsely claimed to be my representative.)

Immediately upon landing I make clear to the local press that no
one will take advantage of this visit. We have come with the sole
object of uncovering the facts and making them known. At the president's palace there is another press conference with Cosic. I repeat
our demand that our visit not be used for propaganda purposes. Cosic
says: "All we want is for you to know the truth."

He takes me by the arm, and I think he is going to accompany
me to the door. Wrong. He leads me to a sumptuous dining room
where a huge banquet has been laid out. I find it difficult to restrain
my frustration and anger. From the very beginning, I had asked specifically that the program not include any lunches, dinners, receptions,
or cocktail parties without which, evidently, diplomatic life would
founder. But I am not a diplomat. I sit down across from the president
and ask for the floor, not to propose a toast but to make a short statement: "I am a Jew, and this is Friday evening; my place is not here but
in the synagogue. . . ." I stand up, shake a few hands, and leave, followed by the whole delegation.

The synagogue, destroyed during the Occupation and recently
restored, has few members. Many have left for Israel; the community
is disintegrating. The Chief Rabbi, a frail and sad old man, officiates in
a low voice. He reminds me of the frightened rabbi I met in Moscow
in the sixties.

I share a pleasant Shabbat dinner with the congregation. There
are prayers, speeches, small talk. And what about the war? People
mention it, of course, but in abstract terms. A well-spoken woman,
fortyish, says: "You must help us." Who are "us"? The Jews? "No, us the
Serbs; we are reviled, slandered, presented as monsters." A Jew in
Sarajevo tells us: "You should help us." "Us," who? The Jews? No. "The
Bosnians; we are the martyrs of this era. We are persecuted, we are
massacred, and the world refuses to intervene."

The next day at the U.S. Embassy, the articles that have
appeared in the local press are translated for me. I had expected the
press to be biased but not so downright mendacious. I am scandalized
by the crass manner in which it presents our visit's main motivation as
assisting Federal Yugoslavia, that is, Serbia, in the task of improving
its international image. I protest publicly several times.

That's not all. In spite of our agreement, our program includes a luncheon with the mayor, another with some minister, a reception somewhere else. How can I cancel them all without creating an incident? But I do cancel them; never mind the susceptibilities of the high officials in charge of public affairs.

There is another, more serious source of friction: I am told how complicated, difficult, and dangerous it would be to go to Sarajevo and visit the prison camps. We are told again and again that we shall have to obtain all sorts of flight authorizations from the U.N.—a matter of air corridors, security measures. I call General Philippe Morillon in Sarajevo, General Nambier in Zagreb. Hours go by; the tension mounts. We are taken to a local museum showing the atrocities perpetrated by the Croats during the World War II Occupation and very recent ones committed by the Muslims. Our guide shows us a picture of the corpse of a man clubbed to death; a woman in black on my left bursts into tears: his widow. In another photo we see a man stabbed to death; his orphans, behind me, are sobbing. And then there are children, murdered children. The innocence of their death is thrown into our faces as though to mark the death of our own innocence. We are shattered. Perhaps it is meant to condition us, to "explain" to us the reason for certain "excesses" on the Serbian side. To "explain" hate is too easy. By explaining you risk justifying.

Will we finally obtain permission to visit the camps?

There is an atmosphere of duplicity, of delaying tactics. Serbian officials are deliberately dragging their feet. They obviously wish to prevent us from going where we might uncover unpleasant truths. But what about Cosic's promise granting us total freedom of movement? We send a message to the officials that if we do not take off in the next hour we shall head home. At once all obstacles are removed. Two hours later, we are en route to Banja Luka. Cosic has promised us that he will close the camp we are about to visit.

The notorious Manjaca camp is plunged in darkness. At five in the afternoon, against a background of whitish snow, night has already fallen over the barracks, where three thousand prisoners are locked up. Only the infirmary is lighted.

We see six hundred prone shadows. The camp commander, Bozidar Popovic, bellows orders to make them move. His flashlight lights up their faces. I choose fifteen at random. They follow me to the infirmary. I ask to talk to them alone, far from the eyes and ears of their guards. Earlier I had insisted on a solemn pledge from the commander that there would be no reprisals, even if they complain, even if they say things he won't like. He gives me his word. The foreign correspondents based in Belgrade tell me this Popovic is a real professional; authoritarian, strict when it comes to discipline, he yells and hollers, but he is not mean. Why is he so forthcoming, so respectful of me? The explanation turns up by accident in the course of our conversation: He has mistaken me for Simon Wiesenthal, whom he admires.

The prisoners tell us that the food is not too bad, the conditions in general bearable. Yes, they suffer from the cold—temperatures can reach 35° Celsius below zero—and from being confined, but on the whole their situation is better than at the beginning. What are their main complaints? To be out of touch with their relatives, their people. To be cut off from the outside world. To live on the sidelines, to feel superfluous. And then the uncertainty, never knowing what the next day will bring.

There is a young German among them. He is blond and thin and stands very straight. He was taken prisoner by the Serbs. Why? How does this war concern him? "Oh, I didn't come to fight," he answers, shrugging his shoulders, "but to write a book." A book about what? "About the war, of course." And that's why the Serbs arrested you? "Well, it's that . . . they caught me with a Kalashnikov [rifle] in my hand." I am bewildered: "And it was with a Kalashnikov that you were going to write a book? Have pens gone out of fashion?"

The faces are lifeless, resigned, drained of their vitality. Looking at them, we feel guilty. We are a different species: free. How can we best help them? How can we express our solidarity? In this place "solidarity" is a word that rings empty.

When we leave, we promise not to forget them. For prisoners, it is crucial to know that people at least think of them.

As a result of our visit the camp *is* shut down; most of the prisoners are freed. But five hundred of them are not handed over to the International Red Cross. They disappear into a "disciplinary" camp. The worst of it is that the group we had spoken with in the infirmary *was* punished and transferred to an even tougher, even more rigorous camp, Batkovic.

Disappointment, anger, outrage. All these unkept promises. All the broken commitments. And what about Popovic's word of honor? The men we came to help and encourage are now worse off than before. What kind of humanitarian missions are these if in the end the victims pay the price?

. . .

Sarajevo is a city that is tragedy incarnate, among the saddest, most desolate, most devastated cities in the world. I am told that it once was one of the most beautiful and most peaceful.

It looks not unlike Dresden in 1945—ruins and debris, gaping, haunted-looking houses. Here and there you see a man, a woman, a child collecting wood from beneath the snow, their faces closed.

General Morillon welcomes us. His is a professorial, ascetic face. This warrior for peace is the pride of France and of the U.N. His behavior in Srebrenica has won him universal admiration.

He tells me about Sarajevo. Life and terror in Sarajevo. Hunger. Death.

How do its inhabitants live in this besieged city? Even far away from "Sniper Alley" there is a risk of being struck by a stray bullet at any moment. And yet whenever there's a letup people walk heads high, almost normally, even as their eyes check the ground before them. But they seem to be going nowhere. The schools are closed, as are the stores. "The worst," we are told, "is that life in Sarajevo seems purposeless. You get up, you go out, you come back, you say something, you answer, and it's all for nothing."

At the Victor-Bubanj prison, in the high, narrow, lime-covered cells, we are allowed to see twenty inmates. Standing in a line, heads lowered, humbled, humiliated, they are waiting to be interrogated. Name, age, place of birth, profession—they answer without looking up. Behind us the guards and officials comment on their answers. All of them have been arrested legally, they tell us. All will have their day in court. A "criminal arrested for war crimes and genocide" is pointed out. I recognize him: His picture had been published in the *New York Times* a few weeks earlier. His name is Borislav Herak. He had confessed to having assassinated thirty-five men and having raped thirteen women, all Muslims. His acts are an abomination, but why call them genocide? (He will be condemned to death and executed.)

President Alija Izetbegovic is our guide in this phantom capital, where visitors circulate only in armored cars. At one point he shows us a small square and says: "It was here that Gavrilo Princip shot Archduke Francis Ferdinand in 1914; it was to be the first bullet of the First World War." And to think that a third European if not world war may well start in this region. . . .

Whatever else he may be, Izetbegovic is brave. His bodyguards try to restrain his enthusiasm. He walks with us, his face exposed, with inadequate protection, disdainful of the risks. Surely he knows that we make perfect targets for sharpshooters who may hide anywhere. Abe Rosenthal remarks on this, and we hurry back to our cars and continue our guided tour.

Here is the National Library, or what's left of it. The walls are riddled with holes from bullets and shells. On many floors you see dark traces of a conflagration; the building must have burned for a very long time.

In the drawing room of the presidential residence, a gaunt man with a dark, tormented face turns to me: "I am a writer. It seems you are going to visit someone who pretends also to be a writer. Ask him why he set fire to the beautiful library of Sarajevo." I promise.

Sitting opposite Radovan Karadjic, master of Serbian Bosnia, I ask him why he burned the library. His face red with indignation, he starts "demonstrating" to me that the accusation is false, an absolute falsehood. It was the Muslims who set it on fire so as to accuse him. I protest: I saw the library just an hour ago. I saw the walls, the traces of artillery fire. Clearly the building was attacked from the outside. Karadjic tells me I understand nothing of such things.

Is Karadjic guilty? Of course. As is his commander in chief, General Ratko Mladic. Does this mean that his opponents, the Bosnians and the Croats, are innocent? In this war the first victim is not only truth but innocence as well. Here no one is innocent. Only some are guiltier than others.

And yet. For at least five centuries Sarajevo was an example of urban coexistence. There was cooperation among its Jews, Christians, and Muslims, a harmony marred by not a single racial, ethnic, or religious incident. What provoked the abrupt change?

Before leaving Belgrade, I visit Cosic as agreed. We spend a few hours together. I summarize what I have seen. I tell him of my negative impressions. I try to convince him to end the policy of terror against the Bosnians. He tries to convince me to accept the principle of ethnic separation: "As a Jew you must understand that certain communities cannot live together. Sooner or later, this will happen in Israel, too." So what his opponents say about him is true: He is indeed for the expulsion of the Muslims, by whatever means. I try to explain to him that he is wrong about the Jews, that we have coexisted with so many peoples for so many centuries. He counters all my arguments with his own, insisting on the fact that the time has come for us to be realists. Finally I slip him this piece of advice: On the day marking the New Year, when he undoubtedly will address the nation, why not use the opportunity to order the Serbian army to close all the camps? "I would be disobeyed," he answers. I say: "But at least you will have earned a few lines in the history books. And I don't think you would be taking much of a chance. No one will dare attack you. You will be the hero of the day. You will be applauded by the whole world. You will have the support of all free men." He promises me to think it over. He lacked the courage and probably the conviction, for in his speech he said nothing. And anyway, his opponents replaced him. His enemy Milosevic took his place.

The war goes on in that part of the Balkans. The Serbian conquerors of the early days have been conquered in turn. The gods of war turned away and favored the other side. The Croats have gone on the offensive, and the Serbs themselves have become victims. The U.N. can do little. The power of death is supreme.

What I feel is total frustration and helplessness.

Day after day men keep killing each other; night after night men fall. And everywhere it is the children who lose hope. This is how it is, always. Adults make war, and children suffer. What can one do? Intervene? How? With arms? Make war on war? The debate divides America. A few months after my visit to Sarajevo, I am in Washington for the inauguration of the Holocaust Museum. I interrupt my speech, turn to President Clinton, and urge him to do something—anything—to stop the bloodshed over there. He is moved; he tells me so. Because my appeal corresponds to a sense of expectation in the country, it is taken up by the newspapers, quoted on radio, on television. I did not say that I favored a military intervention, but that is how my statement is interpreted. Charles Krauthammer, the *Time* editorialist, reproaches me for it. A Jew, he says, should not get involved in the Balkan war. According to him, I should not have launched my appeal from the "sacred place" that is the Holocaust Museum. I don't agree, Mr. Krauthammer. First of all, no museum is sacred. Secondly, when men are dying, when innocent people are subjected to rape and torture, when cities are being transformed into cemeteries, Jews do not have the right to be silent.

In 1992, Secretary of State Larry Eagleburger and I discuss the need to establish an international tribunal to judge crimes against humanity. Who knows but that it may discourage a leader, an officer, a uniformed assassin. For this type of crime there is to be no statutory limitation, no right of asylum. A person accused of crimes against humanity risks arrest anywhere at any time. The State Department favors the idea, but Europe is wallowing in hesitation. Finally there is agreement. We make up a first list. Karadjic and Mladic are on it.

We are now at the beginning of August 1995. "It's over," an American journalist tells me. "It's finished," a French diplomat chimes in. Nothing more to do. Sarajevo is lost. And so is Bosnia. The sad conclusion is that, as with Czechoslovakia in 1938, the leaders of this world have once again betrayed a nation whose independence had been recognized internationally. For Bosnia, ravaged and martyred, and to the shame of us all, the page will soon be turned.

And yet. We must carry on. All the humanitarian organizations are aware of this. We must not become resigned; the criminals never do.

Let us look around. History evidently learns nothing from its own lessons. The tragedy of Somalia is not limited to Somalia. The shame born of the war in Bosnia is spreading beyond the borders of former Yugoslavia. The reports of UNICEF disclose that one child dies of hunger or illness every second. And India, that great country dominated by spirituality, will it send its vindictive demons back to their caves? And what is really happening in the collective unconscious of the former Soviet Union? What will replace the notion of egalitarian Communism? How can one silence the hatred that opposes Azeris to Armenians, Romanians to Hungarians, the haves to the have-nots; the rise of racism in Eastern Europe, of xenophobia in Germany, of fanaticism in the Middle East, and of anti-Semitism everywhere? Blood is flowing and the world does not change. Watchman, what of the night?

I am rereading these notes in the beginning of 1996. How many transformations has the former Yugoslavia gone through since last year? How many cease-fires and armistices have been signed and betrayed? Still, the siege of Sarajevo has been lifted, as has that of Srebrenica. Is it because all sides are exhausted? Surely it is the result of Clinton's decision to send twenty thousand American soldiers to preserve the peace agreement, signed, thanks to Richard Holbrooke, in Dayton, Ohio. And then there are in the background the battalions of NATO and of Russia, which are also ready to assume their responsibilities.

The international tribunal in The Hague is gaining importance. Its emissaries have done good work. They have found the mass graves, unearthed the mutilated corpses. Witnesses have named and testified against the war criminals. It has taken a long time but finally international arrest warrants have been issued against Radovan Karadjic and Ratko Mladic.

To what extent is Slobodan Milosevic implicated personally? His story is not finished. Sarajevo has been replaced in the news by Kosovo; a tragedy straight out of the Middle Ages is unfolding there. Tens of thousands of uprooted families are fleeing their destroyed homes and burning villages on foot, on broken-down tractors, and in buses. More than ever before, the civilized world feels the need to intervene.

Television interviews, questions by audiences, articles, and a millennium lecture at the White House provide me with opportunities to offer comments. For kind people, good people want to know: What about the loss of civilian lives? It is Milosevic, not NATO, who bears the responsibility for their tragic deaths.

In May, Milosevic was charged by the international tribunal at The Hague with the ultimate offense—crimes against humanity—and indicted. And though it will not bring back his victims, he must be judged and condemned. The future of peace in the region depends on it.

I wrote the following essay for *Newsweek*. It appeared on April 12, 1999.

President Slobodan Milosevic is a criminal. Those who still believe that there are nonviolent ways to stop his inhuman actions against Albanians are naive. They forget the nature of the century we live in.

Some of the images seem to belong to the not-so-recent past. Summary executions, collective punishment, forced expulsion of tens of thousands of families, frightened children separated from their parents, endless lines of desperate refugees: following Sarajevo and Srebrenica, Kosovo has entered the long and bloody list of tragedies that bring dishonor to the outgoing 20th century.

Some observers call it genocide. According to the original 1951 United Nations definition, it is. Yet I have problems with its application to Kosovo. In my view, genocide is the intent and the desire to annihilate a people. This is not the case here. Massive violations of human rights and the murder of political opponents, as horrible as they may be, are elements of genocide-in-the-making, but they do not constitute genocide. Still, they are evil enough to inspire anger and the will to stop them.

As early as 1992, media coverage of the war in Bosnia mistakenly compared Serbian "ethnic cleansing" to the Holocaust. The Holocaust was conceived to annihilate the last Jew on the planet. Does anyone believe that Milosevic and his accomplices seriously planned to exterminate all the Bosnians, all the Albanians, all the Muslims in the world? Some reports referred to "Auschwitz" in Bosnia. I saw the prison camps at Banja Luka; the conditions were deplorable and the prisoners terrified. But it was not Auschwitz. Auschwitz was an extermination camp, a black hole in history. Victims were taken there to be turned into ashes. Now we are witnessing a nightmare in Kosovo; it demands action, not comparison.

Was NATO's decision to intervene correct? Was Washington right to push for it? The answer to both questions is yes. Faced with Milosevic's stubborn policy of ethnic cleansing, no self-respecting government or nation could knowingly violate the Biblical injunction "Thou shall not stand idly by."

Surely, when human lives are involved, indifference is not an answer. Not to choose is also a choice, said the French philosopher Albert Camus. Neutrality helps the aggressor, not his victims. If NATO had been created only to protect the weak and defenseless, that would be enough to justify its existence.

Critics of the attacks on Milosevic say that sending our army to the former Yugoslavia is not in America's national interest. From an economic or geopolitical viewpoint, the critics may have a point. But a nation is great not because of its wealth or its military might; its greatness is measured by the way it uses or abuses its wealth and power. In other words: its greatness derives from its commitment to moral principle.

Milosevic has followed an intolerable path of violence and destruction that must provoke revulsion in every civilized person. His policies are evil. Even one of his associates, the novelist turned politician Vuk Draskovic, admitted the possibility that "atrocities" are being committed. Naturally, they occur away from public view. The Yugoslav military and police have ordered witnesses to leave the country: for weeks, Kosovo has been turning into a ghetto. Belgrade's objective is now clear: a demographic change of the entire region. Is it too horrible to imagine that at the end of the war, there will be no more Albanians to enjoy their liberation in Kosovo?

I know Milosevic. I met him during the war in Bosnia, first at an international conference on Bosnia in London and later in Belgrade. I have spoken with officials and journalists who knew him well. Their analyses confirmed my impression of the man: a coldblooded cynic who never kept a promise, except when it was in his own best interest. His extremist political philosophy remained cloaked in facile patriotism. It is no accident that he is nicknamed "the butcher." He is ruthless with those who stand in his way. A fanatic, like most dictators whose argument is terror, he believes that the end always justifies the means. That is why he rejected Richard Holbrooke's last-minute efforts to save peace and Yevgeny Primakov's attempts to stop the hostilities: he is determined to consistently defy the international community's quest for a peaceful solution. He is interested not in peace, but in absolute domination.

But what about the cost in lives, including those of his own people? They are of no concern to him; his personal power alone matters. Hence his willingness to sacrifice innocent civilians, burning their homes and destroying their villages. With utter contempt for humanity, he has embarked on a state-sponsored program aimed at the humiliation, persecution and uprooting of an entire ethnic community.

Like all nightmares, this too will come to an end. And then Milosevic's actions in Bosnia will also be remembered. And he will appear before an international tribunal, charged with the ultimate offense: crimes against humanity. That hope must be part of his victims' victory.

And Yet—

A ND YET. One must wager on the future. To save the life of a single child, no effort is superfluous. To make a tired old man smile is to perform an essential task. To defeat injustice and misfortune, if only for one instant, for a single victim, is to invent a new reason to hope.

Oh yes, I know: It is not always easy to hope. Also, hope can become a trap whose victims are as unhappy as victims of despair. I came up against this problem when I was writing *The Forgotten*, which I had trouble finishing. I did not want to leave my young protagonist Malkiel faced with total despair. In all my novels I try to open or at least to indicate a path not toward salvation (does it exist?), but toward encounter, with the Other and also with oneself. In *The Forgotten*, the old hero, Elhanan, deprived of his memory and aware of the incurability of his disease, no longer has any hope of human contact. Who could possibly succeed in making him smile one more time? I saw no solution to the problem and kept the manuscript in a drawer for several months. Then very early one morning, as I was working, I heard my young son in the next room. And suddenly the solution was clear. I needed to help perform a transfusion of memory; as Elhanan's diminished, Malkiel's would be enriched.

At a certain age one becomes attached to certain words. I now love the word "transfusion."

☙

L AST NIGHT, *I saw my father in a dream. I see him more and more often. And before I fall asleep I don't know whether to fear or hope that he will appear. Each time I wake up trembling, a heavy weight on my chest.*

I have read some of my pages to him, particularly those that I have not yet written and that I may never write. Was he listening to me? I was listening to him, and yet he said nothing. Was I not listening properly? It may well be that of everything I have written or thought I had written, the words that reflected his silence will be the ones to remain.

⌘

I also dream about my mother and my little sister. I cry in my sleep. I try to learn about their last moments. Hilda walked with them a few steps more than I did. I want to question her about it. I don't dare. We speak every week but only about her health, her son, Sidney, her grandchildren. Yet I would like to know more about her experiences in the camp. I don't dare ask. It was the same with Bea. I know they were together in Kauferingen, not far from Dachau. When did they leave Birkenau? What cruelties did the Germans inflict on them? Hilda: "I remember that night, our last night in Auschwitz. That night they moved out a transport of twelve hundred women. Naked. Yes, naked. Bea and I were part of the transport. I remember. I remember even the date. In the cattle car, a very pious woman remarked: 'Today is Tisha b'Av, the ninth day of the month of Av, the saddest day of the year.'" What happened before, and later? I curse the reticence that renders me mute. Neither with Bea nor with Hilda have I spoken of our parents or our home. Am I afraid of bursting into tears?

I know that Hilda, just like Bea until her death, constantly thinks of our landscape of long ago. As do I. All the time.

In my study you will find no medals, no diplomas. But over the table where I work there hangs a single photograph. It shows my parents' home in Sighet. When I look up, that is what I see. And it seems to be telling me: "Do not forget where you came from."

I have just turned seventy. It is time to take stock again. The century I have lived through has been more violent and more promising than any other. Mankind has never before proved to be as vulnerable or as generous. Man lives in expectation. Expectation of what? The Jew in me is waiting for Redemption. And waiting for Redemption, he remembers his enemies. I have fought battles and won some, few in number, too few to derive pride and confidence from them. Anyway, I don't think I shall stop now. I trouble some people when I raise my voice, others when I don't speak up. There are people, good people, who often make me feel as though I owe them something. I don't resent it. There are some who understand my itinerary; others never will. I continue to learn—thus to take and give back—to reach out to others, to begin and begin again with every encounter. I have said certain words; I have kept others for future attempts to tell the tale that is waiting and will always be waiting to be told.

And I say to myself that even taking into account my stories and novels, my essays and studies, analyses and reminiscences, I know that it is not enough.

Help me, Father.

Long ago, *over there*, far from the living, we told ourselves over and over that if we were to come out alive, we would devote every moment of our lives to denouncing by word and deed the cynicism and silence of mankind toward victims past and future. Convinced that the free world knew nothing of the cursed and evil kingdom where death reigned, we encouraged one another. The one among us who would survive would testify for all of us. He would speak and demand justice on our behalf; as our spokesman he would make certain that our memory would penetrate that of humanity. He would do nothing else. His days and nights would be devoted to telling the story. He would turn his entire life into a weapon for our collective memory; thanks to him it would not be lost.

I was no exception. There were times after the liberation when I saw myself as a messenger carrying only one message: to say no to forgetting, to forgetting the life and death of the communities swallowed by night and spit back into the sky in flames. My only goal and obsession was to save them from a second death. I didn't know that I was like Kierkegaard's jester who shouted "Fire!" and people thought he was joking.

I saw myself crisscrossing the Earth, going from town to town, from country to country, like the madman in Rebbe Nahman's tales, reminding humans of the good and evil they are capable of, making them see the armies of ghosts hovering around and within us.

Then I stopped running, or let's say that I slowed my pace. I study, I teach, I guide my students toward their careers. I observe the passersby to guess their secrets. I am happy, I am sad. I continue to teach, to write. More books, more novels. In short, I try not to die before I die. Marion and I have founded a home, we have watched our son grow. He fills us with pride and happiness. Together we have tried to do useful things.

Marion, my wife, my ally, my confidante, it is she who often prevents me from making mistakes. It is to her that I owe the wisdom that enables me to follow a certain path. And she has remained young, which I am no longer.

Hilda's son and grandchildren in Israel are doing well. Oren and Orly have completed their military service. Bea's daughter, Sarah, is the mother of six children. Steve and Itzhaka are the parents of two. I was present at their wedding, and escorted Steve to the *Chuppah*. So as not to slide back into memories, I danced with the young bridegroom to the point of exhaustion.

I was both happy and sad. But more happy than sad. The lineage of Sarah and Shlomo Wiesel is not extinct.

In 1970 I spoke of my intention to end my testimony:

> . . . And now, teller of tales, turn the page. Speak to us of other things. Your mad prophets, your old men drunk with nostalgic waiting, your possessed—let them return to their nocturnal enclaves. They have survived their deaths for more than a quarter of a century; that should suffice. If they refuse to go away, at least make them keep quiet. At all costs. By every means. Tell them that silence, more than language, remains the substance and the seal of what was once their universe, and that, like language, it demands to be recognized and transmitted.*

A pessimistic assessment? I believed it then. I had decided not to speak of "it" anymore.

And today? Those born at the time that text was written are now almost thirty years old. They have their whole lives before them. Must we speak to them? Of whom? Of what? Of our past? To make sure that it will not become their future? To silence those who deny our past, those who wish to silence us?

And here I had dreamed of singing of memory and friendship in a world that sadly needs both.

"Remember," the Book commands us. In my tradition, memory

One Generation After (New York: Random House), 1970.

does not set people apart. On the contrary, it binds them one to the other and all to the origins of our common history. It is because I remember where I come from that I feel close to those I meet on the way. It is because man is capable of transforming his burdens into promises that he lives them fully. That is why to live without a past is worse than to live without a future. What would our civilization be if it were stripped of its memory? Memory is more than the sum of images and words, cries and deeds; it is even more than an individual or collective identity; it is the bond that ties us to the mystery of the beginning, this nebulous place where man's memory is reflected in God's.

That is why we stubbornly continue to bear witness.

And yet. Generations later, I confess to doubts. Have I failed my commitment? I have written books, but, with a few exceptions, they deal with other things. As said earlier, I have written on diverse subjects mostly in order not to evoke the one that, for me, has the greatest meaning.

I have been trying for a long time to understand why.

Let us start with the superficial reasons. I worried that I might speak of it poorly or, worse, for the wrong reasons. I feared that I might use the theme rather than be its servant. I was afraid of temptations, disappointments. And so I was content to say that one could say nothing.

Like most survivors, I tried to invent reasons to live, and a new concept of man in this insane world, and a new language. It is a primary language whose only purpose is to describe all that eludes writing, to cry without opening our mouths, to speak to the dead since they can no longer speak to us.

In July 1995, I return to our town. For a few hours I speak to two young visitors who bear your name, Father. I show them their grandparents' room. I stroll with them in the courtyard, in the little garden where Tsipouka liked to play. I can still see the sun's rays making her hair glisten like gold. I see her and, as always when I think of her, my eyes fill with tears. I must hide my face, hide inside my face.

We halt in front of my Grandmother Nissel's house. The window where long ago she waited for a small schoolboy on Fridays, to offer him a special roll, is closed. Seeing Tsipouka, she would smile. And my little sister would smile back. Right now I would so like to be able to speak of my grandmother with her black scarf on her head. And of the little girl with golden hair . . . but I cannot. My heart is pounding. Could I have returned to Sighet to die?

Here is the cemetery. Let us enter. Let us light a candle at the grave of Yetev Lev, one of the first Chief Rabbis of Sighet. May he intercede on your behalf.

How peaceful it is here. I plan to come back here one more time, with Hilda, Sidney, and his children.

And look, over there was the *heder*. My Masters. My friends. We must light candles for them as well. They have no graves.

And over there, across from us, the Borsher Rebbe's Beit Hamidrash. It is a few minutes' walk to the ritual baths; I went there every morning. The yeshiva was a little farther down, next to the Chief Rabbi's house.

I want to say something to my two young companions, but I cannot, for the tears are choking me. They know and discreetly stay behind.

We pray together in the poor, dilapidated synagogue, the only one left. Seated on a bench facing the empty Holy Ark, we open a dusty book we found lying on a lectern and study the pages dealing with the laws of mourning. Will we be the last Jews in this place to immerse ourselves in the study of holy texts?

At the railroad station we remain silent for a long moment. It is here that Jewish life in Sighet came to an end, carried off by the train's smoke.

Birkenau. How can I say to Elisha and Steve, Bea's son, what nobody could say to me. Their silence becomes one with mine. There is nothing left to say. The ramp, the cries, the screams, the night, the last glimpse of Tsipouka—is she crying? What is she saying to her mother? And what is your grandmother's answer? No doubt she is trying to reassure her. Don't be afraid, little girl. No need to be afraid anymore.

Did I say it out loud to my two companions whom I love with all my soul? Ours is the tree of an old Jewish family whose roots touch those of Rashi and King David. And look: Its branches refuse to wither.

We are having trouble finding Auschwitz III, also known as Buna. The last trace of the camp has disappeared. All that is left is a small plaque. A priest points toward a group of houses and buildings: "There." So close? Yes, the camp was that close. How does he know? He lives in the street that was next to it. From his window he could see everything. Everything? Yes, everything. The "roll calls"? Yes. The "exercises," the punishments, and the hangings as well? And it didn't prevent him from eating in the morning, sleeping at night? The priest shrugs his shoulders. I want to say something to my son and my nephew about what their grandfather endured a few steps away from here, but I say nothing.

It is the same in Buchenwald. The "big camp" has remained almost intact, like a museum. I ask our guide: Where is the "little camp"? He takes us to a forest: "Here." There are many trees, underbrush. Yes, that is all that remains of the hell where the Jews evacuated from Auschwitz suffered and died. There is not even a plaque to guide the lost visitor.

I lean against a tree. I close my eyes and look for my father.

Images are surfacing, blurring my sight. The arrival at night. The screams. The freezing water. The huge, stifling barrack. My father. My sick father, humiliated before my eyes. His delirium. His pain. My father, dying. My father, dead.

Nature here is at peace, indifferent to the rain and snow. It is beautiful in the spring, gray in the autumn. The Angel of Death has gone without leaving a trace.

How does one fight against the will to erase it all? And why did God create obscurity? To hide from His creatures? Is that why Giordano Bruno said that light is God's obscurity?

From all sides I am told to turn away from the past, to wager on the future. I am advised not to look back, to come out of *there*, to change key, to deal with other themes. Enough, I am told. You have done enough. Let others take over. Let them be the ones to be insulted. You have been hurt by the cowardly, vile insinuations, admit it. You are entitled to rest.

Should I listen to them, Father? Tell me.

ᘐ

*I*T IS YOU I WANT TO LISTEN TO *since they refuse to hear you. Let them snicker; I shall speak nevertheless. As long as I can breathe, I shall say the words that belong only to you. "Open a door for us," says a prayer in the* Neilah *service, before the end of Yom Kippur, "open a door for us at the hour when all the doors are closing,* *for twilight is upon us." Twilight is approaching, and I know that soon it will clasp me into its mysterious folds. You will be there, and you will lead me to the others, all those I have known and loved. Grandfather Dodye and Grandmother Nissel. And mother. And Tsipouka. And Bea. And all the uncles, the aunts, the cousins, the friends. I know that when I shall join your ranks, I will hear your voice at last.*

∾

As I write these words, I contemplate the photograph of my home; it is always before me, heavy and sealed under the weight of darkness. And yet I want to go back to Sighet one last time. To write the last pages.

I am not afraid of losing my way. Like Elhanan in *The Forgotten,* I am afraid of forgetting. I read, I reread what I have written, what others have written. And God in all that? I stumble on three poignant words in the Book of Lamentations—the prophet says to the Lord, *"Haragta lo khamalta,"* You killed, You had no pity. Earlier the prophet said to the Lord, "In Your anger, You hid and persecuted us." Why, God? Why? I am afraid to know the answer. I am afraid not to. But above all, I tremble at the idea that my memory could become empty, that I could forget the reasons that have allowed me to set one word after the other.

I am afraid to know the end before I begin.

When shall I begin, Father?

I feel like singing, singing of happiness and serenity. I want to love, to laugh, to accompany the lonely on their road to nowhere. I want to pursue the work God started in the heart of man.

How am I to sing, Mother, how am I to sing the songs that your father, Grandfather Dodye, taught us on Rosh Hashana eve?

How can one still love in this life, when you, Tsipouka, my gentle sister whose future was stolen by the enemy, when you entered death so small, so frail, so innocent?

I still have so many questions to ask you, Father. So many doors to open, so many secrets to discover. Will I have the time?

From the other room, or is it the other side of night, a sweet voice breaks into my daydream: "Did you call me, Father?"

I answer: "Yes, my son. I called you."

Glossary⟶

Aggadah	Traditional Jewish literature; commentaries, aphorisms, legends of the Talmud.
ahavat Israel	Love for, devotion to, the Jewish people.
aliyah	1) "Ascent" toward Jerusalem, hence immigration to Israel; 2) the honor of being called up to read a section of the weekly portion of the Torah.
Amidah	The principal daily prayer, recited standing and silently.
Aufruf	The tradition in which a bridegroom is called to the Torah on the Shabbat preceding his wedding.
bar mitzvah	The ceremony marking the assumption of adult religious responsibilities, at age thirteen.
Beit (Ha)midrash	A house of study and prayer; a synagogue.
Besht	Initials of Baal Shem Tov, the "Master of the Good Name," founder of the Hasidic movement.
Bimah	The raised platform used for the reading of the Torah.
B'nai B'rith	A Jewish social and philanthropic organization.
chuppah	At a wedding, the canopy under which the marriage ceremony is performed.
genizah	A hiding place for sacred books and objects.
Haganah	The well-known Jewish paramilitary self-defense organization in Palestine.
Halakhah	The body of rabbinical law.
Halakhic	Relating to Halakhah.
Hasid (Hasidim)	Literally, "pious man." A disciple of the movement founded by the Baal Shem Tov.

Havdalah	The ceremony at the conclusion of Shabbat marking its separation from the rest of the week.
heder	A religious elementary school; Hebrew school.
Irgun	A Jewish nationalist underground organization which fought against the British occupation in Palestine.
Kaddish	The prayer for the dead.
kipa	A skullcap, or yarmulka, worn by Jewish males.
Kol Nidre	The prayer opening the Yom Kippur evening service.
kosher	Ritually pure, in accordance with dietary laws.
Marranos	Spanish Jews who, though forced to convert to Catholicism, continued to practice Judaism clandestinely.
mezuzah	A parchment containing passages from the Pentateuch that is rolled into a case and affixed to the doorpost as an expression of faith.
midrash	A parable; a story that embodies and expresses moral teaching or a tenet of faith; also, a volume of midrashim.
Minha	The afternoon service.
minyan	A quorum of ten men required for a communal religious service.
Mishna	The codification of the Oral Law based upon the laws and commandments of the Torah, and the basis in turn for the Gemara, or Talmud.
mitzvah	A divine commandment.
Musaf	The additional service following the main morning service on the Shabbat and holidays.
Neilah	The concluding service of Yom Kippur.
Palmah	An elite Haganah strike force whose members were recruited from kibbutzim.
Pesach	Passover, the Jewish holiday celebrating the Exodus from Egypt.
Purim	The holiday (marked by games, exchanges of gifts, and skits) commemorating the victory of the Jews of Persia over their enemy Haman.
Rosh Hashana	The Jewish New Year.
rosh yeshiva	The head of a rabbinical academy.
Seder	The ritual meal on Passover, during which the story of the Exodus from Egypt is told.
Sefer Torah	Sacred parchment scroll containing the books of the Pentateuch.
Shaharit	The morning service.

Shavuot	Pentecost; chiefly commemorates the Giving of the Law on Mount Sinai.
shivah	The first period of mourning, which lasts seven days.
shofar	The ram's horn used in Rosh Hashana and Yom Kippur services.
shtetl	A Jewish village in Eastern Europe.
shtibel	A Hasidic place of prayer.
shtreimel	The wide-brimmed fur hat traditionally worn by Hasidim.
siddur	A prayer book.
Simhat Torah	The holiday celebrating the completion of the year-long reading of the Torah, and the renewal of the cycle of readings, beginning with Genesis.
Sukkot	The Feast of Tabernacles.
tallit	A ritual prayer shawl.
Talmud	The vast collection of rabbinical teachings, laws, and commentaries based upon the Mishna (*q.v.*); also called the Gemara.
tefillin	Phylacteries—two small leather boxes containing four passages from the Pentateuch; one is strapped to the left forearm and one to the forehead during weekday morning prayers.
Tisha b'Av	The Ninth of Av, a day of fasting in memory of the destruction of the Temple, which according to tradition occurred on this date.
Torah	The five Books of Moses, or Pentateuch; in the broader sense, the sum total of Jewish lore and learning, of which the Pentateuch is the foundation.
Tsahal	The Israeli army.
Vidui	A confession of sins.
Yad Vashem	The Holocaust museum in Jerusalem.
yahrzeit	The anniversary of the death of a parent.
yeshiva (pl. yeshivot)	A talmudic academy.
Yizkor	A service in memory of the dead, recited on the three festivals of Sukkot, Pesach, and Shavuot, and on Yom Kippur.
Yom Kippur	The Day of Atonement, the culmination of the Ten Days of Penitence which begin with Rosh Hashana, and the most sacred day in the Jewish year.

Index

Aarvik, Egil, 257, 268–71, 282, 289, 375
Abrahamson, Irving, *Against Silence,* 154
Abrams, Elliott, 215
Abramson, Sonny, 223–4, 234, 242–7
Académie Universelle des Cultures, 328–9
Adler, Laure, 328
African Americans, 144, 382
Agnelli, Susanna, 383
Agnew, Spiro, 53
Agranat Commission, 56, 57, 58
Ahlmark, Per, 232, 256–7
Ahrweiler, Hélène, 280, 288
AIDS, 112, 286
Akiba, Rabbi, 145
Allende, Salvador, 53
Allon, Yigal, 315
Alzheimer's disease, 362–4
American-German Commission, 220–1
Améry, Jean, 102–3
Amin, Idi, 76–7
Amiqam, Eliyahu, 9, 39
Amiqam, Ruth, 9
Amir, Yigal, 135
"Anatomy of Hate" conferences, 135, 369–83
Anderson, Gieske, 271, 375
Anielewicz, Mordechai, 104, 118
"*Ani Maamin,* a Song Lost and Found Again," 66–9, 127, 272

anti-Semitism, 18–19, 48, 72, 93, 109, 110, 124, 128, 145, 155, 171, 175, 198, 213, 214, 380, 396; in Austria, 294–5; history of, 48, 103–4; in Japan, 289–90; in Romania, 292–4; Vichy, 329–32; *see also* Holocaust
Antonescu, Ion, 293–4
apartheid, 93–4, 146, 375
Apion the Greek, 48, 174
Arafat, Yasir, 53, 72, 73, 134, 308; visit to Paris, 319–22
Arendt, Hannah, 347
Arens, Moshe, 305–6
Argentina, 97
Arkoun, Mohammed, 370
Armenia, 92, 145, 186, 211, 396
Aron, Raymond, 89
Asahi Shimbun, 96, 383
Aschehoug, 24
Attali, Jacques, 239, 258, 278–82, 320, 331, 333–6; *Verbatim,* 335
Auschwitz, 4, 18, 19, 69, 72, 81, 93, 95–6, 129, 135, 145, 149, 170, 175, 184, 224, 284, 290, 299, 361, 388, 398, 404; Carmelite convent controversy, 124–5, 171–2; EW's return visits to, 191–4, 195, 198, 282; exhibitions, 153; fiftieth-anniversary liberation ceremonies, 194–8, 282; as film subject, 118–22, 123; liberation of, 203–4, 216, 283

Australia, 290
Austria, 128, 294–6; Anschluss, 295

Baader-Meinhof group, 77
Baal Shem Tov, Israel, 28, 29
Babi-Yar, 119, 120, 184, 188, 199–200, 228, 302, 356
Baez, Joan, 89
Baker, James, 379
Balkan war, 387–99
Barbie, Klaus, 299; trial of, 299–302
Barenboim, Daniel, 314
Bar-Lev, Gen. Haim, 20–1, 57
Barthélémy, Michel, 301
Beckett, Samuel, 15
Begin, Menachem, 10, 37, 59, 75, 77, 78, 93, 148, 182, 256, 315; 1977 peace talks, 78–9
Beilin, Yossi, 382
Beit Hatefutsot, 243
Bellow, Saul, 279
Ben-Gurion, David, 27, 36, 40, 58, 256, 315
Ben Jelloun, Tahar, 89
Benkow, Jo, 259, 374
ben Nathan, Asher, 60
Berenbaum, Michael, 184, 189, 247
Bergen-Belsen, 10–11, 216, 229, 233; Reagan's visit to, 240
Berkowitz, Moshe-Chaim, 69, 192
Berlin, 220–1, 340, 350
Bernstein, Irving, 59, 60, 189, 241, 242
Bernstein, Robert, 15, 51
Besançon, Julien, 93
Bettelheim, Bruno, 345, 349
Bialkin, Kenneth, 228, 229
Bible, 3–4, 6, 48, 88, 94, 144, 313, 315, 318
Birkenau, 50, 67, 104, 153, 183, 248, 283, 302, 404, 408; EW's return visits to, 191–4, 195, 198, 282; fiftieth-anniversary liberation cere-monies, 196–8
Bitburg affair, 36, 39, 215, 224, 227–50
Black September movement, 20, 50
Bö, Erik, 258
Böll, Heinrich, 74
Bonner, Elena, 375
Bookbinder, Hyman, 184, 189, 222–3
Borgen, Johan, 24–7
Borowski, Tadeusz, 345

Boschwitz, Rudy, 97
Bosnia, 154–5, 197, 220, 289; war, 387–99
Boston Globe, 382
Boston University, 79, 106–12, 154, 163, 239, 370
Bousquet, René, 313, 329–32, 339
Bousquet affair, 319, 322, 329–40
Boutros-Ghali, Boutros, 388
Brademas, John, 211
Braman, Irma and Norman, 189, 241
Brandt, Willy, 74, 280
Breger, Marshall, 232, 235–6
Brezhnev, Leonid, 200
Brin, Herb, 130
Brod, Max, 107
Brooks, Peter, 110
Brown, Robert McAfee, 52, 222, 241, 373
Bruno, Giordano, 409
Buchanan, Patrick, 228–9, 234, 237
Buchenwald, 79, 119, 121, 131, 193, 409; liberation of, 216
Buddhism, 370
Buna, 24, 345, 408–9
Bunam of Pshiskhe, Rebbe, 107
Burger, David, 290
Burns, Arthur, 233
Bush, George, 237, 281; Gulf War and, 305, 309

Cambodia, 89–91, 272, 279, 284; Khmer Rouge regime, 76, 90
Camus, Albert, 88, 261, 361, 398
Canada, 37
Cargas, Harry, 52, 373
Carter, Jimmy, 33, 89, 129, 374, 375; Holocaust Commission, 33, 179–205, 209–12, 224, 242, 249; Teheran hostage crisis, 211–12
Casaroli, Cardinal, 174
Catholic Church, 124, 146, 167–75, 219, 283, 371
Ceaușescu, Nicolae, 322
Celan, Paul, 345
Centre Rachi lectures, 145, 154, 288
Chauffier, Jean-Martin, 131
China, 21, 52
Chirac, Jacques, 258, 280–1, 288
Christianity, 146, 167–75, 282–3, 371, 394

Churchill, Winston, 381
Cicero, Marcus Tullius, 48
Ciechanover, Joseph "Yossi," 78, 187, 256–7, 272
City College of New York, 49, 106
Clinton, Bill, 194, 249; Balkan policy, 395, 396
Clinton, Hillary, 382
Cohen, Gaby, 219
Cohen, Yehoshua, 58
collective guilt, 152, 235, 347
Communism, 15, 28, 64, 87, 90, 189, 195, 263, 267, 322, 327, 379, 381, 396
Congress, U.S., 179, 183–4, 188, 210–13, 223, 228, 230
Congressional Gold Medal ceremony, 229–39
Conrad, Joseph, 361
Copenhagen, 93, 204, 272–3
Cosic, Dobrica, 388–91, 294–5
Council of Jewish Federations, 1971 convention of, 34–6
"Courage to Care" conference, 218–20
Craig, Marian, 184, 232, 246
Croatia, 155, 387–99
Crusades, 103, 167
Cuomo, Mario, 381
Czechoslovakia, 14, 396
Czerniakow, Adam, 104

Dachau, 50, 216, 240
Dagbladet (newspaper), 254, 256
Daoud, Abu, 79–81
Dayan, Moshe, 54, 58–9, 66, 78, 256
Day of Remembrance, annual, 183–4, 187–8, 211–14, 220, 233, 243, 320
Deaver, Michael, 232–4, 237
de Gaulle, Charles, 15, 20, 334
Democritus, 48
Denmark, 93, 204
Derogy (Jacques) and Carmel (Hesi), *Le siècle d'Israël*, 58
Derwich, Mahmoud, 125
Diaspora Jews, 59–64, 72, 93, 134–7, 190, 273, 307–8, 373
Dickens, Charles, 361
displaced persons, 24, 103
Dobrynin, Anatoly, 188
Dodd, Christopher, 97
Doi, Takako, 383

Domenach, Jean-Marie, 124–5
Dostoyevsky, Fyodor, 361; *The Possessed*, 95
Dubinin, Yuri, 324
Dubnow, Simon, 61–2
Durand, Claude, 335

Eagleburger, Lawrence, 383, 395–6
Eban, Abba, 36–40, 55, 58, 75, 88, 89
Edelman, Lily, 15, 34, 205
Eder, Richard, 92
Egypt, 54, 56, 75, 132; 1977 peace talks, 78
Eichmann, Adolf, 9, 119, 128, 169, 221; trial of, 9, 37, 118, 141
Einav, Zalman, 224, 234
Einstein, Albert, 40
Eisenhower, Dwight D., 40
Eitinger, Leo (Sjua), 24–5, 271, 289, 372
Eizenstat, Stu, 181–2, 209–11
Eleazar, "Dado," 57–8
Elisha ben Abuya, 83
El Salvador, 94
Ennis, Jean, 15
Entebbe Airport incident, 76–7
Estes, Simon, 375
Ethics of Our Fathers, The, 131, 154

Fayard, 335
Feig, Dodye, 28, 30, 410
Figaro, Le, 72
Figaro Littéraire, 131, 132
Fischman, Bernie, 187, 282
Fisher, Max, 35–6, 228, 229
Flinker, Moshe, 104
Flynn, Bill, 279
Ford, Gerald, 35, 74, 75
Ford, Henry, III, 222
Fortas, Abe, 15
Foss, Lukas, 66, 375
Foundation for Humanity, 277–9, 281, 289, 369–83; conferences, 96, 135, 277–87, 369–83
Fox, Richard, 228
France, 10, 15, 49, 52, 54, 74, 94, 102, 124, 145, 167–8, 214, 219, 258, 267, 288, 348; Barbie trial, 299–302; Abu Daoud affair, 79–81; deportation of Jewry, 313, 322, 329, 330, 331; Mitterrand, and Jewish

France (cont'd)
  memory, 313–42; Nobel laureate
  conference (1987), 277–87; Palestinian relations with, 319–22; Vichy
  regime, 319, 329–32, 336–7
France-Culture, 313
Frank, Anne, 104
Freed, James Ingo, 244, 248
Freedman, Monroe, 209–11, 212, 218,
  243
Frost, David, 37
"Future of Hope" conference (1995),
  96, 383

Galbraith, John Kenneth, 374, 376
Galway, James, 375
Gay and Lesbian Anti-Violence Project, 381–2
Gedalia, Rebbe, 291
Gelb, Arthur, 232, 235, 237, 349, 375,
  380
genocide colloquium (1982), 220
Genocide Treaty, 96–7
Germany, 25, 54, 74, 81, 93, 210, 220,
  307, 340, 350, 396; guilt issue, 146,
  152, 228, 235; Munich Olympics
  (1972), 50, 59, 81; persecution of
  Jews, 18, 37, 53, 93, 95–6, 119,
  128–9, 149, 186, 221, 228, 249,
  356–7; Reagan trip to Bitburg,
  227–47; reunification, 131; terror-
  ism, 76–7; see also Nazism
Ghetto (play), 123
Ghetto Fighters Kibbutz, 147–8
Giamatti, Bart, 110
Giscard d'Estaing, Valéry, 74, 79–81
Gitlis, Ivry, 288
"Global Survival" conference (1990),
  145
God, 318; EW's attitude toward, 147,
  272, 286, 309, 358, 360–5, 371,
  409–10; see also specific religions
Goldberg, Arthur, 75, 180, 185, 186,
  188, 209
Goldenberg's restaurant attack, 322
Goldman, Dr. Bollek, 56, 57
Goldstein, Maurice, 195
Goldstone, Richard, 382
Goodfriend, Isaac, 213
Gorbachev, Mikhail, 145, 153, 262,

  265–7, 378–81; EW's relationship
    with, 379–81; 1991 arrest of, 323–8
Gorbachev, Raissa, 381
Gordimer, Nadine, 288, 376
Gottschalk, Alfred, 246
Gouri, Haïm, 8
Gradowski, Zalmen, 104, 105
Grass, Günter, 374
Grasset, 336
Great Britain, 54
Greek Jews, 302
Greenberg, Yitz, 49, 106, 109, 182,
  184, 186, 188–9, 246, 370
Greve, Tim, 232
Grinwald, Marie-Odile, 358
Gros, François, 280
Gross, Ted, 49, 106
Grosser, Alfred, 124
Guatemala, 94
Gulf War, 134, 135, 305–9
Gur, Motta, 16–18, 77
Gyllenstein, Lars, 272
Gypsies, 130, 186, 211

HaCohen of Avignon, Mordechai, 103
Hadrian, Emperor, 103
Haganah, 9
Haider, Jorg, 294
Haifa University conference, 373
Haig, Alexander, 215
Halevy, Binyamin, 9–10
Halevy, Ofra, 9
Halevy, Yehuda, 54
Halfon, Samy, 164
Hallo, Bill, 111
Halperin, Irving, 52
Halperin, Sam, 245
Hamas, 95
Hamburg, David, 370
Hanin, Roger, 314
Harel, Issar, 128
Hartman, Geoffrey, 110
Hasidism, 3, 6, 16, 21, 27–30, 42, 69,
  107, 143, 144, 154, 291–2, 309, 316,
  364
hate, EW's views on, 369–83
Havel, Václav, 374, 376
Hearst, Patty, 74
Helms, Jesse, 96–7
Hepburn, Audrey, 272, 375

Hertzberg, Arthur, 93
Herzog, Chaim, 249, 258, 273
Hesburgh, Theodore, 33, 185
Heschel, Abraham Joshua, 6, 12, 14, 41, 42
Heschel, Sylvia, 12
Heydrich, Reinhard, 221
Heyerdahl, Gerd Host, 25
Himmler, Heinrich, 119, 198
Hiroshima, 95–6, 148; "The Future of Hope" conference (1995), 96, 383
Hitler, Adolf, 48, 72, 73, 93, 95, 96, 129, 149, 168, 169, 294, 295
Ho Chi Minh, 53
Holbrooke, Richard, 194, 197, 396, 399
Hollander, Eli, 307
Holocaust, 11, 18, 29, 33, 67, 95–6, 167; burning of living children, 238; Day of Remembrance for, 183–4, 187–8, 211–14, 220, 233, 243, 320; "deniers," 268, 294, 388; EW's personal experience of, 216–17, 219, 238, 253–4, 270–1, 274, 301–2, 345–6, 404, 405, 408–9; EW's teaching of, 102–5; EW's views on, 18–19, 67–70, 72–3, 102–5, 117–30, 135, 144, 148–52, 179–205, 209–24, 355–65, 398, 405; exhibitions, 153, 243, 248; gassing of camp inmates, 105, 119, 120, 122, 129, 150, 193, 248, 356; guilt issue, 146, 152, 228, 235, 347; hidden children, 149–52, 219; Jewish passivity during, 68, 118, 192, 249, 302, 356–7; liberation of camps, 194, 203–4, 215–18, 282, 283; as literary subject, 104–5, 120, 123, 124, 345–51, 355–65; memory issue, 104–5, 117–22, 129–30, 175, 179–205, 209–24, 227–50, 268, 319–42, 345, 357, 406–7; as television and film subject, 117–23; terminology, 18; Warsaw Ghetto, 60, 67–8, 104, 118, 147–8, 189–90, 230, 238, 248, 249, 302, 319; *see also* anti-Semitism; Holocaust Memorial Council; Holocaust survivors; Nazism; *and individual camps*
Holocaust Memorial Council, 130, 205, 209–24, 230–50, 262; Bitburg affair and, 230–47; EW's resignation from, 245–9; fundraising, 222–4, 247; museum project, 234, 243–50, 395
Holocaust survivors, 18, 102–3, 123, 147–8, 271; Bergen-Belsen, 10–11; Bitburg affair and, 227–50; children of, 21, 22, 55, 102–3, 358; criticism of, 124–31; EW's dedication to, 19, 102–5, 122, 123, 129–30, 149–52, 179–205, 209–24, 269, 290, 302, 405, 407; forgiveness issue, 22, 129–30, 194; guilt experienced by, 254, 345, 347; hidden children, 149–52, 219; liberation and readjustment, 204, 215–18; psychosomatic problems, 24–5, 345, 346, 349; suicides, 345–51; writings of, 105, 345–51, 356–7; *see also* Holocaust
Huberband, Shimon, 104
Hungary, 105, 210, 299, 396
Hussein, Rashid, 305–8
Huth, Pierre, 196

Iasi pogrom, 292
Iliescu, Pres., of Romania, 293–4
India, 95, 396
Inquisition, 167
International Auschwitz Committee, 195
International Committee for Jerusalem, 8
International Rescue Committee, 89, 272
Intifada, 132, 134, 285, 320
Iran, 211–12
Iraq, 305–9
Israel, 8, 9, 10, 28, 51, 62–3, 131, 172, 243, 293, 318, 373, 375, 380, 394; -Arab problem, 20, 92–3, 125–7, 132, 267–8, 273, 285, 318, 319–22, 373, 382; Begin government, 78–9, 93; criticism of, 60–5, 92–3, 124–5, 131–7, 273; Diaspora and, 60–5, 134–7; Eban scandal, 36–40; EW's visits to, 8–10, 55–8, 92–3, 126–7, 136, 147, 181, 204, 272–4, 305–9; Gulf War and, 305–9; Lebanese war, 92–3; Meir government, 36–40, 54–8; mid-1970s, 74–83; 1977

Israel (*cont'd*)
  peace talks, 78–9; nuclear capabili-
    ties, 55; Peres government, 321;
    Rabin government, 56, 75, 77, 78,
    320–1; Shamir government, 267–8,
    273, 305, 309, 315, 319–20; Six-
    Day War, 16–17, 50, 57, 65–6, 93;
    and Teheran hostage crisis, 212; UN
    policy on, 88–9; war of attrition,
    20–1, 49–50; Yom Kippur War,
    52–9, 60, 75, 78, 79; *see also*
    Jerusalem; Palestine
Israel Defense Forces (IDF), 74, 76;
  Ugandan operation, 76–7
Israeli emigrants, 263, 327
Israeli Supreme Court, 56, 127
Italy, 168, 345, 382
Izetbegovic, Alija, 388, 389, 393–4

Jackson, Henry "Scoop," 185
Jackson, Jesse, 240
Jackson, Dr. Leonard (brother-in-law),
  8, 50, 70
Jackson, Steve (nephew), 8, 66, 70, 71,
  293, 306, 406, 408
Jacob, Odile, 332, 335–7, 340
Jacobson, Gershon, 14
Jaffe, Dick, 101
Jakubowicz, Alain, 299, 301
Japan, 95–6, 383; EW's visits to, 96,
  289–90, 300, 301, 383
Jaruzelski, Gen., 281–3
Jasmin, Claude, 153
Jaspers, Karl, 347
Jennifer (stepdaughter), 11
Jerusalem, 4, 7, 9, 15, 16, 56, 132,
  273–4, 318, 363; EW's feelings for,
  16–17, 49, 64, 134, 136, 148–9, 153,
  258, 318–19; temples ransacked, 18;
  terrorism in, 95; Yad Vashem, 183,
  204, 219, 220
Jewish Agency, 60–5
Jewish Daily Forward (*Forverts*), 14, 348
Jews, 34, 48, 59, 170, 319; American,
  34–6, 55, 145, 153, 233; in antiquity, 48; converted, 167–75, 290;
  ethics of, 146; Judeocentrism accusation, 124–5, 129–30; memory
  issue, 36, 37, 48, 104–5, 117–22,
  129–30, 175, 179–205, 209–24,
  227–50, 268, 319–42, 345, 357,

406–7; opponents of EW, 127–31,
  235–6, 273, 308, 322; *see also* anti-
  Semitism; Diaspora Jews; Hasidism;
  Holocaust; Holocaust survivors;
  Soviet Jews
Johansen, Jan Otto, 258
John Paul II, Pope, 167, 175–6, 294
John XXIII, Pope, 168
Jordan, 20, 74
Josephus, Flavius, 48, 174
Joxe, Pierre, 316
Judkowski, Dov, 9, 14, 141, 258, 273
Judkowski, Lea, 9

Kabbalah, 173
Kaddish, 89–91, 175, 186, 195, 198,
  282
Kafka, Franz, 63, 70, 107, 163, 346,
  361
Kahan, Haim-Hersh, 25, 257
Kalman (Kabbalist), 4, 25
Kalugin, Gen. Oleg, 379
Kamhi of Narbonne, Rabbi Joseph, 174
Kamm, Henry, 90
Kant, Immanuel, 142
Kaplan, Chaim, 104
Karadjic, Radovan, 388, 389, 394, 396,
  397
kashrut, 315
Kastner, Rudolf, 9–10
Katzir, Aharon, 50
Kauferingen, 404
Kazantzakis, Nikos, 25–6, 163, 361;
  Zorba the Greek, 25
Kennedy, Edward, 15
Kennedy, John F., 40, 187
Kennedy Foundation, 145
Khadumi, Faruq, 321
Kiev, 199–200, 290
Kissinger, Henry, 52, 53, 74–6, 212,
  228, 258, 279–80, 284, 305; Israeli
  policy, 74–5
Klarsfeld, Beate and Serge, 301
Klein, Menashe, 90, 273–4, 309
Koch, Ed, 259
Koenig of Safad, Rabbi, 291
Koestler, Arthur, 108
Kohl, Helmut, 130, 227, 294, 340;
  Bitburg affair, 227–34, 237, 240
Kollek, Teddy, 7–8, 273
Konrad, György, 374–5

Koppel, Ted, 389
Korotich, Vitaly, 380
Kosinski, Jerzy, 347–9
Kosovo, 397–9
Kouchner, Bernard, 154, 383
Kraus, Moishe, 51
Krauthammer, Charles, 395
Kravetz, Marc, 299, 301, 389
Kreisky, Bruno, 54
Krieger, Richard, 243, 247
Kristallnacht, 119, 152
Kudler, Nathan (brother-in-law), 51
Kurds, 124, 308
Kuwait, 305

Landbergis, Vytautas, 374
Lang, Jack, 277–8, 313, 323, 324, 328,
　　333, 383
Langer, Lawrence, 52
Langford, Jim, 33
Langfus, Reb Arye Laib, 104, 105
Lanzmann, Claude, 28, 122–3
Latarget, Bernard, 328
Lauder, Ronald, 281
Lautenberg, Frank, 210, 235, 242
Lauvergeon, Anne, 331, 332, 338–9
"Leaders of Tomorrow" conference
　　(1995), 382–3
Lebanon, 74, 95, 308; war in, 92–3
Lecanuet, Jean, 325, 326, 327
Lederberg, Joshua, 279, 283
Len (brother-in-law), 8, 50, 70
Léotard, François, 378
Lerman, Miles, 188, 210, 222, 242–7,
　　249
Le Seuil, 49, 102, 335–6
Leventhal, Zalmen, 104
Levi, Primo, 108, 345–7
Levinas, Emmanuel, 174
Levitte, Georges, 43
Lévy, Bernard-Henri, 90, 124, 299, 300
Lévy-Willard, Annette, 337
Libération, 301, 337
Liberators' Conference (1981), 204,
　　215–18, 219
Lieberman, Saul, 4, 6, 8, 12, 14, 31, 42,
　　60, 67, 83, 109, 130, 168, 169, 187,
　　273
Lifton, Robert Jay, 372–3
Lithuania, 210, 273
Lookstein, Joseph, 53

Lubavitcher Rebbe, 41–2, 258, 309
Lubavitcher sect, 4, 14
Lublin, 216
Lubrani, Uri, 382
Lundestad, Geir, 374
Lustiger, Jean-Marie, Cardinal, 167–75
Lyon, 299–302

Maalot massacre, 74, 95
Maimonides, 88
Majdanek, 18, 216
Malka, Shlomo, 174
Malraux, André, 8, 10
Mandela, Nelson, 374, 375
Mann, Thomas, 361
Marash, David, 389
Markish, Peretz, 88
Markish, Shimon, 88, 145, 189
Mauriac, François, 26, 133–4, 169, 361
Mauthausen, 216
McGovern, George, 51–2
Meed, Benjamin, 179, 189–90, 234
Meir, Golda, 20, 36, 56, 75, 78; EW's
　　relationship with, 20, 58, 60, 126,
　　127; Yom Kippur War and, 54–5, 58
Melchior, Bent, 272
Melchior, Michael, 256–7, 262, 271,
　　272, 374
Mendel of Kotzk, Rebbe, 29, 30, 107
Mendelovich, Iosif, 201
Mendelssohn, Moses, 12–14
Menem, Carlos, 97
Mengele, Josef, 128, 169, 193
Meyerhoff, Bud, 224, 242–7, 249
Michnik, Adam, 378
Milhaud, Darius, 66, 67
Milosevic, Slobodan, 388, 389, 395–9
Minsk, 228
Miskito Indians, 91–2
Mitterrand, Danielle, 270, 315
Mitterrand, François, 74, 92, 168, 174,
　　214–15, 239, 258, 266–7, 277–81,
　　374, 375; Arafat and, 319–22; Bous-
　　quet affair, 329–40; death of, 341–2;
　　EW's "dialogues" with, 319–20,
　　331–2, 333–40; EW's relationship
　　with, 214–15, 277–87, 313–42;
　　Nobel laureate conference and,
　　277–81, 283–7; Soviet coup d'état
　　and (1991), 323–8; Vichy past,
　　329–32, 336–8

Mladic, Ratko, 396, 397
Mombaz, Jack, 37
Momjian, Set, 211
Monde, Le, 125, 172, 340, 348
Monod, Jacques, 145
Morgaine, Daniel, 290
Morillon, Jacques, 375
Morillon, Gen. Philippe, 391, 393
Moscow, 145, 188, 200–4, 261–7;
  "Anatomy of Hate" conference
  (1991), 378–80; "Global Survival"
  conference (1990), 145; 1991 coup
  d'état, 323–8
Moshe the beadle (the madman), 4, 5
Mossad, 77, 128, 212
Moussa, Amr, 305
Mozes, Noah, 9, 14
Mozes, Paula, 9
Munich Olympics (1972), 50, 59, 81
Munteanu, Aurel, 292
Muslims, 198, 371, 373, 391, 394
mysticism, 316, 351

Nahmanides, 174
Nahman of Bratzlav, Rebbe, 30, 50, 53,
  59–60, 83, 101, 108–9, 290–2, 331,
  350, 405; "The Seven Beggars," 108
Nathan (brother-in-law), 51
Nathan of Nemirov, Rebbe, 109
NATO, 211, 227, 396, 398
Nazism, 18, 37, 53, 95–6, 105, 119,
  128–9, 169, 186, 204, 221, 228, 249,
  294, 302, 371, 378; Nuremberg
  trials, 9, 95, 200–2, 228, 240; SS
  activities, 227–50, 331, 356–7; *see
  also* Holocaust
Netanyahu, Ben-Zion, 77
Netanyahu, Yoni, 77
New Leader, 349
Newsweek, 238, 397
New York, 38, 49, 65, 82, 141, 220,
  254, 259, 316; 92nd Street "Y" lec-
  tures, 82–3, 154, 259; "To Save Our
  Children" conference (1992), 381–2
New York Times, 16, 40, 72, 90, 92, 93,
  117, 122, 128, 134, 143, 153, 168,
  175, 195, 232, 238, 258, 261, 339,
  347, 375, 393
New York University, 112
Nicaragua, 91–2
Nicholas (friend of EW), 9

92nd Street "Y" lectures, 82–3, 154,
  259
Nister, Der, 88, 145, 189
Nixon, Richard, 15, 35, 53, 60, 75;
  1972 reelection, 51–2; Watergate
  scandal, 52, 53, 73–4
Nobel laureate conference (1988),
  277–87, 369
Nobel Prize, 124, 129, 130, 218,
  253–74, 277, 323, 374; ceremony,
  268–72; effects of, for EW, 277–96
Nordhausen, 216
Northern Ireland, 95
Norway, 24–6, 254, 289, 336; EW
  awarded Nobel Prize, 254–72
Notre Dame Press, 33
Nouvel Observateur, Le, 322, 330, 335
nuclear weapons, 55, 95–6, 229, 286,
  318
Nudel, Ida, 262
Nuremberg trials, 9, 95, 200–2, 228,
  240

O'Brien, Conor Cruise, 374
O'Connor, John, Cardinal, 174
Okamoto, Kozo, 50
Olav V, King of Norway, 268
Olmert, Ehud, 374
Olympic Games (1972, Munich), 50,
  59, 81
O'Neill, Thomas P. "Tip," 179
Ortega, Daniel, 91, 92
Oslo, 24–6, 125, 256, 258, 267–72,
  289; "The Anatomy of Hate and
  Conflict Resolution" conference
  (1990), 374–8
Oslo Declaration, 376–7
Ozick, Cynthia, 52

Palestine, 321, 322, 363; *see also* Israel;
  Palestinians
Palestine Liberation Organization
  (PLO), 76, 134, 320, 321
Palestinians, 20, 64, 93, 125–6, 131,
  267–8; EW's feelings toward, 125–7,
  134–7, 256, 268, 273, 285, 373–4;
  Intifada, 132, 134, 285, 320; -Israeli
  problem, 20, 92–3, 125–7, 132,
  267–8, 273, 285, 318, 319–22, 373,
  382; as prisoners, 125–7; terrorism,
  50, 54, 73, 76, 79, 320, 321

Paris, 83, 145, 154, 168, 288, 299, 313–15, 317, 323, 337, 349–50; Arafat in, 319–22; deportation of Jewry, 313, 322, 329, 330, 331; Nobel laureate conference (1988), 277–87

Passover, 8, 355

Péan, Pierre, 319, 329; *Une jeunesse française*, 329–30

Peck, Gregory, 375

Pei, I. M., 244

Penthouse, 130

Perechodnik, Calel, 356

Peres, Shimon, 77, 78, 95, 181, 258, 273, 315, 321

Pétain, Henri, 319, 329, 332

Petersen, Peter, 220, 234

Petrenko, Vassily, 203–4

Pfefferkorn, Eli, 247

Pincus, David, 289

Pinhas of Koretz, Rebbe, 107

Pius XII, Pope, 167, 169

Pivot, Bernard, 338, 339

plane hijackings, of 1970s, 20, 27, 76

Plath, Sylvia, 107

Podwal, Mark, 230, 355

Poland, 153, 168, 185, 186, 188, 210, 229, 348, 378; EW's visits to, 188–99, 281–3; fiftieth-anniversary Auschwitz liberation ceremonies, 194–8, 282; postwar de-Judaization, 194–8; *see also* Auschwitz; Birkenau; Warsaw Ghetto

Pol Pot, 76, 90

Pompidou, Georges, 74

Pope, Marvin, 111

Popovic, Bozidar, 391–2

Pouget, Christine, 341

President's Commission on the Holocaust, 33, 179–205, 209

Prix Médicis, 288

Protestantism, 168, 371

Protocols of the Elders of Zion, The, 93, 289

Pundik, Herbert, 375

Rabin, Yitzhak, 9, 38, 56, 75, 77, 78, 185, 285, 309; Arafat and, 320; assassination of, 135, 137

Rafael, Gideon, 38

Rager, Itzhak, 382

Random House, 15–16, 51

Ravensbrück, 216

Rawicz, Piotr, 345, 348, 349–51; *Blood of the Sky*, 349; suicide of, 349–51

Reagan, Ronald, 153, 212, 316; Bitburg affair, 227–47; EW's relationship with, 213–15, 228–40, 246; Holocaust Memorial Council and, 212–15

Recanati, Raphael and Dina, 77, 78

refugees, sanctuary for, 94

Regan, Donald, 228–9, 236, 237, 239, 246

Resistance, French, 124–5, 187, 238, 317, 319

Rey, Nicholas, 194

Ringelblum, Emmanuel, 60, 104

Rittner, Dr. Carol, 218–19, 243

Rizhin, Rabbi Israel of, 82, 155

Rohmer, Eric, 164

Rollins, Ed, 228–9

Romania, 144, 322, 396; EW's visit to, 292–4; *see also* Sighet, Romania

Ronald, Al, 66–7

Roosevelt, Franklin D., 183

Rose, Jennifer (stepdaughter), 11

Rosen, Moses, 152, 292

Rosenbaum, Eli, *Betrayal*, 130

Rosenne, Meir, 235

Rosensaft, Hadassah, 185, 240, 241

Rosensaft, Menachem, 240

Rosensaft, Yossel, 10, 185, 191, 240

Rosenthal, Abe, 232, 235, 236, 237, 375, 378, 379, 380, 389, 394

Rostropovitch, Slava, 284, 326

Roth, John, 52, 373

Roth, Sol, 261

Rubinstein, Amnon, 56

Rubinstein, Artur, 88

Rudenko, Roman, 200–2

Russia, *see* Soviet Union

Rustin, Bayard, 89, 185

Rwanda, 289

Sadat, Anwar, 55, 59, 75, 78; 1977 peace talks, 78–9

Sadat, Camelia, 79

Sakharov, Andrei, 262, 264, 266, 267, 277, 327, 375

sanctuary, 94

Sand, Mikhaïl, 28

Sanders, Ed, 182–4

Sapir, Pinhas, 65

Sarah (niece), 8, 66, 70, 71, 406

Sarajevo, 387–99
Sarfati, Abraham, 89
Sawhill, John, 112
Schemla, Elizabeth, 322
Schmidt, Helmut, 74, 378
Schneerson, Menachem-Mendel, 12
Schutz, Klaus, 220
Schwarz-Bart, André, 56, 65
"Science and Conscience" conference, 145
Seidman, Dr. Hillel, 41
Sejersted, Francis, 272
Senate Foreign Relations Committee, U.S., 96–7, 308
Seneca, 48, 108, 142
Serbia, 154–5, 197, 387–99; ethnic cleansing, 388–99
Sevella, Efrem, 28
Sexton, Anne, 108
Shamir, Yitzhak, 145, 256, 258, 267, 273, 305, 309, 315, 319–20
Sharon, Ariel, 55, 75, 78
Shcharansky, Anatoly, 153, 201, 264, 273, 327
Shevardnadze, Edward, 326, 379
Shilon, Dan, 258
Shoah (documentary), 122–3
Shultz, George, 219, 233
Shushani (Mordechai Rosenbaum), 4, 109
Sidney (nephew), 8, 404, 406, 408
Sighet, Romania, 4, 5–6, 11, 24, 25, 51, 71, 148, 159, 180, 237, 253, 290, 302, 309, 404; EW's return visits to, 152, 154, 293, 407–10
Silber, David, 112–13
Silber, John, 91, 106, 109–10, 112–13, 256, 259, 381–2, 383
Silberman, Jim, 15, 41
Sinai, 75
Singer, Isaac Bashevis, 190, 261
Singer, Israel, 388
Siniora, Hanna, 374
Six-Day War, 16–17, 50, 57, 65–6, 93
Slepak, Masha and Vladimir, 153, 262, 263, 264, 327
Sneh, Ephraim, 9
Sneh, Moshe, 9
Sobibor, 119, 121
Sobol, Joshua, 123
Socialism, 55, 201, 314, 333

Solzhenitsyn, Alexander, 74, 279, 325
Somalia, 396
Sophie's Choice (film), 123
Sorbonne lectures, 83, 154, 287, 288, 314
South Africa, 93–4, 146, 375
Soviet Jews, 24, 27, 33, 34, 54, 63, 64, 88, 153; EW's concern for, 88, 189, 200–4, 262–7, 271, 273, 277, 327, 380; Leningrad trials, 27–8
Soviet Union, 3, 20, 21, 27–8, 52, 75, 87, 95, 145, 340, 378–81; EW's visits to, 145, 188–9, 200–4, 261–7, 323–7, 378–81; KGB, 378–9; 1991 coup d'état, 323–8; nuclear capabilities, 318; post-Gorbachev, 380–1, 396; Stalin-era trials, 145; *see also* Soviet Jews
Spain, 146
Speer, Albert, 130
Sperber, Jenka, 10
Sperber, Manès, 10, 21, 88
Spiegel, Der, 131
Spielberg, Stephen, 242
Spinoza, Baruch, 142, 261
Stalin, Joseph, 9, 48, 88, 145, 291
Steinberg, Elan, 388
Stendhal, 361
Stendhal, Bshp. Krister, 370
Stern, Isaac, 41, 88
Stern Gang, 58
Sternhell, Zeev, 124
Steve (nephew), 8, 66, 70, 71, 293, 306, 406, 408
Stockholm, 272
Strochlitz, Sigmund, 55–6, 179, 182, 184–9, 196, 202, 222–4, 230–2, 237, 241–7, 249, 256–7, 262, 305
Struthof, 216
Styron, William, 123
Suarès, Guy, 90
Suez Canal, 54
Sverdrup, Jakub, 257
Syria, 74, 132

Tacitus, 48
Talisman, Mark, 184, 222–3
Talmud, 6, 7, 13, 22, 47, 48, 91, 137, 144, 145, 184, 194, 201, 278, 302, 316, 364–5
Tamir, Shmuel, 10

Tanenbaum, Marc, 90
Tau, Max, 24, 25
Teheran hostage crisis, 211–12
Teresa, Mother, 145, 271
terrorism, 94–5, 97, 382; German,
    76–7; Iranian, 211–12; Irish, 382;
    Munich Olympics (1972), 50, 59,
    81; Palestinian, 50, 54, 73, 76, 79,
    320, 321; *see also specific regimes*
Thaler, Arnold, 381
The Hague, 396–7
Theresienstadt, 104, 119, 121, 216
Tho, Le Duc, 53
Tishman, Peggy, 236
Tito, Mshl. Josip Broz, 387
Tolstoy, Leo, 108
Torah, 184
Torquemada, 48
"To Save Our Children" conference
    (1992), 381–2
Treblinka, 18, 67, 105, 121, 184
Truman, Harry, 40
Tudjman, Franjo, 155, 388
Turkey, 92, 211
Tutu, Bshp. Desmond, 279

Ueberroth, Peter, 259–60
Uganda, 76–7
Ukraine, 186, 188, 199–200, 210, 228,
    290–2
Ullmann, Liv, 89, 272
Uman, 290–2
UNESCO, 88–9, 153
UNICEF, 272, 396
Union of Soviet Writers, 189
United Jewish Appeal (UJA), 50, 59–60
United Nations, 7, 14, 101, 128, 153,
    175; on Balkan war, 388, 391, 395;
    General Assembly, 72; Israel and,
    88–9
United States: Bitburg affair, 227–50;
    Holocaust Memorial Council, 130,
    205, 209–24, 230–50; Jews in, 34–6,
    55, 145, 153, 233; Liberators' Con-
    ference (1981), 204, 215–18; Presi-
    dent's Commission on the
    Holocaust, 179–205, 209
Urbach, Ephraim, 375

Valladares, Armando, 374
Vallquist, Gunnel, 272

Vargas Llosa, Mario, 89, 383
Vaturi, Clément, 290
Vauzelle, Michel, 325, 326, 327
Vergelis, Aaron, 189
Vienna, 294–6
Viernik, Yankel, 105
Vietnam, 76, 284
Vietnam War, 15, 52, 53, 76
Village Voice, 349
Vishniac, Roman, 190, 230
Voice of Israel, 258
Voices in the Night, 105, 122
von Stade, Frederica, 375

Waldheim, Kurt, 128, 130, 174, 294,
    295
Walesa, Lech, 194–8, 281–3; anti-
    Semitism, 197, 198, 282
Wallach, Eli, 143
Wallenberg, Raoul, 379
Wannsee Conference, 129, 221
Warsaw, 152–3, 190, 194, 199, 222,
    228
Warsaw Ghetto, 60, 67–8, 104, 118,
    147–8, 189–90, 230, 238, 248, 249,
    302, 319
Washington Post, 16, 238, 244
Watergate scandal, 52, 53, 73–4
Weinberg, Shaike, 243, 247
Weisgal, Meyer, 40–1, 144
Weiss, Shevah, 196, 197
Weizman, Ezer, 20–1, 78, 136
Weizmann, Chaim, 40, 144
Welles, Orson, 164
Werzberger, Benno, 345
Wessels, Leon, 375
Westling, Jon, 110
West Point, N.Y., 146–7
Wiesel, Bea (sister), 6, 8, 192, 306,
    404, 410; death of, 70–2; illness of,
    50–1, 66
Wiesel, Elie: academic career, 49, 50,
    79, 101–13, 239, 355, 405; activism
    of, 10, 19, 33–4, 48, 55, 79–81,
    88–97, 126, 153, 209, 269, 277, 369,
    391–8, 405; on Balkan war, 387–99;
    Barbie trial and, 299–302; Bitburg
    affair and, 227–50; Bousquet affair
    and, 329–40; celebrity of, 288–9;
    childhood, 4, 28, 70, 180, 192, 216,
    219, 237, 253–4, 260, 270, 301–2,

Wiesel, Elie (*cont'd*)
309, 404, 407–10; on Christianity,
167–75, 282–3, 371; Congressional
Gold Medal ceremony, 229–39;
criticism of Israel, 60–5, 134–7, 273;
critics on, 16, 107, 124–31, 273,
322, 405; death of sister Bea, 70–2;
on Diaspora, 59–64, 134–7, 307–8,
373; dreams of, 19–20, 47, 87, 253,
287, 403–4; Eban scandal and,
36–40; ethics of, 146, 154; fact-
finding mission to Eastern Europe
(1979), 188–94, 199–205; on fanaticism, 361, 370–2; as a father, 41–3,
49, 54, 129, 187, 237–8, 258, 260–1,
270, 324, 406, 408, 410; forgiveness
issue, 25, 194, 270; foundation of,
277–9, 281, 289, 369–83; on freedom, 147; on Gulf War, 305–9; on
Hasidism, 27–30, 107, 143, 144,
154, 292, 309, 364; on hate, 369–83;
on Holocaust, 18–19, 67–70, 72–3,
102–5, 117–30, 135, 144, 148–52,
179–205, 209–24, 355–65, 398,
405; Holocaust experience of,
216–17, 219, 238, 253–4, 270–1,
274, 301–2, 345–6, 404, 405, 408–9;
Holocaust Memorial Council and,
205, 209–24, 230–50; on human
rights, 87–97, 126, 153, 214, 269,
272, 286–7, 369–83, 387–99; Jewish
opponents of, 127–31, 235–6, 273,
308, 322; liberation from Buchenwald, 216–17; literary career, 5,
14–16, 22–5, 28, 31, 47–8, 52, 82,
87–8, 92, 97, 106, 142, 164, 261,
288, 300, 316, 355–65, 380, 405; on
madmen and visionaries, 159–64;
marriage of, 4, 6, 7–12, 196, 406;
memory issue, 104–5, 117–22,
129–30, 179–205, 209–24, 227–50,
268, 319–42, 345, 357, 362–4, 403,
406–7; Nobel Prize, and effects of,
124, 129, 130, 218, 253–74, 277–96;
President's Commission on the
Holocaust and, 179–205, 209; public speaking of, 19, 31, 33–4, 50, 53,
60–5, 82–3, 92, 94, 106, 110, 125,
141–55, 162, 180, 211, 213–18, 221,
232, 233, 238–9, 249, 270, 272, 286,
288, 289, 295; return visits to concentration camps, 191–8, 282;
reviews and polemics, 117–37, 172;
as "soul matchmaker," 220, 284;
television appearances, 8–9, 234,
235, 238, 240, 258, 260, 285, 330;
visits to Israel, 8–10, 55–8, 92–3,
126–7, 136, 147, 181, 204, 272–4,
305–9; wedding day, 7–12; women
and, 142, 143, 160; World Series
ball thrown by, 259–61; Yom Kippur
War and, 52–8, 59, 60
Wiesel, Elie, works of: *The Accident,* 164;
All Rivers Run to the Sea, 4, 6, 28, 109,
329; *A Beggar in Jerusalem,* 15–16, 125,
164, 288, 357; *Dawn,* 164; *The Fifth
Son,* 22, 103, 356–8; film adaptations, 163–4; *The Forgotten,* 22, 52,
362–4, 403, 410; *The Gates of the Forest,*
164; *The Jews of Silence,* 24, 82–3, 313;
journalism and book reviews, 14, 49,
72, 117–22, 128, 131–3, 141, 153,
168, 172, 235, 347–9, 397–9; *Messengers of God,* 31, 33, 313; Mitterrand's
"dialogues" with, 319–20, 331–2,
333–40; *Night,* 70, 141, 142, 164,
270; *The Oath,* 10, 41, 49, 52–3; *One
Generation After,* 16–18, 21–4, 406;
publishers of, 15–16, 24, 33, 49,
102, 288, 332, 335–7; *Sages and
Dreamers,* 364–5; sales of, 288; *Somewhere a Master,* 29–30; *Souls on Fire,* 28;
The Testament, 28, 87, 164, 188;
themes of, 355–65; *To a Concerned
Friend,* 132–3; *The Town Beyond the
Wall,* 18–19, 24, 83, 362; transla-
tions of, 265; *The Trial of God,* 309,
358–61; "The Trial of Krasnograd,"
28; *Twilight,* 278, 362; "Why I Am
Afraid: Ominous Signs and
Unspeakable Thoughts," 72–3
Wiesel, Elisha (son), 41–3, 51, 56, 71,
188, 203, 290, 323, 341, 406; birth
and circumcision, 41–3; childhood,
49, 54, 129, 187, 203, 232, 235,
237–8, 255, 260, 316; at EW's
Nobel Prize ceremony, 268–70;
EW's relationship with, 237–8, 255,
258, 260–1, 268, 270, 324, 406,
408, 410
Wiesel, Hilda (sister), 6, 8, 51, 70, 71,
192, 256, 258, 404, 406, 408

Wiesel, Marion (wife), 4–12, 36, 49, 57, 71, 96, 97, 112, 168, 182–8, 191, 196, 202, 218, 222, 235, 237, 242, 246, 249, 290, 315, 323, 324, 335, 336, 338, 406; childhood, 295; EW's Nobel Prize and, 256–9, 261, 268, 270, 273, 277; as Foundation for Humanity director, 369, 375, 381; help with EW's work, 15, 52, 179, 232; as a mother, 11, 42–3, 187, 406; in Soviet Union, 262–7; wedding day, 7–12

Wiesel, Nissel (grandmother), 407, 410

Wiesel, Sarah Feig (mother), 42, 71, 270, 301, 404, 406, 408, 410

Wiesel, Shlomo (father), 42–3, 71, 89, 186, 253, 270–1, 287, 403–4, 406, 409–10; Beit Hamidrash named for, 273; death of, 270–1, 409

Wiesel, Tsiporah, "Tsipouka" (sister), 270, 287, 301, 404, 407–8, 410

Wiesenthal, Simon, 127–31, 153, 187–8, 392

Wilde, Oscar, 253

Williams, Betty, 284

Wilzig, Siggi, 210, 241, 245

Winds of War, The (TV series), 123

World Jewish Congress, 130, 195, 388

World War I, 211, 227, 393

World War II, 48, 93, 227, 319, 378, 391

World Zionist movement, 40

Wouk, Herman, 123

Yad Vashem (Holocaust Memorial), 183, 204, 219, 220

Yakovlev, Alexander, 378

Yale University, 101–2, 110–11, 314

Yavin, Haïm, 8

Yedioth Ahronoth (newspaper), 9, 14, 38, 49, 65, 141, 273

Yehoshua, A. B., 373

Yeltsin, Boris, 323, 325–8, 340, 379, 380

Yom Kippur War, 52–8, 59, 60, 75, 78, 79

Young Presidents Organization, 146

Yugoslavia, 387–99

Zaks, Gordon, 228, 229

Zalman, Shneur, 3

Zeitlin, Aharon, 190

Zuckerman, Yitzhak, 147–8

Zweig, Stefan, 108

Zygelbojm, Arthur, 185

A NOTE ABOUT THE AUTHOR

Elie Wiesel is the author of more than forty books, including his unforgettable international best-sellers Night *and* A Beggar in Jerusalem, *winner of the Prix Médicis. He has been awarded the Presidential Medal of Freedom, the United States Congressional Gold Medal, and the French Legion of Honor with the rank of Grand Officer. In 1986, he received the Nobel Peace Prize. He is Andrew W. Mellon Professor in the Humanities and University Professor at Boston University. He lives with his wife, Marion, and their son, Elisha, in New York City.*

A NOTE ON THE TYPE

The text of this book was set in Weiss, a typeface designed in Germany by Emil Rudolph Weiss (1875–1942). The design of the roman was completed in 1928 and that of the italic in 1931. Both are well balanced and even in color, and both reflect the subtle skill of a fine calligrapher.

Composed by North Market Street Graphics, Lancaster, Pennsylvania

Printed and bound by Quebecor Printing, Martinsburg, West Virginia

Designed by Iris Weinstein